Instant Macromedia Flash™ 5

Jim Caldwell
Samuel Wan

Osborne/McGraw-Hill

New York   Chicago   San Francisco
Lisbon   London   Madrid   Mexico City
Milan   New Delhi   San Juan
Seoul   Singapore   Sydney   Toronto

About the Authors

Jim Caldwell is a self-taught and ambition-driven creative developer. His background lies within corporate surroundings working for communications giants such as BellSouth and MCI WorldCom. At present, he is a Senior Applications Developer with MCI WorldCom. Although he has been responsible for MCI's intranet applications, his passion is creating new uses for Flash. Jim is known for his determination to make his designs incredibly download friendly, and most of his projects can be updated without altering Flash files. His own design studio, Innovative FX, LLC (www.innovativefx.com), is still in its growth stage, but is contributing to his success by allowing him to serve clients such as Cisco Systems, Inc. Jim has always been a large part of the design community, moderating at forums such as Ultrashock (www.ultrashock.com), Were-here (www.were-here.com), and Flashmove (www.flashmove.com). He owes his accomplishments to the many great designers within the community for their lasting advice and support.

Samuel Wan has worked extensively in complex Flash design and architecture since the first appearance of ActionScript. His experience with interactive programming—both as a designer and as a programmer—has resulted in several highly regarded publications and speaking engagements.

Osborne/McGraw-Hill
2600 Tenth Street
Berkeley, California 94710
U.S.A.

To arrange bulk purchase discounts for sales promotions, premiums, or fund-raisers, please contact Osborne/**McGraw-Hill** at the above address. For information on translations or book distributors outside the U.S.A., please see the International Contact Information page immediately following the index of this book.

Instant Macromedia Flash™ 5

1234567890 FGR FGR 01987654321

Book p/n 0-07-213142-X and CD p/n 0-07-213143-8
parts of
ISBN 0-07-213144-6

Publisher	Brandon A. Nordin
Vice President & Associate Publisher	Scott Rogers
Acquisitions Editor	Jim Schachterle
Project Editor	Laura Stone
Acquisitions Coordinator	Timothy Madrid
Technical Editor	Jim Cranford
Copy Editor	Marilyn Smith
Proofreader	Linda Medoff
Indexer	Irv Hershman
Computer Designer	Carie Abrew, Lucie Ericksen
Illustrator	Michael Mueller, Lyssa Sieben-Wald
Cover Series Design	Greg Scott
Cover Illustration	Eliot Bergman

This book was composed with Corel VENTURA™ Publisher.

I'd like to dedicate this book to my late sister, Katherine Denise Holmes. She always believed in me and helped me push myself to become a better person. I only wish she could be here to see my success.

—Jim Caldwell

Contents

Acknowledgments

I've received much help and support along the way while writing this book. Without this help, I don't see how I would've ever been able to write it. My wife Mary probably had to suffer more than anyone; she tells me that she has almost forgotten what I look like over the past six months. Even through this, she would provide me with ideas and inspiration that made this book possible.

The staff at Osborne/McGraw-Hill has been extremely helpful in helping me pull together my ideas and actually get a book on the shelf. Jim Schachterle came to me in December with the idea of the book, and I immediately responded. I was excited about the concept, and with his help, we came up with this outline that we felt happy with. Tim Madrid helped me along the way by coordinating all of my technical edits and keeping the content organized.

Before the book was completely finished, Laura Stone and Marilyn Smith brought me back to English 101. After the amount of time they spent proofreading and working on my chapters, I'm sure they know Flash better than anyone.

—Jim Caldwell

Introduction

About This Book

Many emerging designers are tormented with the problem of developing innovative ideas for the Web. Throughout these chapters, you will learn techniques and time-saving applications that will enable you to experiment with new ideas.

While there are many principles of design that should be followed, you will learn in this book that breaking or expanding those principles is what design is about. Each project for this book took more time to think up than it took to actually implement. I started each project with a simple idea, and expanded it into a complex, yet effective Flash application. I wrote Chapters 3 through 14 to exhibit the broad possibilities of Flash. I asked Samuel Wan, Lisa Kushins, and Christine Smart to contribute chapters for this book as well, to showcase their great talents in Flash.

Samuel Wan and Lisa Kushins demonstrate great Flash programming in Chapters 2 and 15 through 19, while Christine Smart explains design layouts like none other in Chapter 1. Using several people to help with this book reveals the vast differences in design and programming preferences. Perhaps you'll relate to one of the programming or design styles used.

The one thing that remains constant throughout each chapter is the heart of each person who wrote it. Writing can be an outlet for creative energy, just as Flash can be. Each word of each sentence must be carefully thought out, just as a line or fill must be carefully thought out in Flash to create a masterpiece. This process uses the creative thoughts in your mind to portray your ideas.

I believe everyone is creative, but only a small portion of people know how to express their creativity. I did not use my potential for many years because I did not think I would be able to find jobs or be successful. After I began working in a creative environment, my life began to change. Little by little I began to express my creativity like I had always dreamed. I was able to use the beauty I saw in real objects for the graphics I designed. However, these graphics did not provide an outlet for my artistic ability to see motion as an art. Moving cars, clouds, and even grass were inspiration only for the creative world in my mind. I could see the potential of movement for design, but did not have a way to use it in my graphics.

The most common motion-design tools were intended for television. Most jobs required many years of schooling and experience, which I did not have. I felt I was ready to use my skills in motion, but lacked the opportunity. Then I received an email about a revolutionary site that came to be the inspiration of many emerging designers. This incredible site was gabocorp.com. The minute I saw the site, I started considering the possibilities of Web design. I immediately downloaded the trial version of Macromedia Flash and began working on my first motion experiments.

Starting small, I used Flash to create banners and intros for the business where I worked. It enhanced the overall appearance and increased the number of hits to the site. Keep in mind that this was three years ago, when Flash was still widely unheard of. People couldn't get enough of it. Our design sales increased and everyone was looking for a catchy intro or enhancement for their Web site. It did not take long until I was beginning to make fully interactive Flash sites, using navigations that were virtually impossible only months before. I admit now, a lot of the Flash work I did in the beginning was a waste of bandwidth for many users, but it was a great learning experience for me. I knew the program inside out, but I was not building sites that were optimized for my target audiences. This lesson is only learned through experience and cannot be taught. Searching for the style that works for you, and your target audience, can take several months or even years.

The key to finding your creative style is to try experimenting with different environmental settings. Try to play music that you do not usually listen to, or go to a park and receive inspiration from nature. Art in design is achieved by finding the beauty of an object and portraying it so that your audience can see the beauty.

Before I start on any Flash project, I try to surround myself with an environment that I feel will inspire my creative thoughts. A recent project I finished called for a navigation that would appeal to the music industry, while not scaring off the non-music crowd. Instead of turning on MTV to listen to the latest music and trends, I listened to Beethoven. While this may seem odd, it actually helped me achieve my goal. Many modern-day rock bands have received inspiration from Beethoven's remarkable music.

While considering your client, look at the advertising and marketing plan of the company your are about to promote online. This will give you great insight on your target audience, the people who will receive the message you portray in your design. It will also give you ideas for placing the message within your design—always remember what you are trying to get across to the viewer.

Anticipate changes early on. That is another reason to review the advertising or marketing plans if they are available. In most cases these are a solid tool for you.

The plans are meant to be followed and implemented, which gives maximum results. These plans are unlikely to change, so they are great outlines for your inspiration. This also allows you to learn more about the company you will be providing your services to. If you know the product and can communicate well to the client about the product, you demonstrate that you are the right person or company for the job. Macromedia Flash can benefit some projects, but it can cripple other projects if it is not used effectively.

While these methods or techniques may not apply to you personally, every person can benefit from experimenting with different moods and setting when working in Flash, or design in general. Each chapter in this book that I wrote was inspired in some way by my surroundings. An example is Chapter 14; it covers sound techniques in Flash. The idea to write a sound chapter was the same from the beginning, but after watching a plane fly overhead the week of writing the chapter, I decided to use a plane to demonstrate the possibilities of the sound object. The positioning of the plane determines the pan and volume of the engine sound, to simulate the movement of the plane.

Reading This Book

While reading this book, you will note CD-ROM icons with references to filenames. These accompanying files are located on the CD-ROM included with this book. Having these files open while reading this book can help you visualize the projects as they are being built. Each project is separated on the CD-ROM according to chapter number.

The back of the book has one appendix containing some useful sites about Flash.

Who Should Read This Book

While reading through these pages, do not limit yourself to the way the projects are portrayed in this book. Using these ideas and samples, you can create your own unique interfaces or motion-design techniques. Most of the projects are targeted for intermediate to advanced Flash developers, but even relatively new users can pick up on the techniques to enhance their skills, or adapt the solutions for their own use.

Each project is broken into an individual file or files, with references in the chapter. It may be helpful to have the file open while reading the chapter, so you can see what each chapter is accomplishing along the way. Because this book has more than one author, you will probably notice slightly different programming styles, but each remains consistent with the same high standards of quality.

What This Book Covers

This book contains 19 chapters that range from design basics to XML parsing in Flash. The projects in each chapter are built using modular code that can be easily adjusted to work in many other environments.

Chapter 1, "Designing in Flash," was written by Christine Smart. This chapter covers techniques used in the design aspect of Flash. This chapter is broken down into sections such as color theory and designs that work, which can be helpful for anyone who is just getting into design, or for people who want to broaden their design skills.

Chapter 2, "Simulating an MP3 Player," was written by Samuel Wan. This chapter deconstructs a Flash MP3 Player. Using externally loaded SWF files, you can simulate all of the features found in common MP3 Players, and use it over the Web.

Chapter 3, "Real-Time Preloader," was written by Jim Caldwell. This chapter uses new Flash 5 features to build a preloader that shows advanced output such as percentage loading and how fast the connection is downloading.

Chapter 4, "Resizable Windows," was written by Jim Caldwell. This chapter expands the capabilities of standard windows made in Flash. With resizable windows, more content can be placed within windows, as in standard operating systems.

Chapter 5, "Drop-Down Menu Navigation," was written by Jim Caldwell. Many people use ActionScripting to expand the capabilities of their Web sites, but many overlook optimization of code. This menu demonstrates organic movement, with object-oriented coding.

Chapter 6, "Drag-and-Drop Navigation," was written by Jim Caldwell. Drag-and-drop navigation has been around since the release of Flash 4. With Flash 5's new `hitTest()` command, these navigational ideas can expand to new horizons.

Chapter 7, "Picture Album," was written by Jim Caldwell. This experiment came to life from the need to display many pictures at once while minimizing space.

Chapter 8, "Advanced Scrollbars," was written by Jim Caldwell. So many projects now call for scrollbars in Flash. The scrollbars used in this project are robustly designed so that little modification is required to edit for future projects.

Chapter 9, "Duplicating Movie Clips," was written by Jim Caldwell. With users still connecting via dial-up modems, duplicating movie clips can save valuable file size. This project duplicates nearly 100 objects on the screen at once, while maintaining extremely low file sizes.

Chapter 10, "Swap Depths," was written by Jim Caldwell. The newly added Flash 5 command, `swapDepths()`, reduces the amount of work required with Flash 4 Action Scripting. Now you can dynamically place movie clips in new depths via scripting.

Chapter 11, "Flash JavaScript Interaction," was written by Jim Caldwell. Many projects require more than what Flash can handle; therefore, it is important to be able to call JavaScript commands and functions within Flash.

Chapter 12, "Corporate Intro Movie," was written by Jim Caldwell. The recent "coming soon" intro designed for the Innovative FX Web site is deconstructed in this chapter. Many Flash secrets used to produce broadcast-style effects are explained in detail.

Chapter 13, "Sound Object," was written by Jim Caldwell. Try flying this 3-D plane through space on the screen and listen as the sound follows with a true 3-D experience.

Chapter 14, "Flying Through Time," was written by Jim Caldwell. Lots of code and even more movie clips show how frames aren't always necessary to produce blazing motion graphics. Using values read from the Date object, the Flash movie builds dynamically showing the date and time.

Chapter 15, "Map Interface," was written by Samuel Wan. This chapter deconstructs the popular minimap navigation used on www.innovativefx.com. Using fast, object-oriented code, this chapter can easily be followed to produce amazing results.

Chapter 16, "The Links Generator Smart Clip," was written by Samuel Wan. Smart Clips allow you to build Flash content that can be easily updated by anyone with basic Flash experience.

Chapter 17, "XML Address Book," was written by Samuel Wan. Everyone seems to be interested in the new Flash XML object. It allows you to read through XML data and pull structured values into Flash.

Chapter 18, "Animating with ActionScript," was written by Lisa Kushins. Many tutorials cover how to animate objects in Flash, but they rarely explain why it works. This chapter goes into detail on why and how to code in Flash.

Chapter 19, "Programming a Game in Flash," was written by Lisa Kushins. A big interest in Flash has been the gaming capabilities. Each year more complex games are being developed, using more powerful code and techniques. This chapter covers a Pac-Man style game.

Designing in Flash

IN THIS CHAPTER:

▶ Understand some basic principles of design

▶ Create appealing, high-impact sites with Flash

▶ Use style and color to unite your site design

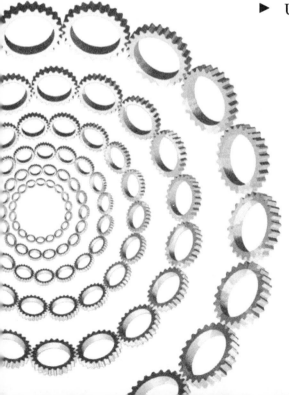

I remember seeing my first site made with Flash on the Internet. I was in awe. I saw that Flash is a wonderful way to create Web sites—the interaction and creative techniques were remarkable. I believe that building creative designs in Macromedia Flash is just as important as formulating advanced ActionScript.

Consider that all the world is by design, from the chair you sit in to the car you drive to the book you are reading now. Design is the creative exploitation of emotion, the communication of messages, and the expression of concepts through shapes and color—all with the goal of creating a desired reaction. A great designer is continually working to hone creative development through a detailed focus on well-defined convictions; to strive to think and create beyond the typical; and to purely construct distinct, reaction-based, concept-driven design.

This chapter will give you some insight on how to create a Flash site that offers the visitor a congruent image from frame to frame and from color to color. You will be introduced to the unique world of Flash design and learn how to plan and lay out a Flash site. This chapter also covers the basics of designing with color and type.

Planning the Site Design

All designs start with the white screen, which can be intimidating to even the best designers. Getting over the "blank-page syndrome" can be a hard task. However, following some simple rules will help you to get started producing creative, outstanding sites.

When planning a site, the best place to start is with the content that will be included on the site. Next, you need to decide how to organize that content. Planning the content organization meticulously before you begin prevents reorganization problems in the middle of the project. Following organization, the next step is to create a storyboard for your project. The storyboard's main purpose is to show the content placement, design style, actions, and objective of the site. Creating a proper storyboard outline will allow your client to see the actual steps and approach you will be taking on a project. At this point, your client can review the site design concept and make critical decisions regarding the workflow.

Here are the main steps in the site planning process:

► Interpret the client's requirements

► Define the site's purpose

► Define the site's visual style

- ▶ Choose a color palette
- ▶ Select the type styles
- ▶ Create a storyline
- ▶ Develop a storyboard

Interpreting the Client's Requirements

Your starting point is to create a basic outline of the client's requests for the site: the information, content, message being communicated, and audience for the message. This is the ground floor of the project, and the success of your project can depend on it.

Working on a project that is not clearly defined will make for a long, drawn-out process that may have a confusing end result. For example, your definition of simple and the client's definition of simple may be totally diverse, and the consequences of that will be time, money, and frustration. Hone your interpretation skills, and make sure that you thoroughly understand the client's requirements. The creative part of your design can flow from there.

Defining the Site's Purpose

As a designer, considering your purpose with the project is very important. How do you want the visitor to see the site? You are the director of the visitor's experience, and taking full advantage of that is critical. At this stage, you should outline your intent and comprehend the best way to achieve your intent as the designer.

Another main factor at this point is defining the end user's capabilities. For this, you may need to do some research about your client's market. A market made up of more technically advanced users would be more apt to find hidden buttons, use sliding menus, and handle a unique navigation system. A less technical user would not be inclined to be so adventurous, so maintaining a more predictable approach may be in your client's best interest. You must balance your desires to push the limits of technology with the needs of the users.

Defining the Visual Style

After you've defined the purpose of the site, your next step is to create an outline of the visual style. This phase will determine the look and feel of the site, the imagery, and how to accomplish the goal that was defined in the interpreting stage. Visual design is the finished building, and the interaction and motion design are the bolts that hold the building together.

The importance of creating the visual style of the site is enormous. The visual impact of the site depends on the site's style. Equate it to the fashion imagery of the music artists you see on MTV. If there were no visual style created for the artists, the artists would somehow seem less interesting.

As an example, compare the site styles shown in Figure 1-1. The site at the top shows the original Creative Ceed site with an impractical navigation scheme and unappealing layout. The site lacks a dominant visual image, and it is unclear how to find the company's information. The site shown at the bottom integrates a navigation scheme with a strong visual style. The style is more modern and meets the client's requirements for the company's identity. In fact, an entire advertising campaign was built around the new identity created in this site.

Choosing a Color Palette

It is important to define a color palette at this time. Choosing and identifying the colors up front prevents time-consuming changes later. Color design issues are covered later in this chapter, in the "Designing with Color" section. This section addresses some basic details for saving and importing your color palette for your Flash projects.

When you initially open a Flash movie, the default color palette is the Web-safe palette of 216 colors. While designing your Flash movie and creating new colors and gradients, your Flash file will contain and save its own color palette. You can add colors to the current color palette using the Mixer panel. Additionally, if you have a palette that has been predetermined, you can import, export, and modify your color palette. You can also import and export color palettes between Flash files, as well as between other applications. To import a color palette, you can use Flash Color Set files (CLR), Color Table files (ACT), or color palettes from GIF files.

You can import or export a color palette as follows:

▶   **Import a color palette**   Open the Swatches palette and click the pop-up menu in the upper-right corner. If you want to append the imported colors to the current palette, choose Add Colors. If you want to replace the current palette with the imported colors, choose Replace Colors. Select the desired file and click OK.

▶   **Export a color palette**   Open the Swatches panel and click the pop-up menu in the upper-right corner. Select Save Colors. In the dialog box that appears, choose a name for the palette. For Save As Type (Windows) or Format (Macintosh), choose Flash Color Set or Color. Click OK and Save.

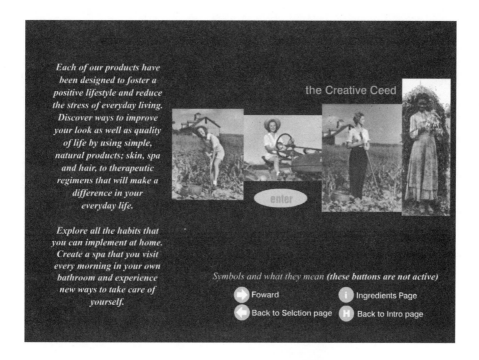

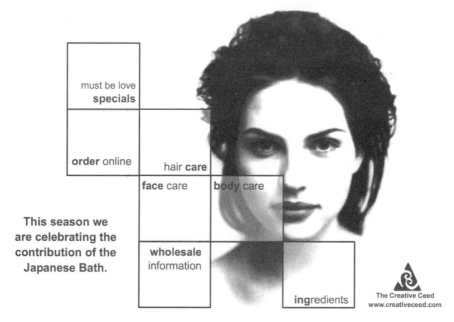

Figure 1-1   *The original Creative Ceed site (top) is not visually appealing, whereas the revised Creative Ceed site (bottom) has visual style.*

NOTE

Web-safe colors in Flash are drawn by the proprietary plug-in, not by the browser, so there will be no graphic versus code-produced color issues. The colors you select will shift when viewed in a High Color system, but there will not be any interruption between the graphic and code-produced color.

Selecting the Type Styles

The next step is to decide which fonts will be used in the project. Choose your fonts for each area of the site, and make a chart that describes the font name, the size, and the other font attributes, as shown in the following illustration. These attributes include font family, type size, style, color, tracking, auto kerning, and baseline shift. Choose fonts for headlines, text, subsections, and other areas, such as buttons and menus.

Font Selections

Arial Bold 16 pt	**Headlines**
Arial 14 pt	Sub-Headings
Arial 12 pt	Text
Times New Roman 11 pt	quotations

The font listing should be followed strictly for the best site management and results, as shown in Figure 1-2. Imagine completing the site, and then needing to go through each movie clip and change font styles! Creating and adhering to a font list will allow for a practical and clear-cut production flow. Some typography design issues are covered later in this chapter, in the "Designing with Type" section. This section addresses some issues of dealing with type in Flash projects.

Small Fonts

One of the biggest issues with type in Flash is the use of small fonts, because they become blurry, making them difficult to read. This happens because, by default, Flash uses anti-aliased text in type blocks. The solution is to use a text field instead of a type block. Text used in text fields is not anti-aliased by default. Text fields are normally used for text entry, but you can make them noneditable. A text field will display small text much cleaner than a type block will. Also, using text fields to display text decreases the file size, because font outlines are not included in the final movie.

>PrePressInformation >Film

Headlines   Sub-Headings

Arial Bold 16 pt   Arial 14 pt

DO NOT USE RGB FILES FOR PRINTED OUTPUT. Graphics intended for color reproduction should always be CMYK; for black and white reproduction, grayscale.

BE CAREFUL WITH DUOTONES. If you create a duotone, make sure the colors are named the same way they are named in your page layout program. For example, if the duotone is Pantone 242 and Black, make sure the colors are labeled "PANTONE 242 CV" and "Black" (not "PANTONE Process Black"). Page layout programs cannot process-separate duotones. If you want your duotone to process separate, convert it to CMYK in Photoshop

Text

Arial 12 pt

quotations

Times New Roman 12 pt

We make magic happen in beautiful color. Ask us how.

INCLUDE ALL SUPPORTING Files. For proper output, we need all of the placed graphics files. Most page layout programs have a way to ensure that all files are included; in Quark, it's "Collect for Output," in PageMaker, it's the "Copy Files" function in the "Save As..." dialog box. Even if the file is embedded in the layout program, include it! Otherwise, we can't trap it or fix problems with it.

Figure 1-2   *Font map in use*

NOTE

Anti-aliasing is a method of smoothing the curved and diagonal edges in fonts and images. Intermediate pixels along edges are filled to smooth the transition between the edges and the surrounding image, thus creating a smooth edge.

Some bitmapped fonts are still aliased in text fields. If you run into this problem, the best solution is to use an imported graphic.

TIP

Flash 5 has the ability to apply HTML formatting styles to text fields. Styling tags and URL links can be applied to a word or group of words within a text field.

Embedded Fonts

Embedded fonts are fonts installed on your system used in your Flash movie. Flash embeds the font information in the SWF file when exporting the movie, ensuring that the font displays properly in the Flash Player. To optimize the movie, select only the characters used for embedded fonts, rather than including the entire font.

Not all fonts displayed in Flash can be exported with a movie. Confirm that a font can be exported by previewing the text. Select View | Anti-alias. If you see jagged type, this signifies that Flash does not recognize that font's outline and will not export the text.

Device Fonts

As a substitute for embedding font information, you can use special fonts in Flash called *device fonts*. Device fonts are not embedded in the SWF file. Instead, the Flash Player uses whatever font on the local computer most closely resembles the device font. Because device font information is not embedded, using device fonts produces a smaller Flash movie file size. Device fonts will be sharper and more readable than embedded fonts at small type sizes.

Flash includes three device fonts, named _sans (like Helvetica or Arial), _serif (like Times Roman), and _typewriter (like Courier). To use a device font, select one in the Character panel or choose Use Device Fonts in the Text Options panel.

Creating a Storyline

A site with a storyline is almost guaranteed to influence and capture the attention of the visitor. At this point in the planning process, you should create a very detailed story idea. Become a storyteller. By personalizing the product or service being offered, you can create an environment that grabs the visitor's attention. Try not to be obvious in your interpretation of the story; you want the visitors to be interested enough in the storyline to explore the site.

For instance, take a look at designer Joen Asmussen's site, www.turtleshell.com, shown in Figure 1-3. The whole site, from beginning to end, is a story. From the color scheme to the sounds, Turtleshell.com has a deep-rooted feeling and purpose. Another site that creates a great storytelling experience is www.nike.com/features/bowerman, designed by IO Research. This site is a good example of storytelling through visuals, storyline, and flow.

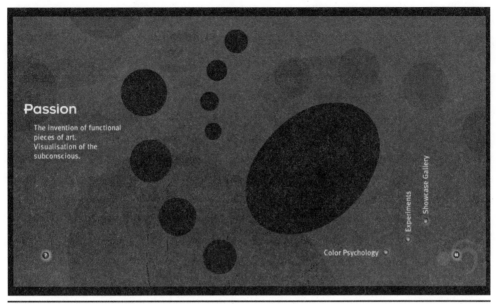

Figure 1-3   *The Turtleshell site tells a story*

Developing a Storyboard

Now you're ready to develop the site, using all of the elements you defined in the preceding steps. Even for the most experimental sites, with confusion and chaos as the strategy, there is always an underlying organization. The importance of following a single plan for your site cannot be emphasized enough. The imagery, buttons, individual sections, and every other element must be harmonized and in union to meet the goal of a well-designed site.

Development of the site is through storyboarding. A *storyboard* is a pictorial or text guide detailing the site in the finished order, as shown in Figure 1-4.

Each frame of the storyboard should contain the following:

▶ **Screen sketches or shots**   Draw what a particular screen or episode of your project will look like. Number the screen and try to group related screens together. Include information about the screen dimensions as well.

▶ **Interaction, effect, and transition effect information**   *Interaction* usually refers to user interaction, in which a user can input information or push a button. The *effect* is what happens after the user makes an interaction take place. The *transition effect* is what happens as the interaction takes place. Write down exactly what you want to happen for each of these.

▶ **Graphics, animation, sound, music, and text information**   For each element, list the filename and write a brief description. Animation refers to any movement or changes. Sound includes any sound effects that are conditional or specific to a certain interaction, movie clip, or effect. Music includes any background music.

Make sure that your storyboard indicates all major elements of the site. The elements should be clearly labeled. The sequence of the elements should be clear and logical, without any gaps or dead ends.

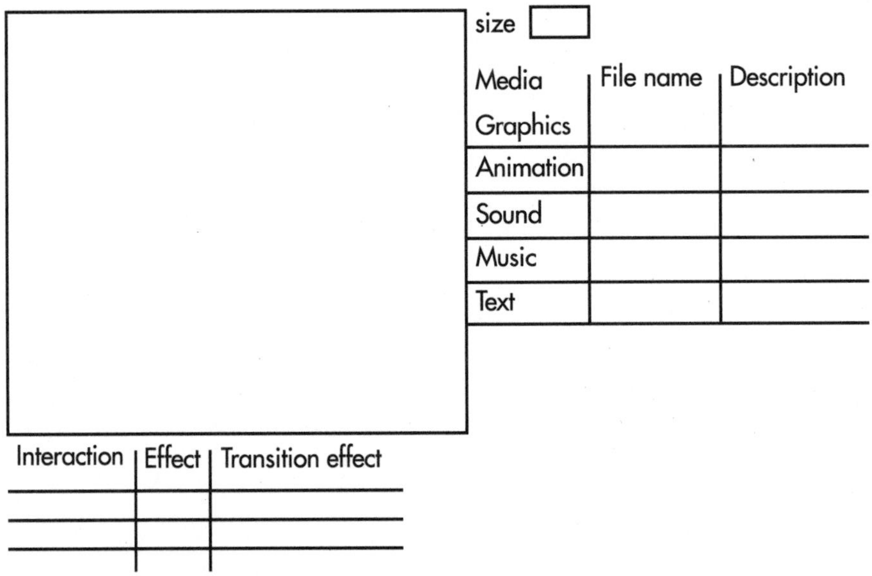

size		
Media	File name	Description
Graphics		
Animation		
Sound		
Music		
Text		

Interaction	Effect	Transition effect

Figure 1-4   *A storyboard frame*

Laying Out a Flash Site

When people visit a site that has been poorly designed—with navigation problems, spacing issues, unreadable fonts, and an unfriendly user interface—they instinctively respond negatively to the site. They get the impression that the company is unprofessional and disorganized. The best test is to surf the Web and see your reaction to both poorly and precisely designed sites. Ask yourself if you would use the services or buy products from the sites, or trust the messages that they are communicating.

Working in Flash is different from working in the static HTML environment. This is mainly because of the motion capabilities. Creating a site driven by motion can be difficult. Detailing your motion design in the form of storyboarding is a simple task that will save you a lot of frustration. The issues to consider are shapes, interaction, usability, positive and negative space, and centered elements.

Using Shapes

Shapes in a design create a feeling. As in logo design, shapes create meanings for companies. The same is true for shapes used in sites. The shapes used in a site should follow the defined visual style of the site.

As shown in Figure 1-5, shapes and lines evoke emotion. Study how just the shapes of the elements create the defining mood of the image shown.

Using Functioning Motion in Interactive Design

Interactive design describes how the user engages, responds to, and comprehends interactions between sections. This design should give the users the tools they need to work with the site clearly and naturally. Your storyboard should detail how motion will come into play and tell a story to the user, leaving an impression. You want to avoid using Flash in a way that is clunky, confusing, or disruptive to the flow of the site.

Functional motion follows an innate purpose. To understand if your motion is functional within your site, look to nature as your model. Consider the natural flow of the ocean and its tides: A wake turns into a wave, folds over and crashes into the

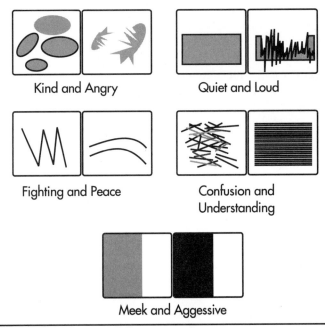

Kind and Angry

Quiet and Loud

Fighting and Peace

Confusion and
Understanding

Meek and Aggessive

Figure 1-5 *Different shapes evoke different moods.*

water, and flows forward into the whitewash. Check the flow and smoothness of your
design. If a shape goes off the left side of the screen in a straight line, does it appear
to come back in on the right side of the screen in the same way, or do you have it coming
in from the top corner? It's important that the functional motion in your site makes
sense to the user.

Designing for Usability

Site usability means many things to different people. It can represent how fast a site
loads, how easy a menu is to use, or how quickly a user can navigate through a site. You
should try to balance the requirements for usability with those for scripting and design.
In commercial design, usability is the key to making a site successful for a client. The
more designers take usability in Flash as a serious issue, the easier it will be to promote
Flash as a practical tool for site design.

There are a few key issues to file under usability, including the ability to skip
introductions, ease of navigation, consistency in the user interface, reduction of
download time, and reduction of CPU requirements.

Skipping the Introduction

Some sites include long introductions without a Skip Intro button or a client-side JavaScript cookie that will automatically bypass the introduction the next time the user visits the site. Yes, the introductory animations that you see in well-developed sites can be very stimulating, but they also can hinder the visitors' access to the information they are looking for. Visitors may find their experience unpleasant and decide not to return to the site. Most designers would not define this as a successful achievement. If the site has a lengthy introduction, give the users some way to avoid it.

Orienting the User

Easy and logical navigation and interactivity are primary to site usability. It is important to keep the visitors oriented to where they are when traveling through the site. This can be done through headings or section titles. Always display an easy way back to the user's previous location and a straightforward path to other places on the site. You might also consider supporting the Back button navigation on the browser by dividing Flash movies into separate movies and placing them on individual HTML pages. However, this approach can be distracting and time-consuming, for both the site designer and the visitor.

Navigation structures should be kept in an organized and apparent system. It is important to show primary site navigational elements first by using the streaming capabilities of Flash. Also, remember that all of your buttons should have a well-defined hit area.

To check the usability of your site, test, test, and test some more. Have someone impartial test your site to make sure that it accomplishes both user and site objectives. Retest the site each time you make even minor changes. Make sure that the testers reflect the demographics of your site's audience—especially if the expected audience includes a wide range of users.

Designing a Consistent User Interface

Consistency in the user interface (UI) is the best way to enhance a site's function. When you reuse architectural elements, design elements, and naming conventions, the visitors don't need to figure out how to use the interface. This frees them to develop an interest in your message while they navigate to their goal. You can use Smart Clips to reuse interactive elements throughout the site, and have words and images from initial navigation links reappear on destination pages.

Considering Low-Bandwidth Users

The shorter the download time for your site, the better the user will feel about visiting. The initial screen download should be no more than 45KB, including the Flash files, HTML, and images. To reduce download time, limit the amount of images and sounds. Anything that would blow the file size up should not be used in the opening movie. Using the Load Movie action when specific files are requested eases the loading delay as well. If a wait is unavoidable, provide a load-time sequence with a progress indicator, and have your navigation system load in the first 5 seconds whenever possible. You can see a sample of a progress indicator at www.beingsmart.com.

Considering CPU Speed

Another usability issue to consider is low CPU speed. Taking advantage of all the wonderful scripting can take a toll on a processor. Unless your audience consists of other designers or only high-end computer users, designing for lower CPU speeds is important. If possible, test your scripting on several different machines and go for the lowest common denominator. This is important when the smoothness and speed of a design depend on the power of the processor.

   Even if your movie is only 28KB, the processor demands can be much greater than lower-end CPUs can handle. The following is a good test for understanding the CPU speed a movie requires.

Creating a Reusable Frame-Counter Module   The following steps will create a reusable frame counter module:

1. Open Flash and start from an empty document.
2. Create a text field and type **0** in this field. Set it to Dynamic Text in the Text Options panel. Select the Center option in the Paragraph panel. Use any font you want. In the Text Options panel, name this text field's variable **fps**.
3. Turn this text field into a movie clip by selecting it and choosing Insert | Convert to Symbol.
4. Make sure the Behavior option is set to Movie Clip. Type the name **counter text**. Click OK.
5. Now that your text field is a movie clip, you can attach some object actions to it. To do so, select it and open the Actions panel. Make sure that the words "Object Actions" are displayed at the top of your Actions panel.

6. Add the following code to attach actions to the movie clip:

```
onClipEvent (load) {
      // change the value of movieFps (20 by default) to your
      // own fps setting (movie property)
      movieFps = 20;
      frame = 0;
}
onClipEvent (enterFrame) {
      if (Number(frame) < 1 or Number(frame) > Number(movieFps)) {
      frame = 1;
      startTime = getTimer() / 1000;

      } else if (Number(frame) == Number(movieFps)) {
      endTime = getTimer() / 1000;
      elapsedTime = endTime - startTime;
      fps = int(movieFps / elapsedTime);
frame = 0;
      } else {
            frame = Number(frame) + 1;
       }
}
```

7. Now you need to "nest" this whole movie clip and its actions inside a shell.
    This protects your code from being lost or altered when you use it in a future
    project. Select the movie clip and select Insert | Convert to Symbol. Make sure
    the Behavior option is set to Movie Clip, type in the name **counter module**,
    and click OK.

8. Save your project (choose File | Save As) as **framerate counter module**.

Reusing a Module   You can now use the framerate module in any Flash movie at any
time, using these steps:

1. Open any Flash project

2. Create a new layer at the top of the main timeline. Name it **temporary
    fps counter**.

3. Open your counter project as a library (select File | Open as Library).
    You should see a Library window containing the counter text and counter
    module symbols.

4. Select the counter module symbol and drag it to your stage, into the new
    layer you created in step 2.

5. Test your movie (select Control | Test Movie). You should see the counter
    on top of everything else in your movie, and it should be constantly updating.

With this module, you can easily see where your Flash project is slowing down. You will learn what to modify in your layout in order to make the user's experience smoother. Furthermore, you will be able to see the playback performance on different computers before you deliver the project to your client or show it to your audience. You can e-mail a few friends and ask them to check your movie on the Internet and report what frame rate they get; where the movie is slowing down on their machine; and, finally, what machine they have.

Using Positive and Negative Space

It is important to use positive and negative space correctly so that the visitor can understand the design and information given on the site. *Positive space* is generally the space occupied by your objects. Conversely, *negative space* is the space that is not occupied by your objects. The negative space is defined by the edges of the positive space and the edge of the movie stage. So, part of your negative space is bounded by the stage, and another part is bounded by the positive space. Sometimes, the negative space is completely bounded by the positive space. Yes, this can be confusing. An important concept to note is that the negative space also defines your objects.

You want to use positive and negative space to direct the visitor's attention to particular information on the page, as shown in the following illustration.

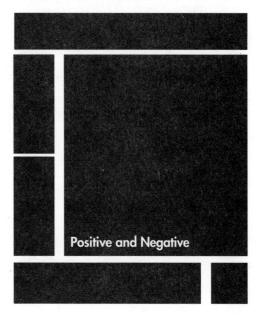

Where does your eye go?

A composition works when it achieves a balance between the positive and the negative. A major factor in controlling this balance is the stage or border of the site. While the balance idea is easy to grasp, the involvement of the "frame," or the site's edge, is harder to grasp and harder to clarify.

The frame is the edge of the site boundaries. If you are laying your Flash movie in a larger HTML site, then the frame is the boundaries of that larger site, if it blends into the design. You need to account for the frame in composing a layout with balanced positive and negative space.

By using the space on the page correctly, you can create expressions and illusions in the layout. Experiment with various exercises that will test your techniques in expression and motion. For example, create a layout that illustrates speed, one for growth, one for confusion, and so on, as shown in Figure 1-6. It is quite amazing how a shift in spacing and shape can change the whole feeling of a site.

Using Centering

Using centering in a design can be a tricky issue. To use centering successfully, you need to maintain the balance of the layout. If the page is totally centered, with nothing heavier in another area to capture interest, the visitor has no focus and no launch point for the eye to follow.

If you look at the www.postcardgraphics.com front page, shown in Figure 1-7, you will see that the navigation is centered in the middle of the page. What keeps it from looking weak is the different shading of the navigation buttons, the use of the images in a nonuniform method, and the longer bar that breaks up the boxes.

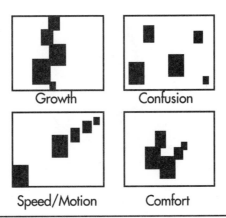

Figure 1-6   *Showing spacing and emotion*

Figure 1-7 *The postcardgraphics site*

Now take a look at the same site navigation without the images and shading differences, as shown in Figure 1-8. You will see this framework does not hold interest to the viewer. There is no story for the eye to uncover.

Designing with Color

"Color is a sensation and not a substance." This statement was made by Joseph Friedman in *History of Color Photography* (1947). It hits the nail on the head when speaking about the importance of color in design.

Color in design for the Internet is an amazing tool. With the exception of images, there is nothing that will create the emotional impact that color can produce. Color can be a make-it or break-it factor in creating a premise for a site.

Figure 1-8   *Centering used ineffectively*

What Is RGB?

Color on your computer monitor or television screen is shown by variations of light. If you were to magnify your monitor, you will notice that only three colors are used: red, green, and blue (RGB). Red, green, and blue are the three primary colors of light. These three colors in different combinations are perceived as many different colors.

The numbers that you see in the RGB area of your Flash color palette equate to the hexadecimal code for the color you choose. Hexadecimal color codes are used in HTML, whereas decimal numbers are used for Flash. Understanding how to get the hexadecimal value to correlate with the decimal value is important. First, a bit of background on the hexadecimal system: it is the alphanumeric system used to specify colors on the Web. For example, the hexadecimal equivalent of white is FFFFFF, and black is 000000. Each hexadecimal color code consists of six characters. The first two characters are a hexadecimal number representing the intensity of red light in the color, in a range between 00 (zero, no red) and FF (255, or 100% red). The second two characters show the intensity of green light in the color, and the last two characters represent the blue light. The following table shows some examples of decimal numbers, the equivalent hexadecimal codes, and the intensity of color (red, green, or blue) that the number represents.

Decimal Number	Hexadecimal Code	Color Intensity
0	00	0%
51	33	20%
102	66	40%
153	99	60%
204	CC	80%
255	FF	100%

To convert the two characters of a hexadecimal number to decimal, take the first number of the pair, multiply it by 16, and then add the second number of the pair. This comes in handy when you want to create seamless color in a Flash movie in an HTML document. Remember that hexadecimal is a *base16* numbering system.

Color Terminology

The following are some of the terms used to describe color and how it works:

► **Hue**   The attribute of color associated with a dominant spectrum wavelength.

► **Primary colors**   Red, green, and blue for computer monitors. These colors are used to make all of the colors. In traditional color wheels, red, yellow, and blue are the primary colors. Primary colors are basic and cannot be mixed from any other color.

► **Orange, green, and violet.** These colors are created from two primary colors. Yellow and red make orange. Red and blue make purple. Blue and yellow make green.

► **Tertiary colors**   Orange-red, yellow-orange, yellow-green, blue-green, blue-violet, and red-violet. Each of these colors is the mixture of a primary and the secondary color next to it on the color wheel.

- ▶ **Complementary colors**   Colors that are 176 degrees opposite from each other on the color wheel. These colors are in extreme contrast to each other, yet they help make each other more active. Purple and yellow are complementary colors.

- ▶ **Spectrum**   The distribution of colors, arranged in order of wavelengths, which make up the light from any particular source. The simplest example of this concept is a rainbow, which is a natural display of the visible spectrum.

- ▶ **Additive color**   The system for screen colors, using red, green, and blue. Different intensities of each color create the secondary color, making all other colors besides red, green, and blue in the additive color system. Red, green, and blue mixed together in equal intensity make white.

- ▶ **Subtractive color**   The system for printing color, using cyan, magenta, yellow, and black (cyan, magenta, and yellow inks mixed in equal intensity make black).

- ▶ **Chrome**   Refers to the intensity or the degree of purity or grayness of a color. Chromacity is not to be confused with the value (lightness and darkness).

- ▶ **Tone**   A color that has been neutralized by the addition of gray.

- ▶ **Value**   The degree of lightness or darkness in a color.

In hexadecimal, you count all the way to 15 before using double digits. After 9, start using letters: 10 is A, 11 is B, 12 is C, and so on, to 15, which is F.

Using Color to Target an Audience

The rules of engagement for color are based on particular social understandings. What a design firm such as www.skilla.com can use for color is far different from the colors that work on a site that is servicing the corporate world, like www.wsj.com. If the *Wall Street Journal* were to have a hot pink and green site, the seriousness of the site would be lost, as well as the male-oriented target audience. You must find a color palette that will work for your targeted audience and the image your client wishes to project. This palette will define the colors for the background, buttons, text, images (if you are creating duotones), and other elements.

Here are some guidelines for color design:

▶ Color must work productively on several levels at the same time.

▶ Technically, the colors must be as accurate as the existing hardware and software will allow.

▶ Once a set of colors has caught and held the visitor's attention, these colors must succeed in conveying the appropriate information.

▶ Colors must work competently as the primary structural element in the client's image reflected by the site. In this capacity, color must create appropriate spatial and navigational effects on the page and the site as a whole.

▶ As the primary aesthetic tool, the colors must create a sense of visual harmony, sustaining and enhancing a visitor's experience.

The following are some great sites for seeing how color is used to gear the site to the targeted audience:

▶ **www.girlshop.com**   A great use of color for its target female audience

▶ **www.wholetruth.com**   Creates a feeling of dark mystery and the unknown

▶ **www.nick.com**   Obviously designed for kids

▶ **www.billabong-usa.com**   Works for its young male audience

▶ **www.purusdesign.com**   Offers a soothing approach for modernism

▶ **www.h73.com**   Has a progressive approach to color

These sites are just a few examples of many that explore the use of color in an effective way.

Using Colors Together

When you isolate a color, the color itself is, in a sense, neutral. The intensity must always be thought of in relationship to the intensities and values of the colors that surround it.

For example, suppose that you create a site with light orange as a background. If you make the other elements yellow, they will be lost in the light-orange background. If you changed the background to black, the yellow would stand out more strongly. If you used dark green for the background, the yellow would stand out, but it also would be very harmonious, because green and yellow are close on the color wheel.

On the opposite side of the color wheel to yellow is purple. Using purple as the background would cause the yellow to really pop out, emphasizing the yellowness of the yellow more than any other color could.

The most important rule for choosing colors for your site is to aim for simplicity. Try not to use a large number of colors all at once. Understanding the three following color arrangements when creating your color palette will allow simplicity to reign in your design:

▶ **Analogous colors**   A scheme that uses colors next to one another on the color wheel. For example an analogous color scheme might include yellow-green, yellow, and yellow-orange. The only rule is that none of the colors may be opposite one another on the wheel. You could not add orange-red to the example, because red is opposite green on the wheel, and yellow-green is one of the colors.

▶ **Harmonious colors**   A scheme that uses adjoining colors on the color wheel. Two adjoining colors obviously harmonize easily because they are almost monochromatic; but such a scheme can be monotonous, unless the two colors are used with many value contrasts. A scheme with three adjoining colors would be far more interesting because it would have more color contrast within the harmony.

▶ **Complementary colors**   A scheme that uses complementary colors on the color wheel. If the mood of your site requires a less harmonious color scheme, you can build a color palette based on complementary colors. For example, the yellow and purple palette mentioned earlier will generate visual excitement, even though it has only two colors. In the same way, a touch of orange will make your blues more vibrant.

When using these color palettes, it is best to have either a cool or warm palette for the majority of your color. A cool color palette has blue as the base color—even the red used in a cool color palette would be a blue-red. A warm color palette has a yellow-orange base to it. You can mix the two palettes, but one should always be dominant.

Color's structure and excitement comes from intensity, value, and color. Creating tension through polarities is fundamental in color and design. Coupled with movement, one of the following basic color structures will give your design greater dynamics and a solid impact:

▶ Light versus dark

▶ Bright versus dull intensities

▶ Opposing hues

▶ The radiation of colors, such as the way that a red projects forward and a blue recedes

▶ Contrast of extension, such as a red dot in a large black area

Your eye naturally recognizes particular colors and contrasts; perception of other colors require logical thinking and attention. Studying how color interacts in nature is a great place to start understanding how to use multiple colors to create visual results. On the Web, www.visibone.com is a great resource and includes an interactive page for creating color palettes.

Designing with Type

When your content is mostly text, typography plays a big role. Typography is the art of making a design pattern on the page. The overall pattern of the page, not the title or other details, is the first thing that the visitor will see when visiting your page. The visitor's eye will scan the page for a graphic pattern, and then begin to follow and decipher type and page elements.

The regular patterns established through meticulously organized pages of text and graphics help the reader quickly establish the location and organization of your information, and increase the overall legibility of your site. Various typography styles and text headers will make it difficult for the user to see major patterns promptly, and will make it almost impossible for the user to quickly foresee where information is likely to be located in unfamiliar documents. Choose your fonts with the overall pattern in mind.

A definitive rule of typography when working in design is that the letters that show a unified straight form, such as all capital letters, are great for display, but not for paragraph text. We do not read letter to letter, we read words. Grasping the word as a whole is difficult when there is too much unity in lettering. Avoid using only capital letters, because they are equal in height and volume, and typically also equal in width.

A rule that is often violated in Web design is one of the most basic in book and magazine typography. The lines of text in most Web sites are much too long to be easily read. Most magazine and book columns are limited for physiological purposes: at standard reading distances, the eye's span of movement is only about 3 inches (8 centimeters) wide. Designers try to keep compact blocks of text in columns no wider than the reader's comfortable eye span. Wider lines of text require the readers to move their heads slightly or to strain their eye muscles to track over the long lines of text.

When you are designing a site that is text intensive, keep the rules of typography in mind. You want the viewer to be interested in your site and also be able to comprehend all that text.

Finding Inspiration

Inspiration for designing your next project can come from just about anywhere. I find a lot of my inspiration from other sites—seeing what other designers have done. It's always wonderful to find new methods and concepts. Following is a listing of some inspiring Flash sites:

- ► www.amontobin.com
- ► www.juxtinteractive.com
- ► www.turbonium.com
- ► www.barneys.com
- ► www.turtleshell.com
- ► www.skilla.com
- ► mtv2.co.uk
- ► www.yugop.com
- ► www.gmunk.com
- ► www.droppod.com
- ► www.viaduct.co.uk
- ► www.aidio.com
- ► www.webstyles.net

There are many others Flash sites that are sensational, but the listed sites left a tremendous impression on me. Also, a great place to see an updated listing of excellent sites is www.coolhomepages.com.

Inspiration can come from other places beyond the Internet. Search for something innovative and distinctive from other areas of creative expression, such as architecture, painting, writing, films, and even television commercials. Study the lines and movements of these creative works. Try to analyze the thought processes that led to the final version of the project.

With the release of Flash 5, there is a whole new edge to inspire the designer. It adds the new ActionScripting capabilities and enhanced capabilities for creating stunning interactivity. Also, other features—such as JavaScript-like syntax, XML transfer support, HTML text support, and Smart Clips—make for an extensive playground of creativity. The projects that are detailed in this book will be a great tool for inspiration as well. With all of the exercises that have been outlined in the following chapters, creating a project that will make a enormous impact will be an easy task.

What to Take Away from This Chapter

Beyond what has been covered in this chapter, there is one ultimate key to successful design: your imagination. When you approach a project, listen to your instincts about how to form a site. Try not to be caged into a mindset or a style. Develop your own personal style, but don't be hesitant to experiment with different techniques and styles. An enormous part of being an innovator is the ability to let go of the trend and look of today and create something that will be the trend and look of tomorrow.

Simulating an MP3 Player

IN THIS CHAPTER:

▶ Streaming audio in Flash

▶ Build a music player's display

▶ Load Flash movies in levels

▶ Create a music list

▶ Create volume and panning control sliders

▶ Create tracker and loading bars

Thereare many possibilities for interface design when you combine the interactive capabilities of ActionScript with the regular streaming features of Flash movies. To demonstrate one of these possibilities, the examples in this chapter will walk you through the construction of a Flash interface that simulates an MP3 player. Although the final result will look and feel like an MP3 player, the actual music files are separate Flash movies in the small web format (SWF), because Flash cannot play MP3 files. Instead, the MP3 files are imported into a Flash movie, and then the movie is exported as a streaming SWF file.

When Flash exports a movie with audio, users have an option of using the MP3-encoding algorithm inside the Flash editor to compress audio files into a Flash movie. Consequently, Flash movies containing MP3-compressed audio can stream with a speed and quality comparable to regular MP3 streaming, as long as the user's browser contains the Flash plug-in.

By this point, you may be wondering why you should bother building an MP3 player in Flash if it only plays SWF movies. The use of SWF movies for music playing has several advantages. A file in SWF format can provide a degree of protection for copyright music because it's not easy to extract audio elements from an SWF file. A designer can easily build an attractive interface to control or load music Flash files with just a bit of ActionScript, and both the interface and music files will play on any browser regardless of its platform, as long as the computer has the Flash plug-in installed. Also, building a regular MP3 player requires the use of much more complex programming languages, such as Visual C++ or Visual Basic.

Streaming Audio in Flash 5

There are several ways to load external SWF movies into a Flash movie, but not all of them are well suited to the task of streaming music. The project described in this chapter uses the simplest approach possible, which is to create an SWF movie with an embedded music file (.raw, .wav, or .mp3), and then load this external SWF movie onto level 2 of the main Flash movie. This external SWF movie will contain only audio, nothing visual.

Let's call this interface a music player instead of an MP3 player, because it plays SWF audio movies instead of MP3s. The main music player will load into the browser with an interface to control the music, while several external SWF movies containing MP3-compressed audio clips will exist on the server, waiting for the user to choose to load them into the music player.

TIP

There are many free and commercial tools that automate the process of turning an MP3 music file into an SWF Flash movie. Several of these tools are listed at the end of the chapter, and most of them will run on a regular Web server with a server-side scripting language such as Active Server Pages (ASP), PHP, or some other server-side programming language built in. Uploading a batch of MP3 players and then converting them into SWF movies can be done dynamically or manually with one of the free tools.

In order to load an external music movie, you'll need some music first. The project described in this chapter uses a demo track I composed, entitled "Arabian Rain." The music is stored and compressed inside the SWF movie named ArabianRain.swf. Very long audio clips such as this one should use the streaming option, so that the Flash Player can begin to play the audio clip while the rest of it is still downloading into the player.

ArabianRain.fla

Open the ArabianRain.fla file, and you will see a sound imported into the first frame of the main timeline. The default location of the Sound panel in Flash 5 is in the lower panel window, next to the Frame and Instance panels. Select the first frame on the main timeline, and then open the Sound panel. Here, you will see that the sound ArabianRain.wav has been imported into the first frame, and that the sync is set to Stream.

NOTE

ArabianRain.fla is a processor-intensive Flash file due to the long music stream. It could use up to 50MB of memory to run.

Select File | Publish Settings and note the settings for Audio Stream. For this movie, the Audio Stream settings use MP3 compression to achieve the highest compression possible, and the audio quality is set to Best at a bit rate of 20Kbps. These settings provide an optimum balance between speed and quality for streaming audio in Flash.

Testing the movie's playback in Flash 5 allows you to evaluate its streaming behavior. To see how well the movie will stream, select Control | Test Movie. For this project, choose Debug | 56K to test for the popular 56Kbps modem's bandwidth, and choose View | Show Streaming to see the actual speed of the file as it streams into a simulated modem.

NOTE

The subject of digital music composition is beyond the scope of this book, but for curious readers who want to know, I composed and produced the soundtrack "Arabian Rain" using the free Jeskola Buzz Tracker and a commercial sound-editing program called Sound Forge 4.5, from Sonic Foundry. The music was saved as a WAV file at 44KHz and 16-bit mono, and then imported into Flash.

Planning the Music Player's Interface

Before you begin to build an interface, you should plan a list of interface components. This will save a lot of time and speed up the design process.

So what kind of interface elements are commonly found on a music player such as a CD player or MP3 player? For playback control, many machines have play, stop, rewind, forward, and pause buttons. Other common features include volume, panning, and mute controls.

Streaming audio players have a unique interface requirement, because the user needs some way to select a music file from a list, and then begin loading it to the player. Therefore, you want to include a music list. The interface should also contain a display to show the name of the music file currently playing, a tracker to show how far the music has played, and a loader to show how much of the music has currently streamed/downloaded to the browser.

Creating the Playback Buttons and Display

MusicPlayer_01.fla

The easiest interface components to build for the music player are the play, stop, rewind, forward, pause, and mute controls. Because these components only require the user to click them once, you can make them buttons, as shown in Figure 2-1. The source file for this step, which contains the playback control buttons and display, can be found on the CD-ROM as MusicPlayer_01.fla.

Adding the Play and Stop Buttons

The play button is a simple triangle pointing toward the right, 40 pixels wide and 40 pixels high. The lines of the triangle edges are stroked with a stroke height of 2, and each stroke has a different lightness of gray to make the button appear beveled, or raised. The fill color of the triangle is a simple radial gradient from white to black, to give it a polished-metal look. After drawing the shape, select the entire triangle with its edges and press F8 to convert the triangle into a symbol. Choose the Button behavior option to make it a button, and give it the name **PlayButton**.

The stop button is a simple square 40 pixels wide and 40 pixels high. The lines of the square are again stroked at different colors of gray to give a beveled appearance, and filled with a radial gradient from white to black. Draw the shape, and then select the entire square with its edges and press F8 to convert the square into a symbol. Choose the Button behavior option to make it a button, and give it the name **StopButton**.

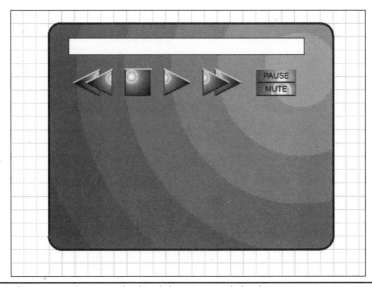

Figure 2-1   *The music player's playback buttons and display*

Adding the Forward and Rewind Buttons

To save time, reuse the graphics from the play button for the forward button. Select the play button, and then copy and paste it somewhere else on the screen. With the button still selected, choose Modify | Break Apart to break the button into a vector image again. Next, highlight the entire new image and select Edit | Copy | Paste In Place. This positions a copy of the image directly on top of the original image. Press the left arrow key to move the new copy toward the left.

You now have two overlapped triangles with beveled edges. Highlight the entire image and press F8 to convert the overlapped triangles into a new symbol. Choose the Button behavior option to make it a button, and give it the name **ForwardButton**.

Use the same technique to create a new button for the rewind button. Make another copy of the ForwardButton button somewhere on the screen, and then select Modify | Break Apart again. With the graphics still selected, choose Modify | Transform | Flip Horizontal to reverse the graphic on the screen. Highlight the image, press F8 to convert the graphic into a symbol, choose Button, and name it **RewindButton**.

Adding Pause and Mute Buttons

For the pause button, create another beveled rectangle by using a radiant fill from white to black and different shades of gray. Use a stroke height of 2 pixels to make the beveled edges. Using the Arial font at 12 points in black, type **PAUSE**, and drag the text over the rectangle. Select both the rectangle and the text, and press F8 to convert them into a symbol. Choose Button and name it **PauseButton**.

The mute button can be built by simply duplicating the pause button and changing the text. In the Flash Library, select the PauseButton, select the Duplicate command from the Library's pull-down menu, and name the new button **MuteButton**. Double-click the new button and change the text inside from PAUSE to **MUTE**.

Rollover Highlighting

For the final touch, adjust the buttons so that they appear highlighted whenever the mouse cursor rolls over the buttons. Go through all of the new buttons in the Library and create a new keyframe in the frame labeled Over. Then change all the lines in the over frame to white by changing the stroke color to white. For example, the Forward Button should have a keyframe in the over frame, with white lines outlining the arrow shapes, as shown in Figure 2-2.

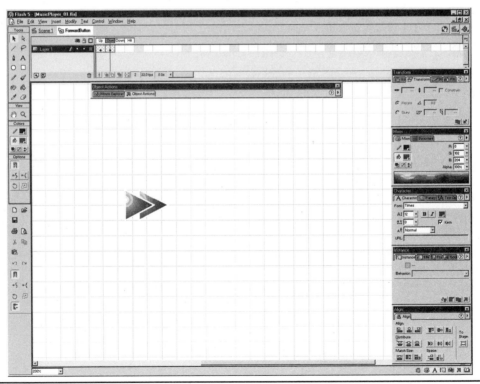

Figure 2-2   *Add white outlines for the button in the Over keyframe.*

Creating the Display

For the display, which will show the name of the current music SWF movie being played, a simple text field will stack on top of a gradient rectangle. First, create a text field with Arial font at 19 points, and extend it across the stage so that the text field is approximately 360 pixels wide. In the Text Options panel, choose Dynamic Text, make it single-line, and give the text field a variable name of **display**. Make sure that the text field's Border/BG check box is checked, so that it will have a white background with a black border.

So far, all of these buttons and the text field exist on a single layer in the main timeline of the movie. Name this layer **Buttons**, and then create another layer beneath the Buttons layer. Name the new layer **Background Shape**, and then draw a simple rectangle with smooth curves to give the interface a background shape. You won't need to make any changes to the Background Shape layer, so lock the layer on the main timeline.

Creating the Music List

Thus far, you've built an interface for the playback control buttons and the display text field. In addition, the external SWF movie ArabianRain.swf already exists to contain the music for the music player. The next step in this project is to bring both files together by allowing the music player interface to load ArabianRain.swf into the main Flash movie. This is accomplished through a list of available music. The user will be able to click the title of a song and load the external SWF movie into the main movie.

Building the Music Menu Bar

A list of music titles must do two things: display the title of the song and allow the user to click a button to load the song into the movie. In order to meet these two goals, build a new movie clip that contains a dynamic text field to display the title of the song and a button that will load the song when clicked by the mouse. This new movie clip will act as a labeled button.

First, create a new layer in the main timeline called Music List. In the first frame of the new layer, insert a text field approximately 180 pixels wide, with the Arial font at 12 points. In the Text Options panel, make the text field Dynamic Text and give the text field a variable name of **title**. Now that a text field exists to contain the title of the song, convert it into a movie clip by pressing F8 and selecting the Movie

Clip behavior option. Give the new movie clip the name **MusicMenuBar**. Then double-click it to edit the contents.

The MusicMenuBar movie clip already includes a text field, so the next step is to create a button inside the movie clip. Insert a new layer beneath the text field layer, and then draw a rectangle with the same dimensions as the text field. For effect, you can use the same beveling technique with lines that was used for the playback buttons to make the button appear raised. Select the rectangle, and then press F8 to convert it into a button named **MusicMenuBar_Button**. The final result should look like the button shown in Figure 2-3.

Back on the main timeline, select this new button, and in the Instance panel, give the movie clip an instance name of **MusicBar**, so that it can be referred to in ActionScript code later on.

NOTE

It's important to assign an instance name to the movie clip; otherwise, ActionScript will not know which movie clip to reference when you build a Music List menu.

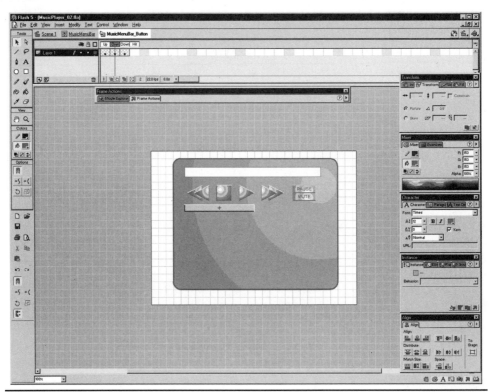

Figure 2-3   *The final structure of the MusicMenuBar_Button*

Building a Music List

In order to create a music list from which the user can select a song to load, you need to create duplicates of the MusicMenuBar movie clip and stack them up into a list of song titles with buttons, as shown in Figure 2-4. Several steps are involved in this process. First, you need to store the title of the song and the location of the corresponding SWF movie file inside ActionScript variables. Using these variables, you must then duplicate a stack of MusicMenuBar movie clips and insert the title and location information inside those movie clips, so that they will load the correct song.

Back in the main timeline, insert a new layer at the top, named Actions. Back in the first frame of the Actions layer, double-click the frame to open the Action panel.

TIP

It's always a good idea to separate your ActionScript from the rest of the content in a timeline. The separation will prevent the ActionScript from being deleted as you manipulate the timeline. Also, it helps to know exactly where to edit your ActionScript code.

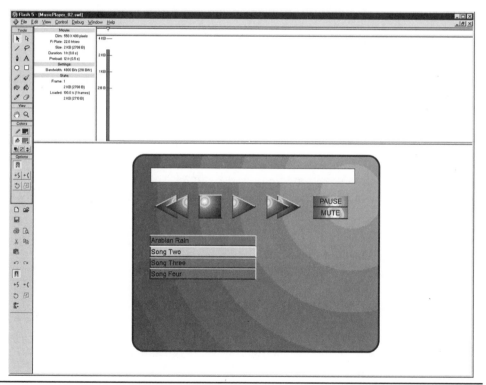

Figure 2-4   *The music list for the music player*

MusicPlayer_02.fla

Inside the Action panel, type in the following ActionScript code, as shown in Figure 2-5, which we will explore shortly (to skip this step, you can open the MusicPlayer_02.fla file on this book's CD-ROM):

L 2-1
```
function addSong(songName, fileName)
{
        duplicateMovieClip("musicbar", "bar" + index, index);
        var reference = eval("bar" + index);
        reference.title = songName
        reference.location = fileName;
        reference._y = musicbar._y + musicbar._height * index;
        index = index + 1;
}

index = 1;
addSong("Arabian Rain", "ArabianRain.swf");
addSong("Song Two", "ArabianRain.swf");
addSong("Song Three", "ArabianRain.swf");
addSong("Song Four", "ArabianRain.swf");

musicbar._visible = false;
musicbar._x = 2000;
```

Near the bottom of the ActionScript code, you see four lines that add a new song to the interface using the addSong() command. Flash 5 ActionScript doesn't have a command called addSong(), but you can create one by defining a function. A function in ActionScript acts as a group of commands that can be called in sequence by simply calling the name of the function. A parameter of a function allows the user to pass along data while the function is being called.

Creating the addSong() Function

The first portion of this code defines the addSong() function, beginning with its name and parameters:

L 2-2
```
function addSong(songName, fileName)
```

The function's two parameters are songName and fileName. Any ActionScript code can pass the name of the song to the function by placing the name inside the

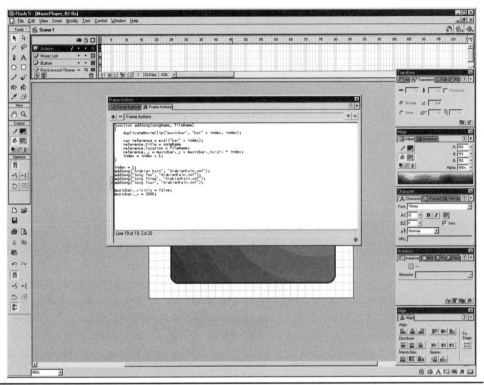

Figure 2-5   *The ActionScript for the music list*

`songName` parameter. The location of the SWF music file can also be passed into the function through the second parameter, `fileName`.

The next steps for the function involve duplicating the MusicMenuBar movie clip created earlier and stacking the duplicates into a list of buttons that allow the user to select and load a song. The `duplicateMovieClip()` command creates a new duplicate of the MusicMenuBar, which has an instance name of musicbar.

L 2-3

```
duplicateMovieClip("musicbar", "bar" + index, index);
```

The new duplicate is given an instance name of bar joined with the value of the `index` variable, so if this were the first song added, the new duplicate would have an instance name of bar1. If it were the second song added, the new duplicate would have an instance name of bar2, and so forth. The `index` variable is also used to specify the depth of the duplicate movie clip, so that each duplicate's depth will be different when the `index` variable increases by a value of 1 (at the end of this function definition).

Next, the new movie clip is assigned to a variable named `reference` using the `eval("bar" + index)` command to assign the instance name of the movie clip.

L 2-4

```
var reference = eval("bar" + index);
```

You use the name `reference` because the value of this variable contains a reference to the newly duplicated movie clip. In other words, the `reference` variable is a shortcut, or a representation, of the duplicated movie clip.

You can create new variables inside the referenced movie clip by assigning new properties to the reference variable, like so:

L 2-5

```
reference.title = songName;
reference.location = fileName;
```

The properties `title` and `location` are defined for each movie clip by assigning to them the value of the function parameters of `songName` and `filename`.

At this point, remember that the MusicMenuBar movie clip contains a text field with the variable named `title`, so any changes made to the reference variable's `title` property will essentially display the title of the song in the text field of the new duplicate movie clip.

In the last two lines of the `addSong()` function, the y position of the new movie clip is defined.

L 2-6

```
reference._y = musicbar._y + musicbar._height * index;
index = index + 1;
```

Because each subsequent duplicate must be positioned below its previous movie clip, you can find the y position of each new movie clip by positioning it according to the y position of the original MusicBar movie clip, and adding a product of the movie clip's height times the number of duplicates already created. After positioning the new movie clip, the `index` variable is incremented by one, so that it will know how many movie clips have been duplicated when the `addSong()` function is called again next time.

Adding the Songs and Displaying the Music Bar

The rest of the ActionScript code in this keyframe simply initializes the `index` variable and then calls the `addSong()` function to add new songs and new MusicBar movie clips to the interface. First, the variable named `index` is declared to keep track of how many songs have already been added to the interface.

L 2-7

```
index = 1;
```

The `index` variable is initialized with a value of 1, so that the first song loaded will know that it's the first song on the list.

Next are the calls to the `addSong()` function.

L 2-8

```
addSong("Arabian Rain", "ArabianRain.swf");
addSong("Song Two", "ArabianRain.swf");
addSong("Song Three", "ArabianRain.swf");
addSong("Song Four", "ArabianRain.swf");
```

These songs have the names Arabian Rain, Song Two, Song Three, and Song Four; however, they all point to the same music file, ArabianRain.swf. This is because this project uses only one music file.

The last two lines of code make the original MusicBar movie clip invisible, and set it off to the side so that it won't interfere with the main interface.

L 2-9

```
musicbar._visible = false;
musicbar._x = 2000;
```

Adding ActionScript to the MusicMenuBar Button

Now that each movie clip contains information about the title and the location of the music SWF file, the buttons inside the movie clip need to know how to load the music SWF file. In the Flash Library, double-click the MusicMenuBar movie clip and select the beveled rectangular button by locking all the other layers and then highlighting the button. Then open the Action panel for the button, either by right-clicking the button or by selecting Window | Action.

Remember that the `addSong()` function will insert the filename of each song into each duplicated movie clip's `location` variable, so the external SWF file that matches the `location` variable of each movie clip should load into the Flash movie when the user clicks the button of a MusicMenuBar movie clip. To accomplish this, insert the following lines of code into the button:

L 2-10

```
on (release) {
    loadMovieNum (location, 2);
}
```

Here, you can see that the ActionScript command `loadMovieNum()` will execute as soon as the user's mouse is released over the button. The `loadMovieNum()` function will load an external SWF file whose name matches the `location` variable,

Using Levels

Flash movies may actually load external movies on top of themselves as levels. These levels are similar to depths in Flash, because only one external SWF movie may exist in a level at a time. However, they are different from depths because movies inside levels actually exist outside the main Flash movie, like a stacked deck of SWF movies resting on top of each other.

The main Flash movie always exists at level 0. Whenever you load an external SWF file into level 2, the SWF file currently loaded into level 2 is removed from the browser's memory and replaced by the new external SWF. In order to refer to a movie on level 2, ActionScript must use the prefix `_level2`.

and the loaded movie will exist in level 2 of the Flash movie. The next section describes how to add ActionScript to the playback control buttons of the interface to control the playback of the music movie on level 2.

At this point, try testing the movie to observe how each duplicated MusicMenuBar will load the ArabianRain.swf file with a different title displayed in the interface. Figure 2-6 shows the main movie playing, with Song Three selected as the current song.

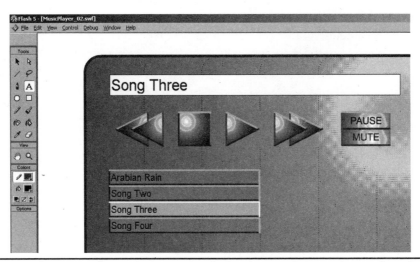

Figure 2-6   *The Music Player playing in the Flash editor, with Song Three selected*

Adding ActionScript to the Interface

This next steps are to add ActionScript to the music player's playback control buttons. Because these are buttons, their actions should occur when the user clicks them. A mouse click typically uses the `on(release)` event handler for a button, because a mouse click logically doesn't happen until the user presses and then releases the mouse button.

Scripting the Stop, Play, Pause, Rewind, and Forward Buttons

When the external SWF file ArabianRain.swf loads into level 2 of the Flash movie, it begins playing immediately. The stop button contains the following code in the `on(release)` event handler to stop the movie in level 2 and return it to the first frame:

L 2-11
```
on (release) {
    _level2.gotoAndStop(1);
}
```

In order to force the movie in level 2 to continue playing after it has stopped, the play button contains the following code in the `on(release)` event handler:

L 2-12
```
on (release) {
    _level2.play();
}
```

You can pause the music by telling the level 2 movie to stop at its current frame. This is accomplished by inserting the following code inside the `on(release)` event handler for the pause button:

L 2-13
```
on (release) {
    _level2.stop();
}
```

The rewind button works by finding the current frame of the movie in level 2, and then telling the movie to jump 20 frames before its current frame and start playing from that frame:

L 2-14
```
on (release) {
    _level2.gotoAndPlay(_level2._currentFrame - 20);
}
```

The forward button finds the current frame of the movie in level 2, and then tells the movie to start playing 20 frames after its current frame:

L 2-15
```
on (release) {
       _level2.gotoAndPlay(_level2._currentFrame + 20);
}
```

Using the Sound Object for the Mute Button

The functionality of the mute button actually requires much more complex programming than the previous buttons for two reasons:

▶   The mute button must prevent the level 2 movie (ArabianRain.swf) from making any sound, while still allowing the movie to continue playing.

▶   The mute button must toggle the volume of the level 2 movie clip so that the volume will either go to 0 or 100 each time the mute button is pressed.

In order to have the mute button accomplish its tasks, the ActionScript code will need to use the Sound object in Flash 5.

The Sound object in ActionScript creates a reference to an attached sound in the Library or a reference to another movie clip in the Flash movie. In the case of the music player, a new Sound object must be created to represent the sound properties of the movie loaded into level 2.

L 2-16
```
on (release) {
       if(music == null or music.getVolume() > 0) {
             music = new Sound(_level2);
             music.setVolume(0);
       } else if(music.getVolume() == 0) {
             music.setVolume(100);
       }
}
```

Here, the on(release) event handler executes the code between its curly braces every time the mouse cursor is released over the button. There are two possible conditions for the ActionScript code. The first section of ActionScript will create a new Sound object called music, and use the music object to refer to the audio properties of the movie in level 2. Then the next step in the first section of ActionScript will set the music's volume to 0 if the music object hasn't been defined yet or if the music object's volume is still greater than 0. The second section of ActionScript will set the `music` object's volume back to 100 if the music object's volume had previously been set to 0.

Creating a Slider for Volume and Panning Control

The next logical step after the introduction of the Sound object is the creation of a slider to control the volume and left/right panning of the music. A slider consists of two elements:

▶ The slider button, which allows the user to drag the slider up and down with the mouse

▶ The bar, which defines the constraints of the slider's dragging area

The slider built for the volume and panning controls will use the most simple design possible, so that you can adapt a single generic slider for both controls.

Creating the Slider's Bar and Button

Begin by inserting a new layer on the main timeline called Sliders. The first step is to create the bar for the slider. Draw a black rectangle 10 pixels wide and 100 pixels high on the stage, as shown in Figure 2-7. Convert this black rectangle into a movie clip with the name **SliderBar**, and then give it an instance name of **SliderBar** in the Instance panel. Double-click the new SliderBar movie clip. Now, position the bar so that its top edge is at the center of the movie clip by opening the Info panel and assigning a value of 0.0 to the black rectangle's y position.

Go back to the main timeline and select the Sliders layer again. Create the slider button by making a beveled, gray square approximately 20 pixels wide and 10 pixels high. (Use the same beveling techniques that were used to create the other buttons for the interface, as described in "Creating the Playback Buttons and Display," earlier in this chapter.) Convert this square graphic into a button with the name **SliderButton**. Then press F8 with the SliderButton selected and convert it into a movie clip with the name **DragBox**. Give the DragBox move clip an instance name of **DragBox** in the Instance panel.

Now you have a black rectangle movie clip with the instance name SliderBar and a movie clip called DragBox that contains a button called SliderButton. Select both the SliderBar and DragBox together, and convert them into a single movie clip called **ScrollBar**, with the instance name ScrollBar.

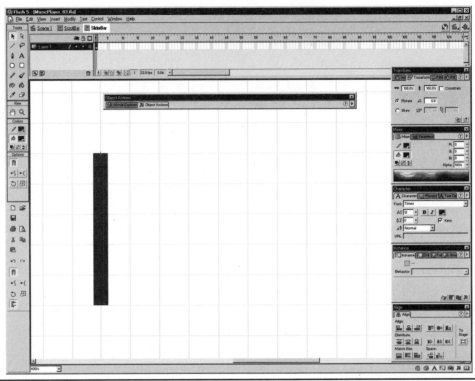

Figure 2-7   *The rectangle for the slider bar*

The positioning of the slider bar and button inside the new ScrollBar movie clip is very important. As shown in Figure 2-8, the center of the black rectangle is actually the top of the black rectangle, using crosshairs to mark the center. The center of the black rectangle must be positioned at the center of the ScrollBar movie clip. The center of the DragBox movie clip must also be positioned at the center of the ScrollBar movie clip. By putting the button at the top of the bar, the highest volume setting becomes the default starting position. To position an object to the center of the movie clip, simply set its x and y positions to 0, 0 in the Info panel.

Scripting the Slider Button

Inside the ScrollBar movie clip, double-click the DragBox to edit the SliderButton within it. You want to set up the button so that the user can press the DragBox to

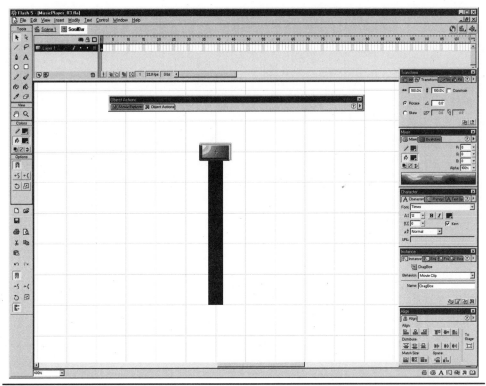

Figure 2-8   *Centering the slider bar and button in the movie clip*

drag it up and down the same length of the ScrollBar movie clip, but not from side to side. Here is the ActionScript code for the button's on (press) event handler:

L 2-17
```
on (press) {
        startDrag (this, false, 0, 0, 0, 100);
        isDragging = true;
}
```

The startDrag() command allows the user to drag a movie clip. The first parameter is the target of the drag operation. Here, this refers to the parent movie clip, DragBox. The second parameter is false, which means that the mouse will not be locked to the center of the movie clip to be dragged. The next four parameters set the constraints for the drag operation.

When the mouse button is finally released, a `stopDrag()` command should be
called to stop the DragBox movie clip from being dragged anymore.

L 2-18

```
on (release) {
      stopDrag();
      isDragging = false;
}
```

Throughout the `on(press)` and `on(release)` event handlers, the variable
`isDragging` is set to either `true` or `false`, depending on whether the DragBox
is actually being dragged by the user's mouse. The purpose of having a true/false
variable called `isDragging` is to know whether the mouse is just moving around
the screen or if it's actually dragging the DragBox movie clip to change the volume
of the movie in level 2.

Scripting the Volume Control

Go back to the ScrollBar movie clip and open the Action panel for the DragBox movie
clip. Insert the following code to control the volume of the level 2 movie by dragging
the DragBox movie clip:

L 2-19

```
onClipEvent (mouseMove) {
      if(isDragging == true)
      {
            music = new Sound(_level2);
            music.setVolume(100 - this._y);
      }
}
```

All of the ActionScript is located inside the `onClipEvent(mouseMove)` event
handler, which will execute its ActionScript code whenever the mouse moves. However,
you only want to execute the volume-control code when the mouse is moving *and*
when the `isDragging` variable is true at the same time. To handle this, create a
Sound object called music, to reference the sound properties of the movie in level 2.

L 2-20

```
music = new Sound(_level2);
```

The final line of code for this slider sets the volume of the movie in level 2 by
subtracting the current y position of the DragBox movie clip from 100.

L 2-21

```
music.setVolume(100 - this._y);
```

Because the DragBox is located at the center, and the drag constraints for its inner button are set from 0 to 100, you need to reverse the value of the position for it to apply to the volume bar. By subtracting the y position from 100, you can convert the top constraint of the dragging into a maximum volume of 100 and the bottom constraint of the dragging into a minimum volume of 0.

Finally, the ScrollBar movie clip needs a label to show what it does, so add a text label underneath the movie clip named "Volume." The layout for the ScrollBar movie clip should look like Figure 2-9, with a Volume label beneath it.

At this point, try testing the movie to see how the volume control works.

Creating the Panning Slider

Once you've verified that the volume slider works, the next step is to create a duplicate of it and turn the new duplicate into a panning slider to pan the music left or right. Open the Library and duplicate the ScrollBar movie clip by selecting the Duplicate

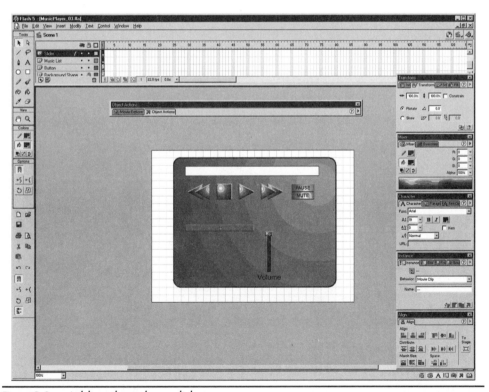

Figure 2-9 *Adding the volume slider*

command from the Library's pull-down menu. Give the new movie clip the name **PanningControl**. Double-click the PanningControl movie clip to make some changes that will allow this movie clip to control the left and right panning of the sound.

The Sound object supports a method called `setPan()`. This method takes an integer parameter between –100 to 100, where –100 pans the sound entirely to the left speakers, and 100 pans the sound entirely to the right speakers. Because the default center for panning is 0, move the DragBox movie clip toward the center of the black bar for its starting position, as shown in Figure 2-10.

The ActionScript also changes a bit from the one used for the volume slider, to use the `setPan()` method instead of the `setVolume()` method for the DragBox movie clip. Inside the PanningControl movie clip, select the DragBox movie clip. Open its Action panel and insert the following code:

L 2-22
```
onClipEvent (mouseMove) {
      if(isDragging == true)
      {
            music = new Sound(_level2);
            music.setPan((50 - this._y) * 2);
      }
}
```

The only noticeable difference from the ActionScript of the volume control is the last line, where the `setVolume()` command has been replaced with the `setPan()` method. The only other change is the new calculation of the y position, which actually calculates the difference between the DragBox's y position (ranging from 0 to 100) and 50, so that the resulting difference can range between –50 and 50. Multiplying this possible range of calculations by two will increase the range of the `setPan()` parameters between –100 and 100, from full left to full right panning.

Drag the PanningControl movie clip from the Library onto the stage in the Slider layer, and then add some text to label it "Panning," as shown in Figure 2-11. To make the interface more user friendly, you can add some text to show that the PanningControl can slide from L (left) to R (right).

Creating Tracker and Loader Bars

MusicPlayer_03.fla

For the final components of the music player's interface, build two tracking bars: one to display how much of the music has played, and the other to show the progress

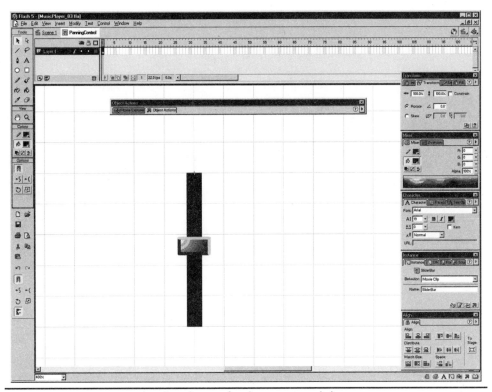

Figure 2-10   *Positioning the drag button for the panning slider*

of loading the music into the browser. Like the volume and panning controls, these two bars will use the same movie clip, but their ActionScript will have a few slight differences. The Flash source files for this section are available on the CD-ROM as MusicPlayer_03.fla .

Building the Music Tracker

The music tracker consists of a blue bar that will stretch from 0 pixels to 360 pixels, depending on how long the music has been playing. Begin by inserting a new layer on the main timeline called Trackers. Then draw a rectangle with black borders and blue fill, 360 pixels wide and 10 pixels high. Select this new rectangle and its black borders, and then press F8 to convert the rectangle into a movie clip with the name **MusicTracker**. Give the new movie clip an instance name **MusicTracker** in the Instance panel, and then double-click the movie clip to edit its contents.

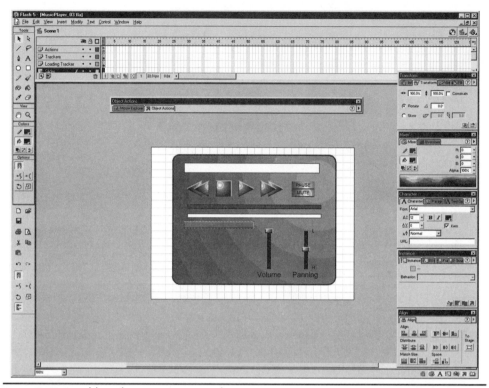

Figure 2-11   *Adding the panning control*

In order for ActionScript to resize the MusicTracker bar without repositioning the rectangle, you need to position the left edge of the rectangle to the center of the movie clip. Centering the left edge can be done by selecting the rectangle and border lines inside the movie clip, and then assigning the x position of 0 in the Info panel, as shown in Figure 2-12. Go back to the main timeline and reposition the movie clip to the center of the screen.

Next, you need to add some ActionScript to resize the MusicTracker's width according to how far into the external SWF the music has played. If the external SWF on level 2 has just begun playing at frame 1, then the MusicTracker should be almost invisible. If the external SWF on level 2 is almost finished playing at its last frame, then the MusicTracker bar should reach its full width. Open the Action panel for the MusicTracker movie clip and add the following code:

L 2-23
```
onClipEvent (enterFrame) {
      this._xscale = (_level2._currentFrame / _level2._totalFrames)
      * 100;
}
```

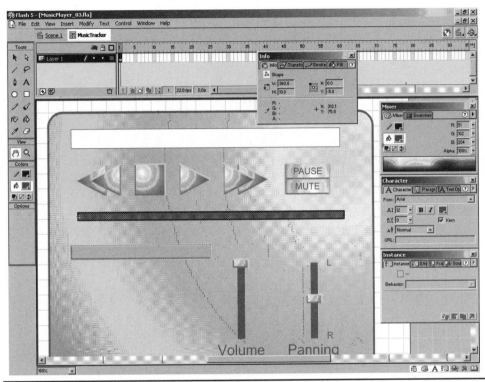

Figure 2-12   *Building the MusicTracker movie clip as a simple rectangle with borders*

The `onClipEvent (enterFrame)` event handler will execute all the ActionScript between its curly braces again and again, in a continuous fashion, at the same speed as the Flash movie's frame rate. The main purpose of this `enterFrame` event handler is to resize the width of the MusicTracker movie clip according to the current frame playing in the level 2 movie.

In order to resize the movie clip, the script uses the `_xscale` property, which sets the width of the movie clip from 0 to 100 percent of its original width. The calculation of a percentage involves finding a fraction, and then multiplying that fraction by 100. The calculation for this ActionScript code finds the current frame number of the movie in level 2, divides the frame number by the total number of frames in the movie, and then multiplies the result by 100, to create a percentage that ranges from 0 to 100. If the level 2 movie has reached its end, its `_currentFrame` will be equal to the `_totalFrames`, and dividing `_currentFrame` by `_totalFrames` will yield a value of 1, which will still give a product of 100 when multiplied times 100.

You can see how this works by testing the movie, loading a song into the player, and then using the forward or rewind button to change the current frame of the external SWF movie in level 2. You'll notice that the MusicTracker movie clip will stretch according to the current frame of the level 2 movie.

Building the Loading Tracker

Next, create another movie clip bar to track the loading progress of the external SWF in level 2. As you saw with the panning control, duplicating a similar movie clip and then making the necessary changes will save a lot of time. In the Library, choose the MusicTracker movie clip and select the Duplicate command from the Library's pull-down menu. Name the new movie clip **LoadingTracker**. Double-click the symbol to edit the movie clip, and make a simple change by filling the rectangle with white instead of blue.

Insert a new layer called Loading Tracker on the main timeline, beneath the Trackers layer. Then drag the LoadingTracker movie clip from the Library onto the Loading Tracker layer. Position the LoadingTracker movie clip below the MusicTracker movie clip, so that you can view the music progress and loading progress at the same time. Add the following ActionScript to the LoadingTracker's Action panel:

L 2-24
```
onClipEvent (enterFrame) {
        this._xscale = (_level2._framesLoaded / _level2._totalFrames)
        * 100;
}
```

The sole difference between the ActionScript for the LoadingTracker movie clip and the MusicTracker movie clip is the replacement of the _currentFrame property with the _framesLoaded property. The _framesLoaded property allows the Flash Player to detect how much of the movie clip has downloaded to the browser at a specific time. Dividing the _framesLoaded value by the total number of frames allows the ActionScript code to calculate the percentage of the level 2 movie clip's loading progress.

If you test the movie on your own computer, the LoadingTracker bar will always show 100 percent, because the external SWF movie will load instantly into the Flash Player. However, try to upload the ArabianRain.swf and MusicPlayer.swf files onto a server, and test the music player on a modem connection. If you do so, you will see the LoadingTracker slowly expand as the external ArabianRain.swf file streams into the browser.

What to Take Away from This Chapter

The music player project explored some of the possibilities of integrating a Flash interface with streaming movies. Along the way, this project involved the construction of several different interface components, such as buttons, scrollbars, and duplicated movie clip elements for the music list. The interface elements were often created by simply duplicating and modifying symbols in the Flash library, which saves time. The project also demonstrated how to use the same interface element, such as the slider control, to perform different tasks by assigning different ActionScript commands to different instances of the same movies.

The music player described here is only a simulation of an MP3 player. Using more complex programming techniques, you can create an actual MP3 player using Flash. However, these techniques require programming languages and technologies beyond the scope of this book, such as C++, PHP, and Macromedia Generator. For readers who are interested in further exploration of dynamic MP3 conversion with SWF wrappers, I recommend three possible solutions:

► The Macromedia Generator solution, available at www.macromedia.com

► The free and very powerful Swift-3D tool for various Web server platforms, available at www.swift-tools.com

► The open-source (LGPL licensed) PHP library called Ming, which can dynamically write SWF format files as a PHP module, available at www.php.net

CHAPTER

3

Real-Time Preloader

IN THIS CHAPTER:

▶ Build a preloader into your Flash Movies to maximize playability

▶ Determine whether or not to use a preloader

▶ Use new Flash 5 features such as .getBytesLoaded() and .getBytesTotal() to display exact file sizes and determine connection speeds

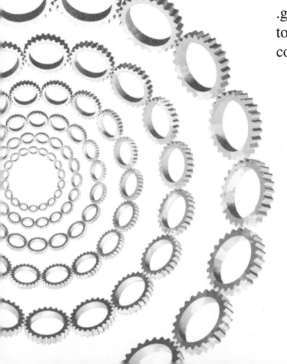

U sing a preloader for a Flash Movie can allow you to download the movie into the user's cache before the user views it. There are two main advantages to the use of preloaders:

▶ Downloading the entire movie before viewing it will prevent a jerky or shaky playback if the Flash movie's connection is streaming at a bytes-per-second bandwidth.

▶ Preloading the entire contents of the movie—including its main timeline and all of the visual/audio elements—enables the Flash movie to use all of its elements and to skip around the timeline without waiting for those sections to download.

The second advantage is especially useful in Flash-based applications or Flash-based games, where complete download of the Flash interface elements has a higher priority than streaming animation. Generally, preloading a movie allows you to make a Flash movie viewable on a 33.6KB-per-second connection at the same quality as a Flash movie viewed on a broadband connection.

The standard preloader, used since the release of Flash 2, checked the total number of frames loaded and then proceeded to the specified frame, if it was loaded, or continued to the next frame. The next frame contained a simple go-to-previous-frame command, thereby creating a loop that ended only when the specified frame was loaded.

With the addition of the new Flash 5 `.getBytes()` method, you can now check exactly how much of the Flash movie has been loaded before proceeding past the preloader, and you can also calculate the rate of download in terms of bytes per second. The new ability to detect download speed is especially useful if the Web site contains two versions of multimedia content for visitors with high-bandwidth and low-bandwidth connections.

Structuring Your Flash Movie Preloader
ch03_01.fla

Flash movies load a complete scene before continuing to the next. This can work to your advantage for preloaders. When adding a preloader to a Flash movie, I always separate the movie into two scenes: The first scene contains the preloader script and objects, and the second scene contains the content of the site, as shown in Figure 3-1. Separating the preloader content and main content into two different scenes helps keep the movie organized and ensures that the preloader is the only object loading in the first frames.

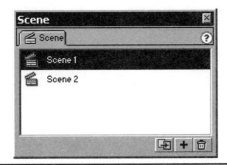

Figure 3-1   *Separating a Flash movie into a scene for the preloader script and a scene for the main content*

Placing all of the contents of the preloader in its own scene will ensure that the preloader loads quickly, without the delay of loading other elements of the site at the same time. The first priority is to load the preloader scene as soon as possible, so that the user can see a visible preload report or animation immediately, while the rest of the movie continues to load.

Preloaders are usually used for loading content that cannot be streamed smoothly. If the site will be viewed over different Internet or intranet connections, a preloader can help ensure that all viewers see the movie in the same way, no matter what type of connection they are using.

In general, all of my preloader scenes are constructed in the same way. I separate them into three layers: script, text, and preloader clip, as shown in Figure 3-2. Using layers to separate the objects makes it easier to edit the scene later. Assigning a descriptive layer name that refers to the object in that layer also makes it easy to locate an object on a timeline for future reference.

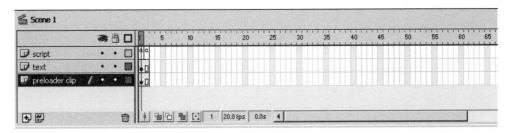

Figure 3-2   *A preloader scene divided into script, text, and preloader layers*

Creating the Script Layer

The first layer of the preloader scene contains the standard preloader script, which consists of two frames looping back and forth. This looping technique, commonly known as the "two-frame loop," is used to determine the total number of frames loaded on the main timeline, and it continues to loop until the specified frame is loaded.

The specified frame does not need to be the last frame of the movie. You should preload only the amount of frames needed to obtain a smooth playback. Continually testing your movie, and using the Bandwidth Profiler, shown in Figure 3-3, will help you determine the best frame for your needs. The Bandwidth Profiler lets you see where larger downloads will occur.

The first frame needs to contain the ActionScript to determine whether the specified frame is loaded, as shown here:

L 3-1
```
ifFrameLoaded ("Scene 2", 1) {
    gotoAndStop ("Scene 2", 1);
}
```

This ActionScript checks to see whether the first frame in scene 2 is loaded. If scene 2, frame 1 has been loaded, then the movie goes to frame 1 of scene 2 and stops. If the frame is not loaded, it will move to the next frame of scene 1 and continue looping until the first frame of scene 2 has been loaded into the browser.

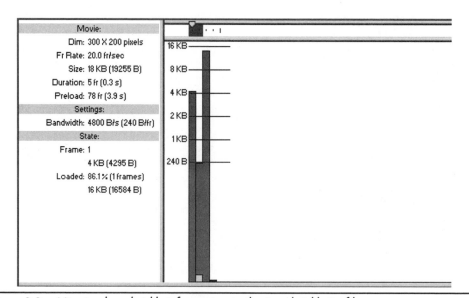

Figure 3-3   *Viewing bandwidth information in the Bandwidth Profiler*

The second frame needs to contain a script to tell the Flash movie to return to frame 1 and play through the detection process again. This code is shown here:

L 3-2
```
gotoAndPlay (1);
```

Creating the Text Layer

The text layer in scene 1 contains the text or graphics that let the user know the Flash movie has begun downloading into the cache. This layer can contain any type of animation to keep the user informed and occupied, ranging from a simple line of text to a more complex trailer. It is a good idea to make the preloader interesting for the viewer, to keep the viewer from becoming impatient before the site loads. The text or graphics should be relatively small in file size to improve the initial download time, so you won't need a preloader for your preloader.

I simply added the text "Loading Movie" into the text layer for this chapter's project. For a larger file, I would have probably added a more interactive preloader that introduced or promoted the forthcoming content in some relevant way.

Creating the Preloader Clip Layer

In Flash 5, scripts can now be added to the movie clip, which is much more organized and effective than the old method of adding scripts to multiple frames inside the movie clips. The preloader clip layer contains the movie clip used to hold all of the ActionScripting for the following data, also shown in Figure 3-4:

- ▶ The total file size of the Flash movie
- ▶ The amount of bytes downloaded
- ▶ The percentage downloaded
- ▶ The amount of bytes left to download
- ▶ The bytes-per-second download speed
- ▶ The kilobytes-per-second download speed
- ▶ The amount of time the user has waited, in seconds

To create the movie clip for this layer, press CTRL-F8 (COMMAND-F8 for Macs) to create a new object, select Movie Clip from the list of options, and name it

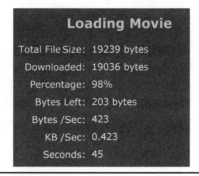

Figure 3-4   *The data output of the preloader*

preloader. Drag an instance of this movie clip onto the main stage for editing. Open the Instance panel and give the movie clip an instance name of **preloader**. Providing an instance name for a movie clip will allow the ActionScript to refer to the movie clip by referring to its instance name.

When using scripts on movie clips, be sure to select the appropriate `onClipEvent`. Select `enterFrame` for this project to allow the script to continue running until the object is removed from the stage. The `enterFrame` event handler basically executes all of the ActionScript within its brackets again and again, in a continuous loop at the same speed as the Flash movie's frame rate. In the case of the preloader, the ActionScript code inside the `enterFrame` event handler will constantly update the text fields with information until the movie moves to scene 2.

Adding Text Fields

First, open the preloader movie clip. This movie clip will contain all of the dynamic and static text. Adding all of the text inside the movie clip makes it possible to reuse this preloader in other Flash movies by simply copying and pasting the entire movie clip.

Static Text Fields

Start by creating the static text fields. These static text fields just contain the text labels for the preloader's data output, and they never change. Add the following fields (see Figure 3-4, shown earlier):

▶   Total File Size
▶   Downloaded

- ► Percentage
- ► Bytes Left
- ► Bytes/Sec
- ► KB/Sec
- ► Seconds

Dynamic Text Fields

Next, create the dynamic text fields used to retrieve data from the ActionScript. The unique aspect of dynamic text fields in Flash movies is that the text field and the variable are the same thing. If you change the value of a variable on a Flash timeline, any text field with the same name will reflect the change in the value. You can think of a dynamic text field and a variable within the same timeline as the same thing, but *only* if they have the same name.

Start by opening the Text Options panel and selecting Dynamic Text from the first drop-down list. Remove the check mark from Selectable check box, so the user cannot select the text field. Enter `total_filesize` in the Variable text box, as shown in Figure 3-5. This is the name of the first script variable you will create, as explained in the next section.

Next, draw a text field on the stage large enough to hold all the characters in the largest variable. Draw the text fields a little longer than the largest string variable that you plan to use for this project. You can go back and resize the text fields later if they are not large enough. This is especially important when you might change the font for a text field later on, because different fonts may use more or less space. To ensure that the text fields will be lined up and the text is displayed at the same size, I just copied (CTRL-C/COMMAND-C) and pasted (SHIFT-CTRL-V/SHIFT-COMMAND-V) the text field in place six times, and then used the arrow keys to move each text field down the stage at even intervals.

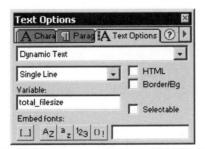

Figure 3-5   *Selecting Dynamic Text in the Text Options panel*

For each text field, open the Text Options panel again and change the text field's variable name to match the variable names used in the ActionScript code:

- ▶ `total_filesize`
- ▶ `downloaded`
- ▶ `bytes_left`
- ▶ `percentage`
- ▶ `bytes_per_sec`
- ▶ `kb_per_sec`
- ▶ `sec`

These and the other variables used in the ActionScript are discussed in the next sections.

Creating Variables

The preloader script variables are used to display information in the dynamic text fields. Two of the dynamic text fields, `bytes_per_sec` and `kb_per_sec`, will show a message to inform the user that the connection speed is being detected if the timer has not yet reached one second. That scripting is described in the "Adding If-Else Statements" section, later in the chapter.

The Total_filesize Variable

The first variable, `total_filesize`, determines the total file size of the Flash movie. You can retrieve the total file size of the movie, in bytes, by using the new `.getBytesTotal()` method available in Flash 5.

When targeting the main timeline using the new dot syntax in Flash 5, you should use `_root` for the target name. This is necessary for this project because you want to determine the total bytes for the main timeline in the Flash movie. The method becomes `_root.getBytesTotal()`.

The text field named Total File Size refers to the same value as the variable named `total_filesize`. Because the file size is returned in bytes, the text field should also show the word *bytes* after the value of the movie file size. To accomplish this, add the string `" bytes"` to the results of the `_root.getBytesTotal()` method. Any part of a script contained in quotation marks will output the exact contents of the characters between the quotation marks. Adding a string of characters to other characters is called *concatenation*. In this case, you want to concatenate the string " bytes" to the number returned by the getBytesTotal() method, to create a string variable called total_filesize:

L 3-3
```
total_filesize = _root.getBytesTotal() + " bytes";
```

The Downloaded Variable

The next variable, downloaded, determines how many bytes have been loaded into the user's cache already. This is done using the new .getBytesLoaded() method available in Flash 5, as shown in Figure 3-6.

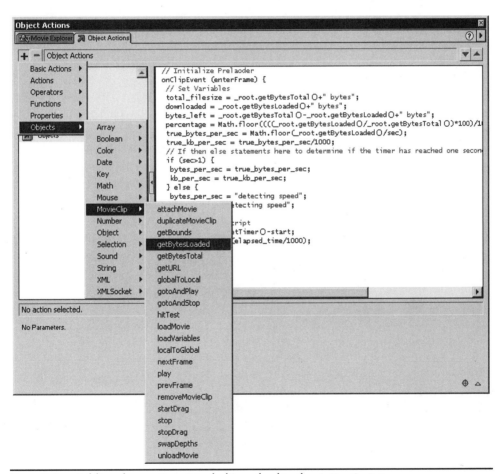

Figure 3-6 *Adding the .getBytesLoaded() method to the ActionScript*

As with the `getBytesTotal()` method, you need to use `_root` for the target name, because you want to determine the loaded bytes for the main timeline in the Flash movie. Also, you want to display the word *bytes* after the value in the text field, so concatenate the string " `bytes`" to the number returned by the `getBytesLoaded()` method, to create a string variable called `downloaded`:

L 3-4
```
downloaded = _root.getBytesLoaded() + " bytes";
```

The Bytes_left Variable

Next, make a variable to determine how many bytes are remaining to be downloaded. This is done by simply subtracting the number of bytes already loaded from the total number of bytes in the Flash movie:

L 3-5
```
bytes_left = _root.getBytesTotal() - _root.getBytesLoaded() + " bytes";
```

The Percentage Variable

The `percentage` variable is used to determine the percentage of the total file size that has been loaded. You can create this variable by dividing the loaded bytes by the total bytes, and then multiplying by 100. This outputs a large number with several decimal places. To go one step further, round off this number to eliminate the decimal places. This is done by using the new `Math.floor` function in Flash 5, as shown in Figure 3-7. The `floor` function rounds the number down to the closest integer that is less than or equal to the value of the variable. For example, the expression `Math.floor(20.5)` will return a value of 20. Finally, concatenate the symbol % to display a percentage sign following the number in the text field:

L 3-6
```
percentage = Math.floor((_root.getBytesLoaded() /
_root.getBytesTotal()) * 100) + "%";
```

The True_bytes_per_sec Variable

Next, create a formula to determine the user's connection speed. This shows how fast the user is downloading the data in the Flash movie. The result of the variable is not equal to the user's connection to the Internet, but the user's connection to the site containing the Flash movie.

To create the `true_bytes_per_sec` variable, divide the total bytes loaded by the amount of seconds that the user has been downloading the Flash movie. The method used for getting the seconds is explained later in this chapter, in the "Adding If-Else

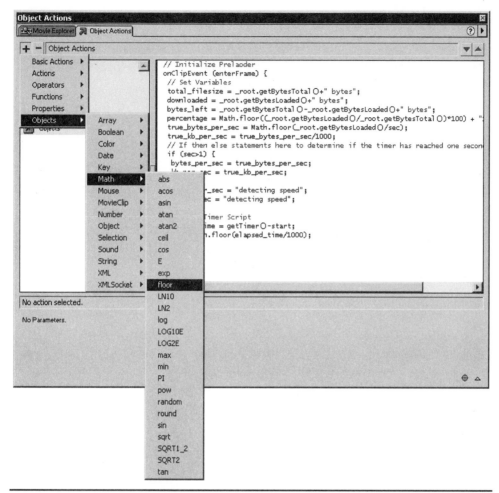

Figure 3-7   *Using the Math.floor function*

Statements" section. Again, use the new `Math.floor` function to round the variable down to an integer.

L 3-7   `true_bytes_per_sec = Math.floor(_root.getBytesLoaded() / sec);`

NOTE

The preloader must work for at least one second to provide an accurate connection speed. The formula divides the total bytes loaded by the time; dividing anything by zero will result in an Infinity output.

The True_kb_per_sec Variable

The `true_kb_per_sec` variable shows the user's connection speed to the Flash movie site in kilobytes per second. This is done by simply dividing the previous variable, `true_bytes_per_sec`, by 1000.

L 3-8
```
true_kb_per_sec = true_bytes_per_sec / 1000;
```

The variable for the final dynamic field of the preloader, `sec`, is defined after the `if-else` statements for checking the timer.

Adding If-Else Statements

There is a timer clock built into Flash, and the clock starts ticking in milliseconds as soon as the Flash movie loads into the browser or Flash player. The next part of the script determines whether the timer has reached one second yet and displays the appropriate information by using two new variables: `bytes_per_sec` and `kb_per_sec`.

If the timer has reached one second, the output for the `bytes_per_sec` and `kb_per_sec` variables is the same as the calculations for the `true_bytes_ per_sec` and `true_ kb_per_sec` variables, described in the previous sections. If the timer has not yet reached one second, the dynamic text fields show a message to inform the user that the connection speed is being detected. This is necessary because if the loaded bytes are divided by zero, the output will always be infinity, which is an illegal value.

The if-else portion of the script is shown here:

L 3-9
```
if (sec > 1) {
    bytes_per_sec = true_bytes_per_sec;
    kb_per_sec = true_kb_per_sec;
} else {
    bytes_per_sec = "detecting speed";
    kb_per_sec = "detecting speed";
}
```

In the first section of the preceding script, the variables on the right side of the equal sign are not contained in quotation marks. When using variables, they must be read as an expression, or the variable name, not the value of the expression, will be the output. All nonexpression data, such as the text to be displayed in the dynamic text field (in the second part of the preceding script) must be contained within quotation marks so that it is output as text.

Setting the Timer

The final step to construct the preloader clip is to use the timer. In order to count the elapsed time between one moment and another moment, you need to record the starting time for your counter as the start variable, and then subtract the start time from the current time to calculate the time elapsed in between. You can set the `start` variable to the current time by using the `getTimer()` function, as shown in Figure 3-8. Calculating the difference in time is done by subtracting the value of `start` from the current time of the Flash clock. Once the timer is initialized, it will need to be reset to zero, by setting the `start` variable to the current time again, using `getTimer()`.

Next, use the `sec` variable to display the actual seconds. The time is output in milliseconds, so it needs to be divided by 1000 to display seconds. Again, use the `Math.floor` function to round the seconds off to the closest lower integer.

L 3-10
```
elapsed_time = getTimer() - start;
sec = Math.floor(elapsed_time / 1000);
```

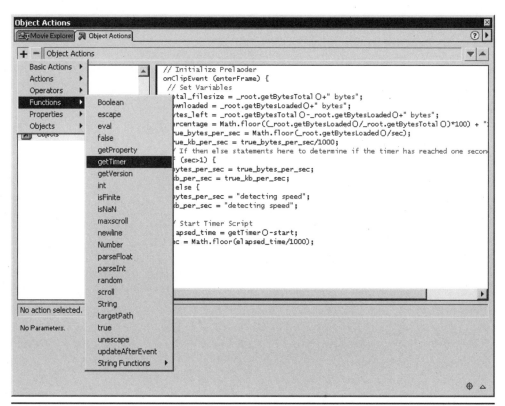

Figure 3-8   *Selecting the getTimer() function*

Putting the Script Together in the Clip

The final task is initialize the script, which is done in the `enterFrame onClip Event`. This has the script update continuously to provide a real-time instance.

Here is the complete script, with comments added for each section of the script.

L 3-11
```
onClipEvent (enterFrame) {
    // Set variables
    total_filesize = _root.getBytesTotal() + " bytes";
    downloaded = _root.getBytesLoaded() + " bytes";
    bytes_left = _root.getBytesTotal() - _root.getBytesLoaded() +
    " bytes";
    percentage = Math.floor(((( _root.getBytesLoaded() /
    _root.getBytesTotal()) * 100) / 100) * 100) + "%";
    true_bytes_per_sec = Math.floor(_root.getBytesLoaded() / sec);
    true_kb_per_sec = true_bytes_per_sec / 1000;
    // If then else statements here to determine if the timer
    // has reached one second yet
    if (sec > 1) {
        bytes_per_sec = true_bytes_per_sec;
        kb_per_sec = true_kb_per_sec;
    } else {
        bytes_per_sec = "detecting speed";
        kb_per_sec = "detecting speed";
    }
    // Start timer script
    elapsed_time = getTimer() - start;
    sec = Math.floor(elapsed_time / 1000);
}
```

Creating the Content Scene

The content scene is where you place the normal Flash movie actions and content. In this example, the content is an imported graphic made in a raster program. Open the Flash Library by pressing CTRL-L (COMMAND-L for Macs) and locate the newly imported graphic. Right-click (COMMAND-click for Macs) the graphic, and go to the Properties option to open the Bitmap Properties dialog box. In the Bitmap Properties dialog box, set the compression to Lossless (PNG/GIF) to create a larger file size so you can test how the preloader works, as shown in Figure 3-9.

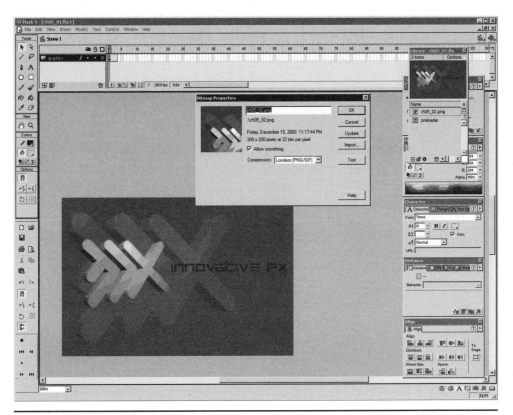

Figure 3-9   *Setting image properties*

Using the Library to optimize each graphic can dramatically reduce the file size of your Flash movie. Use PNG/GIF compression for images that use less than 256 colors and for drawn art. Use JPG compression for photographs and more complex images. Optimize each image with a JPG compression rate of somewhere between 40 and 70. Images that are small in size and with few colors can be optimized at much lower compression rates.

In a full Flash site or a Flash introduction to a site, the file size could vary. Your Flash movie may not need a preloader, or it may need several preloaders for sections of a site. You don't want to make viewers sit at a preloader scene for a long time when they first reach your site. To avoid this, it is a good idea to break larger files up into smaller sections and load them into place as needed. This is done using the `loadMovie()` command discussed in more detail in Chapter 7 of this book.

What to Take Away from This Chapter

When using Flash for the Web, you should always try to make the final file size acceptable to your target audience. Preloaders can help benefit Flash movies by ensuring that the proper number of frames are cached ahead of time, but they have other advantages as well. They allow you to present your users with content while waiting on the main portion of the site to load. This seems to be a common problem among many Flash sites; the users get tired of waiting and just leave.

In this chapter, you learned how to build a real-time preloader in Flash, determine a user's connection to the site, use new Flash 5 features to display actual bytes loaded and loading, and use the Flash Library to set image compression.

Resizable Windows

IN THIS CHAPTER:

▶ Build a draggable window constrained inside a Flash movie

▶ Update constraints depending on the size of the movie clip

▶ Resize the movie clip using a draggable movie clip

▶ Show and hide movie clips to simulate minimized, maximized, and closed windows

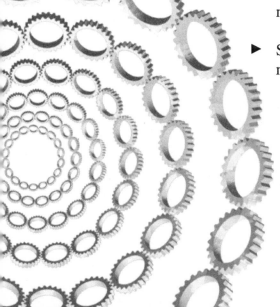

Flash 5's new ActionScripting language has revolutionized the way we develop Web content. ActionScript uses properties and variables to dynamically change the many aspects of objects in Flash. With the release of Flash 5, you can now add scripts directly to movie clips, as mentioned in Chapter 3. This eliminates the need for adding extra frames and layers just for scripting, resulting in a more organized Flash movie.

This chapter describes how to construct a draggable, resizable window that contains features similar to those in window interfaces found in many operating systems today. This project focuses on opening, minimizing, maximizing, resizing, and closing a window.

ch04_01.fla

Start by creating a new Flash movie and setting the stage dimensions to 780 pixels wide and 400 pixels tall. Separating a Flash movie into subcomponents makes the movie easier to manage and easier to modify in the future. The resizable window described in this chapter is designed in four layers: the bar, open window, text output, and window layers.

Adding the Bar Layer

The layer on the bottom of the stack is simply for adding the drag bar across the top of the movie. Draw the rectangle for the drag bar on the main stage. Then use the Info panel to set the bar's dimensions to 780 pixels wide by 20 pixels high, as shown in Figure 4-1.

Next, press CTRL-K (COMMAND-K on Macs) to open the Align panel. Choose to center the rectangle to the movie horizontally (the second button from the left under Align), aligned to the top edge, as shown in Figure 4-2.

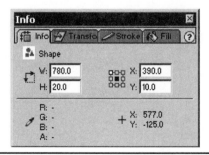

Figure 4-1 *Setting the drag bar's dimensions in the Info panel*

TIP

Using the Info and Align panels will save you countless hours trying to zoom in and align or resize objects manually.

Adding the Open Window Layer

The open window layer in the main timeline of the resizable window project (ch04_01.fla) contains the movie clip labeled open_window_clip. This is the movie clip that opens the window once it has been closed.

When the Flash movie first loads, it sets the visibility of the open_window_clip to 0, which is invisible. This is explained in more detail later in this chapter, in the "Window Scripting in Flash 5" section.

The open_window_clip contains only one frame and one object: the open_window button. This button contains actions to set the visibility of the window movie clip to 1. This will simulate the effect of closing and opening the window. If the window movie clip has its visibility set to 0 (not visible), then the button will still set the visibility of the open_window_clip back to 1 (visible).

The open_window button contains the script shown here:

```
on (release) {
    setProperty ("_root.window", _visible, "1");
    setProperty ("_root.open_window_clip", _visible, "0");
}
```

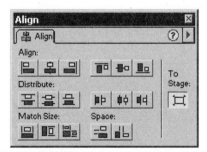

Figure 4-2 *Setting the drag bar's alignment in the Align panel*

Adding the Text_Ouput Layer

The text_output layer is included just for learning purposes. It contains four dynamic text fields that read and display the variables set by the window clip. (See Chapter 3 for more information about dynamic text fields.)

Open the Text Options panel and select Dynamic Text from the first drop-down menu. Next, draw a text field on the movie stage. Once you have the text field sized, select it and open the Text Options panel again. In the Variable field, type the name of the variable that you would like to display, making sure to include the path to the variable. In this case, all of the variables are located in the window clip, so they are referenced from the window movie clip's `enterFrame` event handler (defining and referencing the variables are described later in this chapter, in the "On Load Event Handling" section). The first variable is `_root.window.window_width`, as shown in Figure 4-3.

Repeat the same procedure until you have four text fields. The variables for the four text fields are as follows:

- ▶   `_root.window.window_width`
- ▶   `_root.window.window_height`
- ▶   `_root.window.corner_x`
- ▶   `_root.window.corner_y`

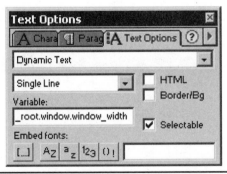

Figure 4-3   *Setting the dynamic text field variable in the Text Options panel*

Adding the Window Layer

The window layer contains all of the script and elements to create the resizable window. Combining all of the elements in one movie clip helps to keep the variables and objects organized, and this approach usually requires less work and coding.

The window clip has six layers, each containing an element of the resizable window: the middle, corner, top, minimize, maximize, and close layers. Positioning of the elements is very important for this project. You must set the position of each element carefully in order to make sure that the objects resize evenly.

Press CTRL-F8 (COMMAND-F8 for Macs) to create a new object. Select MovieClip from the list of options and name the movie clip **window**. Open the Library (CTRL-L/ COMMAND-L) and drag an instance of the movie clip onto the main timeline from the Library. Then open the Instance panel (CTRL-I/COMMAND-I) and enter **window** in the Name field.

Right-click (COMMAND-click for Macs) the movie clip and select Edit to add the elements of the movie clip. Inside the movie clip, you will separate the different objects onto their own layers and name the layers to reference the objects. This will make it easier to identify the layer in which each object resides, both for future reference and editing.

Creating the Middle Layer

This project uses many variables depending on the size of the window, so it is vital to determine the window size early in the process. For this project, use a 100-by-100-pixel window. The top 10 pixels will be occupied by the top draggable bar.

Draw a rectangle, and then use the Info panel to resize it to 100 by 90 pixels. Open the Stroke panel and set the stroke to hairline, as shown in Figure 4-4. This will keep the lines from stretching when the window is resized.

Next, press F8 to make the rectangle into a movie clip. In the Instance panel, give the movie clip an instance name by entering **middle_clip** in the Name field, as shown in Figure 4-5. As explained in Chapter 3, giving a movie clip an instance name allows the movie clip to be targeted by an ActionScript.

By default, the rectangle is aligned to the center in the movie clip. Open the movie clip and use the Align panel (see Figure 4-2, earlier in this chapter) to align the rectangle to the left edge and the top edge (the first button on the left under Align). This positioning is necessary for the window to resize properly. Figure 4-6 shows the middle_clip positioning.

Use the Info panel to set the middle_clip's x coordinate to 0 and its y coordinate to 10.

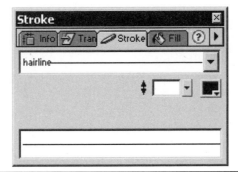

Figure 4-4 *Setting the window rectangle's stroke size in the Stroke panel*

Creating the Corner Layer

The corner layer contains the draggable movie clip, corner_clip, in the bottom-right corner of the window. This is the button that is dragged to resize the window. Using movie clips allows nested buttons to be dynamically repositioned when the window is resized.

Draw a rectangle on the stage. As with the middle_clip, use the Stroke panel to set the stroke width to hairline, to prevent the lines from scaling. Next, select the Line tool, hold down the SHIFT key, and draw a line constrained at 45 degrees through the middle of the rectangle. Delete the lines and fill on the top left of the rectangle to create a triangle, as shown in Figure 4-7.

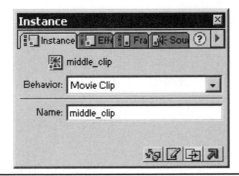

Figure 4-5 *Giving the movie clip an instance name in the Instance panel*

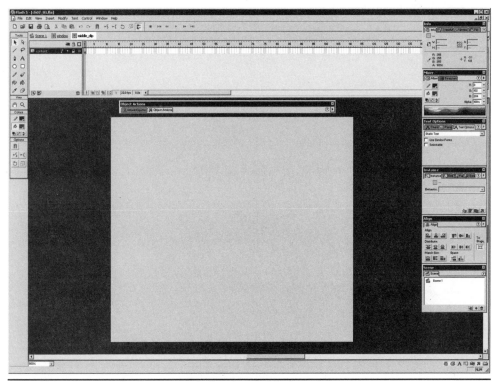

Figure 4-6   *Positioning the rectangle for the middle layer*

Next, select the triangle with the cursor, press F8, and select Button from the Behavior options. This will make the triangle into a button, so that actions can be applied to it. Then press F8 again and select Movie Clip from the Behavior options. This will make a movie clip with a button nested inside. The button will contain the original triangle shape.

With the new movie clip selected, open the Instance panel and give the new movie clip an instance name of **corner_clip**. Open the movie clip and use the Align panel (CTRL-K/COMMAND-K) to align the button to the bottom edge and the right edge (the third button from the left under Align). This will keep the button positioned at the bottom-right edge of the window when the window is resized. Figure 4-8 shows the alignment.

Next, open the button and insert a keyframe in the over frame. In this frame, change the color of the triangle, to make the button change colors when the mouse rolls over it.

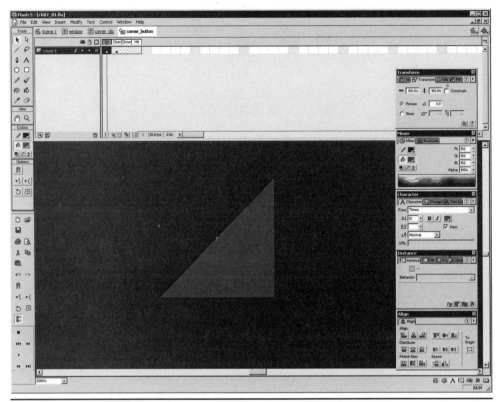

Figure 4-7 *Creating the triangle for the corner layer*

Now, to make the corner_clip draggable, add these actions to the button:

```
on (press) {
    startDrag ("_root.window.corner_clip", false, 75, 50, 250, 200);
}
```

The script starts the drag operation on the mouse event `press`, as shown in the first line of the script. The second line sets the parameters and identifies which movie clip is to be dragged. In this case, the corner_clip will be dragged. The next part determines whether or not to lock the mouse to the center of the movie clip to be dragged. Since it is not necessary in this case, set this to `false`. The final part of the script constrains the draggable movie clip to a set dimension. I set this to 75 pixels for the top border, 50 pixels for the left border, 250 pixels for the right border, and 200 pixels for the bottom border. This will limit the size of the window to no smaller than 75 by 50 pixels and no larger than 250 by 200 pixels.

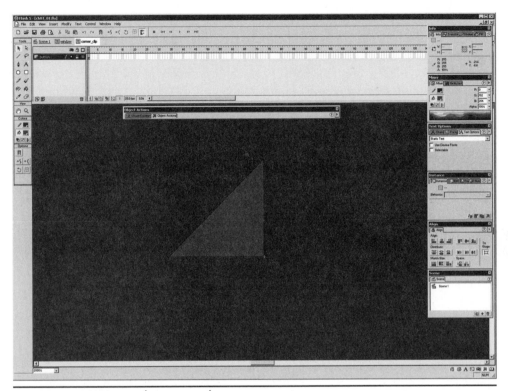

Figure 4-8   *Positioning the corner_clip*

NOTE

Locking the mouse to the center of a drag operation by setting the startDrag *parameter value to* true *will move the object centered to the mouse position. This creates a jerking effect for larger objects that require more memory usage and raster images, so it is not often used for them. However, this method can be useful for smaller objects that contain simple lines or vector drawings or for having objects follow the mouse coordinates.*

The next part of the script stops the drag operation:

```
on (release) {
    stopDrag ();
}
```

This script takes place on the release mouse event, as shown in the first line of the script. The mouse event release executes the code within its brackets whenever Flash detects that the mouse button has been released after it has been pressed. The second line simply contains `stopDrag ()`. This stops any drag operation being performed. In Flash, only one movie clip drag operation can be performed at any given time using this method.

Finally, you need to align the corner_clip in the window movie clip. In the Info panel, set both the x and y coordinates to 100. Figure 4-9 shows the final corner positioning.

Creating the Top Layer

The top layer contains the top section of the window. Like the corner_clip, it is a nested button within a movie clip.

Start by drawing a rectangle. Then use the Info panel to set the dimensions to 100 pixels wide by 10 pixels tall. Again, use the Stroke panel to set the stroke to hairline, to prevent the scaling of the lines. While the rectangle is selected, press F8, and then select the Button option. Press F8 again, and select MovieClip from the options. Open the Instance panel, and in the Name field, set the instance name to **top_clip**.

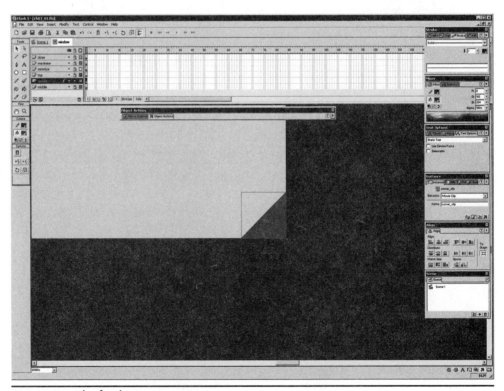

Figure 4-9   *The final corner positioning*

Open the movie clip and use the Align panel to align the button to the top edge and the left edge. This is necessary for the window to resize properly.

Next, open the button and add a keyframe at the over frame. In this frame, change the color of the rectangle. (As you learned in the previous section, setting a different color for the over frame makes the button change color when the mouse is rolled over it.)

Now, to make the top_clip draggable, add these actions to the button:

```
on (press) {
    startDrag ("_root.window", false, _root.window.left,
_root.window.top, _root.window.right, _root.window.bottom);
}
```

The first line of the script starts the drag operation on the `press` mouse event. The drag operation on the second line moves the corresponding movie clip according to the position of the mouse, to duplicate the effect of dragging a window with the mouse. In this case, the top `_root.window` movie clip will be dragged. As in the script for the corner_clip, the next parameter is set to `false`, to indicate that the mouse should not be locked to the center of the movie clip during a drag operation. The final parameters constrain the draggable movie clip to a set dimension of left, top, right, and bottom boundaries for the dragging action.

Unlike the constraints used for the corner_clip, the constraints for the top_clip are based on variables instead of fixed numbers (defining the variables is described in the "On Enter Frame Event Handling" section, later in this chapter). You need to use variable constraints for the window to allow the window to be dragged to the edges of the stage and for the window to stay within the size of the stage when it's being resized.

The next part of the script stops the drag operation:

```
on (release) {
    stopDrag ();
}
```

This script is the same as the one used to stop the drag operation for the corner_clip.

Finally, align the top_clip in the window movie clip. Use the Info panel to set both the x and y coordinates to 0. Figure 4-10 shows the final position of the top_clip.

Creating the Minimize Layer

The minimize layer contains the minimize button. Draw a rectangle and use the Info panel to size it to 5 pixels wide by 5 pixels tall. Set the stroke width to hairline. Use the Align panel to align the rectangle horizontally and vertically to the stage. Next,

Figure 4-10   *The final top_clip positioning*

draw a horizontal line approximately 3.5 pixels wide. Use the Align panel to align the line horizontally and vertically to the stage. This will place the line in the center of the rectangle.

While the rectangle and line are selected, press F8, and then select Button from the Behavior options. Press F8 again and select Movie Clip from the Behavior options. Open the Instance panel and name the instance **minimize_clip**.

Now open the minimize_clip and add these actions to the button:

```
on (release) {
    setProperty ("_root.window.middle_clip", _visible, "0");
    setProperty ("_root.window.corner_clip", _visible, "0");
}
```

This script takes place on the `release` mouse event. The second line sets the visibility of the middle_clip to 0, and the third line sets the visibility of the corner_clip to 0 also. This will simulate the main part of the window and corner to be minimized, while keeping the top_clip visible.

Finally, use the Info panel to position the minimize_clip to x coordinate 75 and y coordinate 5. Figure 4-11 shows the minimize_clip positioning.

Creating the Maximize Layer

The maximize layer contains the maximize button, another nested button. Start by drawing a rectangle, and then use the Info panel to size it to 5 pixels wide by 5 pixels tall. Set the stroke to hairline, and align the rectangle horizontally and vertically to the stage.

Next draw a square on the stage approximately 3.5 pixels tall and 3.5 pixels wide to represent a maximize button seen on most common operating systems used today. Use the Align panel to align the square horizontally and vertically to the stage.

While the rectangle and lines are selected, press F8 and select the Button from the Behavior options. This will make the combined rectangle and lines a single button so that actions can be applied to the button. Then press F8 again and select Movie Clip from the options. In the Instance panel, enter **maximize_clip** in the Name field.

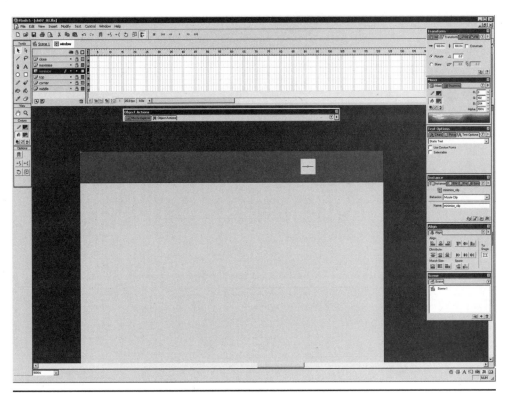

Figure 4-11   *The minimize_clip positioning*

Open the maximize_clip and add these actions to the button:

```
on (release) {
    setProperty ("_root.window.middle_clip", _visible, "1");
    setProperty ("_root.window.corner_clip", _visible, "1");
}
```

The setProperty lines set the visibility of the middle_clip and corner_clip to 1. This will simulate the main part of the window and corner to be maximized.

Finally, use the Info panel to position the maximize_clip to x coordinate 85 and y coordinate 5. Figure 4-12 shows the maximize_clip position.

Figure 4-12   *The maximize_clip positioning*

Creating the Close Layer

The final layer of the window contains the close button. As you did for the minimize and maximize buttons, draw a rectangle, size it to 5 pixels wide by 5 pixels tall, set the stroke width to hairline. and align the rectangle horizontally and vertically to the stage.

Next, draw a horizontal line approximately 3.5 pixels wide. Then draw a vertical line of the same size. Select both lines, and use the Info panel to rotate both lines 45 degrees. Again, use the Align panel to align the lines horizontally and vertically to the stage. This will place the lines in the center of the rectangle so they form an X.

While the rectangle and lines are selected, press F8 and select Button from the Behavior options. Press F8 again and select Movie Clip from the Behavior options. Give the clip the instance name **close_clip**.

Open the close_clip and add these actions to the button:

```
on (release) {
    setProperty ("_root.window", _visible, "0");
    setProperty ("_root.open_window_clip", _visible, "1");
}
```

The `setProperty` lines set the visibility of the window clip to 0 and the visibility of the open_window_clip to 1. This will simulate the window being closed, and it will make the open_window_clip button visible so it can be clicked.

Finally, use the Info panel to position the close_clip to x coordinate 95 and y coordinate 5. Figure 4-13 shows the close_clip positioning.

Window Scripting in Flash 5

To complete the resizable window project, you need to add the scripting to the window movie clip. Adding the script to the movie clip's event handlers instead of to the timeline will make the movie much easier to update and organize.

The script can be divided into two main sections that exist inside two event handlers: on load and on enter frame.

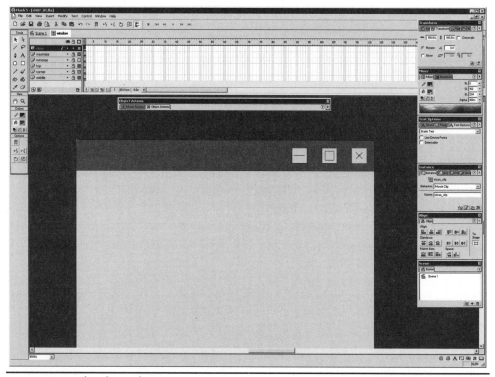

Figure 4-13   *The close_clip positioning*

On Load Event Handling

When the window clip is first loaded, the first thing that needs to be done is to hide the open_window_clip. Preventing users from seeing the open_window_clip will keep them from trying to click the button when the window is already opened. By placing the open_window_clip under the onClipEvent (load) event, the movie clip's ActionScript will execute once, and only once. The script is very simple:

```
onClipEvent (load) {
    setProperty ("_root.open_window_clip", _visible, "0");
}
```

This script will execute when the movie clip has completely loaded into the browser, so the script takes place in the onClipEvent (load) event, as shown on the first line of the script. The second line sets the visibility of the open_window_clip to 0.

On Enter Frame Event Handling

Scripts placed under the `onClipEvent (enterFrame)` event will be updated. This technique is necessary for this project because the window will be dynamically resized. This section can be broken down into three subsections: variables, constraints, and properties.

Setting Variables

Before you apply actions, you should set variables to avoid needing to type the same script repeatedly. This project uses four variables:

```
window_width = Math.floor(getProperty(_root.window, _width));
window_height = Math.floor(getProperty(_root.window, _height));
corner_x = Math.floor(getProperty(_root.window.corner_clip, _x));
corner_y = Math.floor(getProperty(_root.window.corner_clip, _y));
```

Each variable is coded to use the `Math.floor` function to round the number to the next lowest integer.

The first two lines of code set the `window_width` and `window_height` variables. They use the `getProperty` command to find the window movie clip's width and height, respectively.

The third and fourth lines of code set the `corner_x` and `corner_y` variables. They use the `getProperty` command to find the corner_clip's x position and y position, respectively.

Setting Draggable Window Constraints

This section of the script contains the constraints for the draggable window. As mentioned earlier, the constraints will keep the window within the dimensions of the stage, even when resized.

```
left = "0";
top = "20";
right = 780 - (window_width);
bottom = 400 - (window_height);
```

The first line of code sets the `left` variable to an initial value of 0. The second line sets the `top` variable to an initial value of 20. Because the window is resized by repositioning the bottom-right corner of its dimensions, the left position and the top border of the window will never change.

NOTE

The top border of the window dimensions could be set to 0, but I wanted to keep it below the edge of the draggable bar shape at the top of the movie, so I used 20 instead.

The third line of code sets the `right` variable, whose value is dynamically assigned, depending on the width of the window. Calculating the position of the right border of the window is done by subtracting the `window_width` from the width of the entire Flash movie, which is 780 pixels.

The last line of code dynamically sets the `bottom` variable depending upon the height of the window. This is done by subtracting the `window_height` from the movie height, which is 400 pixels.

Setting Properties

The final section of the script contains the ActionScript that sets the window dimension properties. Because you set the `window_width`, `window_height`, `corner_x`, and `corner_y` variables earlier, you can use the variable names in this part of the script, which shortens the length of your final code.

```
setProperty ("_root.window.middle_clip", _width, corner_x);
setProperty ("_root.window.middle_clip", _height, corner_y - 10);
setProperty ("_root.window._root.window.top_clip", _width,
corner_x);
setProperty ("_root.window.minimize_clip", _x, corner_x - 25);
setProperty ("_root.window.maximize_clip", _x, corner_x - 15);
setProperty ("_root.window.close_clip", _x, corner_x - 5);
```

These lines set the window properties as follows:

▶ The first line sets the width of the middle_clip equal to the x position of the corner_clip.

▶ The second line sets the height of the middle_clip equal to the y position of the corner_clip.

▶ The third line sets the width of the top_clip equal to the x position of the corner_clip.

▶ The fourth line sets the x position of the minimize_clip by subtracting 25 from the corner_x variable, which represents the x position of the corner_clip. This will keep the movie clip 25 pixels away from the right edge of the window.

▶ The fifth line sets the x position of the maximize_clip by subtracting 15 from the corner_x variable. This will keep the movie clip 15 pixels away from the right edge of the window.

▶ The last line sets the x position of the close_clip by subtracting 5 from the corner_x variable. This will keep the movie clip 5 pixels away from the right edge of the window.

NOTE

I did not make the height of the top_clip change. This will keep the top_clip the same size, resembling the top of windows used in many operating systems.

The Completed Script

Here is the entire script for the window movie clip, including comments:

```
// This sets the open window button invisibility when the movie is
// first loaded
onClipEvent (load) {
    setProperty ("_root.open_window_clip", _visible, "0");
}
// These events will update because they are using enterFrame
onClipEvent (enterFrame) {
    // These are the variables used to get the properties
    // of the movie clips
    window_width = Math.floor(getProperty(_root.window, _width));
    window_height = Math.floor(getProperty(_root.window, _height));
    corner_x = Math.floor(getProperty(_root.window.corner_clip, _x));
    corner_y = Math.floor(getProperty(_root.window.corner_clip, _y));
    // These set the limits of the draggable window
    left = "0";
    top = "20";
    right = 780 - (window_width);
    bottom = 400 - (window_height);
    // These set the size of the window and the positioning of the
    // buttons, based on the position of the corner button
    setProperty ("_root.window.middle_clip", _width, corner_x);
    setProperty ("_root.window.middle_clip", _height, corner_y - 10);
    setProperty ("_root.window._root.window.top_clip", _width,
    corner_x);
    setProperty ("_root.window.minimize_clip", _x, corner_x - 25);
    setProperty ("_root.window.maximize_clip", _x, corner_x - 15);
    setProperty ("_root.window.close_clip", _x, corner_x - 5);
}
```

With all of the elements in place, the window should look like the one shown in Figure 4-14.

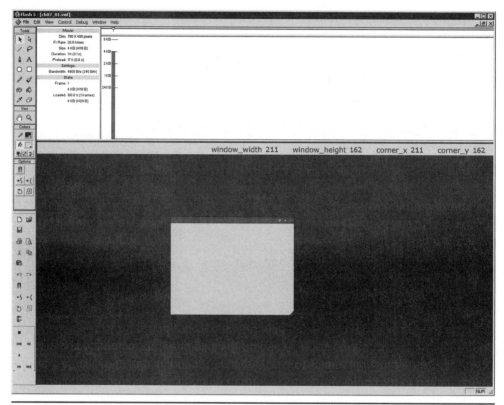

Figure 4-14 *The finished resizable window project*

What to Take Away from This Chapter

The resizable window project presented in this chapter used the fundamentals of properties and variables to add more functionality to a Flash movie. It demonstrated how to add resizable elements. These techniques can be applied to other movies to achieve greater functionality and to decrease file size.

CHAPTER 5

Drop-Down Menu Navigation

IN THIS CHAPTER:

▶ Build a drop-down menu using ActionScripting

▶ Use duplicate movie clips to reduce file size

▶ Dynamically reposition duplicated clips

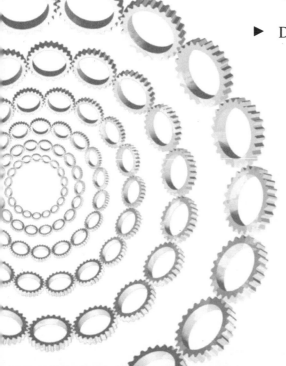

One of the most resourceful features of Flash is the capability to use duplicate movie clips. Reusing the same object can dramatically reduce the file size, and it also makes it much easier to modify the file in the future. Any changes you make to the original movie clip will also be applied to all of the duplicated movie clips.

This chapter describes how to build a drop-down menu using duplicated movie clips. Two projects are presented. Both result in a similar final product, with a small but significant difference: the first file uses a variable in the scripting to determine the amount of menu items to display, and the other file allows user input to set the number of menu items.

Building a Dynamic Drop-Down Menu

ch05_01.fla

The ch05_01.fla file is a draggable menu consisting of duplicated movie clips. The ability to dynamically adjust an interface element, such as the number of buttons in a drop-down menu, makes it easy to create elements that can be reused in other applications. With minor modifications, the drop-down menu can be used for any Flash site. The project uses local variables to determine the button names and positioning. This approach results in a smaller final file size and allows the file to be easily updated and edited.

This project consists of four layers: the actions, button1, button0, and clip layers. Each of these layers is discussed in detail in the following sections.

Adding the Actions Layer

I usually add an actions layer to every Flash movie I make. This layer typically contains actions that declare variables or stop actions. Using a layer just for these actions keeps the Flash movie more organized. Another advantage of separating layers with ActionScripts and layers with animation is that you can drag, copy, cut, and paste any keyframe with ActionScript, without affecting the animation in a timeline.

NOTE

In Flash 4, all actions needed to be placed on the timeline, forcing you to add extra frames and make special movie clips just for scripts. Flash 5 allows you to add scripts directly to movie clips. I try to place all of my scripts, except stop commands and global variables, in movie clips.

For this project, I added a `stop ()` action to the frame. While this is not necessary for a single-frame Flash movie, it is usually best to add it anyway. This way, if you later decide to add a preloader or an additional scene, this scene will still work correctly.

Next, I made the variables to constrain the draggable menu inside the stage area. Defining variables on the main timeline instead of inside another movie clip makes it easier to address the variables in other movie clips, if necessary. An ActionScript command at any location in the Flash structure can simply reference a variable in the main timeline by using the `_root` suffix before the variable name, such as `_root.right` or `_root.top`.

In the first frame of the actions layer in the main timeline, four lines of ActionScript retrieve coordinates based on the Flash coordinate system:

L 5-1
```
left = (getProperty (button0, _width)) / 2;
right = 400 - ((getProperty (button0, _width)) / 2);
top = getProperty (button0, _height) / 2;
bottom = 300 - (getProperty (button0, _height) / 2);
```

As you learned in Chapter 4, the `getProperty()` command returns information about the property of a specific object in Flash. The format of the `getProperty()` command requires two parameters between its parentheses: the first parameter names the object to be targeted by the `getProperty()` command, and the second parameter defines the property to be retrieved from the target object.

In the definition of the `left` and `right` variables here, the `getProperty()` command retrieves the `_width` property of a movie clip with the instance name of button0. Note that applying `getProperty()` to another movie clip will work only if you have given the movie clip an instance name. The properties of objects include name, height, width, and other attributes. They are listed under the Properties section of the ActionScript window of Flash, as shown in Figure 5-1.

The `left` variable gets the width of the draggable movie clip with a button inside, named button0 (as explained later in this chapter, in the "Adding the Button0 Layer" section). The `left` variable is then divided by 2. The result of this division will be equal to the distance from the center of the movie clip to the left edge of the movie clip. All objects in Flash are positioned from their center point, which is why this calculation is necessary. The `right` variable uses the same logic as the `left` variable, but is subtracted from the Flash movie width. This will be equal to the distance from the center of the movie clip to the right edge, subtracted from the right pixel coordinate of the Flash movie.

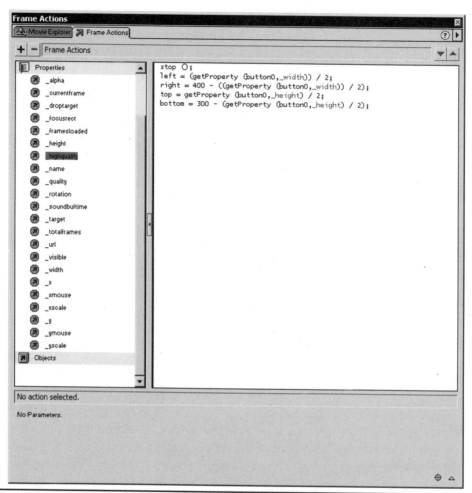

Figure 5-1 *ActionScript properties*

The `top` variable uses the same logic as the `left` variable. The `top` variable gets the height of the draggable button, button0. It is then divided by 2. This will be equal to the distance from the center of the movie clip to the top edge. The `bottom` variable is the same as the `top`, subtracted from the Flash movie height. This will be equal to the distance from the center of the movie clip to the bottom edge, subtracted from the bottom pixel coordinate of the Flash movie.

How Flash Positions Movie Clips

Let's take a quick look at how movie clips are positioned in Flash and how their position properties are determined. If you remember algebra, you know that the position of an object on a flat surface can be divided into its horizontal position (referred to as the x position) and its vertical position (referred to as the y position). The horizontal x position of an object on a flat surface is measured by the X axis, which is an imaginary line moving from the left border of the surface to the right border. The vertical position of an object is measured by the Y axis, which is an imaginary line moving from the top of the surface to the bottom border.

In the main timeline of a Flash movie, the position on the stage ranges from 0 on the left border to the width of the movie clip. If the width of a Flash movie stage is 400 pixels, then the X axis ranges from 0 to 400 from left to right. However, the Y axis goes from 0 at the top to the bottom position, reverse from a regular math coordinate system. If the height of a Flash movie stage is 300, then the Y axis ranges from 0 to 300 from top to bottom.

Inside a movie clip, the X axis and Y axis begin at the center of the screen, where x = 0 and y = 0 at the center. The X axis increases from the center toward the right, and decreases into negative numbers from the center toward the left. The Y axis increases downward from the center toward the bottom of the screen, and it decreases upward into negative numbers.

Adding the Button1 Layer

The button1 layer contains the movie clip that is duplicated to create the menu structure. All variables will be dynamic, because the movie clip will be renamed each time it is duplicated. When the movie clip is duplicated, it is repositioned according to the position of the movie clip preceding it. In this project, each object is positioned to the same x coordinate and 15 pixels below the y coordinate of the preceding movie clip.

Start by pressing CTRL-F8 (COMMAND-F8 for Macs) to create a new object. Select Movie Clip from the list of options and name it **button1_clip**, as shown in Figure 5-2. Drag this object from the library onto the main timeline and name it **button1** in the Instance panel. This will allow the movie clip to be targeted by ActionScripting.

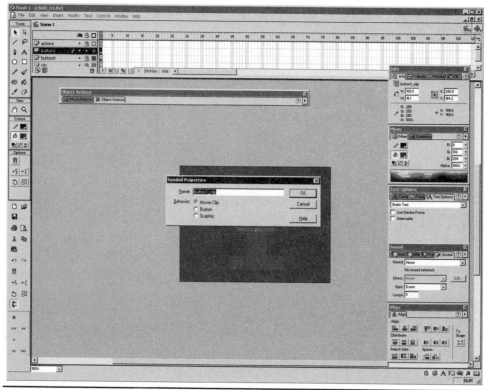

Figure 5-2 *Creating the button1_clip movie clip*

All of the actions on the button1_clip must be updated dynamically, so the movie clips will be repositioned when moved. Select `enterFrame` from the list of clip events, as shown in Figure 5-3. This will update the script every time the frame is played inside the movie clip. Depending on the frame rate selected for your Flash movie, the menu will move slower or faster. For this project, I used 20 fps (frames per second), which is the speed I use for most of my Flash movies.

Determining the Previous Movie Clip

The ActionScript for the menu uses four variables to determine the name of the previous movie clip:

▶ `bname` is the name of the button.

▶ `bname2` sets a string equal to the name of the button.

- ▶ `bname3` extracts the seventh character from the button name.

- ▶ `bname4` adds `"_root.button"` to the seventh character of the button name, minus 1.

Each of these variables is described in more detail in the following sections.

The Bname Variable   When the movie clip is duplicated, it must be given a new instance name to set it apart from the original movie clip. The first task is to determine the name of the movie clip. Using the `getProperty()` command with `this` as the target returns the name of the current movie clip. When using `this` as a target, the Expression check box must be checked next to the target field. In the Property field, select _name. The `bname` variable sets the full name of an object, such as button3.

L 5-2

```
bname = getProperty (this, _name);
```

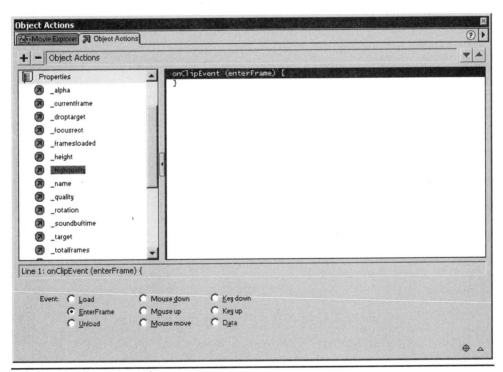

Figure 5-3   *Choosing a clip event action*

The Bname2 Variable Because the button is repositioned according to the button preceding it, you need to determine the name of the preceding button. The button name contains both numbers and letters, so you cannot subtract to determine the name. A solution is to use the `substring()` command to read only the numerical characters. To use the `substring()` command, you first need to prepare a string using the `String()` command. This command converts an object into a string, so it can be referenced by the `substring()` command. The following code sets the variable `bname2` equal to `String (bname)`.

L 5-3

```
bname2 = String (bname);
```

The Bname3 Variable Next, the `substring()` command is used to divide the string into numerical characters.

L 5-4

```
bname3 = substring (bname2, 7, 1);
```

Inside the parentheses, the first part, `bname2`, is the string from which to extract the new string, set on the previous line of code. After the comma, the 7 represents the number of the first character to extract. After the next comma, the 1 represents the number of characters to include in the extracted string, not including the index character.

The Bname4 Variable Finally, subtract 1 from the `bname3` variable to equal the preceding duplicated movie clip trailing number. The text is then added back to the name. In order to add the button-name text to the `bname3` variable, the text must be enclosed in quotation marks. The object also must be referenced as an absolute link, so `_root.` precedes `button`.

L 5-5

```
bname4 = "_root.button" + (bname3 - 1);
```

Determining the Position of the Previous Movie Clip

The next section of the code determines the x and y coordinates of the movie clip set by the `bname4` variable. This is done by using the `getProperty()` command to set the `x_pos` and `y_pos` variables.

L 5-6

```
x_pos = getProperty (bname4, _x);
y_pos = getProperty (bname4, _y);
```

These variables return the x and y coordinates of the movie clip set by `bname4` by using the `_x` and `_y` object properties.

Positioning the Current Movie Clip

The last task is to set the x and y coordinates of the current movie clip according to the position of the preceding movie clip. Using the setProperty() command, you can change the properties of objects in Flash. The x coordinate is set to the same x coordinate as that of the preceding movie clip by setting the property of the movie clip this equal to the x_pos variable. The y coordinate of movie clip this is set equal to the y_pos variable plus 15. This will position the movie clip 15 pixels below the preceding movie clip.

L 5-7
```
setProperty (this, _x, x_pos);
setProperty (this, _y, y_pos + 15);
```

Putting the Script Together

The complete script with comments is shown here.

L 5-8
```
onClipEvent (enterFrame) {
    // substring event to determine the preceding movie clip
    bname = getProperty (this, _name);
    bname2 = String (bname);
    bname3 = substring (bname2, 7, 1);
    bname4 = "_root.button" + (bname3 - 1);
    // get the properties of the preceding movie clip
    x_pos = getProperty (bname4, _x);
    y_pos = getProperty (bname4, _y);
    // reposition this movie clip
    setProperty (this, _x, x_pos);
    setProperty (this, _y, y_pos + 15);
}
```

Dividing the Button1 Movie Clip into Layers

Dividing movie clips into layers helps to identify the objects and organize the project. I broke the button1 movie clip into two layers. One layer contains a button with actions to control the movie clip named clip (described later in this chapter, in the "Adding the Clip Layer" section), and the other contains a dynamic text field.

The Button Layer   The button layer contains a standard button. Draw a rectangle and use the Info panel to resize it to 100 pixels wide by 10 pixels tall. Press F8 to convert the rectangle into an object. Select Button from the list of options, and name it **button1**. To produce a rollover effect, add a keyframe to the over frame and, in the Mixer panel, change the Alpha setting to 80% for the rectangle fill, as shown in Figure 5-4.

Because the movie clip will be duplicated, you cannot assign regular button actions, or else all of the duplicated movie clips will perform the same actions. Using an expression instead of a frame name or frame label allows you to use the same script for each duplicated button, but read a variable declared elsewhere to perform different tasks. This project uses the variable bname3, set in the button1 movie clip actions. This will tell the movie clip to go to the frame number equal to the value of the bname3 variable.

L 5-9
```
on (release) {
    with (_root.clip) {
        gotoAndStop (bname3);
    }
}
```

The Text Layer   The text layer contains a dynamic text field that reads the bname variable. Using this technique displays the movie clip name over each duplicated movie clip. This project displays the button name, but with minor changes. The text can be set by a variable to whatever format is needed. Just set the bname variable to whatever you like, using if statements to determine which is the active movie clip.

CAUTION

When drawing text fields, avoid resizing the field using the Info panel or Resize tool. Doing so will just stretch or skew the text.

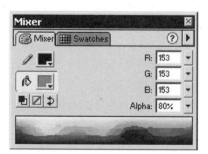

Figure 5-4   *Setting the alpha for the rectangle fill in the Mixer panel*

Adding the Button0 Layer

The second part of this project is duplicating the button1 movie clip to build the menu. These actions take place in the button0_clip. This movie clip is the draggable movie clip that controls the rest of the menu.

Begin by pressing CTRL-F8 (COMMAND-F8 for Macs) to create a new object. Select Movie Clip from the list of options and name it **button0_clip**. Drag this object from the Library onto the main timeline and name it **button0** in the Instance panel.

The actions on the button0_clip must cycle until the menu is completely built. Select enterFrame from the list of clip events. This will make the actions go through an endless loop.

Setting the Menu Button Limit

First, determine how many menu buttons you want to have. Although it isn't necessary, using a variable to set the maximum number of buttons makes it easier to update and edit the script. The limit variable sets the maximum to nine.

L 5-10
```
limit = 9;
```

Naming the Menu Buttons

Next, set the variable that will be used to name the buttons and also limit the number of buttons to duplicate. This is done by adding the variable name followed by two plus signs (++). It will add 1 to itself each time it is cycled. This will name the buttons in consecutive order, 1 through 9.

L 5-11
```
i++;
```

This expression above can only be entered using expert mode. The same result can be achieved using normal mode by setting the i variable equal to $i + 1$, as shown here.

L 5-12
```
i = i + 1;
```

Duplicating the Movie Clip

The next part of the script is an if statement that determineswhether the variable i is less than the limit variable, and also whether it is greater than 1. This will start the loop at 2 to ensure that there are not two button1 movie clips.

The `duplicateMovieClip()` command duplicates a movie clip and assigns it a new name and a new depth level.

L 5-13

```
if (i <= limit & i > 1) {
    duplicateMovieClip ("_root.button1", "button" + i, i);
}
```

The first parameter of the `duplicateMovieClip ()` command sets the target, `"_root.button"`.

The second parameter sets the name of the duplicated clip, `"button" + i`. The quotation marks here are important. This will render the string "button" as text while still treating the variable `i` as an expression. The overall effect is to add the word *button* to the value of the variable `i`, resulting in a sequential list of movie clips containing buttons with instance names of button1 through button9.

The final parameter sets the depth of the duplicated movie clip. Each movie clip must be assigned a new depth, or it will replace the previous duplicated movie clip. To place these movie clips on separate depths, use the `i` variable again.

Putting the Script Together

The complete script with comments is shown here.

L 5-14

```
onClipEvent (enterFrame) {
    // set the amount of buttons in the menu
    limit = 9;
    // variable to add 1 plus itself
    i++;
    // if statement to duplicate button1 movie clip
    if (i <= limit & i > 1) {
        duplicateMovieClip ("_root.button1", "button" + i, i);
    }
}
```

Creating the Button Layer

Next, open the button0_clip and draw a rectangle. Use the Info panel to set the rectangle size to 100 pixels by 15 pixels. Align the object to the center of the stage using the Align panel. While the rectangle is selected, press F8 to convert the rectangle into an object. Select Button from the list of options and name the object **button0**. As for the button in the button1_clip, add a keyframe on the over frame, and then use the Mixer panel to change the alpha of the fill to add a rollover effect for the button.

Next, add the actions to the button to make the button0_clip draggable.

L 5-15
```
on (press) {
    startDrag (this, false, _root.left, _root.top, _root.right,
    _root.bottom);
}
```

This code adds a startDrag() operation on mouse event press. The first parameter sets the target to this. When using this as a target, the Expression check box must be checked. This uses a relative target instead of the standard absolute target. If the name of the movie clip needs to be changed in the future, this part of the script will not need to be edited.

The second startDrag() parameter is false, which means that the mouse will not be locked to the center of the movie clip to be dragged. Locking the mouse to the center (by setting this parameter to true) places the movie clip at the same x and y coordinates as the mouse position. As noted in Chapter 4, this technique is generally not used for large objects, but it can benefit some ActionScript projects, such as mouse trailers.

The next parameters determine the constraining rectangle for the movie clip to be dragged. This code uses the constraints set previously in the actions layer. The constraints will keep the menu from being dragged off the main stage.

The last part of the script is used to stop the drag operation on the release mouse event. This is necessary to keep the button from sticking to the mouse after the mouse button is released.

L 5-16
```
on (release) {
    stopDrag ();
}
```

Adding the Clip Layer

The clip layer contains a movie clip with nine frames. This layer is included for learning purposes, to demonstrate how the button1 reads the bname3 variable to determine which frame to go to in the clip movie clip. Each frame in the movie clip contains a number corresponding to the frame number of the movie clip.

Start by pressing CTRL-F8 (COMMAND-F8 for Macs) to create a new object. Select Movie Clip from the list of options and name it **clip**. Drag this object from the Library onto the main timeline and name it **clip** in the Instance panel.

NOTE

I set the alpha of the movie clip to 10% to keep the text with the frame numbers from interfering with the appearance of the menu.

Figure 5-5   *A numbered frame*

The clip movie clip has two layers: the numbers layer and the actions layer. The numbers layer contains nine frames. Each frame contains a number corresponding to the frame name, as shown in Figure 5-5. Select the Text tool and add the number 1 on frame 1, number 2 on frame 2, and so on. In a full Flash site, these frames could contain content for the site or more actions. The actions layer contains a simple `stop()` command on the first frame to keep the movie clip from playing when the Flash movie is first loaded.

Building an Interactive Drop-Down Menu

ch05_02.fla

The ch05_02.fla file produces a menu that is virtually the same as the one described in the previous sections, with the exception that it allows user input to decide how many menu items to display, as shown in Figure 5-6.

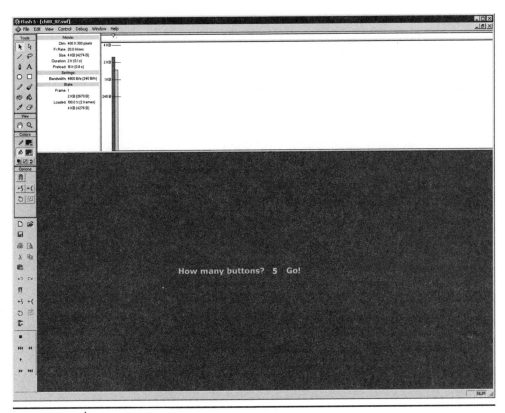

Figure 5-6 *The user input screen*

This type of navigation can be useful when making smart clips, which are discussed in Chapter 16 of this book, and for making user-customized sites, which are becoming more common on the Web.

This Flash movie is two frames long. The first frame asks for the user input, and the second frame renders the amount of buttons from the input.

This project uses modified layers from the previous project. The button1, button0, and clip layers will need a blank keyframe inserted before the current frames containing the objects. That way none of the events take place before the input is completed. The actions layer will need to have an extra keyframe inserted before the current keyframe with a `stop()` action. This will stop the Flash movie at the first frame until the user fills in the text field and clicks the Go button (described in the next section).

Adding the How_Many Layer

The how_many layer contains the movie clip that asks for user input and sets the `limit` variable. Press CTRL-F8 (COMMAND-F8 for Macs) to create a new object. Select Movie Clip from the list of options and name it **how_many**. Drag this object from the Library onto the main timeline and name it **how_many** in the Instance panel.

Creating the Button Layer

The button layer within the how_many movie clip contains the Go button. When the user clicks this button, the Flash movie continues to the next frame and renders the menu buttons.

Type **Go!** on the stage, and then align the text to the center of the stage using the Align panel. While the text is selected, press F8 to convert the text into an object. Select Button from the list of options and name the object **go_button**. Create a rollover effect by adding a keyframe on the over frame and changing the color of the text.

Next, add actions to the button to tell the Flash movie to go to the next frame and hide the how_many movie clip.

L 5-17
```
on (release) {
    with (_root) {
        gotoAndStop (2);
    }
    setProperty ("_root.how_many", _visible, "0");
}
```

In this code, the first command to take place on the `release` mouse event tells the Flash movie main timeline to go to frame 2 and stop. To address the main timeline, use `_root` for the target.

Next, the code uses the `setProperty()` command to change the `_visible` property of the how_many movie clip to 0. The how_many clip must be in the second frame so that the button0 movie clip can read the `limit` variable.

Creating the Text Field Layer

The text field layer contains an input text field. This type of text field allows users to type in text to set variables in a Flash movie.

Start by drawing a text field large enough for one character. In the Text Options panel, select Input Text from the first drop-down menu. Set the Max. Chars field to 1. This will prevent users from being able to enter more than one character into the input text field. In the Variable field, enter **limit**, as shown in Figure 5-7. This will create the `limit` variable equal to the content entered into the text field.

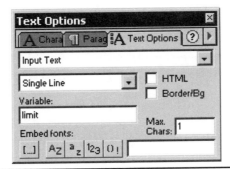

Figure 5-7 *Creating a user input text field in the Text Options panel*

Adding the Content Layer

The content layer contains the text and text field outline. Type **How many buttons?** on the main stage and align it to the left of the text field. Then add a rectangle to serve as an outline behind the text field, so the user will know where to add the input.

> **NOTE**
>
> *The Text Options panel includes an option for drawing borders and background. Rather than use that option, I always choose to draw my own borders and background to match the rest of the Flash movie.*

Modifying the Button0_Clip

The final part of this project is to modify the button0_clip used in the previous project. In that version, the `limit` variable was referenced from within the ActionScripting. Now it needs to reference the `limit` variable set by the text field. This requires two changes to the script. First, the `limit` variable can be removed. (Leaving unused code in a script can result in confusion and possibly problems with the code itself.) Next, the `if` statement reference to the `limit` variable must be changed to read the new `limit` variable set from the text field. The modified script is shown here.

L 5-18
```
onClipEvent (enterFrame) {
    // variable to add 1 plus itself
    i++;
    // if statement to duplicate button1 movie clip
    if (i <= _root.how_many.limit & i > 1) {
        duplicateMovieClip ("_root.button1", "button" + i, i);
    }
}
```

An example of the resulting drop-down menu is shown in Figure 5-8.

What to Take Away from This Chapter

The two projects discussed in this chapter use duplicated movie clips to build an ActionScript-driven drop-down menu. The end results of both files are navigational menus that can be easily updated and changed, while staying very low in file size. The techniques used to create these files can be implemented in many real-world applications to achieve great results in a short amount of time.

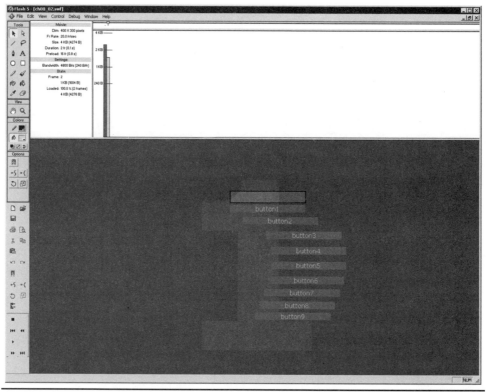

Figure 5-8   *The drop-down menu*

CHAPTER 6

Drag-and-Drop Navigation

IN THIS CHAPTER:

▶ Build a drag-and-drop navigational system using ActionScripting

▶ Use duplicate movie clips to reduce file size

▶ Determine which movie clip is on top with the swapDepths() command

▶ Control the speed and direction of objects with friction and velocity

▶ Lock objects onto targets using the new Flash 5 hitText() command

Drag-and-drop navigation techniques have been around since the release of Flash 4. Drag-and-drop navigation usually consists of one or more objects that can be dragged with the user's mouse and placed or thrown into a target area. Once the object hits that area, then an event would take place as if a button had been pressed. This navigation is similar to dragging a file into a folder in an operating system such as Microsoft Windows. Using common methods and properties such as `dragMovieclip()` and `_droptarget`, you can build a simple navigational system in Flash with the same features.

The drag-and-drop navigation project described in this chapter has some extra functionality and uses some commands that are new to Flash 5. I incorporated the use of friction and velocity to make the navigation more interesting. *Friction* is defined as a force that slows down an object's motion when it rubs against another object. *Velocity* is defined as the combination of speed and direction of an object's motion.

Rather than using `droptarget` to determine whether the navigation box was dropped inside the target, this project uses the new `hitTest()` command. The `_droptarget` property works only when a mouse button is released, but the `hitTest()` method can detect a collision between two movie clips at any time. Using collision detection that is independent of the mouse enables you to use friction and velocity to actually throw the boxes around, as if they were real physical objects, and still lock onto the targets.

The drag-and-drop navigation project consists of six layers: Bounds, Target, Box, Duplication Action, Content, and Actions.

Adding the Bounds Layer

ch06_01.fla

First, determine the size of the Flash movie you want to use. I set the dimensions of the movie to 600 pixels by 400 pixels.

The bounds layer contains an unfilled rectangle to simulate a border and to set the boundaries of the Flash movie. This rectangle will be used to constrain the box movie clips that are explained later in this chapter, in the "Adding the Box Layer" section.

Start by drawing a rectangle without an inner fill, to match the stage size of the Flash movie. Make sure that the stroke is set to hairline in the Stroke panel, as shown in Figure 6-1. This will keep the lines from resizing.

While the rectangle is selected, press F8 to convert the rectangle into an object. Select Movie Clip from the list of behaviors and name the movie clip **bounds**. Next, name the movie clip **bounds** in the Instance panel, so it can be targeted by ActionScripting.

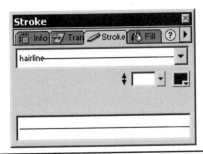

Figure 6-1   *Setting the rectangle's stroke with the Stroke panel*

Open the Align panel (CTRL-K/COMMAND-K). Set the width and height of the **bounds** movie clip to the same dimensions as the Flash movie. To do this, select the Align/ Distribute to Stage button and click the Match Width and Height button. Next, click the Align Horizontal Center button (second button from the left on the top row in the Align Panel), and then click the Align Vertical Center button (fifth button from the left on the top row in the Align Panel) to center the **bounds** movie clip on the stage.

Adding the Target Layer

When making Flash movies, the design of reusable objects and reusable movie clips is key to optimizing your development work. The target layer contains the target movie clip. The target movie clip contains a graphic square and a text field used to label the movie clip dynamically when the movie clip is duplicated.

Creating the Graphic Square

Start by drawing a box and use the Info panel to resize it to 23 pixels by 23 pixels. Then change the color of the top and left lines to a darker color, and the bottom and right lines to a lighter color, to simulate a beveled square, as shown in Figure 6-2. While the square is selected, press F8 to convert the square into an object. Select Movie Clip from the list of behaviors and name the movie clip **target**. Next, give this movie clip an instance name of **target0** in the Instance panel.

Adding the Text Field to the Target Movie Clip

Open the target movie clip and add another layer on top of the layer containing the square. Select Dynamic Text in the Text Options panel, and draw a text field

Figure 6-2   *The beveled square for the target movie clip*

approximately the same size as the box below it. Next, give the text field a variable name of **name3** in the Text Options panel. This sets the text field to the name3 variable. Set the font size so that the value of the name3 variable will fit within the box. I used 12-point Verdana.

Target ActionScripting

While the target movie clip is selected, press CTRL-SHIFT-A (COMMAND-SHIFT-A for Macs) to open the ActionScript editor for that movie clip instance.

The first line of the script sets the onClipEvent event to enterFrame:

L 6-1
```
onClipEvent (enterFrame) {
```

This will make the script run continuously. In this case, the enterFrame event handler is necessary because the movie clips are dynamically duplicated, and each duplicated instance will need to run its own code continuously and independent of the other movie clips.

NOTE

The `enterFrame` event simulates the old method of using multiple keyframe movie clips to perform actions continuously by looping between keyframes. This new method of using an `enterFrame` event handler is much more efficient and saves time if you need to edit the code later.

The next line of code uses the `getProperty()` command to get the name of the movie clip:

L 6-2

```
name = getProperty(this, _name);
```

The `getProperty()` command has two arguments. The first argument contains the instance name of a movie clip from which the property is being retrieved. The second argument contains the property to get from the action. The code here gets the name of the current movie clip (`this`), returning the full name (`_name`), including the text and number, and sets it to the variable `name`.

To be able to use the name information to dynamically name the movie clip, the text needs to removed from the name. This is done by using the `substring()` command. As you learned in Chapter 5, the purpose of `substring()` is to extract a sequence of characters from a string of characters. Before using the `substring()` command, you need to declare a string using the `String()` command, adding the `name` variable as the argument in the parentheses:

L 6-3

```
name2 = String(name);
```

How the Substring Command Works

The arguments of the substring command start with the variable name. The second argument determines which character to extract, and the final argument determines how many characters to extract.

The following example illustrates how the Flash `substring()` function works. Suppose that the variable named `myVariable` contains a string value of "abcdefg." The command `substring(myVariable, 2, 4)` retrieves four characters starting from position 2. The resulting value is equal to *cdef*. Note that the position of characters in string variables start from 0 and end with the length of the string minus 1.

Next, using the `substring()` command, read the seventh character of the name2 variable:

L 6-4

```
name3 = substring(name2, 7, 1);
```

The arguments of the `substring()` command start with the name of the variable whose characters will be extracted by the command (name2). The next argument determines the position of the first character to extract (7), and the final argument determines how many characters to extract after the first extraction position (1).

Here is the complete script:

L 6-5

```
onClipEvent (enterFrame) {
    // substring actions
    name = getProperty(this, _name);
    name2 = String(name);
    name3 = substring(name2, 7, 1);
}
```

Adding the Box Layer

The box layer contains the box movie clip. The box movie clip includes a button and a text field used to label the movie clip dynamically when it is duplicated.

Begin by drawing a filled box. Then use the Info panel to resize it to 23 by 23 pixels. Change the color of the top and left lines to a lighter color, and the bottom and right lines to a darker color, to simulate a raised, beveled square.

While the square is selected, press F8 to convert the square into an object. Select Button from the list of options and name the button **box_button**. Once again, press F8 with the button selected to convert the button into a nested button within a movie clip. Select Movie Clip from the list of options and name the movie **box_clip**. Name the movie clip instance **box0** in the Instance panel.

Adding the Text Field to the Box Movie Clip

Open the movie clip and add another layer on top of the layer that contains the square. Select Dynamic Text in the Text Options panel and draw a text field approximately the same size as the box below it. Next, enter **name3** in the Variable text field in the Text Options panel. As with the text field for the target movie clip, set the font to a size that will fit in the box without overflowing. Again, I used 12-point Verdana.

Coding Button Events

In order to drag a movie clip, the movie clip needs a button that contains ActionScript for the `on (press)` event. This code will execute as soon as the user presses the mouse button while the cursor is on top of the Flash button. The command to drag a movie clip with the cursor is `startDrag()`.

L 6-6
```
on (press) {
    startDrag (
this, false, bounds.xMin + size, bounds.yMin + size,
bounds.xMax - size, bounds.yMax - size
);
```

The first parameter for the `startDrag()` command is the target text field. The script uses relative targeting because the movie clips will be dynamically renamed. Using `this` as the target name and selecting the Expression check box, which is next to the target name field, will start the drag operation on the current movie clip.

> **NOTE**
>
> *Actions for buttons must exist within the curly braces of an* `on (event)` *handler, which executes its ActionScript when triggered by mouse or keyboard events.*

The next parameter determines whether or not to lock the mouse to the center of the movie clip to be dragged. Since it is not necessary in this case, set this to `false`.

The final parameters constrain the draggable movie clip to a set left, top, right, and bottom boundaries for the dragging action, as follows:

► The left boundary is set equal to the `xMin` variable plus the `size` variable.

► The top boundary uses the same logic as the left boundary by setting the limit to the `yMin` variable plus the `size` variable.

► The right boundary is set equal to the `xMax` variable minus the `size` variable.

► The bottom boundary uses the same logic as the right boundary by setting the limit to the `yMax` variable minus the `size` variable.

Check the Constrain to Rectangle check box, which appears in the normal ActionScript editing window when you add the `startDrag()` command. This will keep the drag operation within the specific set boundaries. This script uses the variables set from the bounds box, as explained in the next section.

Next, two variables are updated when the button is pressed:

L 6-7
```
drag = "true";
speed = 1;
```

The first line sets the `drag` variable to `"true"`. This will be used to determine when the movie clip is being dragged. The next line sets the `speed` variable to 1. This is used to set the speed of the button when thrown, as explained in the next section.

Finally, the last function performed when the button is pressed is to swap the depth of the current movie clip so that it will be on top. This is done using the `swapDepths()` command.

L 6-8
```
this.swapDepths(_root.dup_actions.i);
```

The two arguments used are for the target and the variable. The target uses relative targeting because the movie clips will be dynamically renamed. This argument comes before the `swapDepths()` command and is separated from that command by a period. Inside the parentheses, the variable for the depth is set to the `i` variable on the dup_actions movie clip (described in "Adding the Duplicate Actions Layer," later in this chapter). The `i` variable constantly raises by 1, so it will always place the current movie clip above the others.

Here is the final code:

L 6-9
```
on (press) {
    startDrag (
this, false, bounds.xMin + size, bounds.yMin + size,
bounds.xMax - size, bounds.yMax - size
);
    drag = "true";
    speed = 1;
    // sets depth to top
    this.swapDepths(_root.dup_actions.i);
}
```

When the mouse is released, the first action performed is to stop the drag operation using the `stopDrag()` command, which stops all drag operations in the Flash movie. Next, the drag variable is set to `"false"`. This will be used to determine when the movie clip is released.

L 6-10
```
on (release) {
    stopDrag ();
    drag = "false";|
}
```

Box ActionScripting

The ActionScripting for the box_clip contains all of the actions to throw, bounce, and lock the box_clip to the correct target. On the main timeline, select the box_clip movie clip and press CTRL-SHIFT-A (COMMAND-SHIFT-A for Macs) to open the ActionScript editor.

Coding Box On Load Actions

ActionScript commands contained within `clipEvent (load)` actions are performed only when the movie clip is first loaded. Coding `onClipEvent (load)` actions is useful for setting global variables. For this project, four variables are set for the `onClipEvent (load)` event: `friction`, `speed`, `bounds`, and `size`.

The first variable to set is `friction`. This variable determines how much friction the box_clip will have when it is thrown. The lower the number, the shorter the period of time the box will move. Setting a number above 1 will cause the box to gain speed and never stop. I set the variable to 0.98. This resembles friction from a real-life object, such as a pool table.

L 6-11
```
friction = "0.98";
```

Next, set the `speed` variable. This variable determines how fast the object will move when it is first thrown. A higher number will result in a much faster moving object. This variable will be updated when the object is thrown, as described in "Coding Box On Enter Frame Actions," later this chapter.

L 6-12
```
speed = 1;
```

Next, the size of the bounds layer (created earlier in the chapter) must be called to use for the boundary limits. In Flash 5, this is done by using the new `getBounds()` command. Use the `bounds` variable to get the bounds of the bounds movie clip.

L 6-13
```
bounds = _root.bounds.getBounds(_root);
```

When using the `getBounds()` command, target the movie clip with absolute targeting. The target and command are separated by a period, and then the next argument is in parentheses. This argument declares the target coordinate space, or where the target lies.

TIP

Using the `getBounds()` technique is much more effective than using actual numbers. If the size of the movie clip changes, just resize the bounds movie clip. No further changes will be necessary.

Finally, set the `size` variable. This variable uses the `getPropery()` command to get the size of the current movie clip and divide it by 2.

L 6-14
```
size = getProperty(this, _width) / 2;
```

The size will equal the distance from the center of the object to the outer edge. Dividing the width by two is necessary in Flash because all objects are placed from the center of the movie clip, not from the edge. If it were not divided, half of the movie clip would go over the edges of the boundaries. (Because the object is a square, it is not necessary to also get the height of this movie clip.)

Here is the final code:

L 6-15
```
onClipEvent (load) {
    // set variables
    friction = "0.98";
    speed = 1;
    bounds = _root.bounds.getBounds(_root);
    size = getProperty(this, _width) / 2;
}
```

Coding Box On Mouse Down Actions

Actions included in the `onClipEvent (mouseDown)` event will be updated every time the mouse is pressed. When the mouse is first pressed, the timer needs to be addressed to determine what time the mouse was first pressed. The timer built into Flash returns the value in milliseconds. Using milliseconds is not necessary for this project, so divide the results by 1000 to convert the value into seconds.

L 6-16
```
onClipEvent (mouseDown) {
    // get timer when mouse is pressed
    o_time = getTimer() / 1000;
}
```

This `o_time` variable represents the original time.

Coding Box On Mouse Up Actions

Actions included in the `onClipEvent (mouseUp)` event will be updated every time the mouse is released. When the mouse is released, the timer needs to be addressed to determine when the mouse was released. Again, divide the results by 1000 to convert the value into seconds.

```
L 6-17    onClipEvent (mouseUp) {
                // get timer when mouse is released
                n_time = getTimer() / 1000;
          }
```

The n_time variable represents the new time.

Coding Box On Enter Frame Actions

Actions included in the onClipEvent(enterFrame) event will be updated every time the frame is accessed. This replaces the old method of adding actions to frames within movie clips. The result is much more efficient and cleaner code.

Coding Substring Actions   The text field in the box_clip movie clip referenced the name3 variable. This variable is created by using a substring() command to get the final character of the movie clip.

As with the uses of the substring() command you have seen earlier in this chapter and in previous chapters, first use the getProperty() command to get the name of the current movie clip. This enables you to dynamically name the movie clip and determine which target it locks to.

```
L 6-18        name = getProperty(this, _name);
```

Next, use the String() command to declare a string.

```
L 6-19        name2 = String(name);
```

After creating the string, you can use the substring() command to read the fourth character of the name2 variable.

```
L 6-20    name3 = substring(name2, 4, 1);
```

Setting the Visibility of the Content   Next, set the visibility of the content triggered by the current button to 0. This will keep the content hidden until the box is locked into its target. The content section will be explained in "Building the Content Layer," later in this chapter.

```
L 6-21        setProperty ("_root.hit" + name3, _visible, 0);
```

Determining How Fast to Throw the Target   Create the time variable to determine the length of time the movie clip was dragged. This is done by subtracting the new time from the original time, using the two time variables set earlier in this chapter (in the "Coding Box On Mouse Down Actions" and "Coding Box On Mouse Up Actions" sections). The `time` variable is used to determine how hard the movie clip was thrown.

L 6-22

```
time = o_time - n_time;
```

Next, set the `speed` variable to `speed` multiplied by 1.1. This will cause the `speed` variable to slowly rise, to reflect the acceleration from the throw. However, as the speed slowly increases, friction acts on the movie clip to slow it down, and the movie clip will slowly come to a stop. The combination of the acceleration and the friction imitates real-life forces and prevents the movie clip from stopping too abruptly.

L 6-23

```
speed = speed * 1.1;
```

When the box is stopped, the x and y positions are set equal to `o_x_pos` and `o_y_pos`. To do this, just set `o_x_pos` equal to `x_pos` and `o_y_pos` equal to `y_pos`. Because the `x_pos` and `y_pos` variables are set in the next lines of code, this code will set the variables equal to the last-known position:

L 6-24

```
o_x_pos = x_pos;
o_y_pos = y_pos;
```

Next, to get the new x and y position, use the `getProperty()` command to retrieve the x and y coordinates of the current movie clip.

L 6-25

```
x_pos = getProperty(this, _x);
y_pos = getProperty(this, _y);
```

This code uses relative targeting (`this`) to get the property of the current movie clip and returns the _x and _y properties of that movie clip.

Determining Whether the Object Is Being Dragged or Thrown   Next, you need to determine whether the movie clip is being dragged or thrown. This is done by using `if-else` statements.

Start by checking to see if the `drag` variable is equal to `"true"`. If the variable is `true`, set the two velocity variables.

L 6-26

```
if (drag == "true") {
    x_velocity = (x_pos - o_x_pos) * time;
    y_velocity = (y_pos - o_y_pos) * time;
```

NOTE

It is important to use a double equal sign (==) in this `if` statement. A single equal sign is used to set properties. A double equal sign is used to check properties.

The `x_velocity` variable is equal to `x_pos` minus `o_x_pos` multiplied by the amount of time the object has been dragged. The `y_velocity` variable uses the same formula as the `x_velocity` variable, but with the y positions.

If the `drag` variable is not equal to `true`, the code continues to the `else` commands.

L 6-27
```
} else {
    x_pos = x_pos + (x_velocity / speed);
    y_pos = y_pos + (y_velocity / speed);
```

The `x_pos` variable is set equal to `x_pos` plus `x_velocity` divided by the `speed` variable. This is equal to the x position of the object, used for the next section of scripting. The `y_pos` variable uses the same logic as the `x_pos` variable, but using the y position and velocity.

Determining Whether the Box Is Inside the Boundaries   Next, you want to keep the movie clip from bouncing outside the boundaries. Use `if` and `else if` statements to determine whether the movie clip touches or tries to move outside the boundaries.

This code first checks to see if `x_pos` minus the `size` variable is less than or equal to the `xMin` boundary. This will be the case if the box_clip movie clip is touching or overlapping the left edge of the bounds movie clip.

L 6-28
```
if (x_pos - size <= bounds.xMin) {
        x_pos = bounds.xMin + size;
        x_velocity = -x_velocity * friction;
        y_velocity = y_velocity * friction;
```

If this is the case, `x_pos` is set equal to the `xMin` variable plus the `size` variable. Then `x_velocity` is set equal to negative `x_velocity` multiplied by `friction`, causing `x_velocity` to reverse its current value. This will cause the object to bounce off the boundary and then slow down due to the friction variable. Finally, `y_velocity` is set equal to `y_velocity` multiplied by `friction`. This will keep the object moving in the same direction, but, again, the `friction` variable will gradually slow down the object. The following `else if` statements in this portion of the script use the same logic to bounce the object of the boundary and move it slowly away from the boundary.

Next, check to see if the box_clip movie clip is touching or overlapping the right edge of the bounds movie clip. If it is, x_pos is set equal to the xMax variable minus the size variable.

L 6-29
```
} else if (x_pos + size >= bounds.xMax) {
    x_pos = bounds.xMax - size;
    x_velocity = -x_velocity * friction;
    y_velocity = y_velocity * friction;
```

The x_velocity and y_velocity variables are set in the same way they are in the previous if statement.

Then the code determines whether y_pos minus the size variable is less than or equal to the yMin boundary. This will be the case if the box_clip movie clip is touching or overlapping the top edge of the bounds movie clip.

L 6-30
```
} else if (y_pos - size <= bounds.yMin) {
    y_pos = bounds.yMin + size;
    x_velocity = x_velocity * friction;
    y_velocity = -y_velocity * friction;
```

In this case, y_pos is set equal to the yMin variable plus the size variable. The x_velocity variable is set equal to x_velocity multiplied by friction, and the y_velocity variable is set equal to negative y_velocity multiplied by friction.

Next, using the same techniques, check to see if the box_clip movie clip is touching or overlapping the bottom edge of the bounds movie clip. If it is, y_pos is set equal to the yMax variable minus the size variable.

L 6-31
```
} else if (y_pos + size >= bounds.yMax) {
    y_pos = bounds.yMax - size;
    x_velocity = x_velocity * friction;
    y_velocity = -y_velocity * friction;
```

Determining Whether the Object Hits the Target   The next else if statements check to see if the object is touching the target containing the same number as the current movie clip, as shown in Figure 6-3.

This code uses the new Flash 5 hitTest() command.

L 6-32
```
} else if (hitTest("_root.target" + name3)) {
    x_pos = getProperty("_root.target" + name3, _x);
    y_pos = getProperty("_root.target" + name3, _y);
    setProperty ("_root.hit" + name3, _visible, 1);
```

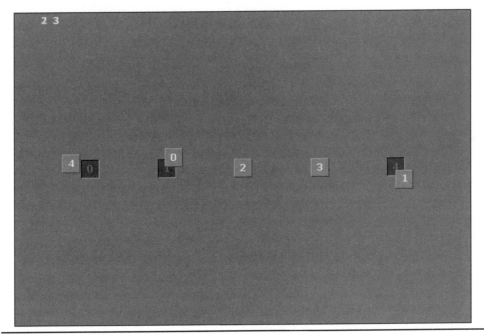

Figure 6-3   *The hit test*

If the movie clip is touching the target with the same suffix number (using the name3 variable), the movie clip will stop and lock into position. The hitTest() command has only one argument, the name of the target.

Next, if the object is touching the target object, the x and y positions are set equal to that of the target. Using the get_Property command, get the property of the target with the same suffix number, by using the name3 substring variable again. Set the x_pos variable equal to this object's x position, and set the y_pos variable equal to this object's y position.

Finally, the code sets the visibility of the corresponding content movie clip to visible, using the setProperty() command. This command has three arguments. The first is the target to be addressed, which, in this case, is _root.hit plus the name3 substring variable. The next argument determines which property to modify, and the last argument sets the property. Here, the _visible property is set to 1, to make the movie clip visible (the other setting for _visible is 0, for invisible).

Setting the Position of the Current Movie Clip   The final task for this script is to set the x and y positions of the current movie clip equal to x_pos and y_pos, respectively, using the setProperty() command.

L 6-33
```
setProperty (this, _x, x_pos);
setProperty (this, _y, y_pos);
```

These setProperty() commands use this as the target, to address the current movie clip. The first line sets the _x property equal to the x_pos variable, and the second line sets the _y property equal to the y_pos variable.

Putting the Script Together   The following is the final ActionScript, with comments:

L 6-34
```
onClipEvent (enterFrame) {
    // substring actions
    name = getProperty(this, _name);
    name2 = String(name);
    name3 = substring(name2, 4, 1);
    // set visibility of hit to zero
    setProperty ("_root.hit" + name3, _visible, 0);
    // actions to determine how fast to throw target
    time = o_time - n_time;
    speed = speed * 1.1;
    o_x_pos = x_pos;
    o_y_pos = y_pos;
    x_pos = getProperty(this, _x);
    y_pos = getProperty(this, _y);
    // determines if object is being dragged or thrown
    if (drag == "true") {
        x_velocity = (x_pos - o_x_pos) * time;
        y_velocity = (y_pos - o_y_pos) * time;
    } else {
        x_pos = x_pos + (x_velocity / speed);
        y_pos = y_pos + (y_velocity / speed);
        // if then else statements to determine if box
        // is inside bounds
        if (x_pos - size <= bounds.xMin) {
            x_pos = bounds.xMin + size;
            x_velocity = -x_velocity * friction;
            y_velocity = y_velocity * friction;
        } else if (x_pos + size >= bounds.xMax) {
            x_pos = bounds.xMax - size;
            x_velocity = -x_velocity * friction;
            y_velocity = y_velocity * friction;
        } else if (y_pos - size <= bounds.yMin) {
            y_pos = bounds.yMin + size;
```

```
        x_velocity = x_velocity * friction;
        y_velocity = -y_velocity * friction;
    } else if (y_pos + size >= bounds.yMax) {
        y_pos = bounds.yMax - size;
        x_velocity = x_velocity * friction;
        y_velocity = -y_velocity * friction;
        // determines if object hits target
    } else if (hitTest("_root.target" + name3)) {
        x_pos = getProperty("_root.target" + name3, _x);
        y_pos = getProperty("_root.target" + name3, _y);
        setProperty ("_root.hit" + name3, _visible, 1);
    }
    setProperty (this, _x, x_pos);
    setProperty (this, _y, y_pos);
    }
}
```

Adding the Duplicate Actions Layer

The duplicate actions layer contains a blank movie clip with actions to duplicate
the box_clip and target_clip movie clips. This code needs to go in its own movie
clip. If it were added to either of the duplicated movie clips, it would run endlessly.

Press CTRL-F8 (COMMAND-F8 for Macs) to create a new object, select Movie Clip
from the list of options, and name it **dup_actions**. In the Instance panel, name this
clip instance **dup_actions**.

For this frame, all actions are assigned in the onClipEvent(enterFrame)
event. This allows the actions to cycle through and duplicate each movie clip. Also,
the i variable is accessed for the swapDepths() command (described earlier in
this chapter, in the "Coding Button Events" section).

L 6-35
```
onClipEvent (enterFrame) {
    i++;
    if (i < 5) {
```

The i variable adds one to itself each time the script loops. This is done by adding
the variable name followed by two plus symbols (the same as i = i + 1). Next, the
if statement is used to determine if i is less than 5. If so, it continues to duplicate
the movie clips. This variable can be modified to add more or fewer movie clips.

Duplicating the Movie Clips

Using the `duplicateMovieClip()` command, duplicate each movie five times. Each time the original movie clip is duplicated, it is renamed and assigned a new depth.

L 6-36
```
duplicateMovieClip ("_root.target0", "target" + i, i);
duplicateMovieClip ("_root.box0", "box" + i, i + 5);
```

The first `duplicateMovieClip()` command copies the target0 movie clip and renames it "target" plus the i variable. Then it assigns the new movie clip a new depth equal to i.

In the second `duplicateMovieClip()` command, the box0 movie clip is duplicated and renamed "box" plus the i variable. Then the new movie clip is assigned a new depth equal to i plus 5. The target movie clips need to be set to i plus 5 so that they will not overwrite the movie clips duplicated from the target0 movie clip.

Positioning the Boxes

Next, to set the box movie clips away from each other, use `setProperty()` commands to assign a new x position and a new y position to the new box movie clips.

L 6-37
```
setProperty ("_root.box" + i, _x, random (600));
setProperty ("_root.box" + i, _y, random (400));
```

Both of these command use `"_root.box"` plus the i variable as the target. The first command sets the _x property to a random number less than 600 (the movie width) by using the `random()` command. The second command sets the _y property to a random number less than 400 (the movie height).

Positioning the Targets

Finally, use the `setProperty()` command to assign a new x position to the new target movie clips.

L 6-38
```
setProperty ("_root.target" + i, _x, (i * 100) + 100);
```

This command addresses the target `"_root.target"` plus the i variable. It sets the x position to i multiplied by 100 plus 100. This sets each movie clip 100 pixels apart from the previous movie clip.

Putting the Duplicate Actions Script Together

The following shows the final code for the duplicate actions layer, with comments:

L 6-39

```
onClipEvent (enterFrame) {
    i++;
    if (i < 5) {
        // duplicates movie clips
        duplicateMovieClip ("_root.target0", "target" + i, i);
        duplicateMovieClip ("_root.box0", "box" + i, i + 5);
        // randomly positions boxes
        setProperty ("_root.box" + i, _x, random (600));
        setProperty ("_root.box" + i, _y, random (400));
        // positions targets
        setProperty ("_root.target" + i, _x, (i * 100) + 100);
    }
}
```

Building the Content Layer

The content layer contains five movie clips to show which box has successfully been dropped into its target. This project has five movie clips, labeled hit0 through hit4. Each movie clip contains a number corresponding to the name of the movie clip, as shown in the example in Figure 6-4. In a full Flash site, this section could be replaced with content.

To make each movie clip, use the Text tool to type a number on the stage. While the text is selected, press F8 to convert it into an object. Select Movie Clip from the list of options, and name each one **hit** plus the number corresponding to the number selected, **hit0** through **hit4**. In the Instance panel, enter the same name in the Name text field, to allow the movie clip to be accessed by ActionScripting.

Adding the Actions Layer

As I noted in Chapter 5, I usually add an actions layer to every Flash movie I make to help organize my movies. This layer usually contains actions that declare variables or stop actions.

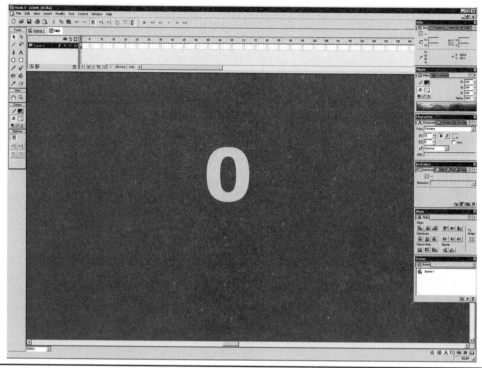

Figure 6-4   *A hit movie clip*

For this project, the actions layer has a `stop ()` action. Although this is not necessary for a single-frame Flash movie, it's still a good idea to add it. If you later decide to add a preloader or an additional scene, this scene will still work correctly.

What to Take Away from This Chapter

This project used duplicated movie clips to build an Action Script-driven, drag-and-drop navigational system. The navigational system includes many additional features, such as the use of friction and velocity to control the speed and direction of objects.

All of these techniques work together to result in a fully updateable and dynamic navigational system. You can implement this navigational system in many projects, modifying it as necessary.

Picture Album

IN THIS CHAPTER:

► Create a Flash picture album

► Reduce load time with external .swf files

► Reduce file size with external .html files

► Use arrays to avoid the need to duplicate variables

► Perform repeated tasks with the function() command

Flash has included the `loadMovie()` command since the release of Flash 2. In the past, Flash developers commonly used the `loadMovie()` function to load smaller movies into the main movie. Breaking up a large Flash Web site into smaller parts helps to shorten the load time by reducing the file size of the main Flash movie.

Flash 4 added the `loadVariables()` command, which works like `loadMovie()`, but loads external text files instead. These external files can help to further reduce file size, as well as make it easier to update the separated data.

Flash 5 includes the same `loadMovie()` function, plus it adds capabilities to the `loadVariables()` command. Now you can load HTML files that support HTML 2.0 tags, as well as text files. This enables you to modify text within paragraphs of external files. Also, hyperlinks within loaded HTML files can be used as navigation links to other URLs.

The project presented in this chapter is a Flash photo album. It enables the user to view relatively small images of all of the photos at once on the screen, as an index. When a user presses the mouse over one of the images, they zoom in closer to view just one picture at a time. At this point, the user is presented with three further options: go to the previous image in the row or column, go to the next image in the row or column, or go back to the index of images. The project uses the `loadMovie()` command to load an external .swf file for the background and the `loadVariables()` command to load an external HTML file for the text positioned over the background.

Adding the Pictures Layer
ch07_01.fla

Begin by creating a new Flash movie and setting the movie dimensions to 325 pixels by 450 pixels. The pictures layer contains all of the interactive components for this project. All of the main ActionScripting is inside the event handlers of the pictures movie clip instance.

TIP

When you add ActionScripting onto frames of the timeline instead of the event handlers of the movie, the code can exist in the same location, rather than being scattered across several keyframes and timelines. Including all of the scripting in the movie clip enables you to just copy and paste the entire movie clip into another Flash movie, and all of the scripting will still work, without any changes. I have a library of Flash movies that contains movie clips that I reuse in many of the sites that I design.

To make the pictures movie clip, press CTRL-F8 (COMMAND-F8 for Macs) to create a new object. Select Movie Clip from the list of options and name it **pictures**. The pictures movie clip contains only one layer, frame_mc, which includes all of the frames for the pictures. For this project, I decided to use 25 pictures, with five rows and five columns.

Creating the Frame_mc Movie Clip

Start by making the frame_mc movie clip. Press CTRL-F8 (COMMAND-F8 for Macs) to make a new object. Select Movie Clip from the list of options and name it **frame_mc**.
The frame_mc movie clip contains six layers:

▶ The frame_button layer contains the button for zooming in on a picture.

▶ The blank_mc layer contains the blank movie clip for loading the .swf file.

▶ The text_mc movie layer contains a text field used for loading the external HTML files.

▶ The back_button, next_button, and index_button layers hold Back, Next, and Index buttons, respectively, for navigating through the picture album.

Each object is on its own layer, which makes it easier to separate the objects for better organization so that they are easier to update later.

Adding the Frame_button Layer

First, determine the size of each picture you will be loading. For this project, I decided the pictures should be 250 by 375 pixels when fully zoomed. The index size is one-fifth of the full size, so I started out by making the individual pictures 50 by 75 pixels.
Draw a rectangle on the stage, and then use the Info panel to resize it to 50 pixels by 75 pixels, as shown in Figure 7-1. Be sure to set the stroke to hairline in the Stroke panel, so that the lines do not scale. (Hairline width is the only stroke selection that will maintain the same 1-pixel screen width during rescaling.) This is not necessary, but it usually provides a much cleaner appearance.
While the rectangle is selected, press F8, select Button from the list of options, and name it **frame_button**. The ActionScripting for this button is described in "Frame_button Scripting," later in this chapter.

Adding the Blank_mc Layer

The blank_mc layer contains a blank movie clip that will be used to load an external .swf file, as described in "Loading the Movie and Variables," later in this chapter.

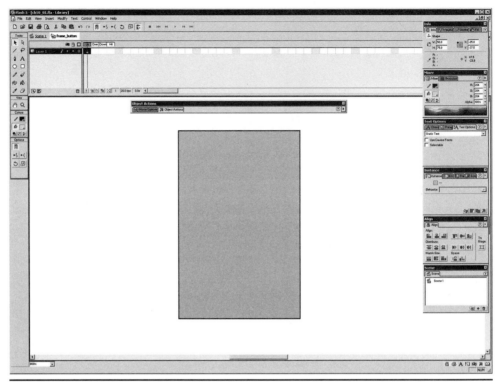

Figure 7-1 *Adding the frame button rectangle*

When an external movie loads into another movie clip, the external movie clip's upper-left boundary aligns with the center of the parent movie clip, which can sometimes shift the external movie clip to an unwanted position. When you load an external file into a movie clip, you can position the loaded file by placing the center of the object where you want the top-left area of the loaded movie to be.

Start by pressing CTRL-F8 (COMMAND-F8 for Macs) to make a new object. Select Movie Clip from the list of options and name it **blank_mc**. In the Instance panel, name the movie clip **blank_mc**. This will allow the movie clip to be targeted by ActionScripting.

Position the blank_mc clip at the top-left corner of the frame_button clip, as shown in Figure 7-2. This will set the top-left area of the externally loaded file even with the top-left corner of the frame_button clip.

Adding the Text_mc Layer

This text_mc layer contains the text_mc movie clip. This movie clip includes a dynamic text field used to load external .txt or .html files into place. Loading external files is

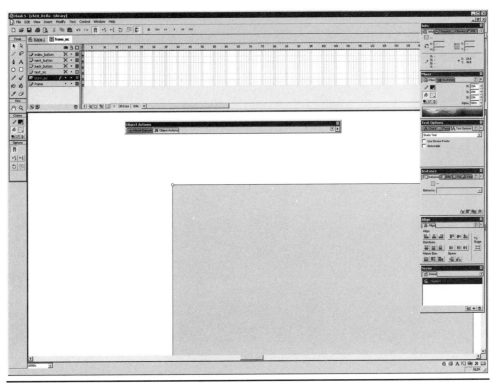

Figure 7-2 *Positioning the blank_mc clip*

a good option for Flash movies that need to be updated regularly, because you can make changes to one part of the Flash Web site without affecting other parts. Loading external files also reduces the movie's file size because you can use dynamic text. I used .html files for this project, so that I could further extend the capabilities of the loaded text with HTML 2.0 standard tags.

Press CTRL-F8 (COMMAND-F8 for Macs) to make a new object. Select Movie Clip from the list of options and name it **text_mc**. Drag an instance of the movie clip onto the main stage from the Library. In the Instance panel, name the movie clip **text_mc**.

Open the text_mc movie clip and then select the Text tool. In the Text Options panel, select Dynamic Text from the drop-down list. Select the HTML check box to allow HTML-formatted text.

Draw a text field on the stage large enough to accommodate the text that will be loaded into place, as shown in Figure 7-3. It's difficult at this point to know how large to make the fields, so they may have to be adjusted later. It's a good idea to

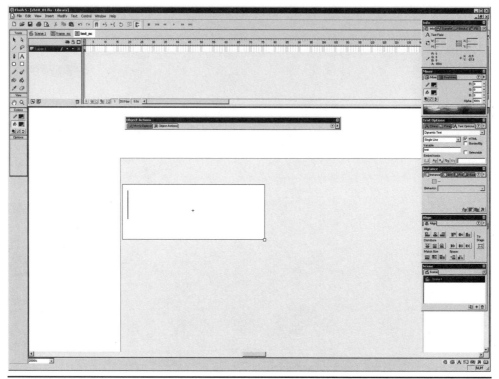

Figure 7-3   *Adding the text field*

draw the text fields slightly oversized to prevent text from being cut off. With the text field selected, open the Text Options panel again and type **text** in the Variable field. This reads the `text` variable from the loaded .html file, as discussed in "Creating the HTML Files," later in this chapter.

Adding the Back_button Layer

The photo album project include buttons to go to the next or previous picture, as well as a button to go to the index. These buttons will allow users to navigate from picture to picture, without needing to return to the main index each time.

Begin by drawing a rectangle on the stage approximately 4 pixels tall and 8 pixels wide. Then use the Rotate tool to skew the rectangle into a rectangle with angled sides, as shown in Figure 7-4. The skewed shape is used merely to enhance the look of the button. Be sure to set the stroke to hairline in the Stroke panel to prevent the lines from scaling when the picture is zoomed in. Next, add the text **Back** above the rectangle to identify the button.

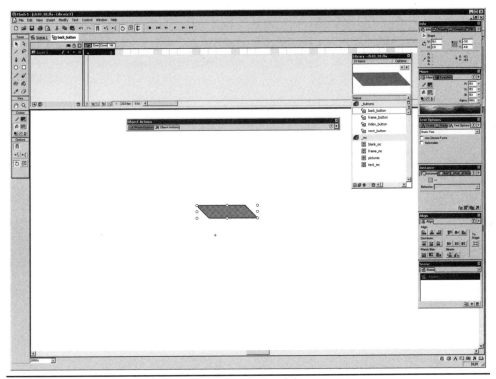

Figure 7-4   *Adding a skewed rectangle for the Back button*

While the rectangle and text are selected, press F8 to convert them into a symbol. Select Button from the list of options and name it **back_button**. Adding ActionScripting to the button is discussed in the "Next_button and Back_button Scripting" section, later in this chapter.

Adding the Next_button Layer

As you did to create the back_button, draw a rectangle on the stage approximately the same size as the back button, use the Rotate tool to skew the rectangle into a rectangle with angled sides, and set the stroke to hairline in the Stroke panel. Then add the text **Next** above the rectangle to identify the button.

While the rectangle and text are selected, press F8 on the keyboard to convert them into a symbol. Select Button from the list of options and name it **next_button**. Adding ActionScripting to the button is discussed in the "Next_button and Back_button Scripting" section, later in this chapter.

The Index_button Layer

Create the index_button in the same manner as the back_button and next_button. Make the rectangle button slightly wider than the other two buttons, to allow the longer text area to fit over the button. Skew the rectangle and set the stroke to hairline. Add the text **Back To Index** above the rectangle to identify the button.

While the rectangle and text are selected, press F8 to convert them into a symbol. Select Button from the list of options and name it **index_button**. Adding ActionScripting to the button is discussed in the "Index_button Scripting" section later in this chapter.

Frame_mc ActionScripting

The ActionScripting for the frame_mc movie clip determines the name of the movie clip and uses a substring to extract specific characters from the name of the movie clip. Also, the `loadMovie()` and `loadVariables()` commands are initialized here.

Open the Library by pressing CTRL-L (COMMAND-L for Macs) and double-click the pictures movie clip to open it. Use the Arrow tool to select the frame_mc movie clip and press CTRL-SHIFT-A (COMMAND-SHIFT-A for Macs) to open the ActionScript editor.

All of the ActionScripting for the frame_mc movie clip is initialized when the clip is first loaded. This is done using the `load` clip event:

L 7-1
```
onClipEvent (load) {
```

Getting the Movie Clip Name

First, you need to get the name of the current movie clip. Set the `name1` variable equal to `this._name`:

L 7-2
```
    name1 = this._name;
```

This is the same as using `getPropery(this, _name)` in normal mode in ActionScripting.

Determining the Row and Column

The instance name of each frame_mc movie clip corresponds to the row and column to which it belongs. For example, the first movie clip in the top row, left column belongs to column 1, row 1. Therefore, the movie clip has a corresponding instance name of frame11. If the movie clip exists on column 2, row 3, it has an instance name of frame23. Based on this instance naming, the `row` variable uses the `substring()` command to extract the sixth character of the name of the current movie clip.

L 7-3
```
row = substring(name1, 6, 1);
```

This sets the `row` variable equal to the current row number. For example, in the case of frame11, `row` will be equal to 1.

To set the `col` variable, use the `substring()` command to extract the seventh character of the name of the current movie clip:

L 7-4
```
col = substring(name1, 7, 1);
```

This sets the `col` variable equal to the current column number. For example, in the case of frame11, the value of `col` will be equal to 1.

Setting the Variables for the Back and Next buttons

The next_button should move the pictures movie clip to show the next frame in the column, or move to the next row when the last picture of a row is accessed. This is accomplished using the `nextrow`, `nextcol`, `prevrow`, and `prevcol` variables.

The `nextrow` variable is set to be equal to the current row plus 1. It is important to use the `Number()` function to read the `row` variable as an integer instead of as text. If this ActionScript expression didn't convert `row` into an integer, the expression would merely concatenate the values of "row + 1," and the resulting value of `nextrow` would be ["3" + "1" = 31] instead of [3 + 1 = 4].

L 7-5
```
nextrow = Number(row) + 1;
```

The `nextcol` variable is set to be equal to the current column plus 1, using the same technique described for the `nextrow` variable. Again, make sure to use the `Number()` function to convert the text into an integer.

L 7-6
```
nextcol = Number(col) + 1;
```

This back_button should move the pictures movie clip to show the previous frame in the column, or move to the previous row when the first picture of a row is accessed. The `prevrow` and `prevcol` variables are set to equal to the current row minus 1 and the current column minus 1, respectively.

L 7-7
```
prevrow = Number (row) - 1;
prevcol = Number (col) - 1;
```

Loading the Movie and Variables

The final scripting for the frame_mc movie clip loads the external files into the blank_mc and text_mc movie clips. Loading the external files will greatly reduce the file size of the main Flash movie, and therefore reduce the initial load time.

Use the `loadMovie()` command to load the bg.swf Flash movie into the blank_mc movie clip. As mentioned earlier in this chapter, the loaded Flash movie will be positioned so that the center of the blank_mc movie clip is where the top-left area of the loaded movie clip is located.

L 7-8
```
loadMovie ("bg.swf", blank_mc);
```

Finally, use the `loadVariables()` command to load the external HTML files into the text_mc movie clip. This command is different from the `loadMovie()` command, in that it loads the variables from a location, rather than loading an entire file. The HTML file must be structured so that it starts with the variable name followed by an equal sign. This is explained in more detail later in this chapter, in the "Creating the HTML Files" section.

L 7-9
```
loadVariables (this._name + ".html", text_mc);
```

Putting the Script Together

Here is the final code with comments:

L 7-10
```
onClipEvent (load) {
    // gets the name of the movie clip
    name1 = this._name;
    // substring events to determine row and column
    row = substring(name1, 6, 1);
    col = substring(name1, 7, 1);
    // variables to be used by back and next buttons
    nextrow = Number (row) + 1;
    nextcol = Number (col) + 1;
    prevrow = Number (row) - 1;
    prevcol = Number (col) - 1;
    // load movie and variables
    loadMovie ("bg.swf", blank_mc);
    loadVariables (this._name + ".html", text_mc);
}
```

Positioning the Frame_mc Movie Clips

As previously mentioned, the picture album project uses 25 pictures, arranged in five rows and five columns. The frame_mc movie clips must be properly positioned in the pictures movie clip to keep the movie clips evenly proportioned.

The pictures movie clip already has one frame_mc movie clip. Copy and paste five movie clips into place using CTRL-SHIFT-V (COMMAND-SHIFT-V for Macs), placing them 64 pixels apart horizontally. This gives you one row with five columns, as shown in Figure 7-5.

Next, copy the entire first row and paste it into place. Position this row 88 pixels below the previous row. Repeat this three more times so that you have five rows and five columns, evenly distributed, as shown in Figure 7-6.

Select all of the frame_mc movie clips and group them together by pressing CTRL-G (COMMAND-G for Macs). Open the Align panel and select Align/Distribute to Stage. Click the Align Horizontal Center and Align Vertical Center buttons. This aligns the entire group of frame_mc movie clips to the center of the pictures movie clip. Finally, press CTRL-B (COMMAND-B for Macs) to ungroup the frame_mc movie clips, so that they can be selected individually.

The last step is to rename all of the movie clips according to the row and column to which they belong. Starting with the frame_mc in the first row and first column, use

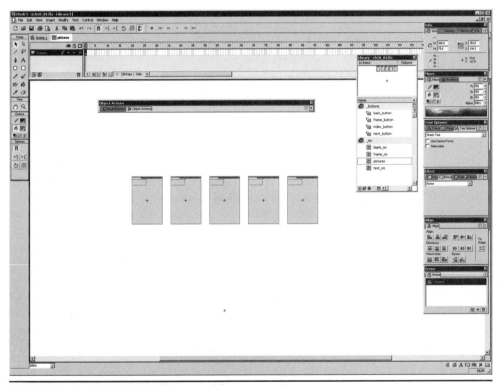

Figure 7-5 *Positioning the first row of frame_mc clips*

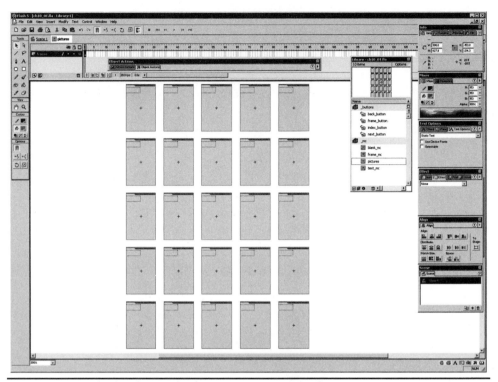

Figure 7-6 *Evenly distributing the frame_mc rows and columns*

the Instance panel to name the instance **frame11**. For the frame_mc in the next column and same row, give the movie clip an instance name of **frame12**. Continue to the end of the row, raising the number by one for each movie clip. For the next row, start by naming the first movie clip instance name, **frame21**. Continue this process until each frame_mc movie clip has its own unique name.

Pictures Movie Clip ActionScripting

Now that you have all of the elements into place, the next step involves adding ActionScripting to the pictures movie clip. This scripting controls the movement of the pictures movie clip, and will be triggered by the three buttons inside of the frame_mc movie clip, as explained in the "Button Scripting" section later this chapter.

On Clip Event Load Scripting

As you've learned, any script that is initialized in the `onClipEvent(load)` event handler runs only one time, when the movie clip is first loaded. This usually includes the variables and actions that will be used many times throughout the Flash movie, as well as actions that should take place when the movie clip is first loaded.

L 7-11
```
onClipEvent (load) {
```

Setting the Initial Variables   The script starts by setting five initial variables: `speed`, `decelerate`, `xpos`, `ypos`, and `scale`.

The `speed` variable determines how fast the pictures movie clip moves. A higher setting results in a much slower-moving action. While this may be unintuitive, the speed variable is just determining what to divide the movement variable by. Setting the `speed` variable to a higher integer slows down the rate at which the movement changes.

L 7-12
```
    speed = 4;
```

The `decelerate` variable determines how much the pictures movie clip will "bounce." The pictures movie clip will go past the destination point, and then bounce back into position, like a rubber band. A lower setting will increase the bouncing effect; anything lower than 1.1 will cause the movie clip to bounce forever. I decided on 1.6, because it provides a smooth bounce effect for this project.

L 7-13
```
    decelerate = 1.6;
```

With the pictures movie clip centered on the main stage and scaled at 100 percent, as shown in Figure 7-7, use the Info panel to check the current scale. The x position of the movie clip shown in the Info panel is the far-left position of the movie clip. Divide the width of the movie clip (in this case, 306) by 2, and add that value to the x position shown in the Info panel. Set the `xpos` variable equal to this number, so it will be centered horizontally on the stage when it is loaded.

L 7-14
```
xpos = 162.5;
```

Now check the y position of the movie clip. Divide the height of the movie clip by 2 and add this value to the number in the Info panel. Set the `ypos` variable equal to this number, so it will be centered vertically on the stage when loaded.

L 7-15
```
    ypos = 225;
```

The `scale` variable is initially set to 100 so that the scale of the pictures movie clip is 100 percent. Later, the `scale` variable will be set to 500 when zoomed in, and then back to 100 when zoomed out.

L 7-16
```
    scale = 100;
```

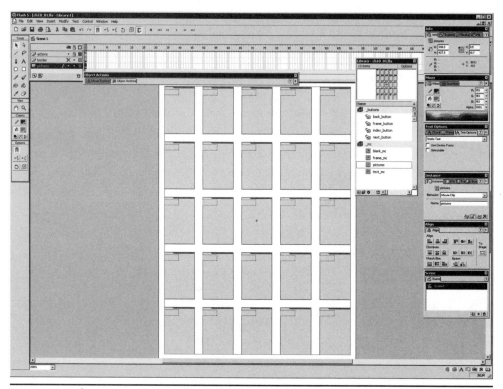

Figure 7-7 *The pictures movie clip at 100 percent*

Setting Array Positions Flash 5 introduced the `Array()` function. Arrays can save a lot of time when using the same variables for multiple events. An *array* is an object whose properties are identified by numbers representing their positions in the array. Arrays start with 0 as the first variable, 1 as the next, and so on. The `xpos_a`, `xpos_y`, and `scale_a` variables use the `Array()` function to position the movie clips.

The numbers stored in the `xpos_a` array are actually the x coordinates of the pictures movie clip. The first number should be equal to the `xpos` variable set earlier. This is the x position of the pictures movie clip at 100 percent, centered on the stage.

The next variables are the x positions to center each picture at 500 percent. The first step in calculating these positions is to multiply the width of the pictures movie clip by 5 to get the width of the pictures movie clip at 500 percent. Next, divide the result of the previous calculation by 2 to find the center position of the pictures movie clip, placing the movie clip at the top-left edge of the stage. Subtract the width of the frame_mc movie clip from the width of the Flash movie. Divide the result of this by

2 to calculate the center position again. Finally, add the center position of the movie clip to the distance from the center of the first frame. This results in 802.5, placing the top-left frame_mc in the horizontal center of the stage.

The movie clips are positioned 64 pixels apart horizontally. Multiply this by 5 to determine how far apart the movie clips are positioned at 500 percent. The result, 320, is how much to decrease the value of each preceding variable. In the end, you should have six values in this array, as shown here.

L 7-17
```
xpos_a = new Array(162.5, 802.5, 482.5, 162.5, -157.5, -477.5);
```

When the xpos_a variable is accessed, an identifier must be used to show which variable to call. For example, when xpos_a(3) is accessed in the array, the result will be 162.5.

The ypos_a array works like the x_pos array, except that it uses the y coordinates of the pictures movie clip. The first number should be equal to the ypos variable set earlier. This is the y position of the pictures movie clip at 100 percent, centered on the stage.

The next variables are the y positions to center each picture at 500 percent. To calculate these positions, first multiply the height of the pictures movie clip by 5. Next, divide the result by 2 to determine the center position of the pictures movie clip, placing the movie clip at the top edge. Subtract the height of the frame_mc from the height of the Flash movie. Divide the result of this by 2 to calculate the center position again. Finally, add the two results together, to come up with 1107.25, placing the top-left frame_mc in the vertical center of the stage.

The movie clips are positioned 88 pixels apart vertically. Multiply this by 5 to find out how far the movie clips are positioned from each other at 500 percent. The result, 440, is how much to decrease the value of each preceding variable. The final ypos_a array should have six values, as shown here.

L 7-18
```
ypos_a = new Array(225, 1107.25, 667.25, 227.25, -212.75, -652.75);
```

The numbers stored in the scale_a array are the scale of the pictures movie clip. The first number is set to 100 to represent 100 percent. When the pictures movie clip is at the index, it is at 100 percent. The second number, 500, represents 500 percent. When the pictures movie clip is zoomed in, it is at 500 percent.

L 7-19
```
scale_a = new Array(100, 500);
```

Calling the Array Positions   Most programming languages contain a function() command. This is a set of statements that you define to perform a certain task. With the release of Flash 5, the function() command was added to the new, much improved ActionScripting language. A function contains parameters enclosed in parentheses. When the function is called, the parameters are also included in parentheses, and they are passed to the statements within the function.

The next part of the onClipEvent (load) scripting defines the slide function:

L 7-20
```
function slide (y, x, s) {
```

Within the slide function, there are three statements. They read the x, y, and s parameters, which are passed from the buttons in the frame_mc movie clip.

The first statement within the slide function sets the ypos variable equal to a value of the ypos_a array.

L 7-21
```
    ypos = ypos_a[y];
```

The y in brackets is the y parameter of the slide function. If the y parameter is equal to 3, then ypos will be equal to 227.25, because position 3 of the ypos_a array is 227.25 (remember that the first position in a Flash array is position 0).

Next, a value of the xpos_a array is assigned to the xpos variable.

L 7-22
```
    xpos = xpos_a[x];
```

The x in brackets is the x parameter of the slide function. If the x parameter is equal to 3, then xpos will be equal to 162.5.

The last statement sets the scale variable equal to a value of the scale_a array.

L 7-23
```
    scale = scale_a[s];
```

The s in brackets is the s parameter of the slide function. If the s parameter is equal to 1, the scale will be equal to 500.

Putting the Script Together   The following is the entire onClipEvent (load) section of the script with comments:

L 7-24
```
onClipEvent (load) {
    // set initial variables
    speed = 4;
    decelerate = 1.6;
    xpos = 162.5;
```

```
    ypos = 225;
    scale = 100;
    // set array positions
    xpos_a = new Array(162.5, 805, 485, 165, -155, -475);
    ypos_a = new Array(225, 1110, 670, 230, -210, -650);
    scale_a = new Array(100, 500);
    // slide function used to call array positions
    function slide (y, x, s) {
        ypos = ypos_a[y];
        xpos = xpos_a[x];
        scale = scale_a[s];
    }
}
```

On Clip Event EnterFrame Scripting

All ActionScript written inside an onClipEvent (enterFrame) event handler will run continuously as fast as the frame rate of the Flash movie. The code inside the onClipEvent (enterFrame) handler will usually contain the variables and actions required for the event handler.

L 7-25
```
onClipEvent (enterFrame) {
```

Getting the Current Positions and Scale   In the first line of the enterFrame event handler, the value of the movieclip's x position, referenced as this._x, is assigned to the variable called current_x.

L 7-26
```
    current_x = this._x;
```

The value of current_x will be used to determine where to move the pictures movie clip along the X axis.

Next, the vertical position of the movie clip, referenced by this._y, is assigned to the current_y variable.

L 7-27
```
    current_y = this. _y;
```

This variable will be used to determine where to move the pictures movie clip along the Y axis.

In this project, the pictures movie clip will be scaled evenly. It isn't necessary to determine the x and y scale of the movie clip, because they both will be the same value. The current_scale is set equal to this._xscale.

L 7-28
```
    current_scale = this._xscale;
```

This variable will be used to determine where to scale the pictures movie clip from.

> ### NOTE
>
> *The* `this.property` *syntax used here works in the same way as using the* `getProperty(this, property)` *method in normal mode in ActionScripting.*

Setting the Difference Between the Current and New Positions and the Scale The `dif_x` variable stores the difference in value between the current x position and the new x position of the movie clip. To calculate the difference in x positions, subtract the `xpos` variable from the `current_x` variable.

L 7-29
```
dif_x = current_x - xpos;
```

This value will be used in the formula to determine how far to move the pictures movie clip along the X axis.

The `dif_y` variable is the difference between the current y position and the new y position. This is calculated by subtracting the `ypos` variable from the `current_y` variable.

L 7-30
```
dif_y = current_y - ypos;
```

This value will be used in the formula to determine how far to move the pictures movie clip along the Y axis.

Using the same logic as the previous two variables, the `dif_scale` variable stores the result of subtracting the new scale from the current scale of the pictures movie clip.

L 7-31
```
dif_scale = current_scale - scale;
```

This value will determine how much the pictures movie clip should increase in size by applying the variables in the `scalespeed` formula, described in the next section.

Setting the Formula for Movie Clip Animation The `xpeed` variable contains the formula that animates the pictures movie clip. To calculate the `xspeed` variable, first divide the `dif_x` variable by the `speed` variable. Then add the `xspeed` variable to that value and finally divide by the `decelerate` variable.

L 7-32
```
xspeed = (dif_x / speed + xspeed) / decelerate;
```

The `decelerate` variable causes the bounce effect by slowly decreasing the `xspeed` variable. The `xspeed` variable updates continuously, resulting in a smooth

ActionScript movement. The effect is gradual because each time the xspeed variable is divided by 1.6, it decreases by a smaller amount than the previous time, as shown here.

10 / 1.6 = 6.25

6.25 / 1.6 = 3.90625

3.90625 / 1.6 = 2.44140625

2.44140625 / 1.6 = 1.52587890625

1.52587890625 / 1.6 = .95367431640625

.95367431640625 / 1.6 = .59604644775390625

.59604644775390625 / 1.6 = .37252902984619140625

.37252902984619140625 / 1.6 = .23283064365386928906925

.23283064365386928906925 / 1.6 = .145519152283668518066640625

.145519152283668518066640625 / 1.6 = .09094947077729282379150390624

The yspeed variable uses the same formula as the xspeed variable, but with the dif_y and yspeed variables.

L 7-33
```
yspeed = (dif_y / speed + yspeed) / decelerate;
```

The scalespeed variable again uses the same formula as the xspeed variable, but with the dif_scale and scalespeed variables.

L 7-34
```
scalespeed = (dif_scale / speed + scalespeed) / decelerate;
```

Setting the Properties of the Movie Clips   The final step is to set the properties of the pictures movie clip equal to the new variables:

▶ The x position is set equal to the xspeed variable using _x -= xspeed.

▶ The y position is set equal to the yspeed variable using _y -= yspeed.

▶ The x scale is set equal to the scalespeed variable using _xscale -= scalespeed.

▶ The y scale is set equal to the scalespeed variable using _yscale -= scalespeed.

Each subtracts 1 from the property and returns the initial value of the property prior to the subtraction.

Putting the Script Together   The following is the entire `onClipEvent`
`(enterFrame)` section of the script with comments:

L 7-35
```
onClipEvent (enterFrame) {
    // get current positions and scale
    current_x = this._x;
    current_y = this._y;
    current_scale = this._xscale;
    // set difference between current and new positions and scale
    dif_x = current_x - xpos;
    dif_y = current_y - ypos;
    dif_scale = current_scale - scale;
    // formula to make movie clip move and bounce
    xspeed = (dif_x/speed + xspeed)/decelerate;
    yspeed = (dif_y/speed + yspeed)/decelerate;
    scalespeed = (dif_scale / speed + scalespeed)/decelerate;
    // set the properties of the movie clip equal to
    // the above variables
    _x -= xspeed;
    _y -= yspeed;
    _xscale -= scalespeed;
    _yscale -= scalespeed;
}
```

Button Scripting

The final scripting for the pictures clip is to initialize the `slide` function when the
buttons are pressed. Open the Library (press CTRL-L/COMMAND-L) and double-click
the frame_mc movie clip.

Frame_button Scripting

For the frame_button, the script just needs to call the `slide` function and read the
`row` and `col` variables. The `row` variable will return the row the button resides on
and call the correct number from the `xpos_a` array. The `col` variable will return
the column the button resides on and call the correct number from the `ypos_a`
array. The final parameter sets the scale. This calls the second variable from the
`scale_a` array.

L 7-36
```
on (release) {
    _root.pictures.slide(row, col, 1);
}
```

Index_button Scripting

The index_button uses the same logic as the frame_button. It calls the `slide` function, but sets all the parameters to 0. This will return the pictures movie clip to 100 percent, centered along the X and Y axis.

L 7-37
```
on (release) {
    _root.pictures.slide(0, 0, 0);
}
```

Next_button and Back_button Scripting

The next_button and back_button require a little more scripting to work properly. They need to determine which row and column they reside on and move to the next or previous frame_mc movie clip.

The back_button uses an `if-else if` statement to determine its location.

L 7-38
```
on (release) {
    if (col > 1) {
        _root.pictures.slide(row, prevcol, 1);
    } else if (col < 2 & row > 1) {
        _root.pictures.slide(prevrow, 5, 1);
    } else if (col < 2 & row < 2) {
        _root.pictures.slide(0, 0, 0);
    }
}
```

First, if the `col` variable is greater than 1, it moves to the previous frame_mc movie clip in its row. If the `col` variable is less than 2 and the `row` variable is greater than 1, it moves to the last frame_mc movie clip on the previous row. This is when the current frame_mc movie clip is the first one in the row. The final `else if` statement checks to see whether the `col` variable is less than 2 and the `row` variable is less than 2. The pictures movie clip is returned to the original 100 percent scale, and centered along the X and Y axes.

The next_button also uses an `if-else if` statement to determine its location.

L 7-39
```
on (release) {
    if (col < 5) {
        _root.pictures.slide(row, nextcol, 1);
    } else if (col > 4 & row < 5) {
        _root.pictures.slide(nextrow, 1, 1);
    } else if (col > 4 & row > 4) {
        _root.pictures.slide(0, 0, 0);
    }
}
```

First, if the `col` variable is less than 5, it moves to the next frame_mc movie clip in its row. If the `col` variable is greater than 4 and the `row` variable is less than 5, it moves to the first frame_mc movie clip on the next row. This is when the current frame_mc movie clip is the last one in the row. The final `else if` statement checks to see whether the `col` variable is greater than 4 and the `row` variable is greater than 4. The pictures movie clip is returned to the original 100 percent scale, and centered along the X and Y axes.

Creating the Border Layer

With all of the elements in place, when zoomed in on one object, you can still see the other frames outside the focused frame_mc movie clip. To cover the other frames, this picture album project uses a border. I use this same technique on most of the Flash movies I design. The border keeps all off-stage elements invisible to the user.

Start by creating a new layer above the pictures. Draw an unfilled rectangle, and then use the Align panel to set the rectangle to match the width and height of the stage. Align the rectangle to the horizontal and vertical center.

Next, create a much larger unfilled rectangle. I scaled mine to be about three times larger than the previous rectangle. Fill the section between the two rectangles, leaving a rectangle with a "hole" the same size as the stage, as shown in Figure 7-8.

Adding the Actions Layer

The actions layer (which I create to separate ActionScript from animation elements for the sake of organization) contains an `fscommand()` to keep the Flash movie from scaling. The picture album project uses too much computer processing power when viewed at larger sizes, because the computer must calculate and render much larger graphics. The following command tells the Flash player to prevent the movie clip from resizing itself.

L 7-40
```
fscommand("allowscale", "false")
```

The actions frame also contains a `stop()` command.

L 7-41
```
stop ();
```

This Flash movie will function properly without the `stop()` command, but I usually include it in case I decide to add an introduction or preloader to a previous scene of the Flash movie.

Figure 7-8 *Creating a border*

Creating the Bg.fla Flash Movie
bg.fla

The loaded bg.swf file is created from the bg.fla file. The structure of this file is important to achieve good-quality graphics for the main Flash movie.

Start by creating a new Flash movie that is 50 by 75 pixels. This is the same size as the frame_mc movie clip at 100 percent. In a raster program, I created a .gif file that is 250 pixels by 375 pixels. This is the size of the frame_mc movie clip at 500 percent. It is necessary to make the original graphic this size so that it still has good quality when viewed at 500 percent in the main Flash movie.

Adding the Graphic Layer

Import the graphic into Flash, and use the Library (CTRL-L/COMMAND-L) to set the optimization. For the Compression setting, I used Lossless (PNG/GIF), as shown in Figure 7-9. I usually use this setting for images that use less than 256 colors. For photos or images with many colors, I use the JPG compression settings.

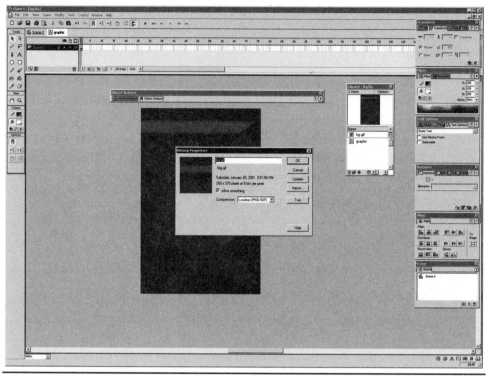

Figure 7-9 *Setting image compression*

Flash always distorts images that are scaled to 100 percent. Many Flash Web sites have this problem—they seem to distort slightly when scaled or when an object with an alpha fill or effect is on top. The solution to prevent this distortion is to scale the image to 99 or 101 percent when first imported. This is the first step I take when importing any image into Flash.

While the image is selected, press F8 to convert it into a symbol. Select Graphic from the list of options and name it **graphic**. Use the Align panel to set the graphic to match the width and height of the stage. Also, align the graphic to the horizontal and vertical center of the stage.

Adding the Border Layer

Next, create a layer above the graphic layer and name it **border**. In this layer, draw an unfilled rectangle, and then use the Align panel to set the rectangle to match the width and height of the stage. Open the Align panel again and align the rectangle to the horizontal and vertical center of the stage. Be sure to change the stroke to hairline in the Stroke panel, to keep the lines from scaling. This creates a small border around the graphic for a cleaner appearance, as shown in Figure 7-10.

Adding the Actions Layer

Finally, add an actions layer to contain the stop() action. As noted earlier, a Flash movie will function properly without the stop() command, but it's a good idea to add one, just in case you want to add an introduction or preloader to a previous scene.

Creating the HTML Files
frame11.html through frame55.html

The HTML files are named to correspond with the frame_mc movie clip names: frame11.html, frame12.html, frame13.html, and so on, for first row of movie clips;

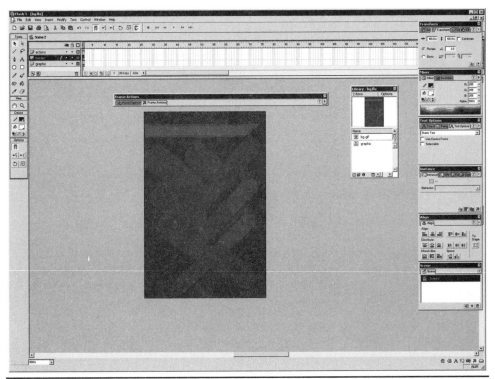

Figure 7-10   *Adding a border to the graphic*

frame21.html, frame22.html, frame23.html, and so on, for the second row; and so on for the third through fifth rows.

The added HTML support of Flash 5 greatly increases the capabilities of text fields. In the past, text fields could only be one font color and one size, and they could not contain any links. The new HTML support allows you to use basic HTML 2.0 tags. The image tag is not included, but tags such as bold, italic, and href can be used.

The first item in the HTML file needs to be the name of the variable. The variable set earlier in the Flash movie is `text`. Start the HTML file as shown here:

L 7-42
```
text=
```

Anything after the equal sign will be read within Flash. All of the HTML files I made are the same, with the exception of the movie clip name.

L 7-43
```
Frame11
```

I added some HTML formatting to the first HTML file, frame11.html:

L 7-44
```
<font color = "#CCCCCC"><u><b><a href =
"http://www.osborne.com">Frame11</a></u></b></font>
```

This results in text that is gray, bolded, underlined, and linked to http://www. osborne.com. Using basic HTML 2.0 tags, the underline is not added automatically to the link, as it is in standard HTML. Figure 7-11 shows the text on the picture as it would appear in the zoomed-in view of the final project. Each picture displays the HTML-formatted text that is loaded through the external files.

What to Take Away from This Chapter

This project used externally loaded files to reduce load time and file size for the main Flash movie. In real-world Flash movies on the Web, file size is an important factor. Many people do not like waiting through long download periods before they see the content of the site. Optimization is one of the key elements of Web design, including Flash Web design.

The techniques discussed in this chapter apply to many Flash movies, and they can be implemented to improve the functionality and appearance of any Flash site.

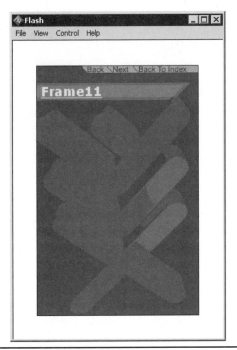

Figure 7-11   *HTML is used to format the text that reads "Frame11."*

CHAPTER 8

Advanced Scrollbars

IN THIS CHAPTER:

- ▶ Build operating system–style scrollbars in Flash

- ▶ Use keyboard commands to control scrolling

- ▶ Add friction and velocity to make scrollbars more interesting

A common problem with Flash movies is not having enough space to accommodate all of the content within the site. Most operating systems have built-in scrollbars for programmers to work with; however, Flash does not have any such function.

The first project described in this chapter emulates an operating-system scrollbar. The next project goes a step further and adds friction and velocity, to allow the scrolling mechanism to be thrown and to bounce off the vertical limits. This can make a dull scrollbar much more interesting, while keeping the original functionality.

Building a Scrollbar
ch08_01.fla

The ch08_01.fla file creates a Flash scrollbar using ActionScript. The project consists of eight layers: the scroll content, mask, outline, bar, slide, scroll arrows, keypress actions, and actions layers. Each of these layers is discussed in detail in the following sections.

Adding the Scroll Content Layer

First, create the content that will be scrolled. For this project, I made a graphic that was 250 by 660 pixels, as shown in Figure 8-1. I set the dimensions of the Flash movie to 300 by 210 pixels. The graphic is much longer than this Flash movie, so there is no way to show the entire graphic on the screen.

I imported the .png file, which I created in a raster program. Then I set the compression in Flash using the Library (CTRL-L/COMMAND-L). For this project, I used JPEG compression, set to 60, as shown in Figure 8-2. This provides a clean, crisp graphic, without a large file size.

NOTE

I usually import my graphics as uncompressed files, such as .png or .bmp. Then, in Flash, I use JPEG compression for photographs or other graphics with a lot of colors. I use PNG/GIF compression for line-art graphics.

After importing the graphic, select the graphic on the stage and press F8 to convert it into a symbol. Select Movie Clip from the list of options and name it **scroll_content**. Open the Instance panel and give the movie clip an instance name of **scroll_content**. This will enable you to target the movie clip by ActionScripting.

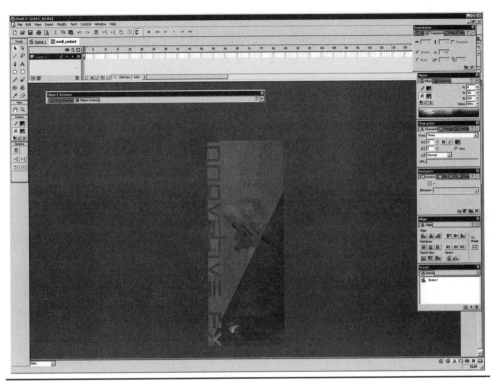

Figure 8-1   *The graphic for scrolling content*

Open the scroll_content movie clip. Resize the graphic's width and height to 101 percent using the Transform panel, as shown in Figure 8-3.

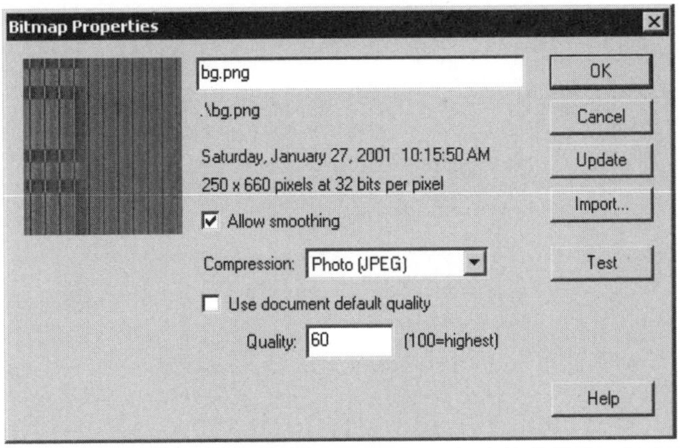

Figure 8-2   *Setting the compression for the graphic*

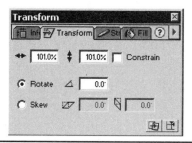

Figure 8-3   *Resizing the graphic with the Transform panel*

TIP

Flash always distorts images that are scaled to 100 percent, which you may notice on many Flash Web sites. The images seem to slightly distort when scaled or if an alpha image is placed over them. The solution is to scale images to anything except 100 percent when they are first imported.

Next, use the Info panel to place the graphic at the 0 y position, as shown in Figure 8-4. This step is necessary for the scrollbar to scroll properly.

Finally, on the main stage, align the graphic to any desired horizontal position. The vertical position is not important, because it will be set with ActionScripting, as described in "Setting the Property of the Content," later in this chapter.

Adding the Mask Layer

The layer above the scroll_content layer contains a rectangle to mask out the content below it. It can be set to any dimension, depending on how much of the graphic you want to show on the screen. I drew mine approximately 250 pixels wide by 175 pixels tall. Using the Info panel, position the rectangle so that it is over the horizontal position of the scroll_content layer and is 15 pixels from the top of the screen. This allows the top edge of the scroll_content layer to be seen when it is scrolled.

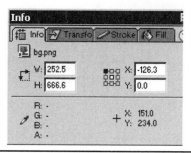

Figure 8-4   *Aligning the graphic with the Info panel*

After the rectangle is in place, right-click (CONTROL-click for Macs) the mask layer, and select Mask from the list of options. This will mask the layer below, so that only the content within the rectangle will be shown.

Adding the Outline Layer

Next, create a layer above the mask layer to add a small border around the scroll_content layer, as shown in Figure 8-5. To ensure that the outline will match the mask area, unlock the mask layer and select the four lines that make up the rectangle. Copy these and use Flash's Paste-in-Place function (CTRL-SHIFT-V/COMMAND-SHIFT-V) to paste the lines into the outline layer. Finally, lock the mask layer again.

Adding the Bar Layer

The bar layer contains the background bar for the slider and scroll buttons. This layer also includes the majority of the code to control the scrolling actions in this movie clip.

NOTE

Many programmers use blank movie clips to contain code. However, I try to include most of my ActionScripting on objects already on the stage.

Start by drawing a rectangle on the stage. Then use the Info panel to resize it to 16 pixels wide by approximately 175 pixels tall. Again, use the Info panel to position the rectangle 15 pixels from the top edge of the Flash movie.

Select the rectangle and press F8 to convert it into a symbol. Select Movie Clip from the list of options and name it **bar**. Open the Instance panel and enter **bar** in the Name field.

Figure 8-5   *Adding a small border*

Next, apply ActionScripting to the bar movie clip. This code is divided into two sections. The first executes only when the movie clip is first loaded, using `onClipEvent (load)`. The second runs continuously by using `onClipEvent(enterFrame)`.

Scripting Bar Load Clip Events

When the movie clip first loads, the top and bottom scroll variables need to be set, and the scroll functions must be built. You initialize the actions when the movie clip loads by using the `onClipEvent (load)` event handler. This prevents the script from unnecessarily repeating throughout the Flash movie.

```
onClipEvent (load) {
```

Setting the Initial Variables   The `topLimit` and `bottomLimit` variables set the top and bottom limits for the slider button created in the "Adding the Slider Layer" section later in this chapter. For this project, I set the `topLimit` variable to 30 and the `bottomLimit` variable to 180. You can modify these variables later if the scrollbar is larger or smaller than expected.

```
topLimit = 30;
bottomLimit = 180;
```

Next, the `ratio` variable is set equal to the height of the scroll_content movie clip divided by the `bottomLimit` variable. This variable is used to determine how fast to scroll the content in relation to the position of the slider.

```
ratio = _root.scroll_content._height / bottomLimit;
```

Determine the height of the scroll_height movie clip by using `_root.scroll_content._height`. This form only works if you are using the expert mode for ActionScripting. To achieve the same result using normal mode, use `getProperty(_root.scroll_content, _height)`.

Building the Functions   The `function()` command is new to Flash 5. It executes a series of other commands and can pass variables from other commands in a Flash movie. Using the `function()` command in Flash eliminates the need for additional movie clips to contain ActionScripting. This results in a much more efficient Flash movie that is easier to maintain. This project uses two functions: the `scrollUp` function and the `scrollDown` function.

The `scrollUp` function scrolls the slider up:

```
function scrollUp (speed) {
    if (scroll > topLimit) {
        scroll = scroll - speed;
        setProperty ("_root.slider", _y, scroll);
    }
}
```

The `function()` command has two parts. The first part contains the function name, which is `scrollUp` in this case. The second sets a variable that will be passed from another action within the Flash movie. The variable for the `scrollUp` function is `speed`, which is the speed at which the scrollbar will move.

Next, to determine whether the scrollbar is not above the `topLimit`, use an `if` statement. If the scroll is greater than `topLimit`, then the `scroll` variable is set equal to `scroll` minus `speed`. Then set the y position of the slider movie clip (discussed in "Adding the Slider Layer," later in this chapter) equal to the `scroll` variable. If `scroll` is less than or equal to the `topLimit` variable, the `scrollUp` function does not perform any task, so the slider movie clip will not move.

The `scrollDown` function scrolls the slider down:

```
function scrollDown (speed) {
    if (scroll < bottomLimit) {
        scroll = scroll + speed;
        setProperty ("_root.slider", _y, scroll);
    }
}
```

Again, use the `speed` variable to set the scrollbar's speed. Then use an `if` statement to determine if `scroll` is less than the `bottomLimit` variable. If it is, then the `scroll` variable is set equal to `scroll` plus `speed`. Next, set the y position of the slider movie clip equal to the `scroll` variable. If `scroll` is greater than or equal to the `bottomLimit` variable, the `scrollDown` function does nothing, and the slider movie clip will not move.

Scripting Bar Enter Frame Clip Events

Events contained within the `enterFrame` section will update continuously, as long as the movie clip is on the stage. This is necessary to dynamically move or position objects, or to get the current position of an object. In Flash 5, `enterFrame` event handling replaces the old method of using blank movie clips with frame scripting to achieve the same results.

Initialize the actions when the movie clip is loaded using the `onClipEvent (enterFrame)` action.

```
onClipEvent (enterFrame) {
```

Setting the Dynamic Variables   Setting the `scroll` variable equal to the y position of the slider movie clip makes it easy to reuse this variable in other scripts. To determine the y position of the slider movie clip, use `_root.slider._y`.

```
scroll = _root.slider._y;
```

The `_root.slider._y` format can be used only in the expert mode for ActionScripting. To achieve the same result using normal mode, use `getProperty(_root.slider,_y)`.

The `y_offset` variable determines how much to scroll the scroll_content movie clip in relation to the slider movie clip. It is set by multiplying `scroll` times negative `ratio`.

```
y_offset = scroll * -ratio;
```

This will basically set the y offset equal to the opposite of the slider movie clip's y position multiplied by the ratio, which will move the object to its full extent. You need to set this because the scroll_content movie clip is larger than the scroll boundaries set for the scroll movie clip.

Setting the Property of the Content   Finally, set the y position of the scroll_content movie clip equal to the `y_offset` variable.

```
setProperty ("_root.scroll_content", _y, y_offset);
```

If all the steps were followed properly, the scroll_content movie clip will scroll to its complete dimensions.

Keeping the Slider Within Its Boundaries   The final section of this code ensures that the slider movie clip does not go beyond its boundaries. For example, if the slider y position is at 34 and you use the `scrollUp` function with the speed variable set to 10, then the slider would move to 24 pixels, going beyond the 30-pixel boundary.

Use an `if` statement to determine whether `scroll` is less than the `topLimit` variable. If so, set the y position of the slider movie clip equal to the `topLimit` variable using the `setProperty()` command.

```
if (scroll < topLimit) {
    setProperty (_root.slider, _y, topLimit);
```

This will bring the movie clip back to its top boundary if it passes that boundary.

Use an else if statement to determine whether scroll is greater than the bottomLimit variable. If so, set the y position of the slider movie clip equal to the bottomLimit variable, using the setProperty() command.

```
} else if (scroll > bottomLimit) {
    setProperty (_root.slider, _y, bottomLimit);
}
```

This will bring the movie clip back to its bottom boundary if it passes that boundary.

Putting the Script Together   Here is the final script with comments:

```
onClipEvent (load) {
    // Set the initial variables that will not change
    // dynamically within the Flash movie
    topLimit = 30;
    bottomLimit = 180;
    ratio = _root.scroll_content._height / bottomLimit;
    // Build the functions for scroll up and scroll down
    function scrollUp (speed) {
        if (scroll > topLimit) {
            scroll = scroll - speed;
            setProperty ("_root.slider", _y, scroll);
        }
    }
    function scrollDown (speed) {
        if (scroll < bottomLimit) {
            scroll = scroll + speed;
            setProperty ("_root.slider", _y, scroll);
        }
    }
}
onClipEvent (enterFrame) {
    // Set the variables that will dynamically update within
    // the Flash movie
    scroll = _root.slider._y;
    y_offset = scroll * -ratio;
    // Set the property of the content in relation to the
    // slider movie clip
    setProperty ("_root.scroll_content", _y, y_offset);
    // Check to see if the slider is beyond the top or bottom limit
    if (scroll < topLimit) {
        setProperty (_root.slider, _y, topLimit);
```

```
    } else if (scroll > bottomLimit) {
        setProperty (_root.slider, _y, bottomLimit);
    }
}
```

Adding the Slider Layer

The slider movie clip is a draggable movie clip used to emulate the scrollbars on an operating system. You can scroll up or down, or drag the slider movie clip to move the position of the scroll_content movie clip.

Start by drawing a rectangle on the stage, approximately the same width as the bar movie clip and 6 pixels tall. With the rectangle selected, press F8 to convert it into a symbol. Select Button from the list of options and name it **slider_button**. With the new button selected, press F8 again to convert it into a symbol. Select Movie Clip from the list of options and name it **slider**. Open the Instance panel and give this movie clip the instance name **slider**. Open the slider movie clip to apply actions to the button.

Scripting Button On Press Events

The button needs to initialize the drag operation when the mouse is pressed. This is accomplished with the `startDrag()` command.

```
on (press) {
    startDrag (
    this, false, 278, _root.bar.topLimit, 278, _root.bar.bottomLimit
    );
}
```

The `startDrag()` command uses `this` as the target, which will target itself for the `startDrag()` operation. Be sure to check the Expression check box, located in the ActionScript editing panel. Also, check the Constrain to Rectangle check box that appears after the `startDrag()` code is added, to prevent the scrollbar from going past the previously set constraints. Set the left and right constraints equal to the x position of the slider movie clip on the main stage. You do not want it to drag beyond the bar movie clip's dimensions.

The top and bottom constraints were previously set with the `topLimit` and `bottomLimit` variables in the bar movie clip. These variables are targeted using `_root.bar.topLimit` and `_root.bar.bottomLimit`. This will set the top and bottom boundaries to 30 and 180, respectively.

Scripting Button On Release Events

When the mouse is released, stop the drag operation by using the `stopDrag()` function.

```
on (release, releaseOutside) {
    stopDrag ();
}
```

This will stop all movie clips from being dragged within the Flash movie.

> **TIP**
>
> *It is a good practice to use* `release` *and* `releaseOutside`. *This way, if the user drags the mouse away from the button and then releases the button, the scroll actions will still stop.*

Adding the Scroll Arrows Layer

The scroll arrows layer contains scroll arrows to go above the top boundary and below the bottom boundary. When pressed, these scroll arrows will scroll the slider and scroll_content layers up and down. These buttons initiate the `scrollUp` and `scrollDown` functions and pass a variable to determine how fast to scroll the objects.

Begin by drawing a rectangle on the stage. Next, use the Info panel to resize the buttons to the same approximate width as the bar movie clip and approximately 10 pixels tall. While the rectangle is selected. press F8 to convert it into a symbol. Select Button from the list of options and name it **scroll_arrow_button**.

Open the scroll_arrow_button button and add a new layer above the layer that contains the rectangle. Draw a simple arrow shape pointing upward, as shown in Figure 8-6. Then add a new frame in the over frame of the rectangle layer. I also changed the color of the rectangle to achieve a rollover effect for the button.

Next, navigate back to the main stage, select the scroll_arrow_button, and press F8 to convert it into a symbol. Select Movie Clip from the list of options and name it **scroll_up**.

Adding the Scroll_Up Movie Clip

The scroll_up movie clip already contains the scroll_arrow_button in the first frame. Add two more frames to this layer. Then add a new layer above this layer and name it **actions**. Each frame of this layer contains blank keyframes with actions to control the scroll functions.

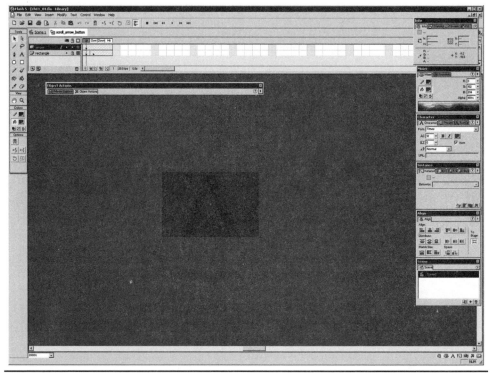

Figure 8-6 *A scroll arrow button*

Scripting Scroll_Arrow_Button Actions

The scroll_arrow_button contains actions for when the mouse is pressed and when the mouse is released.

When the mouse is pressed, the scroll_up movie clip goes to frame 2 of the movie clip and plays. This will create a looping set of actions, as explained in the next section of this chapter.

```
on (press) {
    gotoAndPlay (2);
}
```

When the mouse is released, the scroll_up movie clip returns to frame 1 of the movie clip and stops. This stops the scrolling loop of the movie clip.

```
on (release, releaseOutside) {
    gotoAndStop (1);
}
```

Scripting the Scroll_Up Actions Layer

The actions contained on the actions layer of the scroll_up movie clip actually initialize the `scrollUp` function from the slider movie clip, which was discussed in "Adding the Bar Layer," earlier in this chapter. The first frame contains a `stop()` action to prevent the scroll actions from taking place until the button is pressed.

```
stop ();
```

The second frame of this layer initializes the `scrollUp` action and passes the variable to set the speed at which to scroll content.

```
_root.bar.scrollUp(5);
```

The first portion of the code addresses the function. In this case, the `scrollUp` function is located in the bar movie clip. The number inside the parentheses determines how fast to scroll the scroll_content and slider movie clips. Note that this command must be entered using the expert mode for ActionScripting.

The final frame of this movie clip contains an action to return the scroll_up movie clip to frame 2 and play. This will cause an endless loop until the button is released and the scroll_up movie clip goes back to frame 1.

```
gotoAndPlay (2);
```

Adding the Scroll_Down Movie Clip

The button and actions in the scroll_down movie clip are similar to those in the scroll_up movie clip. To simplify the creation of this movie clip, select the scroll_up movie clip and choose Duplicate Symbol in the Instance panel. In the panel that pops up, name the new movie clip **scroll_down**. Be sure to change the instance name in the Instance Panel to **scroll_down** as well. Use the Transform panel to rotate the new movie clip 180 degrees, as shown in Figure 8-7. Then move the movie clip below the bottom boundary.

Scripting Scroll_Arrow_Button Actions

The scroll_arrow_button contains the same actions as the scroll_up movie clip. When the mouse is pressed, the scroll_down movie clip goes to frame 2 of the movie clip and plays.

```
on (press) {
    gotoAndPlay (2);
}
```

Figure 8-7 *Rotating the duplicated clip with the Transform panel*

When the mouse is released, the scroll_down movie clip returns to frame 1 of the movie clip and stops.

```
on (release, releaseOutside) {
    gotoAndStop (1);
}
```

Scripting the Scroll_Down Actions Layer

The actions contained on the actions layer of the scroll_up movie clip initialize the scrollDown function, which was discussed in the "Adding the Bar Layer" section, earlier in this chapter. The first frame contains a stop() action to keep the scroll actions from taking place until the button is pressed.

```
stop ();
```

The second frame of this layer initializes the scrollDown action and passes the variable to set the speed to scroll.

```
_root.bar.scrollDown(5);
```

As with the scrollUp initialization, the first part of the code addresses the function in the bar movie clip, and the 5 in parentheses sets how fast to scroll the scroll_content and slider movie clips. And, again, this command must be entered in the expert mode.

The final frame of this movie clip contains an action to return the scroll_down movie clip to frame 2 and play. This will cause an endless loop until the button is released and the scroll_down movie clip goes back to frame 1.

```
gotoAndPlay (2);
```

Adding the Keypress Actions Layer

This project allows the user to press keys on the keyboard to scroll the content up or down, as an alternative to using the scroll up and down buttons described in the previous section.

Keypress actions must be contained in a button, so first navigate back to the main timeline and drag one of the scroll_arrow_button buttons onto the main stage. Using the Effect panel, set the Alpha of the movie clip to 0, as shown in Figure 8-8. This makes the movie clip invisible.

Setting the Home Key Action

First, define an action that will scroll the slider movie clip to the top limit when the user presses the HOME key. Use the On Mouse Event action, select Key Press as the action, and press the HOME key. Next, use the setProperty() command to set the y position equal to 30.

```
on (keyPress "<Home>") {
    setProperty ("_root.slider", _y, "30");
}
```

Setting the End Key Action

Next, create an action that will scroll the slider movie clip to the bottom limit when the user presses the END key. Use the On Mouse Event action, select Key Press as the action, and press the END key. Then use the setProperty() command to set the y position equal to 180.

```
on (keyPress "<End>") {
    setProperty ("_root.slider", _y, "180");
}
```

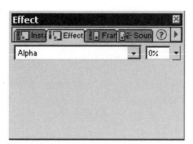

Figure 8-8   *Setting the Alpha of the movie clip to 0 with the Effect panel*

Setting the PageUp and PageDown Key Actions

When the user presses the PAGEUP key, the slider should scroll up the content at a faster speed than occurs when using the scroll button. You can do this with the `scrollUp` function at a higher speed setting.

Use the On Mouse Event action, select Key Press as the action, and press the PAGEUP key. Next, initialize the `scrollUp` function, and set the speed variable to 10. This will move the slider movie clip at twice the speed that it moves with the scroll button.

```
on (keyPress "<PageUp>") {
    _root.bar.scrollUp(10);
}
```

The PAGEDOWN key works in the same way as the PAGEUP key, but uses the `scrollDown` function to scroll through the content.

```
on (keyPress "<PageDown>") {
    _root.bar.scrollDown(10);
}
```

Setting the Up and Down Key Actions

When the user presses the UP key, the slider should scroll up through the content at the same speed as achieved by clicking the scroll button. Use the On Mouse Event action, select Key Press as the action, and press the UP key. Next, initialize the `scrollUp` function and set the speed variable to 5. This will move the slider movie clip at the same speed as the scroll buttons.

```
on (keyPress "<Up>") {
    _root.bar.scrollUp(5);
}
```

The DOWN key works the same as the UP key, but uses the `scrollDown` function to scroll through the content.

```
on (keyPress "<Down>") {
    _root.bar.scrollDown(5);
}
```

Here's the final code:

```
on (keyPress "<Home>") {
    setProperty ("_root.slider", _y, "30");
}
on (keyPress "<End>") {
    setProperty ("_root.slider", _y, "180");
}
on (keyPress "<PageUp>") {
    _root.bar.scrollUp(10);
}
on (keyPress "<PageDown>") {
    _root.bar.scrollDown(10);
}
on (keyPress "<Up>") {
    _root.bar.scrollUp(5);
}
on (keyPress "<Down>") {
    _root.bar.scrollDown(5);
}
```

Adding the Actions Layer

The actions layer contains the fscommand() and stop() commands. I used the fscommand() command to keep the Flash movie from scaling. I wanted to prevent scaling because the bitmap would look pixelated at high resolutions in a full screen.

The fscommand() command works only for stand-alone projectors or .swf files not viewed in the browser. The first argument in the fscommand() command contains the action, whereas the second contains the argument for that action.

```
fscommand ("allowscale", "false");
```

This invokes the allowscale command and sets it to false, to keep the Flash movie from scaling.

The last action is stop(). This isn't necessary for this project, since it has only one frame; but it ensures that if you later decide to add another scene for a preloader or introduction, the scrollbar will still work properly.

```
stop ();
```

Adding Friction and Velocity
ch08_02.fla

Adding friction and velocity to the scrollbar makes it more interesting. With this addition, when the slider is thrown, it will continue to move and then slowly come to a halt. If the slider is thrown and then hits the top or bottom limit, the slider will bounce back.

Revising the Scroll Arrow Button

With the addition of friction and velocity, a few additions need to be made to the scroll_arrow_button's on (press) and on (release) event handling. Navigate to the slider movie clip's timeline and select the button.

Two new variables are updated when the button is pressed. First, a variable named drag is set to "true". This will be used to determine when the movie clip is being dragged. Next, a variable named speed is set to 1. This is used to set the speed of the button when thrown, as explained in "Scripting Slider On Enter Frame Actions," later in this chapter. Here's the final code:

```
on (press) {
    startDrag (
    this, false, 278, _root.bar.topLimit, 278, _root.bar.bottomLimit
    );
    drag = "true";
    speed = 1;
}
```

In the scroll_arrow_button release actions, the drag variable is set to "false". This will be used to determine when the movie clip is released. Here's the final code:

```
on (release, releaseOutside) {
    stopDrag ();
    drag = "false";
}
```

Creating the Slider Movie Clip

The friction and velocity actions are included in the slider movie clip, because the actions apply directly to it. The actions are divided into four sections. The first actions are initialized only when the movie clip is first loaded. Other actions are initialized when the mouse is pressed and when the mouse is released. The final actions are initialized consistently using `enterFrame`.

Scripting Slider On Load Actions

ActionScripting contained within `clipEvent(load)` actions is performed only when the movie clip is first loaded. This is useful for setting global variables. For this project, there are four variables set in the `onClipEvent(load)` event handler: `friction`, `speed`, `top`, and `bottom`.

The `friction` variable determines how much friction the slider movie clip will have when thrown. Set the variable to 0.98 to resemble friction from a real-life object, such as a pool table. Setting the friction variable to a lower number will increase the amount of friction applied to the slider. Setting the friction variable to a value above 1 will cause erratic problems because it puts the slider into infinite motion.

```
friction = "0.98";
```

The `speed` variable determines how fast the objects will move when first thrown. A higher number will result in a much faster moving object. This variable will be updated when the object is thrown, as described in "Scripting Slider On Enter Frame Actions," later in this chapter.

```
speed = 1;
```

The `top` and `bottom` variables are set equal to the `topLimit` and `bottomLimit` variables of the bar movie clip. Although these variables are already set in the bar movie clip, adding the variables here avoids the need to call the full paths of the other variables each time.

```
top = _root.bar.topLimit;
bottom = _root.bar.bottomLimit;
```

Here is the final code:

```
onClipEvent (load) {
    // set variables
    friction = "0.98";
    speed = 1;
    top = _root.bar.topLimit;
    bottom = _root.bar.bottomLimit;
}
```

Scripting Slider On Mouse Down Actions

Actions included in the clipEvent (mouseDown) event handler will be updated every time the mouse is pressed. For this project, when the mouse is first pressed, the timer needs to be addressed to determine what time this occurred. The timer built into Flash returns the value in milliseconds. Divide the result by 1,000 to convert it into actual seconds. The o_time variable represents the original time.

```
onClipEvent (mouseDown) {
    // get timer when mouse is pressed
    o_time = getTimer()/1000;
}
```

Scripting Slider On Mouse Up Actions

Actions included in the clipEvent (mouseUp) event handler will be updated every time the mouse is released. For this project, when the mouse is released, the timer again needs to be addressed to determine when this event happened. The n_time variable represents the new time.

```
onClipEvent (mouseUp) {
    // get timer when mouse is released
    n_time = getTimer()/1000;
}
```

Scripting Slider On Enter Frame Actions

Actions included in the clipEvent (enterFrame) event handler will be updated every time the frame is accessed.

Determining How Fast to Throw the Target   First, you need to determine how long the movie clip was dragged. To do this, subtract the n_time variable from the o_time variable.

```
    time = o_time - n_time;
```

This variable is later used to determine how hard the movie clip was thrown.
  Next, set the speed variable to speed multiplied by 1.1.

```
    speed = speed * 1.1;
```

This will cause the speed variable to slowly rise. With the speed slowly increasing and the friction slowly dropping, the movie clip will slowly come to a stop.

When the slider is stopped, the y position is set equal to the o_y_pos variable.

```
o_y_pos = y_pos;
```

Because the y_pos variable is set in the next lines of code, this will set the variable equal to the last-known position.

Next, to get the new y position, set the y_pos variable equal to this._y.

```
y_pos = this._y;
```

This sets the variable to the _y property of the current movie clip, using expert mode. In normal mode, you can achieve the same result using the getProperty() command.

Determining Whether the Object Is Being Dragged or Thrown   Next, determine whether the movie clip is being dragged or thrown. This is done by using if and else statements.

Start by checking to see whether the drag variable is equal to "true". If the variable is set to true, set the velocity variable. The y_velocity variable is equal to y_pos minus o_y_pos multiplied by the amount of time the object has been dragged.

```
if (drag == "true") {
    y_velocity = (y_pos - o_y_pos) * time;
```

If the drag variable is not equal to true, the code continues to the else command. In this section, the y_pos variable is set equal to the y_pos variable plus the y_velocity variable divided by the speed variable.

```
} else {
    y_pos = y_pos + (y_velocity / speed);
```

Keeping the Box Inside the Boundaries   Next, to keep the movie clip from bouncing outside the boundaries, use if and else if statements to determine whether the movie clip touches or tries to move outside the boundaries. First, check to see whether the y_pos variable is less than or equal to the top variable. If it is, y_pos is set equal to top.

```
if (y_pos <= top) {
    y_pos = top;
```

The y_velocity is set equal to negative y_velocity multiplied by friction.

```
y_velocity = -y_velocity * friction;
```

This will cause the `y_velocity` to reverse its current value, so the object will bounce off the boundary. The `friction` variable is applied to gradually slow down the object.

Next, using the same techniques, check to see whether the slider movie clip is touching or overlapping the bottom variable. If it is, `y_pos` is set equal to the `bottom` variable, and the `y_velocity` is set equal to negative `y_velocity` multiplied by `friction`.

```
} else if (y_pos >= bottom) {
    y_pos = bottom;
    y_velocity = -y_velocity * friction;
```

Setting the Position   The final step is to set the y position of the slider movie clip equal to the `y_pos` variable. This is done using the `setProperty()` command.

```
setProperty (this, _y, y_pos);
```

Putting the Script Together   Here is the final code with comments:

```
onClipEvent (enterFrame) {
    // actions to determine how fast to throw target
    time = o_time - n_time;
    speed = speed * 1.1;
    o_y_pos = y_pos;
    y_pos = this._y;
    // determines if object is being dragged or thrown
    if (drag == "true") {
        y_velocity = (y_pos-o_y_pos) * time;
    } else {
        y_pos = y_pos + (y_velocity/speed);
        // if then else statements to determine if
        // box is inside bounds
        if (y_pos <= top) {
            y_pos = top;
            y_velocity = -y_velocity * friction;
        } else if (y_pos >= bottom) {
            y_pos = bottom;
            y_velocity = -y_velocity * friction;
        }
        // set position
        setProperty (this, _y, y_pos);
    }
}
```

What to Take Away from This Chapter

As shown in this chapter, there are many great ways to present information in a Flash movie. Scrollbars and scrolling content allow for much more information to be displayed within the same amount of space.

The scripts used to build these projects can be implemented in many existing Flash movies or easily modified for new projects. Consider building a library of scripts that you can reuse in your projects.

Duplicating Movie Clips

IN THIS CHAPTER:

▶ Use duplicate movie clips to reduce file size

▶ Create random movement on the stage

▶ Dynamically change properties of movie clips

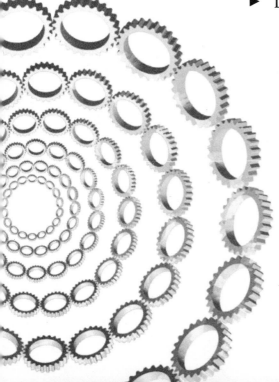

lash has evolved over the years from an animated GIF program to an amazing tool that can create vector-based animated graphics. At some time during this transition, Macromedia decided to add a scripting language to provide interactivity. With each new version, Flash integrated more features to expand its capabilities.

One of the greatest features added to Flash is the ability to duplicate movie clips. This allows you to reuse a movie clip to save file size. Using ActionScripting, you can modify each instance of the movie clip independent of the original movie clip. This enables you to simulate having many different objects on the stage during playback, while having only one actual movie clip during editing.

In this chapter, you will learn how to create a very small file size with nearly 100 movie clips on the stage. Here's the trick: There are actually only four instances duplicated many times and modified through ActionScripting.

Creating the Dup Layer

ch09_01.fla

In all of the previous projects described so far in this book, you have seen how to use movie clips to contain ActionScripting. This project uses the same methods to keep the file size smaller and to make it easier to update scripts. The first layer is a blank movie clip that is used to contain scripting elements.

TIP

Keeping your files organized and cleanly coded is key to becoming a good ActionScripter. This way, you will be able to pass your work onto other designers, and they will be able to easily understand and update your scripts.

Start out by creating a new movie clip. Press CTRL-F8 (COMMAND-F8 for Macs), and name this movie clip **action_clip**. Leave the movie clip empty, creating a blank movie clip.

On Clip Event Load Scripting

Actions placed in a movie clip will execute at different times, depending on the event handler in which they exist. Actions within the `load` event handler take place only when the movie clip first loads. The `onClipEvent (load)` actions usually set variables or perform tasks that do not need to run constantly throughout the Flash movie.

The only action within the `load` event for the action_clip movie clip sets the `limit` variable equal to 15.

L 9-1
```
onClipEvent (load) {
    limit = 15;
}
```

This will limit the amount of duplicated movie clips to 15, as shown in the `if` statement described in the next section.

On Clip Event Enter Frame Scripting

The actions performed in the `enterFrame` event handler run continuously, as long as the movie clip is on the stage. These actions will duplicate the cursor movie clip, which will be built in the next section.

Setting the Position

Start by setting the cursor1 movie clip (described in the next section) x and y positions equal to the mouse x and y positions. Flash 5 added the `_xmouse` and `_ymouse` properties to provide a direct reference to the position of the mouse cursor.

L 9-2
```
_root.cursor1._x = _root._xmouse;
_root.cursor1._y = _root._ymouse;
```

This code uses the `setVariable()` command to set these properties. The first line starts with the name and position of the movie clip, followed by a period and the property to set, `_root.cursor1._x`. This sets the x position of the cursor movie clip on the main stage. Next, set this property equal to the x position of the user's mouse. The mouse is always targeted from the main timeline, so set the cursor1 x position equal to `_root._xmouse`. The next line of script uses the same command to set the y position.

You can also use the `setProperty()` command to achieve the same results. Start by choosing the `setProperty()` command in the Actions drop-down menu of the ActionScript editor. From the Property drop-down menu, select the x position. Type **_root.cursor1** into the Target field. Next, type **_root.x_mouse** into the Value field. This will set the x position of the cursor1 movie clip equal to the x position of the user's mouse. Follow the same steps for the y position, substituting y in place of x.

L 9-3
```
setProperty ("_root.cursor1", _x, "_root._xmouse");
setProperty ("_root.cursor1", _y, "_root._ymouse");
```

ActionScripting Normal Mode Versus Expert Mode

As mentioned in previous chapters, there are two methods to Flash ActionScripting: normal mode and expert mode. Beginners usually find comfort in normal mode. The user-friendly panels make the task of entering commands much easier to understand. Advanced scripters usually opt for expert mode. The freestyle text editor allows a more organized and optimized approach to writing code. Usually, there is less typing involved in expert mode.

Flash designers who use ActionScripting normal mode tend to use the setProperty() command. Designers who use the expert mode tend to use the setVariable() command, because less typing is involved. Either method results in the same output.

Increasing the Integer

The common variable used in programming languages for an increasing integer is i. In expert mode of ActionScripting, this simple expression increases i by one each time the frame is accessed:

L 9-4
```
i++;
```

To achieve the same results in normal mode, set the i variable equal to i plus 1:

L 9-5
```
i = i + 1;
```

This will increase the i integer by 1 each time the frame is accessed.

Determining How Many Clips to Duplicate

When duplicating movie clips, it is important to use an if statement to determine how many movie clips to duplicate. If you do not set a limit, the movie clips will continue to duplicate, until the Flash Player eventually locks up.

Start by checking to see whether the value of the i variable is less than the limit variable by using an if statement. Within the if statement, add the duplicateMovieClip() action.

L 9-6
```
if (i < limit) {
    duplicateMovieClip ("_root.cursor", "cursor" + i, -i);
}
```

In the target field, `_root.cursor` accesses the movie clip created in the next section. Next, `"cursor" + i` is in the new name field. This will name the new clip in order, depending on the `i` variable, such as cursor1, cursor2, cursor3, and so on. Finally, `-i` in the depth field places each duplicated movie clip below the current movie clip. This will result in a trailing effect when the user moves the mouse.

Here's the final code with comments:

L 9-7
```
onClipEvent (enterFrame) {
// Set cursor position
    _root.cursor1._x = _root._xmouse;
    _root.cursor1._y = _root._ymouse;
// Increase i variable
    i++;
// Duplicate cursor movie clip
    if (i < limit) {
        duplicateMovieClip ("_root.cursor", "cursor" + i, -i);
    }
}
```

Creating the Cursor Layer

To start the cursor layer, I went to the new Macromedia Flash Exchange, at http://www.macromedia.com/exchange/flash. In the Navigation Extensions section, there is an extension called OS UI Elements available for PCs. A Mac version may be available in the future. This provides a library of standard operating-system elements, including a mouse cursor arrow that looks like the standard Windows cursor arrow.

Start by dragging the arrow graphic from the library created by the new extension. If you prefer, you can draw the arrow yourself, or you can import a graphic of the mouse cursor. While the object is selected, press F8 (COMMAND-F8 for Macs) to convert the object into a symbol. Choose Movie Clip from the list of options and name the movie clip **cursor**. In the Instance panel, enter **cursor** in the Name field.

Open the cursor movie clip and use the Align panel to align the graphic so that the top-left corner is in the center of the crosshairs, as in Figure 9-1. This simulates the cursor built into most operating systems.

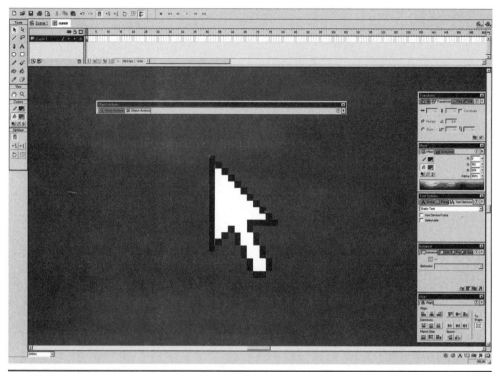

Figure 9-1 *Arrow positioning*

Cursor On Clip Event Load Scripting

On the main stage, click the cursor movie clip, and press CTRL-ALT-A
(COMMAND-OPTION-A for Macs) to open the ActionScript editor. Apply the actions
directly to the movie clip, so the actions will take place on each of the duplicated clips.

Determining the Clip's Names

When using duplicated movie clips, you need to be able to target and identify the
movie clips. Each of the movie clips is named in consecutive order by concatenating
the word *cursor* with a number represented by the i variable. The easiest way to
differentiate between each movie clip is to extract the seventh character and, if it exists,
the eighth character from the movie clip's instance name, using the substring()
command. For example, a movie clip with the instance name of cursor15 could
be identified by extracting the seventh and eighth characters, *15*.

First, use the `setVariable()` command to set the `name` variable equal to the name of the current movie clip.

L 9-8
```
name = this._name;
```

The _name property will return the movie clip name.

Next, use the `substring()` command to extract the seventh and eighth characters, if they exist.

L 9-9
```
name2 = substring(name, 7, 2);
```

The first variable inside the parentheses is the target movie clip, the next variable determines the first character to extract, and the last variable determines how many characters to extract.

The positioning of the cursor movie clips is determined by the preceding movie clip's position. Set the `name3` variable equal to `"_root.cursor"` + (name2 - 1).

L 9-10
```
name3 = "_root.cursor" + (name2 - 1);
```

This returns the name of the movie clip preceding the current movie clip.

Giving the Clips a Tracing Effect

To give the movie clips a fainter appearance, like a tracing, set the alpha of the trailing movie clips to 25. Using the `setVariable()` command in expert mode achieves this effect.

L 9-11
```
this._alpha = "25";
```

The same result can be achieved by using `setProperty()` command to set the _alpha property of `this` equal to 25.

L 9-12
```
setProperty (this, _alpha, "25");
```

Putting the Script Together

Here is the final code with comments:

L 9-13
```
onClipEvent (load) {
    // Determine the clip names
    name = this._name;
    name2 = substring(name, 7, 2);
    name3 = "_root.cursor" + (name2 - 1);
```

```
    // If statement to set alpha of trailing movie clips
    if (name2 > 1) {
        this._alpha = "25";
    }
}
```

Cursor On Clip Event Enter Frame Scripting

The positioning of the cursor movie clips needs to change continuously. Therefore, all of the positioning actions must occur inside the onClipEvent enterFrame event handler. The enterFrame event handler executes the actions in a continuous cycle, as long as the movie clip exists in the timeline.

The position of the current movie clip is set to the last-known position of the preceding movie clip, using the getProperty() command.

L 9-14
```
    this._x = getProperty(name3, _x);
    this._y = getProperty(name3, _y);
```

The first line sets the x position of this movie clip (this._x) equal to the x position of the name3 movie clip. The second line uses the same technique to set the y position.

You can also use the setProperty() command to achieve the same results. Select x position for the property, and enter **this** as the target. Select the Expression check box. In the value field, use the getProperty() command to find the x and y positions of the name3 movie clip.

L 9-15
```
    setProperty (this, _x, getProperty(name3, _x));
    setProperty (this, _y, getProperty(name3, _y));
```

Testing the Movie Clip

To test the movie clip, press CTRL-ENTER (COMMAND-ENTER for Macs). The result should be a cursor arrow that is followed by 14 other arrows when the mouse is moved, as in Figure 9-2. You will notice that there is one additional cursor movie clip that does not move. This is the original cursor movie clip, which is not accessed by ActionScripting.

Close the movie test window and return to Flash editing mode. Move the cursor movie clip outside the stage dimensions. The next section explains how to hide this movie clip below a border.

Figure 9-2   *Following arrows*

Creating the Border Layer

Start by creating a new layer above the cursor layer. Draw an unfilled rectangle on the stage, and then use the Align panel to resize it to the same dimensions as the stage. Align it to the horizontal and vertical center, to create a rectangle around the edge of the stage. Draw another unfilled rectangle, making it much larger than the stage. Zoom the Flash work area to 25 percent to see more of the screen. Next, fill this area between the two rectangles to make a large, filled rectangle with a hole in the center that is the same size as the stage.

While the rectangles and fill are selected, press F8 to convert them into an object. Select Movie Clip from the list of options and name it **border**. This will allow the object to be modified by ActionScripting.

The functionality of layers in Flash is similar to that of layers found in most professional graphic software. The topmost layers lie over the lower layers. Therefore, anything drawn on the border layer will cover the objects on the layer below it. While this usually is the case, you need to go a step further for this project, because it uses duplicate movie clips. When movie clips are duplicated, they are placed into their own depth level. To ensure that the border is always the topmost layer, it is necessary to use the new `swapDepths()` command to bring the border movie clip to the top.

The swapDepths() command can switch the depths between two duplicated movie clips, either by specifying a target depth or by specifying a target movie clip with which to swap depths. For this project, swapDepths() is used to swap the depth of a movie clip with whatever movie clip occupies depth 100.

Select the border movie clip and press CTRL-ALT-A (COMMAND-OPTION-A for Macs) to open the ActionScript editor. The only command that needs to be applied to this movie clip is swapDepths(). Because the swapDepths() command needs to execute only once when the movie clip is first loaded, the most appropriate event handler to execute the command is onClipEvent(load).

L 9-16
```
onClipEvent (load) {
    this.swapDepths(100);
}
```

The swapDepths() command starts with the movie clip name to access. In this case, use this. to target the current movie clip. Next, the command is entered, with the argument inside parentheses. The argument sets the new level for the movie clip. In this case, the new depth is set to 100, in order to ensure that the border will be on the topmost depth when future duplicated clips are added.

Creating the Exit Layer

I originally intended to run this project at full-screen size, instead of embedding the movie in a browser. Providing a way to exit the program is an essential part of creating a stand-alone movie because a stand-alone movie doesn't have the convenience of a browser's Back, Forward, and Close buttons.

Create the new layer, and type the text **Exit** on the stage. While it is selected, press F8 to convert the text into an object. Select Button from the list of options and name it **exit_button**.

TIP

It is good practice to edit the button to provide a rectangle hit area for the hit frame. This way, the users will not need to click exactly on the text.

Open the Actions panel while the button is selected on the main stage. Add the actions to the mouse event release actions. The on (release) event handler will perform the actions when the mouse is released, as in most operating systems. Use the `fscommand()` command with `"quit"` inside the parentheses as the argument. This will close the Flash projector when the button is released.

L 9-17
```
on (release) {
    fscommand ("quit");
}
```

Adding the Actions Layer

Throughout this book, I emphasize adding as much of the scripting as possible to movie clips. I still use an actions layer in all of my Flash projects to perform some of the basic actions, such as the `stop()` command. This project's action layer also includes some commands to prevent the Flash movie from slowing down and to hide the user's mouse.

Preventing Flash Movie Scaling

You can use the `fscommand` command to perform certain tasks for projector files. For this project, set the Flash movie to full screen, but do not let it scale. This ensures that the Flash movie does not slow down when a lot of content is on the stage. The final `fscommand` hides the Flash Projector menu and the right-click menu. This will prevent users from being able to zoom in on the content, possibly causing the Flash movie to slow down.

L 9-18
```
fscommand ("allowscale", "false");
fscommand ("fullscreen", "true");
fscommand ("showmenu", "false");
```

Setting the Quality

Projects that include many duplicated movie clips can tend to be processor intensive. Setting the quality of the Flash movie to either medium or low results is a good balance between quality and speed on slower computers. Setting the quality to the lowest setting still provides crisp, clean graphics while running at a reasonable frame rate. The duplicated movie clips project works best with the quality set to low because of its intense graphics calculations.

L 9-19
```
_quality = "low";
```

Hiding the User's Mouse and Stopping

Flash 5 introduced a new command that allows you to show or hide the default operating system's mouse cursor. Because this project uses duplicate movie clips with graphics to represent the mouse cursor (creating a new cursor for the user), it's important to remove the original cursor, because some users may have different mouse pointers for their operating systems. Use this command to hide the user's mouse cursor:

L 9-20

```
mouse.hide();
```

The final thing to do for this frame action is to add the `stop()` command. While this is not actually necessary for this project, it's a good habit to add the `stop()` command to keyframes that should stop the movie. Reinforcing controls for timeline playing will prepare the Flash movie for future additions of scenes or frames, while saving designers the effort of double-checking how the keyframes will stop or play.

Putting the Script Together

Here is the final code with comments:

L 9-21

```
// Keeps the Flash movie from scaling
fscommand ("allowscale", "false");
// Automatically sets the flash movie to full screen when previewed
fscommand ("fullscreen", "true");
// Disables the right clip menu when previewed
fscommand ("showmenu", "false");
// Sets the quality to low
_quality = "low";
// Hides the user's mouse
mouse.hide();
stop ();
```

Adding the Bar Layer

ch09_02.fla

With all of the previous elements of this project in place, I decided to add a few more objects to increase the amount of activity on the screen and demonstrate how increasing the screen activity with duplicated movie clips barely increases file size. The bar movie clip will be duplicated with the action_clip movie clip, described later in this chapter.

Create a new layer above the dup layer, and name it **bar**. Draw a rectangle slightly taller than the movie clip and approximately 12 pixels wide. While the rectangle is selected, press F8 to convert the graphic into a new symbol. Select Movie Clip from the list of options and name it **bar**. Enter **bar** in the Instance panel's Name field to allow the symbol to be accessed by ActionScripting.

All of the earlier movie clip actions were performed either when the movie clip was first loaded or in the `enterFrame` event handler. The actions on the bar movie clip take place continuously only when the mouse is moved, as handled by the `onClipEvent (mouseMove)` event handler. The actions will start when the mouse is moved and stop when the mouse stops or is moved outside the area of the Flash projector or embedded movie.

While the bar movie clip is selected, press CTRL-ALT-A (COMMAND-OPTION-A for Macs) to open the ActionScript editor. Use the `setProperty()` command to set the x position of the current movie clip to a random position between 0 and 720, the screen width. In the value field, use the `random()` function, with `720` inside the parentheses.

L 9-22
```
setProperty (this, _x, random(720));
```

Again, use the `setProperty()` command to change the properties of the current movie clip. Set the width of the current movie clip to a random width between 0 and 30. In the value field, use the `random()` function with `30` in parentheses.

L 9-23
```
setProperty (this, _width, random(30));
```

Finally, use the `setProperty()` command to set the alpha of the current movie clip to a random alpha state between 0 and 20.

L 9-24
```
setProperty (this, _alpha, random(20));
```

Now, when the user moves the mouse, the bar movie clips will move across the screen, while changing their width and the alpha. Here is the final code:

L 9-25
```
onClipEvent (mouseMove) {
    // Set the positions, width, and alpha of the current movie clip
    // to random values
    setProperty (this, _x, random(720));
    setProperty (this, _width, random(30));
    setProperty (this, _alpha, random(20));
}
```

Creating the Blade Layer

Like the bar movie clip, the blade movie clip will be duplicated with the action_clip movie clip described later in this chapter. Create a new layer above the bar layer and name it **blade**. Draw a rectangle approximately 100 pixels wide by 15 pixels tall. Use the Rotate tool to skew the rectangle slightly, as in Figure 9-3. While the blade is selected, press F8 to convert the graphic into a new symbol. Select Movie Clip from the list of options and name it **blade**, and give it the same name in the Instance panel.

While the blade movie clip is selected, open the ActionScript editor. As with the bar movie clip, the actions on the blade movie clip take place only when the mouse is moved, in the `onClipEvent(mouseMove)` event handler. It includes six `setProperty()` commands that use the `random()` function to change the current movie clip's properties, as follows:

▶ Set the width of the current movie clip to a random width between 0 and 150.

▶ Set the height of the current movie clip to a random height between 0 and 15.

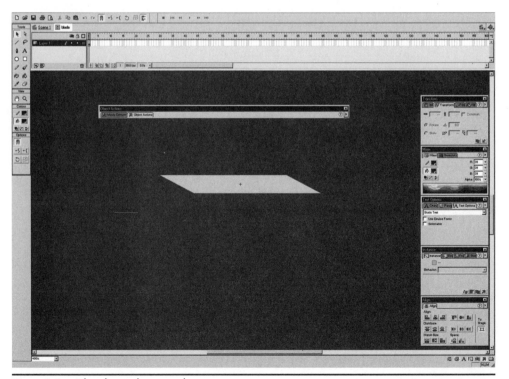

Figure 9-3 *The skewed rectangle*

▶ Set the alpha of the current movie clip to a random alpha state between 0 and 20.

▶ Set the rotation of the current movie clip to a random rotation between 0 and 360, a full circle.

▶ Set the x position of the current movie clip to a random rotation between 0 and 720.

▶ Set the y position of the current movie clip to a random position between 0 and 400.

When the user moves the mouse, the blade movie clips will move all over the screen, while changing their size, rotation, and alpha. Here is the final code:

L 9-26
```
onClipEvent (mouseMove) {
    // Set the positions, width, rotation, and alpha of the current
    // movie clip to random values
    setProperty (this, _width, random(150));
    setProperty (this, _height, random(15));
    setProperty (this, _alpha, random(20));
    setProperty (this, _rotation, random(360));
    setProperty (this, _x, random(720));
    setProperty (this, _y, random(400));
}
```

Creating the Logo Layer

Create a new layer above the blade layer and name it **logo**. Place a logo on the stage (I used my own logo). While the logo is selected, press F8 to convert the graphic into a new symbol. Select Movie Clip from the list of options and name it **logo**. Add **logo** to the Instance panel Name field to allow the symbol to be accessed by ActionScripting.

Next, align the movie clip to the top-left corner of the stage. Right-click (COMMAND-click for Macs) and select Edit-in-Place. Drag the graphic logo (shown in Figure 9-4) to approximately the center of the stage, which can still be seen when using Edit-in-Place—a valuable feature for positioning elements within Flash.

As with the bar and blade movie clips, this movie clip will be duplicated with the action_clip movie clip described later in this chapter, and all of its actions take place in the onClipEvent(mouseMove) event handler. This layer contains three setProperty() commands to set the x position of the current movie clip to a random position between 0 and 10, the y position to a random position between 0 and 10, and the alpha to a random alpha state between 0 and 30. These actions will

Figure 9-4 *The Innovative FX logo*

cause the logo movie clips to shake rapidly while changing the alpha when the mouse is moved. Here is the final code:

L 9-27
```
onClipEvent (mouseMove) {
    // Set the positions and alpha of the current movie clip to
    // random values
    setProperty (this, _x, random(10));
    setProperty (this, _y, random(10));
    setProperty (this, _alpha, random(30));
}
```

Modifying the action_clip Movie Clip

Once the three new movie clips are in place, move them off the main stage, so that they will be under the border, like the cursor movie clip. Select the action_clip movie clip and open the ActionScript editor (CTRL-ALT-A/COMMAND-OPTION-A). You need to add actions to the `if` statement to duplicate the new movie clips.

For each movie clip, use the movie clip's name as the target and set the new name equal to the name plus the `i` variable. For example, set the new name of `_root.bar` to `"bar" + i`. In the depth field, use the `random()` function to place each movie clip into its own layer. This creates a more chaotic, dynamic appearance because all of the movie clips will be on random depths. Enter **99** in the parentheses, to keep the movie clips below the border movie clip.

L 9-28
```
duplicateMovieClip ("_root.bar", "bar" + i, random(99));
duplicateMovieClip ("_root.blade", "blade" + i, random(99));
duplicateMovieClip ("_root.logo", "logo" + i, random(99));
```

Here is the new final code for the action_clip movie clip:

L 9-29
```
onClipEvent (enterFrame) {
    _root.cursor1._x = _root._xmouse;
    _root.cursor1._y = _root._ymouse;
    i++;
    if (i < limit) {
        duplicateMovieClip ("_root.cursor", "cursor" + i, -i);
        duplicateMovieClip ("_root.bar", "bar" + i, random(99));
        duplicateMovieClip ("_root.blade", "blade" + i, random(99));
        duplicateMovieClip ("_root.logo", "logo" + i, random(99));
    }
}
```

What to Take Away from This Chapter

The project described in this chapter focused mainly on duplicating movie clips, but it also used many other features and functions of Flash. Each of these elements helped keep the final resulting file size of the ch09_02.fla-exported .swf file, shown in Figure 9-5, less than 3KB. If you were to present all of these objects (nearly 100!) on the stage without using duplicated clips, the resulting file size would be much larger.

Flash movies can enhance any HTML site or CD-ROM presentation if used correctly. HTML sites have file size limitations, and you should consider your users' connections and patience in designing your site. If the user has a dial-up connection connected at 56Kbps, a 1MB site may take from 10 to 15 minutes to fully load. The faster you can present the data to the targeted users, the better the impression you will make with your site. Try to take advantage of all that Flash has to offer for each project and you will surely raise the quality of your site, along with reducing its file size.

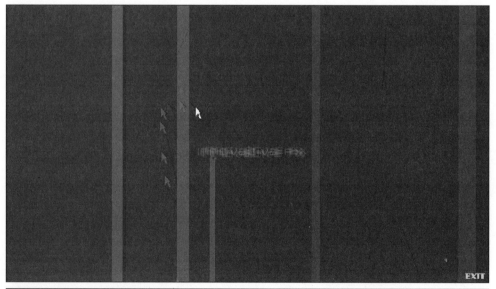

Figure 9-5 *The finished project*

Swap Depths

IN THIS CHAPTER:

- ▶ Control depth of movie clips with swapDepths()

- ▶ Use window-based content to maximize available space

- ▶ Create mouse-sensitive navigation

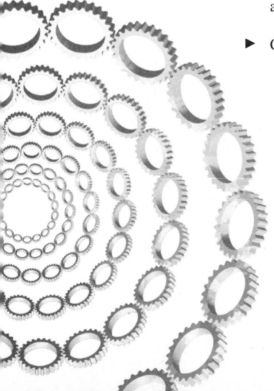

I n the previous versions of Flash, all elements retained a stacking order depending on the layer in which they resided. Flash 4 included a duplicate movie clip function, which allowed you to duplicate an existing movie clip and assign the duplicate movie clip to a new depth. The one drawback of this feature was that you could not modify the depth of the movie clip after using the duplicate movie clip function. Macromedia was kind enough to provide this capability with the release of Flash 5. The new swapDepths() command allows you to assign a new depth to a movie clip dynamically.

In this chapter, you will learn how to use the swapDepths() command to increase the usability and functionality of a window-based interface. This project consists of duplicated window movie clips, whose depths in relation to each other are controlled by using the swapDepths() command. These windows can be dragged around the screen, and each will be brought to the top of the stacking order when the top button on the window is pressed.

Building the Window
ch10_01.fla

Start by creating a new Flash movie and setting the dimensions to 700 pixels wide by 400 pixels tall. First, create the window movie clip. This movie clip will be duplicated to make more windows.

On the stage, create a rectangle approximately one-fourth the size of the main stage. I went one step further by drawing a 45-degree angle on opposite ends and removing the excess to create a slanted rectangle. These adjustments merely serve to enhance the overall look of the window.

Draw a line near the top of the window rectangle to section off an area that will be used as the button to drag the window and to swap the depth of the window. The line should be about 15 pixels below the top line of the window rectangle to allow room for text that will be added later.

Use the Arrow tool and select the entire window. Press F8 to convert these items into an object. Select Movie Clip from the list of options and name it **window**. Open the Instance panel and enter **window** in the Name text field. This allows this movie clip to be accessed by ActionScripting.

Creating the Drag Button

The drag button is created by selecting the filled rectangle area at the top of the window movie clip. Start by right-clicking (CONTROL-clicking for Macs) the window movie clip on the main stage. Choose Edit from the options to open the window for editing on its own timeline.

Select the filled rectangle area between the two top lines of the window. Press CTRL-X (COMMAND-X for Macs) to cut the filled area from the window. This removes the filled area from the rectangle and saves it to the system clipboard. Create a new layer and move it below the layer that contains the rest of the window elements. Use the Paste-in-Place option by pressing CTRL-SHIFT-V (COMMAND-SHIFT-V for Macs) to paste the previously cut filled area into the same position on the new layer.

NOTE

The Paste-in-Place option pastes the object into the same x and y coordinates as it occupied when it was cut or copied.

Use the Arrow tool to select the filled area, and then press F8 to convert it into an object. Select Button from the list of options and name it **drag_button**. Right-click (CONTROL-click for Macs) the new object and select Edit from the list of options. This will open the button timeline for editing.

The button timeline consists of four frames:

▶ The first frame, which already contains a keyframe with the filled-rectangle area, is the up state of the button. This frame will be displayed when the mouse cursor is not over the button.

▶ The second frame is for the over state of the button. Create a new keyframe on the next frame labeled Over. Change the color of the filled-rectangle area to achieve a rollover effect. This frame is displayed when the user's mouse cursor is over the button.

▶ The next frame, labeled Down, is left blank for this project. This frame is displayed when the user presses the mouse button over the button area. If nothing is added to this frame, the over frame will be displayed when the mouse is pressed.

▶ The last frame is labeled Hit. It represents the area that is considered the size of the button. This frame will never be displayed in any state of the button. Leave this frame blank also, so that the hit area is the same size as the up and down area.

Drag Button ActionScripting

Next, you need to apply ActionScripting to the button to make the window draggable and to allow the button to swap the depth of the window. Start by pressing CTRL-L (COMMAND-L for Macs) to open the Library in Flash. (The Library contains all of the symbols inside a Flash movie.) Find the window movie clip and double-click the symbol to open the editing mode for the window movie clip. Use the Arrow tool to select the drag_button symbol, and then press CTRL-ALT-A (COMMAND-OPTION-A for Macs) to open the ActionScript editor.

For this project, you will apply actions for when the mouse is pressed and when the mouse is released. The actions will exist inside event handlers for each corresponding mouse event: on (press) and on (release).

Scripting Button On Press Events

The button needs to initialize the drag operation when the mouse is pressed. This is accomplished with the startDrag() command.

L 10-1
```
on (press) {
    startDrag (
this, false, this._width/2, this._height/2,
700 - this._width/2, 400 - this._height/2
);
```

There are three arguments for the drag operation. The first text field asks for the target movie clip. Type **this** and be sure to check the Expression check box (this uses relative targeting, which is always referenced as an expression).

Next, select the check box for the Constrain to Rectangle function. This will constrain the drag operation to a set rectangular area, which will prevent the window from accidentally being dragged off the stage. There are four limits to set to constrain the dragged movie clip:

▶ Set the left constraint equal to this._width/2. This will keep the window from being dragged off the left side of the stage. It's important to use half of the movie clip's width as the left border to prevent overlap between the movie clip and the stage border. Otherwise, half of the movie clip could leave the visible stage area before the movie clip stops dragging.

▶ Set the top constraint equal to this._height/2. This will keep the window from being dragged off the top of the stage.

▶ Set the right constraint equal to `700 - this._width/2`. The `700` represents the width of the Flash stage, which is 700 pixels wide by 400 pixels high. Half of the width of the current movie clip is subtracted from 700. The resulting number represents the actual distance from the right edge of the Flash stage to the center of the movie clip. Offsetting the right edge of the stage with half of the movie clip's width provides a more accurate calculation of the actual constraints on how far the movie clip can be dragged around. This prevents the movie clip from being dragged partially off the right side of the stage.

▶ Finally, set the bottom constraint is equal to `400 - this._height/2`. The `400` represents the height of the movie. Subtracting this value from half of the height of the current movie clip keeps the window from being dragged off the bottom of the stage.

To make this project as modular as possible, don't call the `swapDepths()` command directly from the button's `on (press)` event. Instead, set a variable on the main timeline.

L 10-2
```
_root.selected = name;
```

By using this approach, you can easily add more items to interact with the window elements. Set the value of the `selected` variable on the main timeline equal to the `name` variable of this movie clip (discussed in "Window ActionScripting," later in this chapter).

Scripting Button On Release Events

When the mouse is released, you should stop the drag operation. This is done using the `stopDrag()` command.

L 10-3
```
on (release, releaseOutside) {
    stopDrag ();
}
```

This command stops all drag operations being performed in the Flash movie.

TIP

It is also a good idea to add `releaseOutside` *to the* `on (release)` *event handler, in case someone moves their mouse faster than the window moves and releases the button. If this happens, the window will continue to be dragged.*

Putting the Script Together

Here is the final code with comments:

L 10-4

```
on (press) {
    // Start drag operation when mouse is pressed.
    startDrag (
this, false, this._width/2, this._height/2,
700 - this._width/2, 400 - this._height/2
);
    // Set the root selected variable equal to the name of this
    // movie clip.
    _root.selected = name;
}
on (release, releaseOutside) {
    // Stop the drag operation when the mouse is released.
    stopDrag ();
}
```

Adding the Text Field

For this project, you will need to use a dynamic text field on the top layer of the window movie clip. This will display the name variable (described in the next section). Displaying the name of the movie clip will help the user identify each movie clip. For a real-world project, you can display different information by setting a variable in Flash or by loading a variable from an external .txt or .html file.

NOTE

Text fields in Flash can be of three different types. Static text fields are for text entered directly into the Flash movie by the developer, and they cannot be updated dynamically. Dynamic text fields contain text that can be dynamically updated using variables within a Flash movie, but their contents cannot be changed by the user. Input text fields are designed for users to input text in forms or surveys.

Use the Text tool to draw a text field on the stage large enough to accommodate the text that will be displayed. In the Text Options panel, select Dynamic Text from the drop-down list. In the Variable field, type **name**. Finally, select the font style and size in the Character panel.

NOTE

If you are using nonsystem fonts or masked text, be sure to include the font outlines, or they will not display correctly.

Window ActionScripting

As you've seen in all of the previous projects in this book, including ActionScripting in movie clips (a capability added to Flash 5) makes your movies more organized and easier to update. The old method of using keyframe actions inside movie clips has been deprecated with Flash 5. While you can still use this method, it's a better idea to use the new technique.

On Clip Event Load Scripting

When the window movie clip is first loaded, you need to get the number at the end of the name to determine which movie clip it is. This is important when applying the ActionScript to swap the depth of these movie clips, because you want to make sure that you're swapping the right movie clips. It is necessary to determine the name of the movie clip only once, so be sure to use the `load` event (selectable at the bottom of the ActionScript editor).

L 10-5
```
onClipEvent (load)
```

Set the `name` variable equal to the last character of the current movie clip name. This is determined by using the `substring()` command to extract specific characters from an object's name.

L 10-6
```
name = substring(this._name, 7, 1);
```

The first `substring()` command argument is the name of the movie clip. For this project, use `this` to access the current movie clip using relative targeting. The second argument determines which character to start with when extracting the characters. In this case, the name of the movie clip is seven characters long, so the argument is 7. The third argument is the number of characters to extract. For this project, you want to extract the number integer at the end of the movie clip name. The number of windows will be limited to a single digit (as explained in "Limiting the Number of Movie Clips," later in this chapter), so this argument is 1 to extract only one character.

On Clip Event Enter Frame Scripting

The other action that needs to take place on this movie clip is to determine whether the current window is selected and to swap the depth if needed. It is necessary to perform these actions constantly, so they are handled in the `onClipEvent (enterFrame)` event handler.

Use an `if` statement to determine whether the selected variable on the main timeline is equal to the `name` variable. Flash runs the statements that follow if the `if` statement is true. Otherwise, the statements are bypassed.

L 10-7
```
if (_root.selected == name)
        this.swapDepths(_root.dup.i);
```

If the `if` statement is true, the next statement swaps the depths of the current movie clip so that it is at the top of the stacking order among the other movie clips. The first part of the action contains the movie clip name. Use `this` to refer to the current movie clip. A period follows the target name, and then the `swapDepths()` command follows. The number of the new depth is passed into the `swapDepths()` command as an argument. Set the depth equal to the `i` variable on the dup movie clip (which is described in the next section). The `i` variable constantly increases by 1, so that when the current movie clip moves to that new depth, it is always on top.

NOTE

The `swapDepths()` *command is found in the movie clip object actions. These object-oriented actions use uncommon scripting methods, which are not usually required for most projects.*

Putting the Script Together

Here is the final code with comments:

L 10-8
```
onClipEvent (load) {
    // Use substring command to determine the numeric character
    // at the end of the name of the current movie clip
    name = substring(this._name, 7, 1);
}
onClipEvent (enterFrame) {
    // Check to see if the selected variable is equal to the
    // name of this movie clip.
    if (_root.selected == name) {
        // Swap the depth of the current movie clip equal to
```

```
    // the i variable on the dup movie clip.
    this.swapDepths(_root.dup.i);
  }
}
```

Creating the Dup Movie Clip

The dup movie clip is a blank movie clip. It contains actions that need to constantly run through the Flash movie, regardless of the main timeline position. Using a blank movie clip keeps the movie more organized for future editing. It will not increase the movie's file size.

To begin, create a new symbol by pressing CTRL-F8 (COMMAND-F8 for Macs). Select Movie Clip from the list of options and name it **dup**. Do not draw any graphics in this movie clip. Press CTRL-L (COMMAND-L for Macs) to open the Library, and then drag an instance of this movie clip onto the main stage. Finally, open the Instance panel and add **dup** for the instance name, so that the movie clip can be accessed by ActionScripting.

Limiting the Number of Movie Clips

When the movie clip is first loaded, the `limit` variable needs to be set. This will limit the number of movie clips that will be duplicated.

NOTE

Setting the limit with a variable will aid the use of the `swapDepths()` *command when there are more symbols on the stage, as explained when the second file of this project is discussed, later in this chapter.*

L 10-9
```
onClipEvent (load) {
    limit = 6;
```

The next actions are handled by the `onClipEvent (enterFrame)` event handler because they need to run constantly as long as the movie clip is on the stage.

First, set the `i` variable, which is a standard variable used by programmers as a counter for loops. By using the expression `i++`, the `i` variable will increase by 1 every time a frame event occurs.

L 10-10
```
onClipEvent (enterFrame) {
    i++;
```

This type of expression can be entered only in the expert mode of ActionScripting. To achieve the same result in the normal mode of ActionScripting, use i = i + 1.

Next, use an if statement to determine whether the i variable is less than or equal to the limit variable, and that it is greater than 0. (Multiple arguments can be used in an if statement by separating them with an operand such as &, or, or not.) If the if statement is true, then Flash will perform the expressions within the if statements. These expressions duplicate the window movie clip into six new window movie clips with new names and new depths.

L 10-11
```
if (i <= limit & i > 0)
        duplicateMovieClip (_root.window, "window" + i, i - limit);
```

Using the duplicateMovieClip() command, the first argument contains the name of the movie clip to be duplicated. Be sure to use the correct targeting to access the window movie clip. In this project, the window movie clip lies on the main timeline, so it is accessed by using _root. for the prefix to refer to the main timeline.

The next field, "window" + i, sets the new name of the duplicated movie clip, renaming each duplicated movie clip consecutively. The quotation marks around window are necessary because it is not a variable. This expression adds the i variable to the end of "window" each time it is duplicated, so the movie clips will be named window1, window2, window3, window4, window5, and window6.

The last argument for the duplicateMovieClip() command determines the depth at which to place the new movie clip. The expression i - limit places the movie clips on a negative depth, on top of each other. This will keep the windows below any other content on the stage (which could be added later).

Repositioning the Movie Clips

Finally, reposition the new movie clips so that they do not lie directly on top of each other. This is accomplished with the setProperty() command:

L 10-12
```
setProperty ("_root.window" + i, _x, (i * 70) + 100);
```

In the Property drop-down list, select x position. This will affect the position of the movie clip along the X axis. In the target text field, enter **"_root.window" + i,** and select the Expression check box. This will access the last duplicated window movie clip.

The value field contains the new position of the movie clip. This is set as (i * 70) + 100, so that the movie clips will cascade 70 pixels apart from each other, starting at 170. Be sure to check the Expression check box.

The y position is set using the same methods, but in the value field use (i * 10) + 150, again being sure to check the Expression check box.

L 10-13

```
setProperty ("_root.window" + i, _y, (i * 10) + 150);
```

This will cascade the windows 10 pixels apart, starting at 160.

Putting the Script Together

Here is the final code with comments:

L 10-14

```
onClipEvent (load) {
    // Set the limit of movie clips to be duplicated.
    limit = 6;
}
onClipEvent (enterFrame) {
    // Raise the i integer by 1 every time that this
    // movie clip is on the stage.
    i++;
    // If statement to determine if i is less than or equal
    // to limit, but greater than 0.
    if (i <= limit & i > 0) {
        // Duplicate the window movie clip
        duplicateMovieClip (_root.window, "window" + i, i - limit);
        // Reposition the window movie clips so they are
        // not stacked on top of each other when duplicated.
        setProperty ("_root.window" + i, _x, (i * 70) + 100);
        setProperty ("_root.window" + i, _y, (i * 10) + 150);
    }
}
```

Adding the Border Layer

With the other elements in place, the Flash movie will be functional. One problem is that the original window movie clip is visible to the left of the stage area. The solution is to add a border movie clip that will hide all of the elements that are off the main stage area.

Start by creating a new layer above the dup layer in the main timeline of the Flash movie. Draw an unfilled rectangle on the stage, and use the Align panel to resize it to the same dimensions as the stage. Align it to the horizontal and vertical center, to create a rectangle around the edge of the stage. Draw another unfilled rectangle and make it much larger than the stage. Zoom the Flash work area to 25 percent to see more of the screen. Next, fill this area between the two rectangles to make a large filled rectangle with a hole in the center the same size as the stage.

While the rectangles and fill are selected, press F8 to convert the graphics into an object. Select Movie Clip from the list of options and name it **border**. This will allow the object to be modified by ActionScripting.

Select the border movie clip and open the ActionScript editor (CTRL-ALT-A/ COMMAND-OPTION-A). The only command that needs to be applied on this movie clip is `swapDepths()`, which ensures that the border is always the topmost layer.

When movie clips are duplicated, they are placed into their own depth level. Depth levels act like virtual layers on a timeline to hold duplicated movie clips. Only one duplicated movie clip can exist in a depth layer, so assigning another duplicated movie clip will make any current movie clip in that depth disappear. Thus, the `swapDepths()` command prevents a movie clip from replacing another movie clip at the same depth by simply switching the depths of two movie clips. Using this command, you can either specify a target movie clip to switch places with or specify a depth layer.

The `swapDepths()` command needs to update continuously to ensure that the border is always on top, so it is placed within the `onClipEvent (enterFrame)` event handler:

L 10-15
```
onClipEvent (enterFrame) {
    this.swapDepths(_root.dup.i + (_root.dup.limit * 2));
}
```

As with the ActionScripting for the window layer, `this` is used as the movie clip name to access, referring to the current movie clip. The argument `_root.dup.i +` `(_root.dup.limit * 2)` sets the new depth of the movie clip. By getting twice the value of the `limit` variable from the `_root.dup` movie clip, you ensure that the border will be on the topmost depth when future duplicated clips are added.

Adding Navigation Elements
ch10_02.fla

After the windows are in place, they can work alone, or a navigation system can be implemented to interact with the window-depth functions to alter the depths dynamically.

When adding a navigation system, another factor to consider is the depth of the navigation. With this project, the navigational elements need to remain on a higher depth than the windows, but still remain below the border movie clip.

Start by drawing a vertical line approximately three times as tall as the movie stage in the nav layer. Use the Align Panel to align it to the vertical center of the stage. Use the Arrow tool to select the line. Press F8 to convert the line into an object. Select Movie Clip from the list of options and name it **nav_line**. Open the Instance panel and enter **nav** in the Name field.

Creating the Nav Button

Start by right-clicking (CONTROL-clicking for Macs) the nav_line movie clip on the main stage. Choose Edit from the options to open the symbol for editing on its own timeline.

Draw an unfilled rectangle approximately 10 pixels wide and 60 pixels tall. Use the Align panel to align the rectangle to the middle of the movie clip. This will result in a small rectangle with a line running directly through the center. Remove the line in the center of the rectangle by clicking the line and pressing DELETE.

Fill the rectangle with the Paint tool and use the arrow tool to select the filled area. Press CTRL-X (COMMAND-X for Macs) to cut the filled area. Create a new layer and move it below the layer that contains the rest of the window elements. Use the Paste-in-Place option (CTRL-SHIFT-V/COMMAND-SHIFT-V) to paste the previously cut filled area into the same position on the new layer.

Use the Arrow tool to select the filled area, and then press F8 to convert it into an object. Select Button from the list of options and name it **nav_button**. Right-click (CONTROL-click for Macs) the new object and select Edit. Follow the steps covered earlier in the "Creating the Drag Button" section to create a rollover effect for the new button.

Navigate back to the nav_line movie clip and select the new button to apply ActionScripting. Press CTRL-ALT-A (COMMAND-OPTION-A) to open the ActionScript editor. The only action that needs to be added to this button is to modify the `selected` variable on the main timeline. Set the `selected` variable equal to the `name2` variable (described in "Navigation ActionScripting," later in this chapter).

L 10-16
```
on (press) {
    _root.selected = name2;
}
```

Adding the Text Field

For this project, you need to use a dynamic text field on the top layer of the nav_line movie clip. This will display the name of the movie clip. (For a real-world project, you can display other information by setting a different variable in Flash or by loading the variable from an external .txt or .html file.)

Use the Text tool to draw a text field on the stage large enough for the text that will be displayed. In the Text Options panel, select Dynamic Text from the drop-down list and type **name** in the Variable field. Finally, select the font style and size in the Character panel.

Navigation ActionScripting

Navigate to the main timeline and select the nav_line movie clip. Open the ActionScript editor (CTRL-ALT-A/COMMAND-OPTION-A) to apply event procedures to this movie clip.

Scripting Navigation Load Actions

In the `onClipEvent (load)` event handler, eight variables are set: `name`, `name2`, `name3`, `ratio`, `o_x_pos`, `o_y_pos`, `top`, and `bottom`.

The first variable that needs to be determined is the `name` variable. This will be used for the text that appears in the movie clip's text field. Set the `name` variable equal to `"button"` + `this._name`.

L 10-17
```
name = "button " + this._name;
```

For example, this will result in an output of "window nav 1" for the first navigation movie clip.

The `name2` variable uses a `substring()` command to extract the numeric character in the `name` variable. This variable will later be used to determine the depth of the current movie clip.

L 10-18
```
name2 = substring(name, 11, 1);
```

The `name3` variable adds 1 to the `name2` variable. This is used for determining the depth of the current movie clip. Use the `Number()` function to convert the `name2` variable into an integer.

L 10-19
```
name3 = Number(name2) + 1;
```

The next variable, o_x_pos, contains the original x position of the current movie clip. This is set equal to the name2 variable multiplied by 100. This variable is used for positioning the current movie clip.

L 10-20
```
o_x_pos = name2 * 100;
```

The o_y_pos variable is the original y position of the current movie clip. This is set to 200, which is the center of the stage.

L 10-21
```
o_y_pos = 200;
```

The ratio variable is used to determine the speed at which to move the current movie clip. The value of the ratio variable must be below 1 and higher than 0 for the ActionScript code to work properly. The higher the number, the faster the movement.

L 10-22
```
ratio = .3;
```

The top and bottom variables are just the top and bottom y coordinates of the stage. These variables will determine when the current movie clip should spring back to its original position.

L 10-23
```
top = 0;
bottom = 400;
```

Here is the code with comments:

L 10-24
```
onClipEvent (load) {
    // Determine name variables.
    name = "button " + this._name;
    name2 = substring(name, 11, 1);
    name3 = Number(name2) + 1;
    // Set the original position of the movie clip.
    o_x_pos = name2 * 100;
    o_y_pos = 200;
    // Speed at which to move the movie clip.
    ratio = .3;
    // The top and bottom limits.
    top = 0;
    bottom = 400;
}
```

Scripting Navigation Enter Frame Actions

As previously mentioned, ActionScript code located inside the braces of an
onClipEvent(enterFrame) event handler will execute continuously at the
same speed as the Flash movie's overall frame rate. A movie clip using 20 frames
per second would perform these actions 20 times within a 1-second duration.

Swapping the Depth of the Current Movie Clip   The navigational elements should appear
in front of the windows, but behind the border movie clip. In this project, all of the
movie clips continuously change their depth, depending on which movie clip is selected
by the user. Therefore, the depth of a movie clip will always move up to the depth
represented by the variable i when selected by the user. The border movie clip is
always set equal to the limit variable on the dup movie clip, multiplied by two
times the i variable. Setting the depth of the border movie clip to the double value
of the i variable will keep the movie clip on top of the other elements, no matter
what value is given to the limit variable.

TIP

*Try to make each project as modular as possible. By creating each object separately, so that it
functions as much as possible by itself, you make future updates and changes much easier. For
example, if you later decided to add two more windows to this project, you would need to change
only one variable. The windows would remain in the appropriate stacking order.*

Set the depth of the current movie clip equal to the i variable on the dup movie
clip plus the name3 variable. This will keep the movie clips on their own depth,
while not interfering with other elements.

L 10-25

```
this.swapDepths(_root.dup.i + name3);
```

Determining the Mouse Position   The navigation for this project moves toward the
user's mouse if the mouse cursor has moved within 50 pixels of either side of the movie
clip, but still exists within the stage dimensions. This is tested by the if statement:

L 10-26

```
if (_root._xmouse > (o_x_pos - 50) & _root._xmouse < (o_x_pos + 50) &
_root._ymouse > top & _root._ymouse < bottom & name2 > 0)
```

This `if` statement contains five arguments, separated by the & operand. Therefore, all of the conditions in the `if` statement must be met before executing the `if` statement's code. The five statements are as follows:

▶ `_root._xmouse > (o_x_pos - 50)` determines whether the user's mouse is greater than the current movie clip's original x position minus 50.

▶ `_root._xmouse < (o_x_pos + 50)` determines whether the user's mouse is less than the current movie clip's original x position plus 50.

▶ `_root._ymouse > top` determines whether the user's mouse is greater than the y coordinate of the top of the movie clip, 0.

▶ `_root._ymouse < bottom` determines whether the user's mouse is less than the y coordinate of the bottom of the movie clip, 400.

▶ `name2 > 0` determines if the `name2` variable is greater than 0.

Setting the Movie Clip's Position When the Conditions Are Met   If these conditions are met, then the statements within the `if` statement are performed. These set the x and y positions of the movie clip to move toward the user's mouse.

L 10-27
```
this._x = x_pos;
x_pos = x_pos - (n_x_pos * ratio);
n_x_pos = x_pos - _root._xmouse;
this._y = y_pos;
y_pos = y_pos - (n_y_pos * ratio);
n_y_pos = y_pos - _root._ymouse;
```

The first statement sets the current movie clip's x position equal to the `x_pos` variable. (This action could also be entered using the `setProperty()` command.)

The `x_pos` variable is actually updated every time the frame is accessed. Basically, it decreases or increases slowly to move toward the user's mouse position. In the next statement, the `x_pos` variable is subtracted from the resulting integer of the `n_x_pos` variable multiplied by the `ratio` variable.

The `n_x_pos` variable is the new x position variable. In the third statement, it is set equal to the `x_pos` variable minus the user's mouse x position. This variable will slowly decrease or increase until the movie clip x position is equal to the user's mouse position.

The last three statements work the same as the first three, except that they set the y position.

Setting the Movie Clip's Position When the Conditions Are Not Met   If all of the conditions in the `if` statement are not met, then none of the previous actions will be performed. Use an `else if` statement to check to see whether the `name2` variable is greater than 0. If it is, the next set of expressions are performed.

L 10-28
```
else if (name2 > 0)
```

The `else if` actions move the movie clip back to the original position if the user's mouse is not within 50 pixels of either side of the original x position of the movie clip, or if the mouse is moved off the stage area.

L 10-29
```
this._x = x_pos;
x_pos = x_pos - (n_x_pos * ratio);
n_x_pos = x_pos - o_x_pos;
this._y = y_pos;
y_pos = y_pos - (n_y_pos * ratio);
n_y_pos = y_pos - o_y_pos;
```

The first two statements work the same as those in the `if` statement's condition. First, set the current movie clip's x position equal to the `x_pos` variable, and then subtract from `x_pos` the result of the `n_x_pos` variable multiplied by the `ratio` variable. The third statement sets `n_x_pos` (the new x position variable) equal to the `x_pos` variable minus the original x position of the current movie clip. This variable will slowly decrease or increase until the movie clip x position is equal to the original movie clip's x position. The last three lines work in the same way to set the y position.

Putting the Script Together   Here is the final code with comments:

L 10-30
```
onClipEvent (enterFrame) {
    // Swap the depth of the current movie clip.
    this.swapDepths(_root.dup.i + name3);
    // If statement to determine if the user's mouse is within
    // 50 pixels of this movie clip's original position,
    // and still on the stage.
    if (_root._xmouse > (o_x_pos - 50) & _root._xmouse <
    (o_x_pos + 50) & _root._ymouse > top & _root._ymouse <
    bottom & name2 > 0) {
```

```
    // Set the x position of the movie clip to move
    // toward the user's mouse.
    this._x = x_pos;
    x_pos = x_pos - (n_x_pos * ratio);
    n_x_pos = x_pos - _root._xmouse;
    // Set the y position of the movie clip to move
    // toward the user's mouse.
    this._y = y_pos;
    y_pos = y_pos - (n_y_pos * ratio);
    n_y_pos = y_pos - _root._ymouse;
    // If statement to determine if the name2 variable is
    // greater than 0, and not within 50 pixels of the current
    // movie clip, or not on the stage.
} else if (name2 > 0) {
    // Set the x position of the movie clip to move
    // toward the original movie clip position.
    this._x = x_pos;
    x_pos = x_pos - (n_x_pos * ratio);
    n_x_pos = x_pos - o_x_pos;
    // Set the y position of the movie clip to move
    // toward the original movie clip position.
    this._y = y_pos;
    y_pos = y_pos - (n_y_pos * ratio);
    n_y_pos = y_pos - o_y_pos;
}
}
```

What to Take Away from This Chapter

This project demonstrated the fundamentals of using the `swapDepths()` command to add functionality to a Flash project. The `swapdepths()` command aided this navigation, so that all of the windows could stay on the stage, without interfering with one another. Using these techniques, you can dynamically stack movie clips in Flash.

Flash JavaScript Interaction

IN THIS CHAPTER:

▶ Change background colors using ActionScripting and JavaScript

▶ Change text field content using ActionScripting and JavaScript

▶ Create a new pop-up browser window using ActionScripting and JavaScript

▶ Move a browser window from Flash

Flash has many capabilities that are not available in other software, but it still has its limits. For example, Flash cannot interact with a user's browser. However, Flash can work with JavaScript to perform many JavaScript tasks, such as opening a browser window or changing the content of a text field.

Flash 5 ActionScripting is based on the JavaScript language. This has made it easier for JavaScript programmers to learn the new ActionScripting language. The same goes for Flash ActionScript programmers, who will find it easy to learn JavaScript.

This chapter focuses on four projects that can be used in many real-world applications to increase the interaction and usability of each project. Each project uses Action-Scripting to call JavaScript functions to perform specific tasks: changing background colors, changing text field content, popping up a new browser window, and moving a browser window. When passing the functions from Flash, variables can be passed as well, to increase the amount of work that can be handled within Flash while using the least amount of JavaScript.

Changing Background Colors

Many Flash Web sites are built so that each section uses different color schemes. The problem is that the HTML page will remain the same color, unless you send the user to another HTML page with a new background color. Using JavaScript, you can dynamically change the background color of an HTML page. This project shows how to call this function from within Flash.

Creating the HTML Page for the Background Color Project

ch11_01.html

The best place to start is usually by building the HTML page and the JavaScript functions. This way, you will know which variables and function to call from within the Flash movie that will be embedded.

TIP

All HTML pages start with the same tags, and I usually start with a prewritten template. Reusing scripts saves time and also reduces the chance of error when you are writing large amounts of code.

Here is the basic HTML document:

L 11-1
```
<html>
<head>
<title>HTML Document</title>
```

```
</head>
<body>
</body>
</html>
```

Creating the JavaScript Bc Function

In the head section of the HTML document, JavaScript needs to be contained within
script tags:

L 11-2
```
<script>
</script>
```

Start by using the `function()` command and setting a name for the function.
In this case, name the function `bc` to indicate background color. Within the parentheses,
specify `newColor` as the variable that will be passed from within the Flash movie.
After the parentheses, use an open curly brace (`{`) to indicate the beginning of a
JavaScript expression.

L 11-3
```
function bc(newColor) {
```

HTML Basics

The basic HTML page consists of eight tags: `<html>`, `<head>`, `<title>`,
`</title>`, `</head>`, `<body>`, `</body>`, and `</html>`. In each case, the
first tag starts the element and the second tag, which is preceded by a slash (`/`),
is the closing tag that ends the element. These tags work as follows:

▶ The html tags open and close the HTML content of an HTML document.

▶ The head tags contain the elements of an HMTL document that will not
be displayed within the browser. This section contains elements such as
the title and JavaScript functions.

▶ The title tags contain the document title that will be displayed at the top
of the browser. It is a good idea to name each of your HTML documents
to allow users to identify which page they are on.

▶ The body tags contain all of the elements that will be shown within the
browser window. JavaScript commands can be called from the head
section within elements of the body.

Expressions written in JavaScript can interact with the HTML document's elements and properties. This expression changes the background color of the current document. Similar to Flash, JavaScript uses a dot syntax for references. When targeting the current document, start the expression with `document`, similar to using `_root` in Flash. Follow `document` with a period, and then add the property to change. In this case, the property is `bgColor`, to access the document's background color. Set this property equal to the `newColor` variable that will be passed from the Flash movie. Be sure to end all JavaScript expressions with a semicolon and a closed curly brace (`}`).

L 11-4

```
document.bgColor=newColor;
}
```

Adding the Body Elements

Elements contained within the body tags are displayed in the user's browser. Also, tags and functions can be added to the body opening tag. These tags and functions will be performed when the HTML page is first loaded.

This project only needs to set the background of the HTML page within the body tag. This will ensure that the user sees the correct color when the page is first loaded. The colors can be entered as hex code or as the name of the color, if you are targeting a 4.0 browser or above. Set this document background color to white by entering `white` or the hex value `"#FFFFFF"`.

L 11-5

```
<body bgcolor="#FFFFFF">
```

NOTE

If the background color is not defined, the user's default background color will be displayed.

Adding a Table   Tables within HTML pages allow you to position elements in rows and columns. This helps with the positioning of elements such as images and the text of Flash movies. For this project, you want to center the table horizontally and vertically in the HTML document, as shown in Figure 11-1.

Start with an opening table tag, and then set the properties of the table. Set the width and height of the table to 100% and the vertical alignment equal to `"middle"`. This will center the elements of the HTML document to the vertical center of the browser.

L 11-6

```
<table width=100% height=100% valign="middle">
```

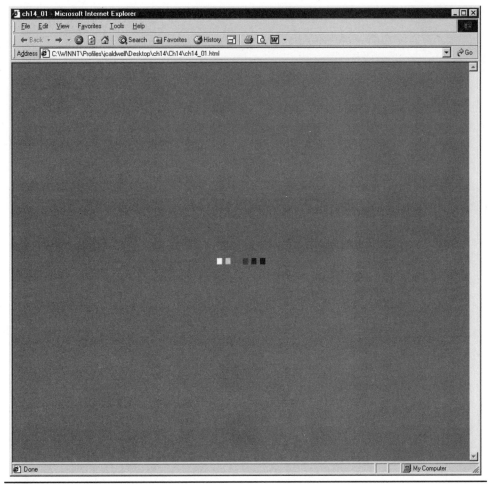

Figure 11-1 *Table positioning*

Once a table is started, you need to start the table row with a tr tag. Each time a new row is started, another tr tag is opened.

L 11-7   `<tr>`

Rows separate the table into horizontal segments, as shown here.

Next, tables are separated into columns, using the td tag. Columns separate a table into vertical segments.

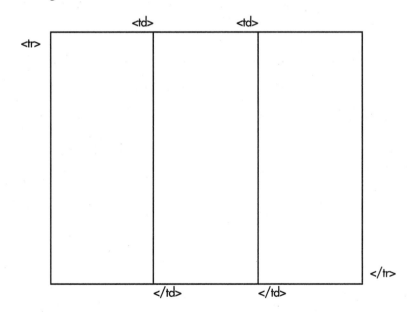

Within the opening td tag, parameters can be set for the column. Set the horizontal alignment equal to `"center"`. This will position the elements within this column to the horizontal center.

L 11-8
```
<td align="center">
```

Inserting the Flash Movie HTML Tags   When inserting a Flash movie into an HTML document, it is necessary to use the object and embed tags to allow the Flash movie to be viewed on the broadest range of browsers.

The object tag inserts the Flash movie for object-based browsers, such as Internet Explorer. The object tag contains parameters that have remained the same since Flash 2, with the exception of the version parameter. When using Flash 5 content, it is important that the version be set equal to 5, 0, 0, 0. The width and height parameters are set within this tag as well. For this project, set the width to 200 and the height to 100.

L 11-9
```
<object classid="clsid:D27CDB6E-AE6D-11cf-96B8-444553540000" codebase=
"http://download.macromedia.com/pub/shockwave/cabs/flash/swflash.cab
#version=5,0,0,0" width=200 height=100>
```

Further parameters can be set for object-based browsers using the param tag. These parameters set the Flash movie to be displayed, the quality of the Flash movie, and whether or not to display the right-click menu. The Flash movie will be named the same as the current HTML document for this project, so set the movie value parameter equal to `"ch11_01.swf"`. Set the quality of the Flash movie to high to ensure that the small lines render properly.

L 11-10
```
<param name=movie value="ch11_01.swf">
<param name=quality value=high>
```

TIP

For processor-intensive projects, setting the quality to medium or low will make the Flash movie run much more smoothly.

The embed tag is used to insert the Flash movie into browsers that do not support the object tag, such as Netscape Navigator. The embed tag sets all of the Flash parameters within the tag. It has not changed since the release of Flash 2.

L 11-11
```
<embed src="ch11_01.swf" quality=high width=200 height=100 type=
"application/x-shockwave-flash" pluginspage="http://www.macromedia.
com/shockwave/download/index.cgi?P1_Prod_Version = ShockwaveFlash">
```

This code can automatically be generated using the Publish feature in Flash. Press CTRL-SHIFT-F12 (COMMAND-SHIFT-F12 for Macs) to open the Publish Settings dialog box; select the HTML tab, as shown in Figure 11-2; and select options from the drop-down menus.

Completing the HTML Document

Check over your HTML document to be sure that there is a close tag after each opening tag. Test the HTML document by opening it in a browser. If there are JavaScript errors in the document, an error message box will pop up. If any HTML tags are missing, a partial HTML tag may be displayed in the browser.

Here is the final HTML document:

L 11-12

```
<html>
<head>
<title>ch11_01</title>
<script>
function bc(newColor){
    document.bgColor=newColor;
}
</script>
</head>
<body bgcolor="#FFFFFF">
<table width=100% height=100% valign="middle">
  <tr>
    <td align="center">
    <object classid="clsid:D27CDB6E-AE6D-11cf-96B8-444553540000"
codebase="http://download.macromedia.com/pub/shockwave/cabs/flash/
swflash.cab#version=5,0,0,0" width=200 height=100>
    <param name=movie value="ch11_01.swf">
    <param name=quality value=high>
    <embed src="ch11_01.swf" quality=high width=200 height=100 type=
"application/x-shockwave-flash" pluginspage="http://www.macromedia.
com/shockwave/download/index.cgi?P1_Prod_Version = ShockwaveFlash">
    </embed>
    </object>
    </td>
  </tr>
</table>
</body>
</html>
```

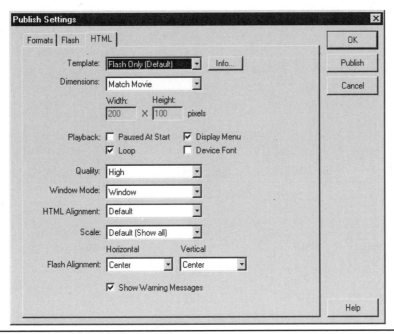

Figure 11-2   *The Publish Settings dialog box*

Building the Flash File for the Background Color Project

ch11_01.fla

Now that the HTML file is complete, it's time to build the Flash file. Start by creating a new Flash movie (CTRL-N/COMMAND-N). Press CTRL-M (COMMAND-M for Macs) to open the Movie Properties dialog box. Set the width of the movie to 200 pixels and the height to 100 pixels, as shown in Figure 11-3. This will match the dimensions set earlier in the HTML document.

TIP

It is a good idea to open the Publish Settings dialog box (CTRL-SHIFT-F12/COMMAND-SHIFT-F12) and uncheck the HTML option. This will ensure that the file does not overwrite the HTML document made in the previous section.

The background color of the Flash movie is not important. This value cannot be changed dynamically, so you need a movie clip on the bottommost layer that will

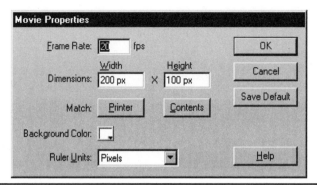

Figure 11-3 *The Movie Properties dialog box*

cover the stage. The colors of this movie clip will change, simulating changing the background color of the Flash movie.

Creating the Bg Movie Clip

Draw a rectangle on the stage with a white fill and without lines. Use the Align panel to set the rectangle to the same width and height as the Flash movie stage. Align the rectangle to the horizontal and vertical center, so that the rectangle completely covers the Flash movie stage.

While the rectangle is selected, press F8 to convert the object into a symbol. Select Movie Clip from the list of options and name the new movie clip **bg**. Open the Instance panel (CTRL-I/COMMAND-I) and type **bg** into the Name text field. This will allow the movie clip to be targeted by ActionScripting.

Creating the Buttons Layer

The buttons layer contains the buttons for changing the background color. Start by creating a square approximately 10 pixels tall by 10 pixels wide. Delete the lines and set the fill color to white. While the square is selected, press F8 to convert the object into a symbol. Select Button from the list of options and name the new symbol **colorButton**.

NOTE

Do not create a rollover state for this button. This button will be used more than once, with a different tint each time. The rollover state would be ignored in this case.

Select the button and open the ActionScript editor (CTRL-ALT-A/COMMAND-OPTION-A). The actions on this button will be performed when the user moves the mouse over the button, using the `on(rollOver)` event handler:

L 11-13
```
on(rollOver){
```

The first action performed when the user's mouse rolls over the button is to set a variable equal to the color object of the bg movie clip. Set the `bgColor` variable equal to `new Color(_root.bg)`.

L 11-14
```
bgColor = new Color(_root.bg);
```

This uses the new object-oriented ActionScripting to set the color of the bg movie clip equal to the `bgColor` variable.

The next action sets the `bgColor` variable to a new color. When the `bgColor` variable is changed, the bg movie clip will change as well. Use the `setRGB()` command found in the Color Object section of the ActionScript editor. This command starts with the variable name (`bgColor`), as other Object actions do. The variable is separated by a period, and contains the argument inside parentheses.

L 11-15
```
bgColor.setRGB(0xFFFFFF);
```

NOTE

When setting a hex value, be sure to include `0x` *before the hex value, such as* `0xFFFFFF`.

Finally, use the `getURL()` command to call the JavaScript function from within Flash. The `getURL()` command performs the same task as the `a href` command in HTML code. The new URL or the JavaScript function to be called is contained within the parentheses. Enter `"javascript:bc('FFFFFF')"` in the URL text field. (It is important to include the hex code color in single quotation marks, or JavaScript will try to read the value as a variable, resulting in a JavaScript error.)

L 11-16
```
getURL("javascript:bc('FFFFFF')");
```

Here is the final code with comments:

L 11-17
```
on (rollOver) {
        // Prepare color object
        bgColor = new Color(_root.bg);
        // Set color of bg movie clip
        bgColor.setRGB(0xFFFFFF);
```

```
// Call JavaScript function to change color of HTML page
getURL("javascript:bc('FFFFFF')");
}
```

Copy and paste the button into place, and move it about 10 to 15 pixels to the right of the previous button. Repeat this six times, each time changing the tint of the button, as shown in Figure 11-4. Change the ActionScript function and JavaScript function to reflect the same color as the new button color, so that when the user rolls the mouse over the button, the background color matches the button color.

Setting HTML Text Field Values

Input text fields in Flash are used to simulate form text fields in regular HTML documents. A problem with using Flash text fields is that JavaScript validation

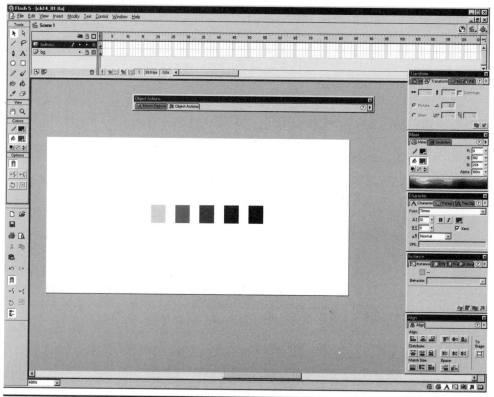

Figure 11-4   *Button placement*

and other JavaScript functions will not work. One solution is to set an HTML input text field equal to the input text field in Flash. The project described here uses Action-Scripting to pass the variable from Flash into a JavaScript function, which then sets the value of an HTML text field.

Creating the HTML Page for the Input Text Field Project

ch11_02.html

As in the background color project described in the previous section, you start by building the HTML page and JavaScript functions. This project uses a similar HTML layout to start with, but adds a form element and a different JavaScript function.

The starting HTML document should resemble this:

L 11-18
```html
<html>
<head>
<title>ch11_02</title>
</head>
<body>
</body>
</html>
```

Creating the JavaScript TextChange Function

The JavaScript function in the head section of the HTML document is contained within script tags, as explained earlier in the "Creating the JavaScript Bc Function" section. For this project, create a function named textChange with textField as the variable that will be passed from within the Flash movie.

L 11-19
```
function textChange(textField) {
```

As explained earlier, expressions written in JavaScript can interact with the HTML document's elements and properties, and JavaScript uses a dot syntax similar to the syntax used in Flash. The expression used here targets the current document (document .) and changes the value of the myText text field in the myForm form (myForm.myText). Set this property equal to the textField variable that will be passed from the Flash movie.

L 11-20
```
document.myForm.myText.value=textField;
}
```

NOTE

Remember to end all JavaScript expressions with a semicolon and a closing curly brace (}).

Adding the Body Elements

Like the previous project, this project only needs to set the background of the HTML page within the body tags, to ensure that correct color appears when the page is first loaded.

L 11-21
```
<body bgcolor="#FFFFFF">
```

The table within the HTML page is also set within the body tags. For this project, place the HTML document in the center, horizontally and vertically. Start by opening the table tag and setting the properties of the table. Set the width of the table equal to 100%. The will allow the table to be the full width of the user's browser window, which is necessary for centering objects in the browser.

L 11-22
```
<table width=100%>
```

Next, start a table row with a tr tag, followed by a td column tag. Set the column's horizontal alignment equal to "center". This will position the elements within this column to the horizontal center.

L 11-23
```
<tr>
<td align="center">
```

The next items within the body tags are the object and embed tags, which allow the Flash movie to be viewed on the broadest range of browsers. This project uses the same settings and parameters as the previous project (with the exception of the movie name), as explained in "Inserting the Flash Movie HTML Tags," earlier in this chapter.

L 11-24
```
<object classid="clsid:D27CDB6E-AE6D-11cf-96B8-444553540000" codebase
="http://download.macromedia.com/pub/shockwave/cabs/flash/swflash.
cab#version=5,0,0,0" width=200 height=100>
<param name=movie value="ch11_02.swf">
<param name=quality value=high>
<embed src="ch11_02.swf" quality=high width=200 height=100 type=
"application/x-shockwave-flash" pluginspage="http://www.macromedia.
com/shockwave/download/index.cgi?P1_Prod_Version = ShockwaveFlash">
```

Inserting the Form Elements   After closing out the column and row of the table cell that holds the Flash movie, create another row and insert a td tag to begin a new column. Set the horizontal alignment for the column equal to `"center"`.

L 11-25

```
<td align="center">
```

Form elements must be contained within a form. Start by inserting an opening form tag. Then name the form so that it can be accessed with JavaScript. Within the form tag, set the name of the form to `"myForm"`.

L 11-26

```
<form name="myForm">
```

Next, add a standard HTML input text field. After the form tag, as with other HTML tags, parameters are included within the opening tag. Set the type equal to `"text"`, the name equal to `"myText"`, and the size equal to 18.

L 11-27

```
<input type="text" name="myText" size=18>
```

Completing the HTML Document

Add closing tags to each of the elements until each contains an opening and closing tag. It is helpful to tab elements so that the opening and closing tags are aligned. This makes it easier to edit and update the file.

Here is the final HTML code:

L 11-28

```
<html>
<head>
<title>ch11_02</title>
<script>
function textChange(textField){
      document.myForm.myText.value=textField;
}
</script>
</head>
<body bgcolor="#FFFFFF">
<table width=100%>
  <tr>
    <td align="center">
    <object classid="clsid:D27CDB6E-AE6D-11cf-96B8-444553540000"
codebase="http://download.macromedia.com/pub/shockwave/cabs/flash/
swflash.cab#version=5,0,0,0" width=200 height=100>
    <param name=movie value="ch11_02.swf">
    <param name=quality value=high>
```

```
        <embed src="ch11_02.swf" quality=high width=200 height=100 type=
"application/x-shockwave-flash" pluginspage="http://www.macromedia.
com/shockwave/download/index.cgi?P1_Prod_Version = ShockwaveFlash">
        </embed>
        </object>
        </td>
    </tr>
    <tr>
        <td align="center">
        <form name="myForm">
        <input type="text" name="myText" size=18>
        </form>
        </td>
    </tr>
</table>
</body>
</html>
```

Building the Flash File for the Input Text Field Project

ch11_02.fla

The Flash file for this project contains the text field. Create a new Flash movie and open the Movie Properties dialog box (CTRL-M/COMMAND-M). Set the width of the movie to 200 pixels and the height to 100 pixels. This will match the dimensions set earlier in the HTML document. Leave the Flash movie background color as white.

Open the Text Options panel and select Input Text from the drop-down menu. This will allow the user to access the text field. Type **textField** into the Variable text field, as shown in Figure 11-5. This will allow the text field to be accessed by ActionScripting.

Include all font outlines as a precaution. If you know the target audience will have one of the specific system fonts, that option could be used. Finally, be sure to include the background and outline, to let the user know where the text field is located.

While the text field is selected, press F8 to convert the object into a symbol. Select Movie Clip from the list of options and name the new movie clip **text_field**. It is not necessary to assign an instance name, because the ActionScript will be targeting itself for this project.

While the text_field movie clip is selected, open the ActionScript editor (CTRL-ALT-A/ COMMAND-OPTION-A). Select the `getUrl()` function from the list of actions. This will automatically insert a clip event for the actions. Change the current clip event to `keyUp`. This will perform the actions every time a key is released after being pressed.

L 11-29   `onClipEvent (keyUp)`

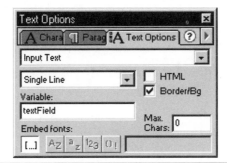

Figure 11-5   *Creating an input text field with the Text Options panel*

The getURL() function looks like this:

L 11-30
```
getURL("javascript:textChange(\"" add textField add "\")");
```

First, enter quotation marks and specify the function name: "javascript: textChange. Then, within a second set of parentheses, start with a backslash to indicate the variable being passed into the JavaScript function is a variable as well. This is followed by a quotation mark, then "add textField add "\")". The add operand indicates that you are adding the following variable to the string to be passed. After the variable name, textField, another add operand appears before the closing forward slash.

Be sure to check the Expression check box to indicate the use of actions within the expression. This is necessary to be able to pass the variable to the JavaScript function.

Here is the final code:

L 11-31
```
onClipEvent (keyUp) {
    // Call JavaScript function to set the HTML text field
    // equal to the Flash text field
    getURL("javascript:textChange(\"" add textField add "\")");
}
```

Creating a JavaScript Pop-Up Window from Flash

JavaScript pop-up windows allow you to open a new HTML document window to a specified size and URL. These windows help present information in a much cleaner and organized manner when used properly. The project described in this section uses

ActionScripting to pass variables from Flash into a JavaScript function, which opens a new pop-up window.

Creating the HTML Page for the Pop-Up Window Project

ch11_03.html

This project uses the same HTML layout as the previous projects described in this chapter, but contains a different JavaScript function:

L 11-32
```
function openWindow(url, winName, w, h) {
```

The function name is `openWindow`, to indicate opening a new window. Within the parentheses, `url`, `winName`, `w`, and `h` indicate the variables that will be passed from within the Flash movie. (Again, after the parentheses, use an opening curly brace to indicate the beginning of a JavaScript expression.)

The expression used in this project opens a new window with a set width and height. When targeting a window, start the expression with `window`. Follow it with a period, and add `open` to indicate opening a new window. Within parentheses, declare the properties for the new window to obtain.

L 11-33
```
window.open(url, winName, "width=" + w + ", height=" + h);
}
```

The first property defines the URL, passed from the `url` variable. Next, the window name is referred to as the `winName` variable. This allows the window to be accessed by JavaScript as needed. The width is read from the `w` variable, and the height is read from the `h` variable. These variables must be set equal to `width` and `height`, respectively.

The body elements are the same as those for the previous projects (with the exception of the value for the movie name). Here is the final HTML document:

L 11-34
```
<html>
<head>
<title>ch11_03</title>
<script>
function openWindow(url, winName, w, h) {
    window.open(url, winName, "width=" + w + ", height=" + h);
}
</script>
</head>
<body bgcolor="#FFFFFF">
```

```
<table width=100% height=100% valign="middle">
  <tr>
    <td align="center">
    <object classid = "clsid:D27CDB6E-AE6D-11cf-96B8-444553540000"
codebase="http://download.macromedia.com/pub/shockwave/cabs/flash/
swflash.cab#version=5,0,0,0" width=200 height=100>
    <param name=movie value="ch11_03.swf">
    <param name=quality value=high>
    <embed src="ch11_03.swf" quality=high width=200 height=100 type=
"application/x-shockwave-flash" pluginspage="http://www.macromedia.
com/shockwave/download/index.cgi?P1_Prod_Version = ShockwaveFlash">
    </embed>
    </object>
    </td>
  </tr>
</table>
</body>
</html>
```

Building the Flash File for the Pop-Up Window Project

ch11_03.fla

The Flash file contains the button for the pop-up window. Start by creating a new Flash movie. Set the width of the movie to 200 pixels and the height to 100 pixels. This will match the dimensions set earlier in the HTML document. Leave the Flash movie background color as white.

Create a static text area on the main stage and type **Pop-up Window**. While the rectangle is selected, press F8 to convert the text into a symbol. Select Button from the list of options and name the new button **popup**. Right-click (CONTROL-click for Macs) the new object and select Edit from the list of options. This will open the button timeline for editing. As explained in Chapter 10, the button timeline consists of four frames for the up, over, and down states, and the hit area of the button.

Now you need to apply ActionScripting to the button so that it will open the pop-up window. For this project, you will apply actions for when the mouse is released. Go to the main timeline and use the Arrow tool to select the pop-up button. Open the ActionScript editor (CTRL-ALT-A/COMMAND-OPTION-A).

When the user presses the mouse button over the pop-up button, and then releases the mouse button while the mouse is still over the pop-up button, the actions should take place. This simulates how most operating system buttons work. Use the on (release) event handler to trigger the action, which is a call to the openWindow function.

L 11-35
```
on (release) {
    // Call JavaScript function to pop up window
    getURL("javaScript:openWindow(
    \"ch11_03.html\", \"newWin\", \"250\", \"150\")\r\n"
    );
}
```

In the URL field of the `getURL()` function, `javaScript:openWindow`
`("ch11_03.html", "newWin", "250", "150")` is specified. Within the
parentheses after the function name, include the variables to be passed. Each variable is
surrounded in quotation marks, to notify the JavaScript function to read the exact data
being sent. The first variable contains the new URL, the second contains the window
name, the third contains the window height, and the last contains the window width.

Moving a Browser Window from Flash

This project uses ActionScripting to pass a variable to JavaScript to move the
document window when a ball is thrown against a wall in Flash. This logic could
be used to move a browser window for added interactivity with games or Web sites.

Creating the HTML Page for the Move Window Project

ch11_04.html

This project uses the same HTML layout as the previous projects described in this
chapter. Again, the difference is the function it uses to accomplish its task.

L 11-36
```
function moveWin(x, y) {
    self.moveBy(x, y);
}
```

The function is named `moveWin` to indicate moving the current browser window.
The variables that will be passed from within the Flash movie are x and y. The
expression moves the current browser window a certain way, depending on which wall
the ball collided with. When targeting the current browser window, start the expression
with `self` (similar to the `this` target in Flash). After the period, `moveBy` indicates
moving a browser window. Within parentheses, declare the properties for the new
window to obtain. The first property defines the amount to move the window along
the X axis, and the second defines the amount to move the window along the Y axis.

The body elements are the same as those for the previous projects (with the exception of the value for the movie name). Here is the final HTML document:

L 11-37
```html
<html>
<head>
<title>ch11_04</title>
<script>
function moveWin(x, y) {
    self.moveBy(x, y);
}
</script>
</head>
<body bgcolor="#FFFFFF">
<table width=100% height=100% valign="middle">
  <tr>
    <td align="center">
    <object classid="clsid:D27CDB6E-AE6D-11cf-96B8-444553540000"
codebase="http://download.macromedia.com/pub/shockwave/cabs/flash/
swflash.cab#version=5,0,0,0" width=600 height=400>
    <param name=movie value="ch11_04.swf">
    <param name=quality value=high>
    <embed src="ch11_04.swf" quality=high width=600 height=400 type=
"application/x-shockwave-flash" pluginspage="http://www.macromedia.
com/shockwave/download/index.cgi?P1_Prod_Version = ShockwaveFlash">
    </embed>
    </object>
    </td>
  </tr>
</table>
</body>
</html>
```

Building the Flash File for the Move Window Project

ch11_04.fla

The Flash movie for this project has two layers: the bounds layer for the boundaries of the movie and the ball layer for the "ball" that will trigger the window movement. Start by creating a new Flash movie. Set the width of the movie to 600 pixels and the height to 400 pixels.

Creating the Bounds Layer

The bounds layer contains an unfilled rectangle to simulate a border and to set the boundaries of the Flash movie. Start by drawing a rectangle without an inner fill. Make sure the stroke is set to hairline in the Stroke panel. This will keep the lines from resizing. While the rectangle is selected, press F8 to convert the rectangle into an object. Select Movie Clip from the list of options and name the movie clip **bounds**. Next, add **bounds** as the name of the movie clip in the Instance panel.

Use the Align panel to set the width and height of the movie clip to the same as the Flash movie by selecting the Align/Distribute to Stage button and clicking Match Width and Height. Next, select Align Horizontal Center, and then Align Vertical Center to center the rectangle on the stage, as shown in Figure 11-6. This rectangle will be used to constrain the ball movie clip, as explained in "Ball ActionScripting," later in this chapter.

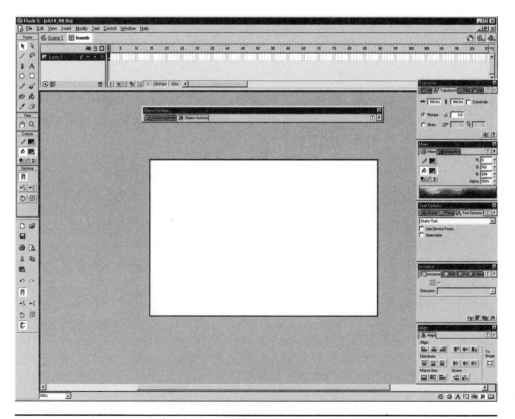

Figure 11-6   *The rectangle for the bounds layer*

Creating the Ball Layer

The ball layer contains the ball button. For this layer, draw a circle approximately 23 pixels wide and 23 pixels tall. Use a gradient fill to give the circle a 3-D look, as shown in Figure 11-7. While the circle is selected, press F8 to convert it into an object. Select Button from the list of options and name the button **ball_button**. Once again, press F8 with the button selected to convert the button into a nested button within a movie clip. Select Movie Clip from the list of options and name the movie **ball**.

Scripting Button On Mouse Press Events

First, actions are added to the button to start the drag operation. This is done by using the startDrag() command.

L 11-38
```
startDrag(this, false, bounds.xMin + size, bounds.yMin + size,
bounds.xMax - size, bounds.yMax - size);
```

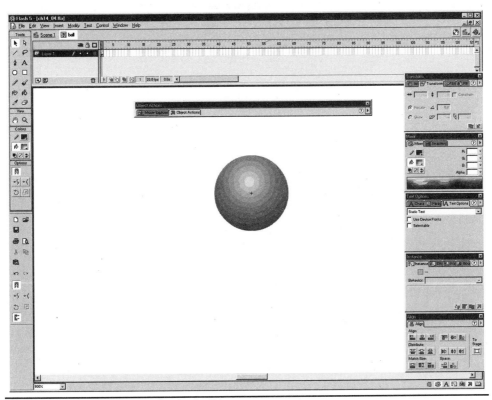

Figure 11-7   *The 3-D circle for the ball layer*

The target text field contains `this` as the target name, using relative targeting (make sure to check the Expression check box) to start the drag operation on the current movie clip. The next parameters are variables for the boundaries. These variables are set from the bounds box, as explained in the next section. Check the Constrain to Rectangle check box to keep the drag operation within specific set boundaries. The boundaries are set as follows:

▶ The left boundary is set equal to the `xMin` variable plus the `size` variable.

▶ The top boundary is set equal to the `yMin` variable plus the `size` variable.

▶ The right boundary is set equal to the `xMax` variable minus the `size` variable.

▶ The bottom boundary is set equal to the `yMax` variable minus the `size` variable.

Next, two variables are updated when the button is pressed. The first is the `drag` variable, which is set to `"true"`. This will be used to determine when the movie clip is being dragged. The next is the `speed` variable, which is set to `1`. This is used to set the speed of the button when thrown, explained in "Ball ActionScripting," later in this chapter.

L 11-39

```
drag = "true";
speed = 1;
```

Here is the final code:

L 11-40

```
on (press) {
    startDrag(
    "", false, bounds.xMin + size, bounds.yMin + size,
    bounds.xMax - size, bounds.yMax - size
    );
    drag = "true";
    speed = 1;
}
```

Scripting Button On Mouse Release Events

When the mouse is released, the first action to be performed is to stop the drag operation. This is done using the `stopDrag()` command. This command does not have any arguments. It stops all drag operations in the Flash movie. Next, the `drag` variable is set to `"false"`. This will be used to determine when the movie clip is released.

L 11-41

```
on (release) {
    stopDrag();
```

```
    drag = "false"; |
}
```

Ball ActionScripting

The ActionScripting contained on the ball movie clip contains all of the actions to throw and bounce the ball. On the main timeline, select the box_clip movie clip and open the ActionScript editor (CTRL-ALT-A/COMMAND-OPTION-A).

Scripting Box On Load Actions

ActionScripting contained within `clipEvent(load)` actions are performed only when the movie clip is first loaded. This is useful for setting global variables. This project uses four global variables: `friction`, `speed`, `bounds`, and `size`.

First set the `friction` variable. This variable determines how much friction the box_clip will have when thrown. The lower the number, the longer the amount of time the box will move. Setting a number above 1 will cause the box to gain speed and never stop. Set the variable to `0.98` to slowly bring the ball to a stop. This resembles friction from a real-life object, such as a pool table.

L 11-42
```
friction = "0.98";
```

Next, set the `speed` variable. This determines how fast the objects will move when first thrown. A higher number will result in a much faster moving object. This variable will be updated when the object is thrown.

L 11-43
```
    speed = 1;
```

The next variable, `bounds`, sets the boundary limits, which it gets from the bounds layer (described earlier in this chapter). This is done by using the new Flash 5 `getBounds()` command. When using the `getBounds()` command, target the movie clip with absolute targeting. The target and command are separated by a period, and then the next argument is in parentheses. This argument declares the target coordinate space, or where the target lies.

L 11-44
```
    bounds = _root.bounds.getBounds(_root);
```

TIP

Using the `getBounds()` command with absolute targeting is much more effective than using actual numbers. If the size of the movie clip changes, just resize the size of the bounds movie clip, and no further changes are necessary.

Finally, set the `size` variable. This variable uses the `getProperty()` command to get the size of the current movie clip, and then divides that value by 2. This will equal the distance from the center of the object to the outer edge. This is necessary in Flash because all objects are placed from the center of the movie clip, not the edge. If it were not divided in half, half of the movie clip would go over the edges of the boundaries. (Because the object is equally wide as it is tall, it is not necessary to get the height and width of this movie clip.)

L 11-45

```
size = getProperty(this, _width) / 2;
```

Here is the final code:

L 11-46

```
onClipEvent (load) {
    // set variables
    friction = "0.98";
    speed = 1;
    bounds = _root.bounds.getBounds(_root);
    size = getProperty(this, _width) / 2;
}
```

Scripting Ball On Mouse Down Actions and On Mouse Up Actions

Actions included in the `clipEvent (mouseDown)` will be updated every time the mouse is pressed. For this project, the timer needs to be addressed to determine what time the mouse was first pressed. The timer built into Flash returns the value in milliseconds. This is not necessary for this project, so divide the results by 1000 to convert it into actual seconds. This variable is named `o_time` to represent the original time.

L 11-47

```
o_time = getTimer() / 1000;
```

Actions included in the `clipEvent (mouseUp)` will be updated every time the mouse is released. When the mouse is released, the timer again needs to be addressed to determine when this happened. This variable is named `n_time` to represent the new time.

L 11-48

```
n_time = getTimer() / 1000;
```

Here is the final code with comments:

L 11-49

```
onClipEvent (mouseDown) {
    // get timer when mouse is pressed
```

```
    o_time = getTimer() / 1000;
}
onClipEvent (mouseUp) {
    // get timer when mouse is released
    n_time = getTimer() / 1000;
}
```

Scripting Ball On Enter Frame Actions

Actions included in `clipEvent (enterFrame)` will be updated every time the frame is accessed. This replaces the old method of adding actions to frames within movie clips, resulting in much more efficient and cleaner coding.

Determining How Fast to Throw the Target   First, determine the time the movie clip was dragged. This is done by subtracting the two time variables described in the preceding section.

L 11-50
```
    time = o_time - n_time;
```

Next, set the `speed` variable to `speed` multiplied by 1.1.

L 11-51
```
    speed = speed * 1.1;
```

This will cause the speed variable to slowly rise. However, as the speed slowly increases, friction acts on the movie clip to slow it down, and the movie clip will slowly come to a stop.

When the ball is stopped, the x and y positions are set equal to `o_x_pos` and `o_y_pos`. This is done by setting `o_x_pos` equal to `x_pos` and `o_y_pos` equal to `y_pos`.

L 11-52
```
    o_x_pos = x_pos;
    o_y_pos = y_pos;
```

Because the `x_pos` and `y_pos` variables are set in the next lines of code, the `o_x_pos` and `o_y_pos` variables will be equal to the last-known position.

Next, set the `x_pos` variable equal to the x position of the current movie clip and the `y_pos` variable equal to the y position of the current movie clip. Use the `setVariable()` command, as follows:

L 11-53
```
    x_pos = this._x;
    y_pos = this._y;
```

This sets the variables to the_x and _y properties of the current movie clip, using expert mode. In normal mode, you can achieve the same result using the getProperty() command.

Determining Whether the Object Is Being Dragged or Thrown   Next, you need to determine whether the movie clip is being dragged or thrown. This is done by using if and else statements.

Start by checking to see whether the drag variable is equal to "true". If the variable is set to true, set the two velocity variables. The x_velocity variable is equal to the x_pos variable minus the o_x_pos variable multiplied by the amount of time the object has been dragged. The y_velocity variable uses the same formula as the x_velocity variable, but with the y positions.

L 11-54

```
if (drag == "true") {
    x_velocity = (x_pos - o_x_pos) * time;
    y_velocity = (y_pos - o_y_pos) * time;
```

NOTE

It is important to use a double equal sign in an if statement. A single equal sign is used to set properties. A double equal sign is used to check properties.

If the drag variable is not equal to true, the code continues to the else commands. In this section, the x_pos variable is set equal to x_pos plus x_velocity divided by the speed variable. This is equal to the x position of the object, used for the next section of scripting. The y_pos variable uses the same logic as the x_pos variable, but with the y positions.

L 11-55

```
} else {
    x_pos = x_pos + (x_velocity / speed);
    y_pos = y_pos + (y_velocity / speed);
```

Keeping the Ball Inside the Boundaries   Next, to keep the movie clip from bouncing outside the boundaries, use if and else if statements to determine whether the movie clip touches or tries to move outside the boundaries. First, check to see whether x_pos minus the size variable is less than or equal to the xMin boundary. This will be the case if the ball movie clip is touching or overlapping the left edge of the bounds movie clip. If it is, the x_pos variable is set equal to the xMin variable plus the size variable.

L 11-56

```
if (x_pos - size <= bounds.xMin) {
    x_pos = bounds.xMin + size;
```

Following this, the x_velocity variable is set equal to negative x_velocity multiplied by friction.

L 11-57
```
x_velocity = -x_velocity * friction;
```

This will cause the x_velocity variable to reverse its current value. The object will bounce off the boundary, and the friction variable will slow down the object.

Then the y_velocity variable is set equal to y_velocity multiplied by friction.

L 11-58
```
y_velocity = y_velocity * friction;
```

This will keep the object moving in the same direction, but applies the friction variable to slow down the object.

Next, use the getURL() function to call the JavaScript moveWin function.

L 11-59
```
getURL("javascript:moveWin(-10, 0)");
```

The -10, 0 in parentheses will move the browser 10 pixels to the left when the ball hits the left boundary.

Next is an else if command. Using the same techniques, check to see whether the ball movie clip is touching or overlapping the right edge of the bounds movie clip. If it is, set the x_pos, x_velocity, and y_velocity variables and use the getURL() function, as in the preceding if command.

L 11-60
```
} else if (x_pos + size >= bounds.xMax) {
    x_pos = bounds.xMax - size;
    x_velocity = -x_velocity * friction;
    y_velocity = y_velocity * friction;
    getURL("javascript:moveWin(10, 0)");
```

The next else if command once again uses the same techniques to check whether the ball movie clip is touching or overlapping the top edge of the bounds movie clip and, if it is, bounce it back.

L 11-61
```
} else if (y_pos - size <= bounds.yMin) {
    y_pos = bounds.yMin + size;
    x_velocity = x_velocity * friction;
    y_velocity = -y_velocity * friction;
    getURL("javascript:moveWin(0, -10)");
```

Finally, check to see whether the ball movie clip is touching or overlapping the bottom edge of the bounds movie clip, and move it back if it is.

L 11-62

```
} else if (y_pos + size >= bounds.yMax) {
    y_pos = bounds.yMax - size;
    x_velocity = x_velocity * friction;
    y_velocity = -y_velocity * friction;
    getURL("javascript:moveWin(0, 10)");
```

Setting the Position   The final thing to do is set the x and y positions of the current movie clip equal to x_pos and y_pos variables, respectively. Use the set Variable() command and set this._x equal to the x_pos variable. Use the same method for the y_pos variable.

L 11-63

```
this._x = x_pos;
this._y = y_pos;
```

Putting the Script Together   Here is the final code with comments:

L 11-64

```
onClipEvent (enterFrame) {
//Determine variable values
    time = o_time - n_time;
    speed = speed * 1.1;
    o_x_pos = x_pos;
    o_y_pos = y_pos;
    x_pos = this._x;
    y_pos = this._y;
//Determine if the ball is being dragged
    if (drag == "true") {
        x_velocity = (x_pos - o_x_pos) * time;
        y_velocity = (y_pos - o_y_pos) * time;
    } else {
//Move ball
        x_pos = x_pos + (x_velocity / speed);
        y_pos = y_pos + (y_velocity / speed);
//Reverse ball, and call JavaScript
        if (x_pos - size <= bounds.xMin) {
            x_pos = bounds.xMin + size;
            x_velocity = -x_velocity * friction;
            y_velocity = y_velocity * friction;
            getURL("javascript:moveWin(-10, 0)");
        } else if (x_pos + size >= bounds.xMax) {
```

```
        x_pos = bounds.xMax - size;
        x_velocity = -x_velocity * friction;
        y_velocity = y_velocity * friction;
        getURL("javascript:moveWin(10, 0)");
    } else if (y_pos - size <= bounds.yMin) {
        y_pos = bounds.yMin + size;
        x_velocity = x_velocity * friction;
        y_velocity = -y_velocity * friction;
        getURL("javascript:moveWin(0, -10)");
    } else if (y_pos + size >= bounds.yMax) {
        y_pos = bounds.yMax - size;
        x_velocity = x_velocity * friction;
        y_velocity = -y_velocity * friction;
        getURL("javascript:moveWin(0, 10)");
    }
    this._x = x_pos;
    this._y = y_pos;
    }
}
```

What to Take Away from This Chapter

This chapter focused on passing variables from ActionScripting into JavaScript functions to allow further interactivity with the browser or with elements within the browser. While the main focus of this book is Flash, JavaScript can definitely aid in building Web sites. The most useful and commonly used example in this chapter is the JavaScript pop-up window. The use of new windows can help display large amounts of content in Flash-based navigational systems.

CHAPTER 2

Corporate Intro Movie

IN THIS CHAPTER:

▶ Create Flash motion graphics

▶ Design Web-capable media

▶ Simulate effects commonly generated by video-editing software

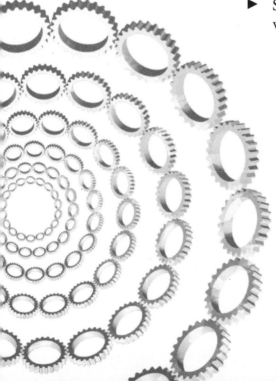

The main focus of this book has been taking advantage of Flash's versatile ActionScript capabilities. Although ActionScripting allows Flash designers to incorporate interaction into their movies, motion design is the most well-known feature of Flash.

Some of the earliest Flash sites set the standards for all the sites to come. An example is the well-known gabocorp.com site. This site used Flash's motion-design capabilities to deliver a powerful site, which helped make Flash such a popular design tool. The designer used the current version of Flash at the time, Flash 3.

As the project described in this chapter demonstrates, adding motion effects can bring a Web site to life. This chapter uses common Flash animation techniques to develop an introductory movie for a corporate site. The project in particular is a "coming soon" intro to www.innovativefx.com, a site that focuses on Flash design and motion. Although the specific steps that I went through for this intro were unique to the project, the basic principles could apply to an intro for any site.

Designing an Intro

Before even opening Flash, you should have developed a concept, or style, to be used for the intro. After you've come up with an idea, you're ready to build the intro using Flash's capabilities. While you're working in Flash, you need to consider ways to improve the speed at which your intro downloads to viewers' computers.

Developing Your Concept

Determining the target audience is vital to designing any intro. When designing a site that will be visited mainly by other Flash designers, you can optimize the site for faster computers and use the latest trends in design. Other sites need to be geared toward the general public, including users with slower computers.

Finding the median between the use of Flash features and the computer requirements for viewing the site can make a site more successful among a wider range of viewers. You'll need to decide whether it's more important to use advanced design techniques or to make your site available to more viewers. Much research may be required to determine your target audience, which varies depending on the site content. Also, your market can change over short time periods, even months. See Chapter 1 for a more in-depth discussion of considerations when designing Flash sites.

Once the concept of the site is established, building the content in Flash is the next step. When you're working on client projects, it is important to follow the storyboard, so that you do not stray from the original concept. For your personal projects, you have much more creative freedom.

Finding Inspiration

Developing a concept for your intro can prove to be the most time-consuming and tedious part of the design process. While different things inspire different people, there are some approaches to inspiration that work for many of us.

Try to conceive of your ideas in a mood-setting environment. For example, if you are designing an intro for a flower company, which would be expected to use beautiful, soft tones, you might find inspiration by sitting in a flower garden and studying the surroundings. If you are planning an intro for a skateboard company, you might visit a loud skate park.

Surrounding yourself with content that will be used in the intro can also serve as an aid when trying to focus. Write down the words you will use for the intro on pieces of paper and attach them to your wall or desk. Laying out pictures or graphics you might use can help as well. This will allow your creativity to feed off the content available in your surroundings.

Write down each of your ideas to see what it looks like on paper. Draw some plans for the screen design. Be prepared to throw away many of your initial ideas, but usually one or two will stand out. This creative process can take longer for some projects than others. Once you have become a more seasoned designer, ideas will begin to come more naturally. Concepts that you have considered in the past may be suitable for future projects. Most experienced designers and programmers develop a library of elements that may be used in many projects with minor adjustments.

During the process of actually building the content in Flash, your ideas will slowly come together, and your design will probably change also. Many designers have produced their greatest work by accident. Early sketches evolve into masterpieces, as elements tend to flow together more smoothly after the initial design process.

Optimizing Movie Streaming

As a designer, you want to keep your file sizes as small as possible while achieving your design goals. One way to optimize an entire Flash movie is by reusing symbols. This way, the user will not need to download repetitive symbols. The result is smaller file sizes.

Even when you are dealing with big file sizes, such as the intro project described in this chapter, you can take some steps to optimize streaming. The Innovative FX Flash intro is too large to stream on a standard 56Kbps modem. However, it is still a good idea to reserve some of the beginning for smaller animations, such as text effects or a logo fading in. When Flash is downloading to a user's cache, it loads from frame 1 until the ending frame, loading each scene before moving to the next. Introduce larger bitmaps or complex animations later, so the user does not need to wait for them to download before even seeing the beginning of the intro.

A helpful Flash tool for optimizing and tweaking the streaming of an intro is the Bandwidth Profiler, shown in Figure 12-1. This tool shows where spikes in the timeline lie.

While in Flash, press CTRL-ENTER (COMMAND-RETURN for Macs) to preview your Flash movie with the player built into Flash. Press CTRL-B (COMMAND-B for

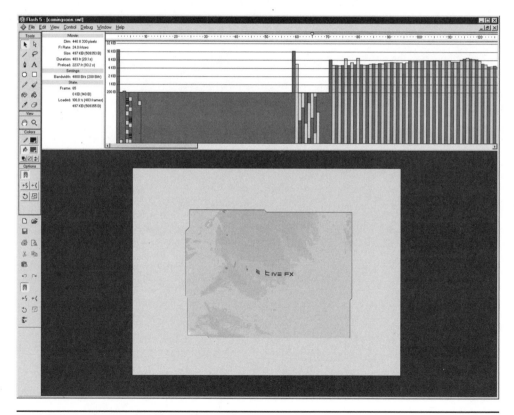

Figure 12-1   *The Bandwidth Profiler in Flash*

Macs) to display the Bandwidth Profiler. While the movie is playing, an indicator will show which frame you are currently seeing. Watch for spikes in the graph that indicate where a large download would occur. Then return to your main Flash-editing environment and try to optimize the frames that contained spikes. While it is virtually impossible to completely eliminate these spikes, you can definitely make some improvements.

It can be difficult to gauge the streaming effects on your computer if your computer is faster than the average computer, and it seems that most designers have above-average computers. I designed the intro project described in this chapter on a fast system with a Pentium 4 processor, but I checked it for speed consistency on a system powered by a Pentium 2 processor. That was sufficient, because the target audience of this site would not be running a slow computer.

Building the Intro

comingsoon.fla

The project described in this chapter is an intro for the Innovative FX site, shown in Figure 12-2. The movie is a "coming soon" preview for the future version of the site. Although the new version of the site is several months away, the title and theme have already been established, so these elements have been incorporated in the intro.

Creating the Background Layer

Start by creating a new Flash movie set to 440 pixels wide by 330 pixels tall. Create a layer labeled **bg**. As you probably guessed, this layer will always reside toward the bottom of the Flash movie.

Next, using the Rectangle tool, draw a rectangle on the stage and resize it to the same dimensions as the Flash movie. While the rectangle is selected, press F8 to convert the rectangle into a symbol, so that it can be reused throughout the Flash movie. Select Graphic from the list of options and assign the graphic a unique name, such as **bg**. This will help distinguish the symbol from others in the Flash Library.

This graphic will determine the background color of the Flash movie. When you want the background color to change, use the Effect panel, shown in Figure 12-3, to change the tint of the bg graphic, as in Figure 12-4. Reusing this symbol throughout the intro will help keep the file size down, because the user will not need to download repetitive symbols.

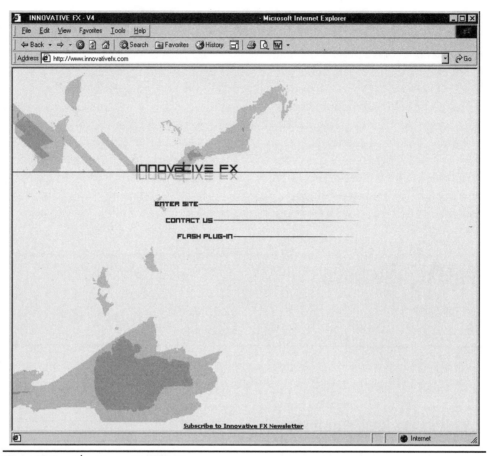

Figure 12-2 *The Innovative FX site*

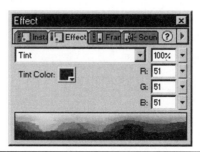

Figure 12-3 *Changing the tint with the Effect panel*

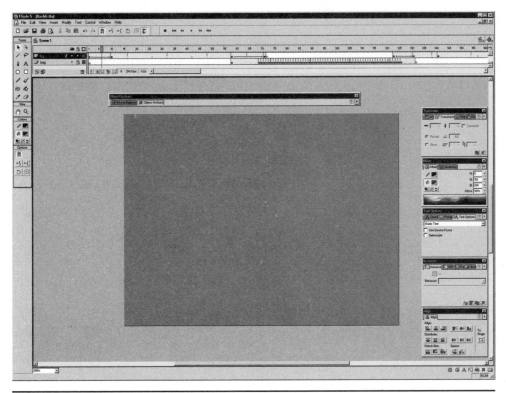

Figure 12-4   *Tinting the bg movie clip*

Adding the Innovative FX Layer

Back on the main timeline, the Innovative FX layer contains the text "Innovative FX." Create this text using the Text tool, and then convert it into a graphic symbol by pressing F8 while the text is selected.

Next, the text animates on the screen with a flickering effect, like on a broken television. In the earlier of the two frames, use the Rotation tool to skew and distort the look and size of the graphic symbol. When previewed, it will appear as if the graphic is distorted, and then regains its original size and position. This frame runs for 55 frames, during which the text "exits" the screen, as explained in the next section.

Creating the Letter Layers

The next 12 layers contain individual letters of "Innovative FX." Instead of bringing the text off the screen the same way it came on, I decided to change the effect. This section covers how to make the text fly off the edge of the stage and fade away.

Copy the Innovative FX layer graphic and paste it onto a layer named **i**. Press CTRL-B (COMMAND-B for Macs) to break the symbol and text apart, so that each letter is its own graphic symbol. Then cut and paste each letter so that it lies on its own layer, labeling each layer the same as the letter it contains.

To animate the letters, they must first be converted into symbols. Select one letter and press F8 to convert it into a symbol. Select Graphic from the list of options and assign it a unique name matching the letter. Repeat this process for each letter. When you get to the third letter, you cannot name it *n*, because a symbol with that name already exists, so name it **n2**. Use the same naming scheme for the second *i* and *v*.

After you convert the letters into symbols, you can animate them. Create two additional keyframes after the first frame. Drag the last frame on each layer over about five frames, flip the letter, and drag it to the top left of the stage. Using the Effect panel, set the Alpha of the symbols to 0 in the end, so they appear to fade away when animated. Stagger the frames, so that the text appears to flow off the stage.

Using Video in a Flash Movie

Once the text flows off the screen, a raster animation fades in. Although it may look like a bitmap animation created in a 3-D modeling program (such as 3D Studio Max), this animation, shown in Figure 12-5, was actually shot with a digital camera with video capabilities. Using camera effects and adding further effects in Adobe Photoshop helped enhance the appearance of the animation.

> ### *NOTE*
> *The image used for the bag layer is actually a plastic bag. I got the idea while watching a plastic bag being blown around by the wind. Later, I recorded the bag in the wind using a Sony Mavica CD1000 digital camera. Using effects such as negative art during the shoot allowed the colors to stand out. Later, during the editing process, I used effects and standard filters in Adobe Photoshop to make the bag more interesting.*

If you want to use a piece of video for an image, you need to extract still-frame images from the video, because Flash cannot import video files. The most commonly

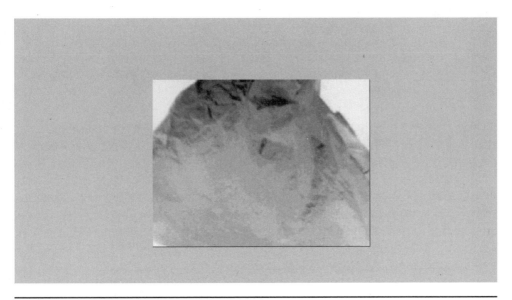

Figure 12-5   *A frame from my raster animation*

used software for this is Adobe Premiere, but it is an expensive package, costing well over $1,000. An alternative is to use VideoMach, which is available for download from gromada.com. This software lets you import many video files, including MPEG, and costs less than $50.

Start by opening the video file that you plan to use for your project in VideoMach. Once the file is imported, you can use the scrub marker to scrub through the frames of the video. *Scrubbing* simply means dragging the slider to display the video frame by frame.

When choosing the file output to be used for the selection, keep in mind where the files will be used for the project. VideoMach can export audio and video files. This project needs to use only the video features, because the intro will have its own sound loop. Select the directory to save the files in, and then select the output format for the files. Using .png files allows you to use alpha transparencies, as well as to set the level of compression for the images within Flash, depending on the target audience. For broadband markets or CD-ROM projects, PNG/lossless compression works quite well. JPG/lossy compression is usually better suited for standard Web projects.

NOTE

Lossless compression allows you present the image at its highest quality. Lossy compression allows you to lower the file size of the image, but the image will lose quality. Finding a setting that suits your project may be best determined by using trial and error, adjusting the settings higher or lower each time, until the desired output is achieved.

In VideoMach's Video tab of the File Settings dialog box, shown in Figure 12-6, rescale the files to the resolution of the Flash movie, 440 by 330 pixels. Also, change the frame rate to 24fps to match the frames per second of the Flash movie. Selecting lower frame rates will result in fewer files output, and make the video run much faster. Selecting higher frame rates will result in more files, making the video run slower. Finally, click the Start Process button to export all of the frames for the video. How long it takes to process the video depends on how many frames it has and the size of the movie. After the files are extracted, use a raster-editing program such as Adobe Photoshop to apply any effects and clean up the images.

Creating the Bag Layer

Navigate back to the Flash authoring environment and create a new layer labeled **bag**. Place a keyframe on frame 57 of the timeline and press CTRL-R (COMMAND-R for Macs) to import the sequence. Select only the first bitmap that needs to be imported and click Open. Flash will tell you that the images appear to be in a sequence and ask if you want to import them in a sequence. Click OK to import all of the images in the sequence at once. Flash will put each image in order on a frame of its own. This saves you the trouble of aligning and reorganizing all of the graphics again.

One common problem when importing graphics this way is that they are not aligned to the stage. If you press CTRL-1 (COMMAND-1 for Macs) to align the stage to the center of the screen before importing, Flash will align the images properly. Otherwise, if you've already imported the files, or if you need to resize or move the entire sequence, you can use Flash's Edit Multiple Frames feature. This feature (whose button is located below the timeline) enables you to select objects across many frames and modify them together. This will ensure that the files align and are scaled evenly.

Creating the Arrow Layers

While the moving bag with the added effects is interesting, something else is needed to enhance the motion. To complement the right-to-left movement of the bag, I added

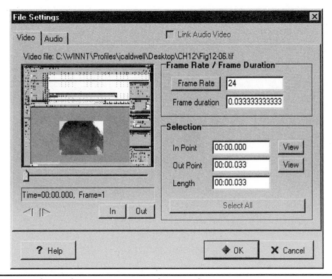

Figure 12-6   *Setting the video output in VideoMach*

arrows to the Flash movie. I created three different arrows in Adobe Photoshop, each one more blurred than the last, to represent different speeds.

Most video-editing software automatically adds motion blur to fast-moving objects to give them a faster appearance than possible with just a regular image. Flash does not do this, because it is a vector-based program. To add this motion blur, you need to create it in a raster-editing program. For example, in Photoshop, you can apply motion blur by selecting Filter | Blur | Motion Blur. Try adjusting the amount of blur to give each arrow a different appearance. Export the image as a transparent .png file so that it will not have any background color.

Once the images are imported into Flash, convert them into graphic symbols by selecting each one in turn and pressing F8. This allows you to use motion tweening, as well as to reuse the symbols, which will reduce the file size.

Create six layers labeled **arrow 1** through **arrow 6**. Add one symbol to each layer, so that you have two copies of each arrow. Now tween the symbol from the right side of the screen to the left. Be sure to use different speeds and different sizes for each arrow. Position each element until the arrows seem to flow smoothly with the bag animation, as shown in Figure 12-7. Getting this how you want it will require much trial and error (it took me nearly two hours).

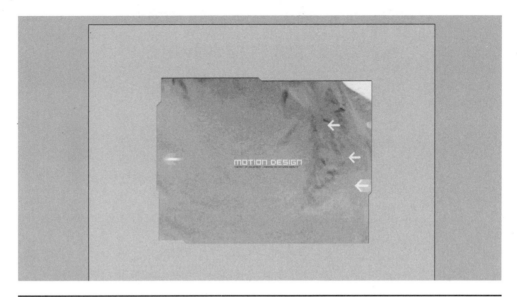

Figure 12-7 *Adding the arrows*

Adding the "Motion Design" Text

After all of the arrows are synchronized with the movement of the bag, the project looks interesting, but it still does not have any useful information. It's time to add some text. Because this is a "coming-soon" intro for the future version of Innovative FX, the text needs to indicate what the next version of the site will contain. Rather than using cliché terms such as "the best in design" or "the new dimension," this project needs something simple yet effective. The phrase that fits is "motion design," because that is the focus of the new version.

Most Flash designers know that Flash seems to "choke" when animating text, especially when many other things are going on. The solution is to add a new layer for only the text, with just a simple keyframe. Create an additional layer to hold the text animation. As was done to create the arrow graphics, create the text (**motion design**) and blur effect in a raster-based program like Photoshop, and then import the image into Flash as a transparent .png file.

Select the text image and press F8 to convert it into a symbol. Select Graphic from the list of options. Use a motion tween from right to left again to move the graphic across the screen. The keyframe containing the standard text should be timed for when the blurred arrow reaches the middle of the screen. Where you want to move the text back off the screen, use more Photoshop blurred text in a sequence to slowly "dissolve" the text away.

TIP

By producing many of your special effects in an image-editing program like Adobe Photoshop, you reduce the CPU processing required to render images in Flash. However, you do need to be careful not to overload the movie with too many bitmap animations at once, or they will run very slow, which would defeat the purpose of using the bitmap animations.

Opening the Next Section

You may have noticed while watching movies and videos that each scene or section contains certain effects that somehow provide a transition into the next one. The most common transition form used in movies is the fade effect. While this effect is fine for long movies, it can be a bit boring for a fast-paced intro. For this project, the transitions should not be so abrupt that they look unnatural, but they should flow with the pace of the movie.

The next section of the Flash intro transitions by opening the new color over the plastic bag. The bg graphic symbol is reused for this portion of the Flash movie, to keep the file smaller.

Resize the bg graphic to the full height of the Flash movie and half of the width. When two copies are placed side by side, you can then swipe them away from the center to give an "opening" appearance. Repeat this three times, to transition from the blue bag, to white, and then to two different shades of gray. This gray color is then used throughout the next section.

Adding the "Prepare Your Mind" Text

Established with version 3 of Innovative FX, "Prepare Your Mind" has become somewhat of a company tagline, so it is appropriate to include it in this intro. Like the "motion design" text, this text is created as a blurred Photoshop graphic.

However, it is blurred to look like the letters are coming toward the viewer instead of across the screen.

Use the same technique of *not* animating the text in Flash to avoid slowing down the playback of the Flash movie. Each word was animated from smaller to larger, using Photoshop effects to make the words look like they are moving faster. Using many Flash alpha or tint effects can hinder the smoothness of the playback.

NOTE

Alpha effects are the most processor-intensive effects in Flash. Tinting weighs in next on CPU usage, while brightness effects use the least amount of resources. In general, it is best to resist the temptation to use many Flash effects for a Flash intro.

Adding the Transition to the "Innovative FX V 5" Section

For the transition to the next section of the Flash movie, it is important to avoid using the same exact effects; otherwise, the Flash movie can become boring and seem very repetitive.

The next section slides black rectangles over the gray rectangles from right to left, using a simple tween animation. One of the blurred arrows follows the black animation across the screen, and completely off to the left. Directly behind this, the bg graphic is used again to reveal a masked image of the bag graphic. Once it reaches the far left, it opens further to reveal more of the image, only to be closed again after "Innovative FX V 5" appears on the screen, as shown in Figure 12-8. Immediately afterward, this text exits the screen and unveils "Coming Soon," which explains the reason for the Flash intro.

The movement of the mask and text takes some time to coordinate. If it is not done correctly, it can look very bad. Try studying the movement of one object, and make the next object accompany the original object's movements.

NOTE

It is not uncommon to spend several hours to prepare several seconds of animated motion, and it may seem like tedious and unforgiving work.

Adding the Transition to the Information Section

At this point, the intro's effects look good and flow smoothly, but the intro still has not shown much useful content. The next section gives a few comments about the

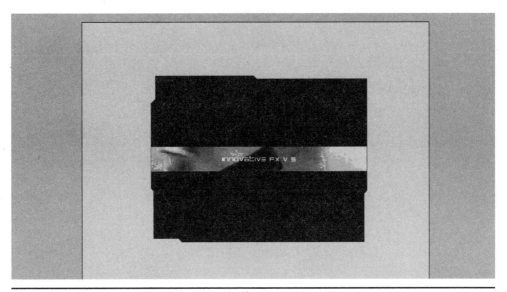

Figure 12-8   *The closing mask*

upcoming site, teasing the viewers so they want to see the site. This type of teaser can entice your audience to come back, but it needs to be followed up with the site you promised!

The information section again reuses the bg graphic, but this time stacked on top of itself three times and converted to a single graphic. This helps keep the number of frames on the main timeline to a manageable amount. At this point, you've already made so many frames that you need to resize and scroll the timeline to see all of them.

The new graphic symbol containing the three bg graphics slides onto the stage from the bottom to split the screen into two colors. This draws the audience's attention to the break in the screen, where the text will lie. Once the graphic stops, the text appears on the stage, without any animation. Again, this keeps the text animation from choking the user's system and causing improper playback.

After a pause, each section scrolls off the screen to reveal the next color break and new text, as shown in Figure 12-9, each time using the same resource-saving techniques. The transition to the next scene happens by scrolling the three colors back off the bottom of the stage.

Figure 12-9 *Revealing more text content*

Adding the Transition to the Follow-Up Section

The follow-up section of the intro was made to quickly "wrap" up the intro, preparing for the ending. The transition to this section needs to be eye-catching, so that viewers do not get bored due to the amount of time they have already spent watching the intro. This is accomplished by using a transition that you do not commonly see in other Flash intros.

In typical Flash intros, you will see a lot of straight and 45-degree angle lines, but not many curved lines. For a unique effect, the transition to the follow-up section has a "flexed" line spring onto the stage.

Flash offers two different types of tweening: motion and shape. The most commonly used type is motion tweening. Shape tweening actually morphs the shape of an object to animate it.

Draw a simple line across the stage and use the Modify menu to convert the line into a shape. (Using shape tweening on lines will not produce the desired effects.) Add an additional keyframe several frames down the timeline and navigate back to the first frame with the line. While the line is not selected, use the Arrow tool to drag the center of the line toward the bottom of the stage.

Rather than the whole line moving, it flexes to form a curved line. Now add a shape tween between the lines to see the line "spring" together. Next, add another keyframe several frames down the timeline after the last frame containing the line. Navigate back to the previous keyframe and again flex the line, this time toward the top of the stage, but not nearly as far as the downward curve.

Add a shape tween between the frames to animate the movement, and then preview the animation. Notice that now the line springs straight, as if it were a string pulled tight quickly, as shown in Figure 12-10.

Create two additional layers above these to contain another line. Draw a line across the stage and convert it into a graphic symbol. Reuse the same line in each frame (again, to reduce the file size). Place the lines so that they overlap each other and lie directly over the lines previously shape tweened. Tween the lines so they "open" the screen slightly to reveal a masked image.

An animated mask reveals the masked image. The mask needs to be resized to match the movement of the lines, so that it appears as if the lines open the screen to show the image. Create a keyframe where the lines are closed together, and create another keyframe when the lines stop. Resize the mask to match the position of the lines. Finally, add a motion tween to expand the mask.

This project also uses four images that were made in Photoshop. Using alpha tweens, these images appear to morph and slowly fade into each other. Drag each layer containing these images below the mask layer, so that they are masked as well. This will ensure that they all are sized and displayed the same way. The section ends with the mask closing back up, and moving the lines to the left of the screen.

Figure 12-10   *Animating a curved line*

Adding the Transition to the Final Section

The final section of the intro contains the Innovative FX logo, along with a contact link and newsletter subscription link. These items follow the same flow of the intro by blurring across the screen and halting to a stop. This process, used throughout the intro, requires careful coordination. You'll probably find that it takes more time to synchronize the animation so that it runs smoothly than it does to create the graphics to use in the animation.

Adding Sound

Most Flash intros use either a sound loop that continues throughout the intro or a sound stream. This project calls for a sound loop, but it also needs to fade the sound down near the end of the intro. Rather than using simple sound editing to set the volume lower or stop the sound loop, it is better to use the Flash Sound object to control the volume depending on the frame.

The Sound object is new with Flash 5 ActionScripting. This object allows you to pull sounds from the Flash library and assign them to a variable. The variable can then be modified to affect the volume, panning, or even where to loop the sound. Using the Sound object ensures that the sound will fade in and out properly, even on slower computers. (See Chapter 13 for details on using the Sound object.)

Importing the Sound

Start by importing a sound loop into Flash. Open the Flash Library and right-click (CONTROL-click for Macs) the sound loop that you want to use in the intro. In the menu that appears, click Linkage. This allows you to assign a linkage identifier to the sound loop so that it can be loaded into the Flash movie, without being dragged onto the frame. Select the Export This Symbol radio button and type **loop** in the Identifier text box, as shown in Figure 12-11.

Navigate to the main timeline and create a new layer labeled **music_clip**. Next, create a blank movie clip by pressing CTRL-F8 (COMMAND-F8 for Macs). Then navigate back to the main timeline and drag an instance of the blank movie clip you just created. In the blank movie clip, you can add ActionScript event handlers to perform further actions. These are scripts that run as long as the movie clip is on the stage.

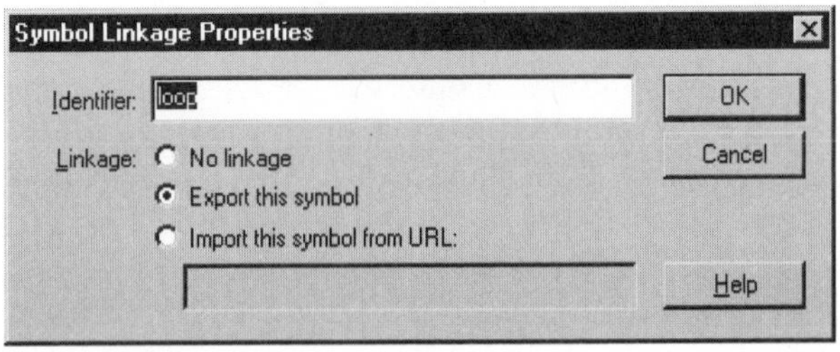

Figure 12-11   *Linking a sound*

Music Clip Scripting

When assigning event handlers to movie clips, the actions can react differently, depending on the event used. The first bit of code for this project needs to take place only when the movie clip is first loaded, so it is handled by the `load` event.

L 12-1
```
onClipEvent (load) {
}
```

Within the `load` procedure, set up the initial variables. The Sound object uses variables to determine the volume of the sound. First, set `i` to `10`, which will be the starting percentage of volume when the movie clip first introduces the music clip.

L 12-2
```
i = 10;
```

To attach a sound to a variable, assign a variable such as `s` to `new Sound(this)`. This specifies that the sound will be attached to this movie clip. When the movie clip or `s` variable on this movie clip is modified, the sound will be affected.

L 12-3
```
s = new Sound(this);
```

Next, the sound needs to be pulled from the Library and assigned to the `s` variable. Do this by using the `attachSound()` command. Preceding the command, type the variable name, followed by a period. Inside the parentheses of the command, enter one argument, enclosed in quotation marks. This argument is the name you typed earlier in the Identifier field when you exported the symbol.

L 12-4
```
s.attachSound("loop");
```

The only thing that needs to be affected for this intro is the volume, so that it fades in and fades back out at the end. Adjust the volume by using the setVolume() command. Again type the sound variable (s) before the command, followed by a period. Set the volume to the i variable by typing the variable name as the argument inside the parentheses.

L 12-5

```
s.setVolume(i);
```

The final command executed in the load event handler starts the music loop. Use the same programming style as before by typing the sound variable name, followed by a period. Next, use the start() command to initialize the music loop. Set two parameters inside the parentheses: where to start the music loop, in this case 0 (the beginning), and how many times to loop the music. Be sure to set this limit high enough to last throughout the intro.

L 12-6

```
s.start(0, 25);
```

After these variables are initialized, some actions need to take place continuously throughout the intro. These actions are placed within the enterFrame event procedure. They will continue to cycle as long as the movie clip exists within the Flash movie.

L 12-7

```
onClipEvent (enterFrame) {
}
```

An if-else if statement is used to start fading the music up when it reaches one frame and start fading the music down once it reaches another frame. When the conditions are met within the if or else if statement, the actions located between the following curly braces take place.

L 12-8

```
if () {
} else if () {
}
```

Within the if statement parentheses, two conditions are checked. The first determines whether the current frame of the intro is less than 76. This is where the sound should level out and stop increasing in volume. The second condition determines whether the i variable is less than 90, so the sound will not be too loud. These conditions are separated by the & operand, so that both conditions must be met before the actions within the curly braces take place.

L 12-9
```
if (_root._currentframe < 76 & i <= 90) {
}
```

Once the conditions within the if statement are met, the volume fades in. Set the i variable to i plus 10, so the sound is increased by 10 each frame. Next, use the setVolume() command to set the volume equal to the i variable.

L 12-10
```
i = i + 10;
s.setVolume(i);
```

Within the else if statement parentheses, two conditions are checked. The first condition determines whether the current frame of the intro is greater than or equal to 462. This is where the sound should start decreasing in volume. The second condition determines whether the i variable is greater than or equal to 10, so the sound does not completely fade away. These conditions are separated by the & operand, so that both conditions must be met.

L 12-11
```
else if (_root._currentframe >= 462 & i >= 10) {
}
```

Once the conditions within the else if statement are met, the volume fades out. Set the i variable to i minus 2, so the sound decreases by 2 each frame. Next, use the setVolume() command to set the volume equal to the i variable.

L 12-12
```
i = i - 2;
s.setVolume(i);
```

Here is the final music script with comments:

L 12-13
```
onClipEvent (load) {
    i = 10;
    // Create Sound object
    s = new Sound(this);
    // Attach sound from Library
    s.attachSound("loop");
    // Set initial volume to 10%
    s.setVolume(i);
    // Start sound loop
    s.start(0, 25);
}
```

```
onClipEvent (enterFrame) {
    if (_root._currentframe < 76 & i <= 90) {
        i = i + 10;
        s.setVolume(i);
    } else if (_root._currentframe >= 462 & i >= 10) {
        i = i - 2;
        s.setVolume(i);
    }
}
```

Optimizing the Intro

Once the entire intro is complete, it's time to optimize the movie. Press CTRL-L (COMMAND-L for Macs) to open the Flash Library. Go through each image file and optimize it individually, so that the graphics look good but do not waste file space. The blurred bitmaps can be optimized more, because the distortion will not show as much. Also, optimize the music loop. The MP3 compression (added with the release of Flash 4) is usually the best compression to use, because it provides great quality.

Once this is complete, you can test your Flash movie, use the Bandwidth Profiler to optimize the intro (as described in "Optimizing Movie Streaming," earlier in this chapter), and prepare your preloader.

What to Take Away from This Chapter

After reading this chapter, you should see how I used my thoughts and ideas to create powerful Flash content and understand some of the considerations necessary when building an intro for a corporate Web site. Every person needs time to find their creative style and put it to use. Using what others teach, you can do what you never imagined possible in Flash.

CHAPTER 3

Sound Object

IN THIS CHAPTER:

► Create 3-D surround sound effects with the Sound object

► Use the Sound object with dynamic content

► Attach Sound files directly from the Flash Library

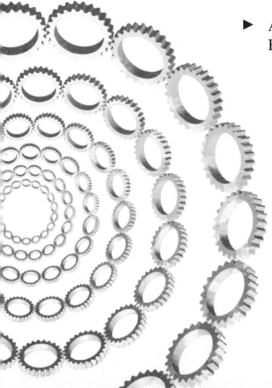

Flash allows you to import sound files and use the Sound editor inside Flash to modify the volume and panning of a sound file. Flash 4 introduced streaming sounds and MP3 compression. These features boosted the use and capabilities of sounds tremendously. Flash 5 has introduced even more sound features and supports more file types (such as importing MP3 files, as you learned in Chapter 2). The most valuable addition to Flash 5 is the inclusion of the Sound object.

The Sound object allows you to assign a sound to a variable and a movie clip. The movie clip is basically a holder for the sound, so that it can be included in the Flash movie. The variable assigned to the sound can be modified and accessed through the Sound object functions.

This chapter describes two projects. The first project uses the Sound object to help create a more realistic demonstration of a static Flash intro. The second project goes a step further to demonstrate how the Sound object can work with dynamic content to provide interactivity with users.

Using a Static Sound Object

ch13_01.fla

The first project for this chapter focuses on moving a movie clip with tweening to change the volume and panning of a sound. The result is that the volume and panning change to match an image's position. The image in this particular project is a 3-D airplane.

Using the Sound object, you can actually "see" where the sound is going to be; therefore, you can control a sound's features on the frame exactly as intended. This is much better than using the Sound editor built into Flash, which does not provide as much control.

Start by creating a new Flash movie and setting the stage dimensions to 640 pixels wide by 480 pixels tall.

Building the Plane Layer

This project uses a plane rendered from a 3-D program. You can build and animate 3-D models in any 3-D package and render them to raster-image sequences.

NOTE

For Web-based projects, bitmaps are not the best choice, because they make the files too large. Ideally, Web-based projects use as many vectors as possible to reduce file size. However, this project was not intended for the Web, but rather for a CD-ROM demo, so I was able to use better-looking raster graphics.

Sound Editor Synchronization Problems

The Sound editor, shown here, allows you to adjust the properties of a sound effect by using a separate sound timeline. Some more complex animations may play slower on other computers and make the sound run out of sync. Just the opposite can happen with less complex animations: faster computers may play the animation faster than the sound plays. The only option previously available was to use streaming audio compression within Flash. Basically, this forces the animation to "drop" frames to keep up with the audio. This method keeps the sound in sync, but can look very choppy on slower computers.

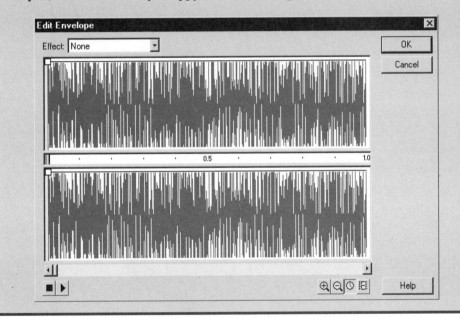

Importing the Images

Exporting the 3-D model as a raster-image sequence saves each individual frame as a new image and names the images in order, such as plane0001.png, plane0002.png, plane0003.png, and so on. When the images are saved in a numbered sequence like this, you can import all of them into Flash at once. Press CTRL-R (COMMAND-R for Macs) to import graphics into Flash. Navigate to the directory where the files are stored and double-click the first image in the sequence. Flash will prompt you that the files appear to be in a sequence and ask whether you want to import all of the files from the sequence. Choose Yes to import each image onto each frame in consecutive order.

NOTE

I usually use .png files when working with Flash, because they allow alpha channels.

The most common problem designers run into when importing sequences is the alignment of the images. If the stage is not centered on the screen when the images are imported, they will hang off to the side. Also, you may need to resize the images to fit the screen. The easiest solution is to use the Edit Multiple Keyframes mode. Pressing the fourth button from the left, below the Flash timeline, activates this feature. When activated, you can select all of the images from each frame and resize and move them at the same time, as shown in Figure 13-1.

Animating the Plane

Once the files are in place, press ENTER (RETURN for Macs) to preview the animation, and see whether there are any unnecessary frames that can be removed. In this plane

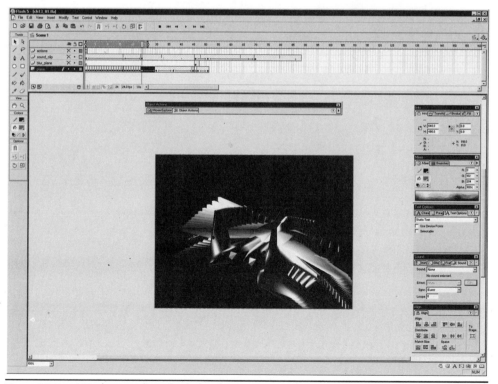

Figure 13-1 *Working with multiple keyframes*

animation, I removed several frames that did not change much and used tweens instead, as illustrated in the timeline shown here. This will reduce the final file size and decrease system resource usage.

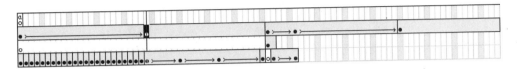

Frame 25 is the end of the initial "fly-in" of the plane. Each frame that follows, up to frame 46, uses the same graphic to simulate the plane hovering. While the graphic is selected, press F8 to convert it into a symbol and select Graphic from the list of options. The next few frames use basic motion tweens to move the plane.

After the plane hovers, it flies off the screen. Add a blank keyframe to frame 46 by pressing F7 while the frame is selected. This frame will contain another graphic on the next layer, as explained in the next section. Frame 47 contains the same symbol used in frames 24 through 45. It is tweened to a smaller size and tinted to black on frame 51. This simulates the plane flying off into the darkness.

TIP

When fading objects away, it is best to use brightness or tint where possible. Alpha fades drastically increase the amount of CPU usage it takes to display the final Flash movie.

Adding the Blur_plane Layer

The blur_plane layer contains one graphic that is used to help make the plane appear to take off faster. The image comes from the same graphic used from frames 24 through 51. Open the graphic in a raster-editing program, such as Adobe Photoshop, and apply the program's motion blur filter. For example, in Photoshop, select Filter | Blur | Motion Blur. Turn the direction to the same direction that the plane is traveling, and increase the amount of blur until the plane is just blurred to the point that it is hard to decipher what it is. Using the Save for Web option, save the image as a transparent .png file, and then import it into Flash.

Place the graphic on frame 46, and add another frame to frame 47 so that the graphic is displayed for the duration of the two frames. Position the graphic so that it is directly over the plane graphic in frame 47. Press ENTER to preview the animation, and notice how the plane seems to look much faster when flying off the screen, as shown in Figure 13-2.

Figure 13-2   *The blurred plane*

Constructing the Sound Clip Layer

The sound clip layer contains the movie clip with scripting used to load and control the Sound object for this project. Start by creating a square approximately 100 pixels by 100 pixels, using a color that is easily distinguished from the other colors used in the movie. This movie clip will later be made invisible, so how it looks is not important.

While the square is selected, press F8 to convert it into a symbol. Select Movie Clip from the list of options and name it **sound_clip**. This movie clip will be used to load the sound and manipulate its volume and pan.

Before writing any script for the sounds, import a sound loop from your computer by pressing CTRL-R (COMMAND-R for Macs). Flash 5 lets you import many types of sound files, such as WAV, MP3, and AIF files. After the sound file is imported, it will be displayed in the Flash Library. Press CTRL-L (COMMAND-L for Macs) to open the Library and right-click (CONTROL-click for Macs) the sound that you want to use. Select Linkage from the list of options that appears and click the Export This Symbol radio button. Type **sound** in the Identifier text field, so that the sound can be later accessed from ActionScripting, as shown in Figure 13-3.

Sound Clip Scripting

The Sound object scripting options are located in the Object section of the ActionScript editor, as shown in Figure 13-4.

As explained in previous chapters, movie clips use event procedures to perform ActionScript functions at different times and after certain actions. The `load` procedure

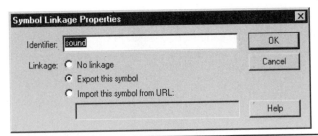

Figure 13-3   *The Symbol Linkage Properties dialog box*

initializes the script only when the movie clip is first loaded. This procedure is useful for initially loading variables and preparing objects.

Figure 13-4   *Scripting options for Sound objects*

Preparing the Sound Object   The first thing that needs to take place when the movie clip loads is to determine a variable to use for the new sound. Set the s variable equal to new Sound(this) to initialize the Sound object.

L 13-1
```
onClipEvent (load)
    s = new Sound(this)
```

This sets the s variable on the sound_clip movie clip as a new sound.

Attaching the Sound   Next, a new movie clip needs to be attached from the Library, using the attachSound() command. This actually attaches the sound as an instance in Flash, so it can be modified and accessed using ActionScript functions. Before the opening period, specify the variable name to assign the sound to—in this case, s. Inside the parentheses, enter the name of the identifier for the sound file in quotation marks ("sound", for this example) to access the exported sound.

L 13-2
```
    s.attachSound("sound")
```

Setting the Sound Volume and Pan   You can set the sound volume by using the setVolume() command. The value within the parentheses can be hard-coded as a numeric value between 0 (muted) up to 100. Also, you can use variables or expressions to obtain an integer. This example uses this._xscale to set the volume equal to the x scale of the current movie clip.

L 13-3
```
    s.setVolume(this._xscale)
```

When the movie clip is resized, the volume will adjust accordingly.

Use the setPan() command to set the pan of the sound to an integer or to an expression that results in an integer. For this project, use the expression this._x / 3.2 - 100 within the parentheses.

L 13-4
```
    s.setPan(this._x / 3.2 - 100)
```

The stage was set to 640 pixels wide for this project; therefore, this expression divides the x position of the current movie clip by 3.2 and then subtracts 100. This will result in the far left of the stage being equal to –100 and the far right of the stage being equal to 100. The center would be equal to 0, which is the center balance of the sound. When the object is moved to the left, the sound pans to the left as well.

Starting and Looping the Sound   The final action that takes place when the clip is loaded is to initialize the sound using the start() command. As with the other sound commands, the variable is placed before the period to determine which sound to start. The `start()` command takes two arguments within the parentheses, separated by a comma:

▶ The first argument determines the second offset of the sound. For example, if you want the sound to start at the tenth second when first initialized, use 10 for the first argument.

▶ The second argument determines how many times to loop the sound. Be sure to set this high enough so that it does not run out before the Flash movie ends—otherwise the sound will abruptly end during the move.

For this project, use 0 for the second offset and 999 for looping.

L 13-5
```
s.start(0, 999)
```

Reinitializing the Sound Volume and Pan   The `enterFrame` procedure initializes the script for every frame, as long as the object is on the stage. This procedure is useful for actions that need to take place continuously throughout the movie. For this project, the `setVolume()` and `setPan()` commands must be reinitialized throughout the movie, so that the volume and pan change with the movement of the object.

L 13-6
```
onClipEvent (enterFrame)
    s.setVolume(this._xscale)
    s.setPan(this._x / 3.2 - 100)
```

Putting the Script Together   Here is the final Sound object code with comments:

L 13-7
```
onClipEvent (load) {
    // Prepare new Sound object
    s = new Sound(this);
    // Attach sound from Library
    s.attachSound("sound");
    // Set sound volume
    s.setVolume(this._xscale);
    // Set sound pan
    s.setPan(this._x / 3.2 - 100);
    // Start sound and loop 999 times
    s.start(0, 999);
}
onClipEvent (enterFrame) {
    // Set sound volume depending on scale of sound_clip movie clip
```

```
        s.setVolume(this._xscale);
        // Set sound pan depending on x position of sound_clip movie clip
        s.setPan(this._x / 3.2 - 100);
}
```

Animating the Sound_clip

Once the code for the sound_clip movie clip is finished, you can reposition the movie clip anywhere on the stage, and the sound will adjust accordingly. Animate the sound_clip as follows:

1. On the first frame, scale the movie clip down to less than 10 percent and move it off to the right of the stage.

2. Add a keyframe at frame 24, where the plane hovers in place. Resize the movie clip to 100 percent and move it directly over the rear of the plane, as shown in Figure 13-5.

3. Add a keyframe on frame 46.

4. Add a keyframe on frame 51. Scale the movie clip down to less than 10 percent again, and move it over the rear of the plane.

5. Add a keyframe on frame 70. Scale the movie down as small as possible.

Figure 13-5   *Resizing and placing the sound clip*

Add motion tweens to frames 1, 46, and 51 by right-clicking (CONTROL-clicking for Macs) the frames and selecting Create Motion Tween. Adjust the image as needed so that the movie clip follows the movements of the plane. This results in the sound panning from left to right with the plane, and decreasing as the plane flies away.

Creating the Actions Layer

As mentioned in earlier chapters, it is always a good habit to add an actions layer to every Flash movie. This allows you to add basic ActionScript commands and easily locate them during future editing.

The only action needed for this project is to hide the sound_clip movie clip. Setting the visibility with scripting allows you to "see" where the sound would be inside Flash, but hides the movie clip when it is previewed or viewed as a .swf file, as shown in Figure 13-6.

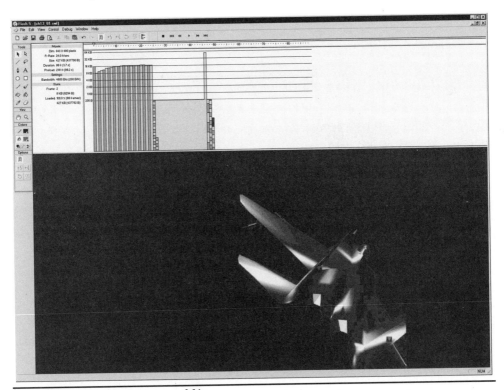

Figure 13-6   *Previewing an .swf file*

In expert mode, you can hide the sound clip as follows:

L 13-8
```
sound_clip._visible = 0
```

In normal mode, use the `setProperty()` command:

L 13-9
```
setProperty(sound_clip, _visible, 0)
```

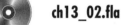

Using a Dynamic Sound Object

ch13_02.fla

The second project for this chapter uses similar techniques to allow for dynamic updating of the Sound object. This project captures the user's arrow keypresses and flies the plane accordingly. The sound is then adjusted, depending on the plane's position and distance. Start by creating a new Flash movie and setting the stage dimensions to 640 pixels wide by 480 pixels tall.

Building the Interactive Plane Layer

The plane layer contains a movie clip with a 3-D plane that rolls from the left to the right. This plane will later become interactive, allowing users to move it with the arrow keys on the keyboard.

The plane layer also contains the bulk of the code for this project. The plane resides on this layer, along with all of the ActionScripting to control the Sound object. It is similar to the plane layer used in the first project discussed in this chapter.

Importing the 3-D Plane

For this project, a 3-D plane was modeled in a 3-D package, and then animated along nine frames. The first frame has the plane positioned so that it is viewed from the rear while rolling left. On frame 5, the plane is positioned so that it is again viewed from the rear, but is level with the ground. On frame 9, the plane is positioned so that it is once again viewed from the rear, but this time rolling to the right. When the video is played, the plane rolls from the left to the right, while being level on frame 5.

Export the 3-D files as a raster-image sequence (with each individual frame as a new raster .png file, named consecutively). Inside Flash, press CTRL-F8 (COMMAND-F8 for Macs) to create a new symbol. Select Movie Clip from the list of options and name it **plane**. This will automatically bring you to the movie clip's timeline. Press CTRL-R (COMMAND-R for Macs) to import images into Flash. Navigate to the directory that contains the rendered .png files and double-click the first one in the sequence. When prompted, select Yes to import each image onto each frame in consecutive order, as shown in Figure 13-7. As noted earlier in the chapter, turn on Edit Multiple Keyframes mode, so that you can select all of the images from each frame and resize and move them at the same time.

Next, import a sound loop (CTRL-R/COMMAND-R). Then open the Library and right-click (CONTROL-click for Macs) the sound that you want to use. Select Linkage from the list of options, and then select the Export This Symbol radio button. Type **sound** in the Identifier text field, so that the sound can be accessed from ActionScripting.

Adding Plane ActionScripting

Navigate back to the main Flash timeline for this project and drag an instance of the plane movie clip onto the stage. Use the Align panel to align the plane to the vertical and horizontal center of the stage, so that the plane will start out centered, as shown in Figure 13-8. Finally, open the Instance panel (CTRL-I/COMMAND-I), and type **plane** in the Name field. Then open the ActionScript editor (CTRL-ALT-A/COMMAND-OPTION-A) .

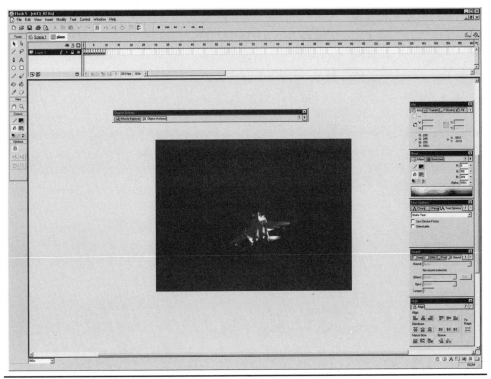

Figure 13-7 *The imported plane*

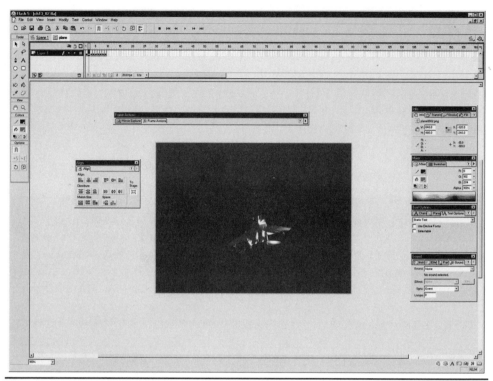

Figure 13-8 *Aligning the plane*

Scripting On Clip Event Load Actions   When the movie clip is first loaded, the movie clip must go to frame 5, which contains the plane graphic that is level with the ground, as shown in Figure 13-9. Use a standard `gotoAndStop()` command, with 5 as the argument within the parentheses.

L 13-10   `gotoAndStop(5);`

This will have the movie clip go to frame 5 when it is first loaded.

Set `i` (the integer variable) equal to 5, the same as the current frame.

L 13-11   `i = 5`

You could go one step further by setting `i` equal to `_currentframe` as well.

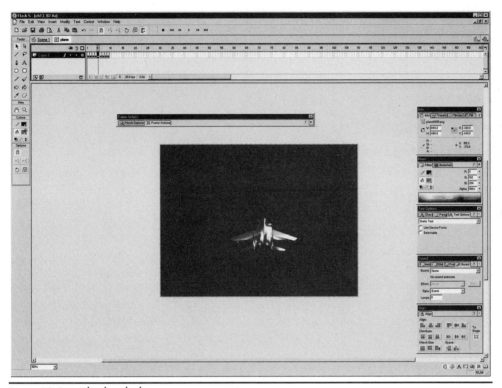

Figure 13-9   *The level plane*

NOTE

Most programmers use i as a variable when working with integers. It is not a rule, but more of a common practice. Doing so makes it easier for other scripters to understand your scripting logic.

Another variable that will be used in this project is `turn`. This variable determines whether the plane is turning or not. The variable is later updated when the user presses a key on the keyboard.

L 13-12   `turn = "false";`

The rest of the load procedures are the same as those used in the previous project (described in "Sound Clip Scripting," earlier in this chapter), to set the s variable as a new sound, attach the new movie clip, set the volume and pan, and finally start and loop the sound.

L 13-13
```
s = new Sound(this);
s.attachSound("sound");
s.start(0, 999);
}
```

Scripting On Clip Event Enter Frame Actions

Also as in the previous project, the setVolume() and setPan() commands must be reinitialized throughout the movie, so that they change with the movement of the object. The first commands within the enterFrame procedure are as follows:

L 13-14
```
s.setVolume(this._xscale)
s.setPan(this._x / 3.2 - 100)
```

The i variable is updated when the plane is moved on the screen. The current frame of the movie clip is determined by the user's key input. As the variable changes, the current frame does as well. Use a gotoandStop() command again, but use i as the argument here.

L 13-15
```
gotoAndStop(i);
```

Next, the plane checks to see whether the plane needs to turn. The turn variable is updated with ActionScripting, as described in "Building the Invis_button Layer," later this chapter. If it is equal to false, the plane needs to slowly turn back until it is level. Add a statement to check whether i is greater or less than 5. If it is less, increase it by 1 until it reaches 5, by using i = i + 1. Just the opposite is done if i is greater than 5. The i variable is decreased by 1 until it reaches 5 by using i = i - 1.

L 13-16
```
if (turn == "false" & i < 5) {
    i = i + 1;
} else if (turn == "false" & i > 5) {
    i = i - 1;
}
```

Scripting On Clip Event Key Up and Key Down Actions

This script also uses keyDown and keyUp event procedures. When the user presses any key, the turn variable is set to true. When the user releases the key, the variable is changed to false. This variable is then read by the earlier enterFrame events.

```
L 13-17    onClipEvent (keyDown) {
               turn = "true";
           }
           onClipEvent (keyUp) {
               turn = "false";
           }
```

Putting the Script Together

The following is the final code with comments:

```
L 13-18    onClipEvent (load) {
               // Tell movie clip to go to frame 5 and stop
               gotoAndStop(5);
               // Set initial i variable
               i = 5;
               // Set turn variable to false to indicate the plane is not turning
               turn = "false";
               // Initialize new Sound object
               s = new Sound(this);
               // Attach sound from Library
               s.attachSound("sound");
               // Start sound and loop 999 times
               s.start(0, 999);
           }
           onClipEvent (enterFrame) {
               // Set sound volume equal to the x scale of this movie clip
               s.setVolume(this._xscale);
               // Set sound pan depending on this movie clip's x position
               s.setPan(this._x / 3.2 - 100);
               // Tell movie clip to go to frame number equal to i
               gotoAndStop(i);
               // if plane is not turning, tell movie clip to go back to frame 5
               if (turn == "false" & i < 5) {
                   i = i + s1;
               } else if (turn == "false" & i > 5) {
                   i = i - 1;
               }
           }
           onClipEvent (keyDown) {
               // When any key is pressed, the turn variable is set to true
               turn = "true";
```

```
}
onClipEvent (keyUp) {
    // When any key is released, the turn variable is set to false
    turn = "false";
}
```

Building the Invis_button Layer

In the previous scripting, the user's keypress was captured to set the `turn` variable. Event procedures allow you to capture when a key is pressed or released, but not to determine which key is pressed. The solution is to use an invisible button to capture the keypresses.

Start by creating a new layer and drawing a simple object. Its appearance is not important, because it will not be displayed in the final movie. While the graphic is selected, press F8 to convert it into a new symbol. Select Button from the list of options and name it **invis_button**.

Double-click the symbol to use the Edit-in-Place feature. Buttons made in Flash use four frames: up, over, down, and hit. Drag the first frame containing the graphic to the fourth frame, as in Figure 13-10. This will make the hit area the size of the graphic, but will be a semi-transparent green color on the main stage. When previewed or viewed as a .swf file, the button will not be visible at all.

Back on the main stage, select the button and open the ActionScript editor (CTRL-ALT-A/COMMAND-OPTION-A). You need to assign actions to the up, down, left, and right arrow keypresses.

Scripting Up Arrow Keypress Actions

When the user presses the up arrow key, the plane flies away. Decreasing the scale of the object simulates this. First, check to see whether the plane's x scale is greater than 10. Doing so will keep the plane from being resized to nothing, and then resized back up. If the plane's x scale is greater than 10, set the plane's x scale equal to the plane's x scale minus 10. Then set the plane's y scale equal to the x scale, so that it scales equally.

L 13-19
```
on (keyPress "<Up>") {
    if (plane._xscale > 10) {
        plane._xscale = plane._xscale - 10;
        plane._yscale = plane._xscale;
    }
}
```

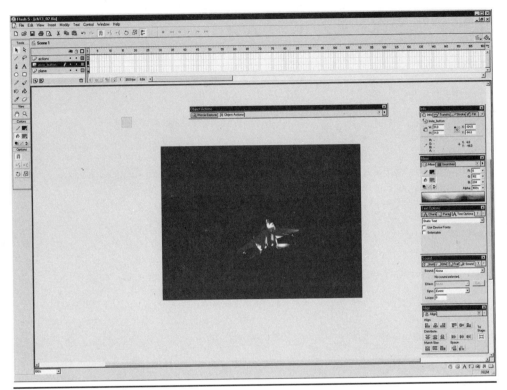

Figure 13-10   *invis_button*

Scripting Down Arrow Keypress Actions

When the user presses the down arrow key, the plane flies closer. Increasing the scale of the object simulates this. First, check to see whether the plane's x scale is less than 100. Doing so will keep the plane from being resized so large that is slows down performance. If the plane's x scale is less than 100, set the plane's x scale equal to the plane's x scale plus 10. Then set the plane's y scale equal to the x scale, so that it scales equally.

L 13-20

```
on (keyPress "<Down>") {
    if (plane._xscale < 100) {
        plane._xscale = plane._xscale + 10;
        plane._yscale = plane._xscale;
    }
}
```

Scripting Left Arrow Keypress Actions

When the user presses the left arrow key, two things are checked:

▶ First, check to see whether the i variable on the plane movie clip is greater than 0. This keeps the i variable from going too low.

▶ Also, check to see whether the plane's x position is greater than 0, so that the plane does not move completely off the screen.

If both statements are true, set the i variable on the plane movie clip equal to the i variable minus 1. This will have the plane slowly roll to the left.

L 13-21
```
on (keyPress "<Left>") {
    if (plane.i > 0 & plane._x > 0) {
        plane.i = plane.i - 1;
    }
```

The next if statement checks to see whether the i variable on the plane movie clip is less than 1. This will mean that the plane is already rolling, so now you can start turning the plane. The next statement checks to see whether the plane's x position is greater than 0, so that it does not move completely off the screen. If both statement are true, set the plane's x position equal to the plane's x position minus 10. This will slowly move the plane to the left.

L 13-22
```
    if (plane.i <= 1 & plane._x > 0) {
        plane._x = plane._x - 10;
    }
}
```

Scripting Right Arrow Keypress Actions

The right arrow keypress actions are similar to the left arrow keypress actions. When the user presses the right arrow key, first check whether the i variable on the plane movie clip is less than 10. This keeps the i variable from rising too high. Also, check whether the plane's x position is less than 640, the screen's right border, so that it does not move completely off the screen. If both statements are true, set the i variable on the plane movie clip equal to the i variable plus 1. This will have the plane slowly roll to the right.

L 13-23
```
on (keyPress "<Right>") {
    if (plane.i < 10 & plane._x < 640) {
        plane.i = plane.i + 1;
    }
```

The next `if` statement checks to see whether the `i` variable on the plane movie clip is greater than 1. If this is true, you can start turning the plane. Then check whether the plane's x position is less than 640. If both statements are true, set the plane's x position equal to the plane's x position plus 10. This will slowly move the plane to the right.

L 13-24
```
if (plane.i >= 9 & plane._x < 640) {
      plane._x = plane._x + 10;
   }
}
```

Putting the Script Together

Here is the final code with comments:

L 13-25
```
on (keyPress "<Up>") {
    // When Up key is pressed, scale the plane smaller to simulate
    // flying away
    if (plane._xscale > 10) {
        plane._xscale = plane._xscale - 10;
        plane._yscale = plane._xscale;
    }
}
on (keyPress "<Down>") {
    // When Down key is pressed, scale the plane larger to simulate
    // flying closer
    if (plane._xscale < 100) {
        plane._xscale = plane._xscale + 10;
        plane._yscale = plane._xscale;
    }
}
on (keyPress "<Left>") {
    // When Left key is pressed, sway plane to left, then move left
    if (plane.i > 0 & plane._x > 0) {
        plane.i = plane.i - 1;
    }
    if (plane.i <= 1 & plane._x > 0) {
        plane._x = plane._x - 10;
    }
}
on (keyPress "<Right>") {
    // When Right key is pressed, sway plane to right, then move right
    if (plane.i < 10 & plane._x < 640) {
```

```
        plane.i = plane.i + 1;
    }
    if (plane.i >= 9 & plane._x < 640) {
        plane._x = plane._x + 10;
    }
}
```

Adding the Actions Layer

In every chapter of this book, I emphasize adding as much of the scripting as possible to movie clips. However, I still use an actions layer on all of my Flash projects to perform some of the basic actions, such as the `stop()` command.

The final thing to do for this frame action is to add the `stop()` command. While this is not actually necessary for this project, it's a good habit to add the `stop()` command to keyframes that should stop the movie. Reinforcing controls for timeline playing will prepare the Flash movie for future additions of scenes or frames, while saving designers the effort of double-checking how the keyframes will stop or play.

What to Take Away from This Chapter

This chapter used the Sound object to demonstrate the plane's position in relation to the screen. The Sound object can be used for many things, including fading in and out of music, or even just to start music for a Flash intro. The ability to do these simple tasks brought Flash 5's sound capabilities to a much higher level, so it is now much easier to control.

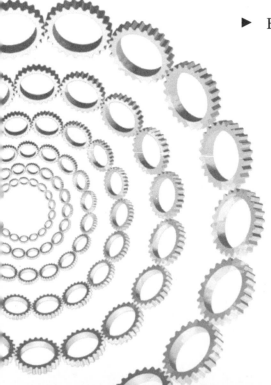

Flying Through Time

IN THIS CHAPTER:

▶ Create an intro that dynamically incorporates the current date

▶ Use ActionScript animations

▶ Build a clock using the Date object

A long with its other new features, Flash 5 includes the Date object, which allows you to read the system clock of a computer. The project described in this chapter uses the Date object to display a "flying through time" intro, based on variables read from the Date object. The Flash movie consists of several keyframes that play the current animation, and then trigger the next keyframe to start when completed. The animation displays the current year and then narrows down the time by months, days, and finally the actual time. Start by creating a new Flash movie and setting the stage dimensions to 600 pixels wide by 400 pixels tall.

Constructing the Date_object_clip Layer
ch14_01.fla

Creating a separate movie clip to hold the Date object variable will make it easier to later debug and modify the code. Each portion of the Date object—such as the month, date, and year—can be set as a unique variable, which can be called from other movie clips or frames in the Flash movie.

Start by creating a new movie clip (CTRL-F8/COMMAND-F8). Select Movie Clip from the list of options and type **date_object_layer** in the text field. Navigate back to the main timeline and drag an instance of the movie clip from the Library onto the stage. In the Instance panel (CTRL-I/COMMAND-I), enter **date_object_layer** in the text field, so that the movie clip can be targeted by ActionScripting.

Preparing the Date Object

Several variables need to be set for the Date object in the `enterFrame` event handler. First, set a variable for the new Date object. This variable will be the full output of the date. Set the variable `myDate` equal to `new Date()`.

L 14-1
```
myDate = new Date();
```

The `myDate` variable displays the full Date object variable. This project needs to read each portion—the year, month, day, hour, minute, and second—separately, so each must be extracted. Extract the year by setting the `year` variable equal to `myDate.getFullYear()`.

L 14-2
```
year = myDate.getFullYear()
```

This will display a four-digit year for the `year` variable.

As with many other ActionScript outputs, the month is output as numbers, starting with January equal to 0, February equal to 1, and so on. To correspond with the normal calendar system, set `month` equal to `myDate.getMonth() + 1`.

L 14-3
```
month = myDate.getMonth() + 1
```

This makes January equal to 1, February equal to 2, and so on.

Next, determine the date of the month. You must set the variable to something other than `date`, or it will not function properly, because `date` is reserved for the Date object. I set it to `dates`.

L 14-4
```
dates = myDate.getDate()
```

The time is also read from the Date object. To extract the hour, minute, and seconds, set each variable accordingly, such as `hour` equal to `myDate.getHours()`.

L 14-5
```
hour = myDate.getHours();
minute = myDate.getMinutes();
second = myDate.getSeconds();
```

The day of the week is output as an integer of 0 through 6, with Sunday equal to 0, Monday equal to 1, and so on. Set `day` equal to `myDate.getDay()`.

L 14-6
```
day = myDate.getDay()
```

This project also dynamically builds a calendar, as explained in "Building the Clock," later in this chapter. To build a calendar that will always work for any month or any year, you need to know when the first of the month is. Set `first` equal to `new Date(year, month - 1, 1)`.

L 14-7
```
first = new Date(year, month - 1, 1)
```

By using `month - 1`, you ensure that the months will output the same as the `month` variable set earlier.

When building the calendar, it is also important to find out what day of the week is the first one in the month. Do this by setting `firstDay` equal to `first.getDay()`.

L 14-8
```
firstDay = first.getDay()
```

Here is the final code with comments:

L 14-9

```
onClipEvent (enterFrame) {
    // Prepare Date object.
    myDate = new Date();
    year = myDate.getFullYear();
    month = myDate.getMonth() + 1;
    dates = myDate.getDate();
    hour = myDate.getHours();
    minute = myDate.getMinutes();
    second = myDate.getSeconds();
    day = myDate.getDay();
    first = new Date(year, month - 1, 1);
    firstDay = first.getDay();
}
```

Adding Text Fields to Show the Date Object Output

To show each of the extracted portions of the date, use dynamic text fields. Draw a text field on the stage and select Dynamic Text in the drop-down list in the Text Options panel. Next, type the variable name in the Variable text box. Be sure to use proper ActionScript targeting. In this case, the text field lies on the main timeline of the movie clip, and the variables are event procedures on the movie clip. For this project, place the text fields within the date_object_clip movie clip. Because the variables lie on the movie clip, just type the variable name. Doing so uses relative targeting. Instead of starting from _root to target the variable or movie clip, you start from the location you are calling the variable or movie clip.

NOTE

You can see what actions are going on during the movie by using the trace() *command to trace variables. The* trace() *command is usually not a good choice for variables that update continuously, because the trace output box will run by too fast when you're previewing the movie. For variables that constantly update, dynamic text fields work best.*

Add a text field for each variable, as shown in Figure 14-1. Navigate back to the main timeline and move the movie clip off the main stage area so that it will not be seen during movie playback.

Finally, add three more frames to this layer, so that the movie clip resides on the main timeline for a duration of four frames. The variables on this movie clip are used on each frame of the movie clip, so it is important to have the movie clip on the stage during these frames.

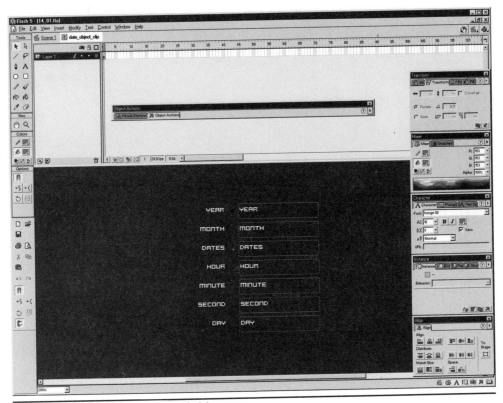

Figure 14-1   *Setting up the text fields*

Adding the Gray_line Layer

The gray_line layer simply contains a line drawn from one edge to the other, centered horizontally and vertically to the stage. Use the Line tool (press N to activate this tool) and draw a line that stretches from the left side of the stage to the right.

While the line is selected, open the Align panel and click the Align to Stage button. In the Match Size section of the panel, click the first button on the left to match the width of the line to the width of the stage. Next, in the Align section of the panel, click the second and fifth buttons to align the line to the horizontal and vertical center of the main stage, as shown in Figure 14-2.

Before continuing, remove the additional frames automatically added by Flash. This object should appear on only the first frame of this movie clip.

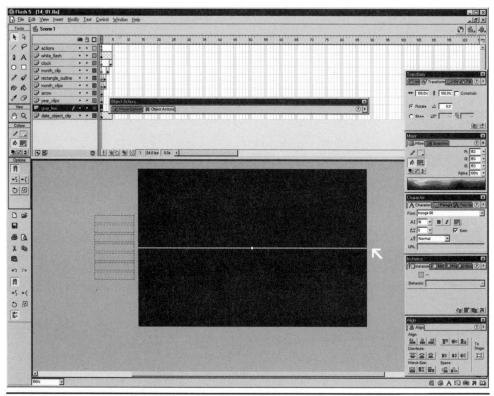

Figure 14-2 *Adding a gray line*

Building the Year_clips Layer

The year_clips layer contains a movie clip that includes nested movie clips with all of the years from 2000 to 2050. When the movie reaches this frame, the movie clips scroll across the stage until the current year reaches the center x position. Each of the years are dynamically built using duplicated movie clips from the original y2000 clip. Start by creating a new layer and labeling it **year_clips**. Remove any frame past the first frame, because the year appears on only the first frame of the movie.

Creating the Year_clip Movie Clip

Start by drawing a vertical line approximately 20 pixels tall on the stage. While the line is selected, press F8 to convert the object into a symbol. Select Movie Clip from the list of options and name it **year_clip**. Open the Instance panel and type **y2000** in the Name text field. This allows the movie clip to be targeted by ActionScripting.

Double-click the year_clip movie clip to edit the movie clip in place. This opens the movie clip's timeline, while still enabling you to see where the movie clip is in relation to the main timeline.

Move the vertical line slightly downward, to leave space for the text. This line will be used as a "stem" pointing toward a text field, which will contain the year for the movie clip, as shown in Figure 14-3.

Create a new layer within the year_clip movie clip and draw a text field large enough to hold four characters. Open the Text Options panel and select Dynamic Text, so that the text can be updated with ActionScript. In the Variable text field, type **name** (this variable will be created in the next section). Position the movie clip so that the bottom end of the line touches the gray line in the gray_line layer (created in the previous section).

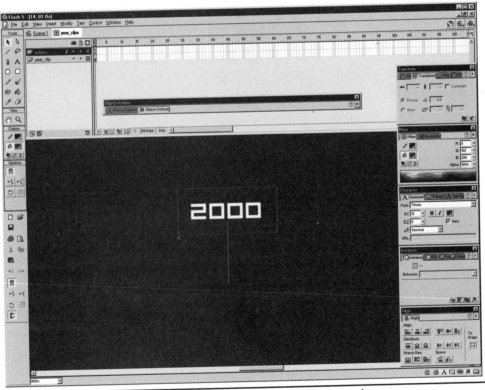

Figure 14-3   *The year_clip will hold the year portion of the Date object.*

NOTE

If you do not have the hooge 08 font installed, the example may not work properly. Just change the font to another font that is installed on your system.

Year_clip Scripting

Navigate back to the main timeline and select the year_clip movie clip. Open the ActionScript editor by pressing CTRL-ALT-A (COMMAND-OPTION-A for Macs) to add event procedures to the movie clip.

The only action that needs to take place on the year_clip movie clip is to extract the year from the movie clip's name. To do this, set the `name` variable using the `substring()` command.

L 14-10
```
onClipEvent (load) {
    // Extract year from clip name.
    name = substring(this._name, 2, 4);
}
```

This `substring()` command extracts characters from the name of the current movie clip (`this._name`), beginning with the second character (2) and extracting four characters (4).

Creating the Year_clips Movie Clip

The year_clips movie clip holds the year_clip movie clip. Inside the year_clips movie clip, the year_clip movie clip is duplicated 50 times to dynamically build all of the years. Duplicating movie clips can save time because you do not need to physically place each individual movie clip on the stage.

While the year_clip movie clip is selected, press F8 to nest the new movie clip inside it. Select Movie Clip from the list of options and type **year_clips** as the movie clip name. Open the Instance panel, and type **year_clips** as the instance name for the movie clip.

Double-click the years_clip movie clip to edit the movie clip in place. Reposition the year_clip movie clip so that the x position of the movie clip is 0.0 and it is centered vertically within the movie clip.

Create a new layer within the year_clips movie clip and label it **actions**. This layer will contain the actions for duplicating the year_clip movie clip.

Setting the Variables

Set year equal to 2000. This variable will be used to determine the name of the movie clip.

L 14-11
```
year = 2000
```

Set i equal to 0. This variable will determine how far away to position the duplicated movie clips.

L 14-12
```
i = 0
```

Set dif equal to 52. This variable determines how far to position the movie clips away from each other. (To increase the distance between the years, just increase this variable.)

L 14-13
```
dif = 52
```

Using a While Statement to Build Content

Most of the projects described in this book use if statements to dynamically build content. This project uses a while statement to build the year movie clips, so that they are built all at the same time. A while statement runs during one frame only, until the argument is not true, and then the movie clip continues to the next frame. This is useful if you do not want the user to see the content being built.

NOTE

A while *statement works differently from an* if *statement. The* while *statement cycles until the argument is not met, all within one frame. This means the actions take place before you can see them, unlike with* if *statements, which cycle every frame.*

While the i variable is less than 50, you want to duplicate the movie clips. This will build 50 additional movie clips, which will be more than enough for this project.

L 14-14
```
while (i < 50)
```

Within the while statement, you must increase the year variable by one each time so that the years are increased, such as 2001, 2002, 2003, and so on.

L 14-15
```
year = year + 1
```

Also, the i variable must be increased by one each time the `while` statement is run. When this variable reaches 50, Flash will break out of the `while` statement.

L 14-16

```
i = i + 1
```

Duplicate the y2000 movie clip to build the other years for this project.

L 14-17

```
duplicateMovieClip("y2000", "y" + year, year)
```

The first argument inside parentheses determines which movie clip to duplicate (`"y2000"`). The next argument, `"y"` + `year`, determines the new name of the duplicated movie clip. The `"y"` will be read as is, and `year` will read the `year` variable. This will increase each movie clip's duplicated name, such as y2001, y2002, y2003, and so forth. The final argument determines the depth to duplicate the new movie clip into. Set this equal to the `year` variable, so that each movie clip is duplicated into its own depth.

The final action within the `while` statement sets the x position of the new movie clip. Use the `setProperty()` action to set the newest duplicated movie clip's x position.

L 14-18

```
setProperty("y" + year, _x, y2000._x + (dif * i))
```

The first argument within the parentheses, `"y"` + `year`, determines which movie clip to modify. The next argument determines which property to modify for the movie clip; in this case, the `_x` property. The final argument, `y2000._x` + `(dif * i)`, determines what to set the property of the movie clip to. By getting the x position of the movie clip and adding the `dif` variable multiplied by the `i` variable, this positions the movie clips 52 pixels from each other.

Putting the Script Together

Here is the final code with comments:

L 14-19

```
// Set initial variables.
year = 2000;
i = 0;
dif = 52;
// Start while statement.
while (i < 50) {
    year = year + 1;
    i = i + 1;
```

```
// Duplicate movie clips to build years.
duplicateMovieClip ("y2000", "y" + year, year);
// Distribute movie clips 52 pixels away from each other.
setProperty("y" + year, _x, y2000._x + (dif * i));
}
```

Adding Year_clips Event Procedures

Navigate back to the main timeline where the year_clips movie clip lies. This movie clip uses its own actions as well, to move the movie clip so that the current year stops at the center of the stage. Move the movie clips to the far left of the screen, past the end of the stage. This will allow the movie clip to move farther across the screen.

On Clip Event Load Scripting

In the onClipEvent (load) event handler, set two variables. To precisely center the year_clip, you need to determine the center point of the movie clip. This is done by dividing the width by 2.

L 14-20
```
year_clip_width = y2000._width / 2
```

This movie clip moves to the center of the stage when loaded. Divide the stage width by 2 to find the center, in this case, 300.

L 14-21
```
movie_center = 300
```

The code looks like this:

L 14-22
```
onClipEvent (load) {
    year_clip_width = y2000._width / 2;
    movie_center = 300;
```

On Clip Event Enter Frame Scripting

In the onClipEvent (enterFrame) event handler, add code to move the movie clip into position. First, set the new_x variable to the new x position of the current movie clip. This is determined by using the substring() command to read the last two digits of the current year. Multiply this value by 52 to determine the x position of the movie clip.

L 14-23
```
new_x = (substring(_root.date_object_clip.year, 3 ,2)) * 52
```

The xpos variable is used to determine the offset of the movie clip, so that it centers the movie clip on the stage. Set the xpos variable equal to the movie_center variable minus the new_x variable, minus the year_clip_width variable.

L 14-24
```
xpos = movie_center - new_x - year_clip_width
```

This will output the xpos variable for the movie clip to center the current year movie clip.

The current_x variable just returns the current x position of this movie clip.

L 14-25
```
current_x = this._x
```

This variable is used to determine how much to move the movie clip each time it cycles.

The dif_x variable subtracts the current x position from the xpos variable.

L 14-26
```
dif_x = current_x - xpos
```

This integer is the amount of distance between the movie clip and its destination point.

Finally, set the x position of the current movie clip equal to the current_x variable subtracted from the dif_x variable, divided by 10.

L 14-27
```
this._x = current_x - (dif_x / 10)
```

This will move the current movie clip one-tenth of the way to the difference of the destination each time the actions cycle. This will cause the movie clip to slowly come to a stop.

Putting the Script Together

Here is the final code with comments:

L 14-28
```
onClipEvent (load) {
    // Determine width of year_clip movie clip.
    year_clip_width = y2000._width / 2;
    // Set center point of stage.
    movie_center = 300;
}
onClipEvent (enterFrame) {
    // Substring the current year.
```

```
new_x = (substring(_root.date_object_clip.year, 3, 2)) * 52;
// Movement actions
xpos = movie_center - new_x - year_clip_width;
current_x = this._x;
dif_x = current_x - xpos;
this._x = current_x - (dif_x / 10);
}
```

Creating the Arrow Layer

The arrow layer contains an arrow that moves toward the center of the screen, so that it points to the current year. Start by creating a new layer and label it **arrow**. Remove any frame beyond the first frame (the arrow only appears on the first frame of the movie). Draw an upward-pointing arrow on the main stage. While this graphic is selected, press F8 to convert it into a symbol. Select Movie Clip from the list of options and name it **arrow**. Open the Instance panel and specify **arrow** as the instance name as well.

Double-click the arrow to edit it in place. Select the arrow graphic and reposition it, so that its tip is at the 0,0 coordinates, as shown in Figure 14-4. This makes it easier later to position the tip of the arrow exactly where you want.

Adding Arrow Event Procedures

Event procedures are added to the arrow movie clip so that it moves toward the center of the screen and stops when it reaches the center. Navigate back to the main timeline, select the arrow movie clip, and open the ActionScript editor.

The xpos variable is the destination position for the arrow movie clip. The arrow should move slowly toward the center of the screen, which is 300, as shown in Figure 14-5.

In the onClipEvent (load) event handler, set xpos to 300.

L 14-29
```
onClipEvent (load)
    xpos = 300
```

In the onClipEvent (enterFrame) event handler, add code to control the movie clip's movement and tell the white_flash movie clip (described in the next section) to play.

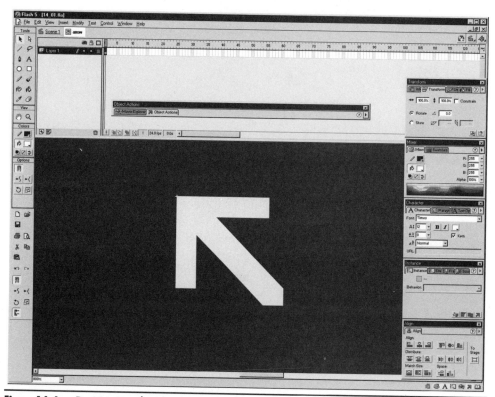

Figure 14-4   *Positioning the arrow movie clip*

The `current_x` variable just returns the current x position of the movie clip. This variable is used to determine how much to move the movie clip each time it cycles.

L 14-30

```
current_x = this._x
```

The `dif_x` variable subtracts the current x position from the `xpos` variable. This integer is the distance between the movie clip and its destination point.

L 14-31

```
dif_x = current_x - xpos
```

Finally, set the x position of the current movie clip equal to the `current_x` variable, subtracted from the `dif_x` variable, divided by 10. This will move the

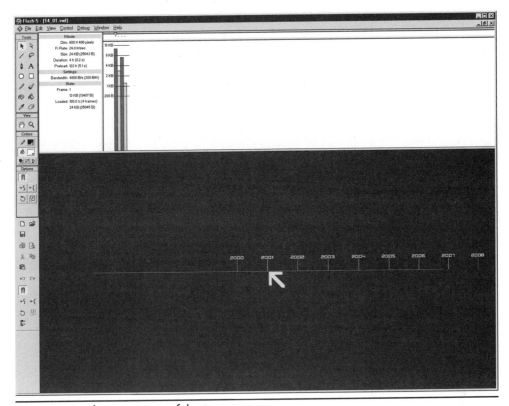

Figure 14-5   *The movement of the arrow*

current movie clip one-tenth of the way to the difference of the destination each
time the actions cycle. This will cause the movement to slowly come to a stop.

L 14-32   `this._x = current_x - (dif_x / 10)`

Once the arrow movie clip arrives at its destination point, the movie clip tells the
white_flash·movie clip to play. This movie clip plays a white flash and tells the main
timeline to move to the next frame.

Use an `if` statement to see whether `current_x` is equal to `xpos`. If so, the
actions within the `if` statement start.

L 14-33   `if (current_x == xpos)`

Use the `with()` command to tell the white_flash movie clip to play.

L 14-34
```
with (_root.white_flash) {
    play ();
}
```

NOTE

Previous versions of Flash used the `tellTarget()` command. This command has not been replaced, but it has been deprecated. The `with()` command is the preferred method to use with Flash 5.

Here is the final code with comments:

L 14-35
```
onClipEvent (load) {
    // Set destination point.
    xpos = 300;
}
onClipEvent (enterFrame) {
    // Movement scripting
    current_x = this._x;
    dif_x = current_x - xpos;
    this._x = current_x - (dif_x/10);
    // If statement to tell white_flash movie clip to play
    if (current_x == xpos) {
        with (_root.white_flash) {
            play ();
        }
    }
}
```

Creating the White_flash Layer

The white_flash layer is essentially used for a transition between frames, as shown in Figure 14-6. It flashes a white square on the stage and moves the main timeline to the next frame. Keep this layer above all of the other layers, so it is always on top of the other graphics.

Create a new layer and label it **white_flash**. Leave the additional frames that Flash adds, so that it can be used on any of the four frames in the Flash movie. Create a white rectangle on the main stage. Then use the Align panel to resize the rectangle to the same size as the stage, and align it to the vertical and horizontal center.

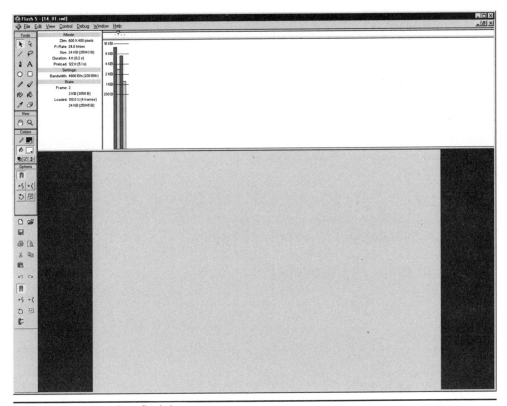

Figure 14-6   *The white flash layer is just a square.*

While the rectangle is selected, press F8 to convert it into a symbol. Select Graphic from the list of options and type **white_flash_graphic** in the text field. Select the rectangle and press F8 again to convert it into another symbol. This time, select Movie Clip from the list of options and name it **white_flash**. Open the Instance panel and type **white_flash** as the instance name.

Animating the Movie Clip

Double-click the white_flash movie clip to edit the movie clip in place. Start by dragging the white_flash_graphic symbol to frame 2. Use the Effect panel to set the Alpha to 0%, so that is completely transparent. Add a keyframe to frame 5 and frame 15. On frame 5, change the Alpha back to 100%, so that it is completely visible.

Next, add a motion tween between these layers by right-clicking (CONTROL-clicking for Mac) the timeline and selecting Motion Tween. This feature animates the movements or effects of an object in Flash. In this case, it animates the alpha effect of the rectangle, so that it flashes onto the screen and then back off.

Adding an Actions Layer to the White_flash Movie Clip

Placing actions on their own layer helps keep the movie clip more organized for future editing. Create a new layer in the white_flash movie clip and label it **actions**. Frame 1 contains only one action, a `stop()` action. This keeps the movie clip from playing until it is called by ActionScripting.

L 14-36
```
stop ()
```

Frame 5 is where the white flash is completely visible on the stage. This is when you want the transition to occur, so that no one can actually see it take place. Use the `with()` command to target the main timeline, `_root`. In the `with()` command, tell the main timeline to go to the next frame.

L 14-37
```
with (_root) {
    nextFrame ();
}
```

Creating the Month_clips Layer

The month_clips layer contains 12 movie clips that represent each month of the year. Create a new layer and add a keyframe to frame 2. Remove frames 3 and 4, because this layer is used only in frame 2.

Draw a rectangle on the stage approximately 125 pixels wide and 70 pixels tall. Then draw a line from the left edge to the right edge, approximately 15 pixels from the top. This area will be used to accompany the name of the month. In the lower section of the rectangle, add five rows and seven columns of x's to represent the dates on a calendar, as shown in Figure 14-7. The dates will be shown later on another calendar view of the Flash movie.

Select the rectangle and all of the x's on the stage, and then press F8 to create a new symbol. Select Movie Clip from the list of options and name it **months_clip**.

Creating the Text Field

Double-click the months_clip movie clip to edit it in place. Create an additional layer and label it text field. Draw a text field as wide as the rectangle and tall enough for

Figure 14-7   *The months_clip movie clip*

one row of text. Make sure that the top of the text field does not go past the top of the rectangle. If the text field is higher than the rectangle, the movie clip will be read as a taller movie clip.

Open the Text Options panel and select Dynamic Text. In the Variable text field, type **name**. When the name variable changes, so will the text field.

Adding Months_clip Scripting

An event procedure is added to the months_clip movie clip to update the text field. The only variable to set in the load procedure is the name variable. This variable is set so the text field will display the correct month name. Set name equal to "JANUARY". (It is important to use quotation marks so Flash does not try to read the month name as an expression.)

L 14-38
```
onClipEvent (load)
     name = "JANUARY"
```

Copy and paste the months_clips movie clip 11 times to create 12 instances of the movie clip. Position the copies in three rows and four columns, as in a calendar layout. On each movie clip, change the name variable to another month name: "FEBRUARY", "MARCH", "APRIL", and so on.

Creating the Rectangle_outline Layer

The rectangle_outline layer is used to box in the current month of the year. Create a new layer and add a keyframe to frame 2. Remove frames 3 and 4, because this layer is used only in frame 2. Draw an unfilled gray rectangle on the stage, the same size as the months_clip movie clip. While selected, press F8 to convert it into a symbol, select Graphic from the list of options, and name it **rectangle_outline_graphic**. Again, select the rectangle and press F8 to convert it into a symbol, but this time select Movie Clip from the list of options and name it **rectangle_outline**.

Double-click the rectangle_outline movie clip to edit the movie clip in place. Add another keyframe to frame 5 and frame 9. On frame 5, open the Effect panel and change the tint of the rectangle to 100% white. Add a motion tween between these layers.

Adding Rectangle_outline Event Procedures

When the Flash movie reaches the second frame, the rectangle_outline zooms in and frames the current month. Navigate back to the main timeline and resize the rectangle_outline movie clip larger than the stage, so that it is not seen when it is first loaded. Then open the ActionScript editor (CTRL-ALT-A/COMMAND-OPTION-A).

In the onClipEvent (enterFrame) event handler, add code to set destinations and control the movie clip's movement. The xpos and ypos variables are the destination x position and y position for the current movie clip, respectively. Use the getProperty() command to get the x and y positions of "_root.m" + _root.date_object_clip.month.

L 14-39
```
xpos = getProperty("_root.m" + _root.date_object_clip.month, _x);
ypos = getProperty("_root.m" + _root.date_object_clip.month, _y);
```

The width and height variables are the destination width and height for the current movie clip, respectively. They are set in the same manner as the xpos and ypos variables.

L 14-40
```
width = getProperty(
                    "_root.m" + _root.date_object_clip.month, _width
);
height = getProperty(
                    "_root.m" + _root.date_object_clip.month, _height
);
```

The current_x, current_y, current_width, and current_height variables just return the current x position, y position, width, and height of this movie clip. These variables are used to determine how much to move the movie clip each time it cycles.

L 14-41
```
current_x = this._x;
current_y = this._y;
```

```
current_width = this._width;
current_height = this._height;
```

The dif_x variable subtracts the current x position from the xpos variable. The dif_y variable does the same for the y position. The dif_width variable subtracts the current width from the width variable, and the dif_height variable subtracts the current width from the height variable. These integers are the amount of distance between the movie clip and its destination point.

L 14-42
```
dif_x = current_x - xpos;
dif_y = current_y - ypos;
dif_width = current_width - width;
dif_height = current_height - height;
```

Finally, set the x position of the current movie clip equal to the current_x variable minus the dif_x variable divided by 5. The y position, width, and height of the movie clip are set using the same method, substituting the appropriate properties. These will move the current movie clip one-twentieth of the way to the difference of the destination each time the actions cycle, causing the movie clip to slowly come to a stop.

L 14-43
```
this._x = current_x - (dif_x / 5)
this._x = current_x - (dif_x / 5);
this._y = current_y - (dif_y / 5);
this._width = current_width - (dif_width / 5);
this._height = current_height - (dif_height / 5);
```

When the rectangle's width is about the same size as the months_clip movie clip, tell the white_flash movie clip to play. Use an if statement to check whether current_width is less than the width variable plus 5. This will trigger the play action just as the movie clip is the same width as the months_clip movie clip.

L 14-44
```
if (current_width < width + 5) {
    with (_root.white_flash) {
        play ();
    }
}
```

Here is the final code with comments:

L 14-45
```
onClipEvent (enterFrame) {
    // Set destinations.
```

```
xpos = getProperty("_root.m" + _root.date_object_clip.month, _x);
ypos = getProperty("_root.m" + _root.date_object_clip.month, _y);
width = getProperty(
                "_root.m" + _root.date_object_clip.month, _width
);
height = getProperty(
                "_root.m" + _root.date_object_clip.month, _height
);
// Movement scripts
current_x = this._x;
current_y = this._y;
current_width = this._width;
current_height = this._height;
dif_x = current_x - xpos;
dif_y = current_y - ypos;
dif_width = current_width - width;
dif_height = current_height - height;
this._x = current_x - (dif_x / 5);
this._y = current_y - (dif_y / 5);
this._width = current_width - (dif_width / 5);
this._height = current_height-(dif_height / 5);
// If statement to trigger white_flash movie clip
if (current_width < width + 5) {
    with (_root.white_flash) {
        play ();
    }
}
}
}
```

Creating the Month_clip Layer

The month_clip layer contains a single-month calendar, with the dates displayed for the month. The dates on the calendar are built dynamically, by determining how many days are in the month and when the first day of the month is.

NOTE

When building this project originally, the hardest part I ran into was determining whether the year was a leap year. Leap years contain 29 days in February, while all of the other years contain 28. With help from Jessica Speigel of webstyles.net, I got past this rough piece of code, as explained in "Adding Month_clip Event Procedures," later in this chapter.

Start by creating a new layer labeled month_clip. Press CTRL-F8 (COMMAND-F8 for Macs) to create a new symbol. Select Movie Clip from the list of options and name it **month_clip**. On the month_clip movie clip's timeline, separate the movie clip into four layers: clips, bg, days, and rect_outline.

Creating the Bg Layer's Content

On the bg layer, draw a rectangle approximately 400 pixels wide by 250 pixels tall. Draw a line across the top section, to represent the top of the calendar, where the month name will appear. Within the bottom section, draw a rectangle divided into five rows and seven columns. Finally, add the days of the week and a text field for the current month that reads data from the `textMonth` variable (described in "Adding Month_ clip Event Procedures," later in this chapter), as shown in Figure 14-8.

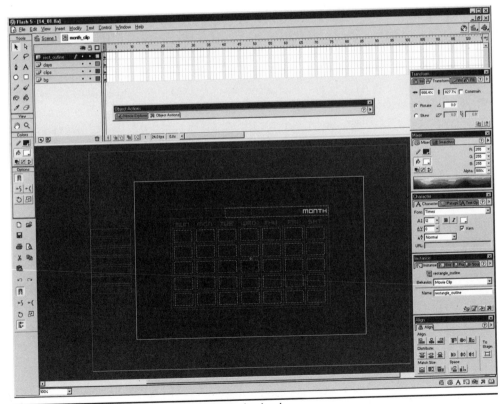

Figure 14-8   *The one-month calendar on the bg layer*

Be sure to keep the blocks evenly proportioned. They will contain the dates for the days of the week.

Creating the Clips Layer

Copy one of the blocks from the calendar on the bg layer and paste it onto this new layer labeled clips. While the block is selected, press F8 to convert it into a symbol. Select Movie Clip from the list of options and name it **day_block**. Then open the Instance panel and type **c1** for the instance name, to represent cell 1.

Copy and paste this symbol, each time moving it to the next block to the right, and moving to the next row when you reach the end of a column. For each copied cell, increase the integer in the name: **c2**, **c3**, **c4**, and so on. Finally, change the Alpha setting of all the movie clips to 0%, so they are not shown when the Flash movie is played.

Creating the Days Layer

Create a text field approximately the same size as the cells on the calendar. Place the first one in the top-left block. Open the Text Options panel and select Dynamic Text from the drop-down list, and then type **d1** for the variable.

Copy and paste this text field, each time moving it to the next block to the right, moving to the next row when you reach the end, as shown in Figure 14-9. For each copied text field, increase the integer for the variable name: **d2**, **d3**, **d4**, and so on.

Creating the rect_outline Layer

The rect_outline layer zooms in and boxes in on the current day, just as the rectangle_outline layer (described earlier) does for the current month. Its event procedures are similar. However, it begins with a `load` event to set the `current` variable equal to the `dates` variable plus the `firstDay` variable. This will result in the proper date integer for the current block (as explained in the next section).

L 14-46
```
onClipEvent (load) {
    current = _root.date_object_clip.dates
            + _root.date_object_clip.firstDay
```

For the `enterFrame` event, begin by setting the `xpos`, `ypos`, `width`, and `height` variables for the destination position for the current movie clip. Use the `getProperty()` command to get the corresponding property of `"_parent.c"` + `current`.

L 14-47
```
xpos = getProperty("_parent.c" + current, _x);
ypos = getProperty("_parent.c" + current, _y);
width = getProperty("_parent.c" + current, _width);
height = getProperty("_parent.c" + current, _height);
```

Next, set the `current_x`, `current_y`, `current_width`, and `current_height` variables to return the current corresponding properties of this movie clip. These variables are used to determine how much to move the movie clip each time it cycles.

L 14-48
```
current_x = this._x;
current_y = this._y;
current_width = this._width;
current_height = this._height;
```

Figure 14-9   *Adding the calendar text fields*

The `dif_x` variable subtracts the current x position from the `xpos` variable. The `dif_y`, `dif_width`, and `dif_height` variables work in the same way with their corresponding properties. These integers are the amount of distance between the movie clip and its destination point.

L 14-49
```
dif_x = current_x - xpos
dif_y = current_y - ypos
dif_width = current_width - width
dif_height = current_height - height
```

Finally, set the x position of the current movie clip equal to the `current_x` variable minus the `dif_x` variable divided by 5. This will move the current movie clip one-twentieth of the way to the difference of the destination each time the actions cycle, causing the movement to slowly stop.

L 14-50
```
this._x = current_x - (dif_x / 5)
```

The y position, width, and height are set using the same methods, substituting the corresponding properties.

When the rectangle's width is about the same size as the months_clip movie clip, tell the white_flash movie clip to play. Use an `if` statement to check whether `current_width` is less than the `width` variable plus 5. This will trigger the play actions when the movie clip is the same width as the months_clip movie clip.

L 14-51
```
if (current_width < width + 5) {
    with (_root.white_flash) {
        play ();
    }
}
```

Here is the final code with comments:

L 14-52
```
onClipEvent (load) {
    // Set initial variable.
    current = _root.date_object_clip.dates +
    _root.date_object_clip.firstDay;
}
onClipEvent (enterFrame) {
    // Movement script
    xpos = getProperty("_parent.c" + current, _x);
    ypos = getProperty("_parent.c" + current, _y);
    width = getProperty("_parent.c" + current, _width);
```

```
height = getProperty("_parent.c" + current, _height);
current_x = this._x;
current_y = this._y;
current_width = this._width;
current_height = this._height;
dif_x = current_x - xpos;
dif_y = current_y - ypos;
dif_width = current_width - width;
dif_height = current_height - height;
this._x = current_x - (dif_x / 5);
this._y = current_y - (dif_y / 5);
this._width = current_width - (dif_width / 5);
this._height = current_height - (dif_height / 5);
// If statement to play white_flash movie clip.
if (current_width < width + 5) {
    with (_root.white_flash) {
        play ();
    }
}
}
}
```

Adding Month_clip Event Procedures

The event procedures added onto the month_clip movie clip are used to determine how many days are in the month and on what days the dates should lie. The script will use the load event because it needs to run only once.

The first section of code is basically a long if-else statement that reads the month variable on the date_object_clip movie clip. Two variables must be set for each month: daysinMonth and textMonth. This is the output for the text field on top of the bg layer of the calendar. Each month uses similar scripting, checking to see whether month is equal to a certain integer, and if so, setting the two variables.

L 14-53
```
if (_root.date_object_clip.month == 1) {
    daysinMonth = 31;
    textMonth = "January";
}
```

The only exception is February. This month can have 28 or 29 days, depending on whether or not it is a leap year (which is every four years). Within the else if statement, another if statement checks to see whether the year variable is divisible by 4 without a remainder, divisible by 100 without a remainder, and divisible by 400

without a remainder. If so, it is a leap year. For leap years, set the `daysinMonth`
variable to 29; for other years, set it to 28.

L 14-54
```
if ((
        (_root.date_object_clip.year % 4 == 0) && !
        (_root.date_object_clip.year % 100 == 0)) ||
        (_root.date_object_clip.year % 400 == 0))
    {
        daysinMonth = 29;
        } else {
        daysinMonth = 28;
        }
    textMonth = "February";
    }
```

Next, all of the text fields that have been added need to be set to a value,
to signify the dates. Set the d1 variable equal to (`_root.date_object_`
`clip.firstDay - 1) * -1`:

L 14-55
```
d1 = (_root.date_object_clip.firstDay - 1) * -1
```

Set the d2 variable equal to (`_root.date_object_clip.firstDay -2)`
`* -1`, the d3 variable equal to (`_root.date_object_clip.firstDay -3)`
`* -1`, and so on, each time increasing the integer subtracted from `firstDay`, until
you reach 35. This will build the calendar, starting with the correct date on the
correct day.

Set the i variable equal to 0 so the following `while` statement will begin. Then
start the `while` statement, by checking whether the i variable is less than 36.

L 14-56
```
    i = 0;
    while (i < 36) {
        i++;
        d = "d" + i;
```

Each cycle increases the i variable (`i++`) until it is not less than 36. The d variable
is set equal to "d" + i each cycle, so it will be equal to d1, d2, d3, and so on. This
variable is used to signify the text field variable names, so that they are set within
this `while` statement.

Within the `while` statement, an `if` statement checks to see whether i is less than
or equal to the `firstDay` variable. If so, the text field is set to " ", which means
it will be blank. The `else if` statement checks to see whether i is greater than the

firstDay variable plus the daysinMonth. If i is greater than the daysinMonth variable, the text field is set to " " so that it will be blank.

L 14-57
```
if (i <= _root.date_object_clip.firstDay) {
    set ("d" + i, " ");
} else if (i > _root.date_object_clip.firstDay + daysinMonth) {
    set ("d" + i, " ");
}
```

Here is the final code with comments:

L 14-58
```
onClipEvent (load) {
    // If statements to determine how many days are in
    // the month, and the month name
    if (_root.date_object_clip.month == 1) {
        daysinMonth = 31;
        textMonth = "January";
    } else if (_root.date_object_clip.month == 2) {
        // February if statement to check for leap year
        if ((
            (_root.date_object_clip.year % 4 == 0) && !
            (_root.date_object_clip.year % 100 == 0)) ||
            (_root.date_object_clip.year % 400 == 0))
        {
            daysinMonth = 29;
        } else {
            daysinMonth = 28;
        }
        textMonth = "February";
    } else if (_root.date_object_clip.month == 3) {
        daysinMonth = 31;
        textMonth = "March";
    } else if (_root.date_object_clip.month == 4) {
        daysinMonth = 30;
        textMonth = "April";
    } else if (_root.date_object_clip.month == 5) {
        daysinMonth = 31;
        textMonth = "May";
    } else if (_root.date_object_clip.month == 6) {
        daysinMonth = 30;
        textMonth = "June";
    } else if (_root.date_object_clip.month == 7) {
        daysinMonth = 31;
```

```
      textMonth = "July";
   } else if (_root.date_object_clip.month == 8) {
      daysinMonth = 31;
      textMonth = "August";
   } else if (_root.date_object_clip.month == 9) {
      daysinMonth = 30;
      textMonth = "September";
   } else if (_root.date_object_clip.month == 10) {
      daysinMonth = 31;
      textMonth = "October";
   } else if (_root.date_object_clip.month == 11) {
      daysinMonth = 30;
      textMonth = "November";
   } else if (_root.date_object_clip.month == 12) {
      daysinMonth = 31;
      textMonth = "December";
   }
   // Set the text field days
   d1 = (_root.date_object_clip.firstDay - 1) * -1;
   d2 = (_root.date_object_clip.firstDay - 2) * -1;
   d3 = (_root.date_object_clip.firstDay - 3) * -1;
   d4 = (_root.date_object_clip.firstDay - 4) * -1;
   d5 = (_root.date_object_clip.firstDay - 5) * -1;
   d6 = (_root.date_object_clip.firstDay - 6) * -1;
   d7 = (_root.date_object_clip.firstDay - 7) * -1;
   d8 = (_root.date_object_clip.firstDay - 8) * -1;
   d9 = (_root.date_object_clip.firstDay - 9) * -1;
   d10 = (_root.date_object_clip.firstDay - 10) * -1;
   d11 = (_root.date_object_clip.firstDay - 11) * -1;
   d12 = (_root.date_object_clip.firstDay - 12) * -1;
   d13 = (_root.date_object_clip.firstDay - 13) * -1;
   d14 = (_root.date_object_clip.firstDay - 14) * -1;
   d15 = (_root.date_object_clip.firstDay - 15) * -1;
   d16 = (_root.date_object_clip.firstDay - 16) * -1;
   d17 = (_root.date_object_clip.firstDay - 17) * -1;
   d18 = (_root.date_object_clip.firstDay - 18) * -1;
   d19 = (_root.date_object_clip.firstDay - 19) * -1;
   d20 = (_root.date_object_clip.firstDay - 20) * -1;
   d21 = (_root.date_object_clip.firstDay - 21) * -1;
   d22 = (_root.date_object_clip.firstDay - 22) * -1;
   d23 = (_root.date_object_clip.firstDay - 23) * -1;
   d24 = (_root.date_object_clip.firstDay - 24) * -1;
   d25 = (_root.date_object_clip.firstDay - 25) * -1;
   d26 = (_root.date_object_clip.firstDay - 26) * -1;
```

```
d27 = (_root.date_object_clip.firstDay - 27) * -1;
d28 = (_root.date_object_clip.firstDay - 28) * -1;
d29 = (_root.date_object_clip.firstDay - 29) * -1;
d30 = (_root.date_object_clip.firstDay - 30) * -1;
d31 = (_root.date_object_clip.firstDay - 31) * -1;
d32 = (_root.date_object_clip.firstDay - 32) * -1;
d33 = (_root.date_object_clip.firstDay - 33) * -1;
d34 = (_root.date_object_clip.firstDay - 34) * -1;
d35 = (_root.date_object_clip.firstDay - 35) * -1;
i = 0;
while (i < 36) {
    i++;
    d = "d" + i;
    // If statement to set unneeded text fields to blank, ""
    if (i <= _root.date_object_clip.firstDay) {
        set ("d" + i, " ");
    } else if (i > _root.date_object_clip.firstDay + daysinMonth) {
        set ("d" + i, " ");
    }
}
}
}
```

Building the Clock

The final frame of this Flash movie displays a clock with the current hours, minutes, and seconds. Rather than using the standard digital output clock, it shows a clock with hands. Start by drawing a circle on the stage approximately 380 pixels by 380 pixels. While this circle is selected, press F8 to convert it into a new symbol. Select Movie Clip from the list of options, and type **clock** as the movie clip name.

Double-click the circle to edit the movie clip in place. Create a new layer labeled numbers. Create 12 static text fields containing the numerals 1 through 12. Using the circle as a guide, place each text field on the stage to imitate a clock, as shown in Figure 14-10. Once completed, delete the layer containing the circle.

Create an additional layer above the numbers layer to hold the clock hands. Draw an object on the stage to represent the second hand. While the object is selected, press F8 to convert it into a symbol, select Movie Clip, and name it **second_hand**. Open the Instance panel and type **second_hand** as the instance name as well. Double-click the second_hand movie clip to edit it in place. Align the hand to the horizontal center and to the bottom edge, to put the pivot point of the movie clip at the end.

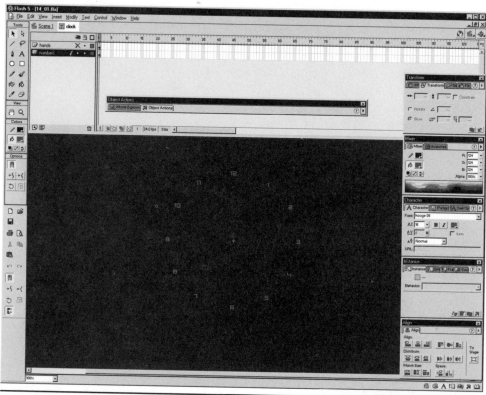

Figure 14-10 *Adding the clock numbers*

Repeat the same steps for the minute and hour hands, naming them **minute_hand** and **hour_hand**, respectively. The minute hand should be shorter than the second hand, and the hour hand should be shorter than the minute hand, like on a common clock, as shown in Figure 14-11.

Adding Clock Event Procedures

The event procedures for the clock use the `enterFrame` event, so the hands will stay in sync with the current time. Navigate back to the main timeline and select the clock movie clip. Then open the ActionScript editor.

Set the rotation of the hour_hand movie clip equal to `(360 / 12) * _root.date_object_clip.hour`. The section in parentheses divides

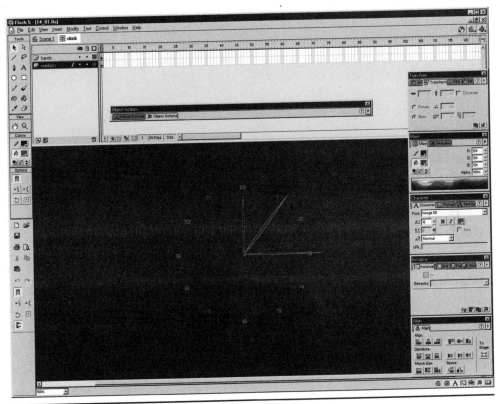

Figure 14-11   *The clock with hands*

the amount of degrees in a circle by the amount of hours, 12. Multiply this by the `hour` variable on the date_object_clip movie clip to move the hand to the current hour.

L 14-59   `hour_hand._rotation = (360 / 12) * _root.date_object_clip.hour`

Set the rotation of the minute_hand movie clip equal to `(360 / 60) * _root.date_object_clip.minute`. The section in parentheses divides the amount of degrees in a circle by the amount of minutes, 60. Multiply this by the `minute` variable on the date_object_clip movie clip to move the hand to the current minute.

L 14-60   `minute_hand._rotation = (360 / 60) * _root.date_object_clip.minute`

Set the rotation of the second_hand movie clip equal to `(360 / 60) *` `_root.date_object_clip.second`. The section in parentheses divides the amount of degrees in a circle by the amount of seconds, 60. Multiply this by the `second` variable on the date_object_clip movie clip to move the hand to the current second.

L 14-61
```
second_hand._rotation = (360 / 60) * _root.date_object_clip.second
```

Here is the final code:

L 14-62
```
onClipEvent (enterFrame) {
    // Set clock hands according to date_object_clip output.
    hour_hand._rotation = (360 / 12) * _root.date_object_clip.hour;
    minute_hand._rotation = (360 / 60) *
                            _root.date_object_clip.minute;
    second_hand._rotation = (360 / 60) *
                            _root.date_object_clip.second;
}
```

Creating the Actions Layer

As mentioned in earlier chapters, it is always a good habit to add an actions layer to every Flash movie. This allows you to add basic ActionScript commands and easily locate them for editing later. The only action needed for this project is to stop the Flash movie from playing when first loaded.

L 14-63
```
stop ();
```

What to Take Away from This Chapter

This chapter used Flash ActionScript and the Date object to decide the outcome of each frame within the Flash movie. Each frame reads the appropriate variable before continuing to the next animation. The concepts demonstrated in this chapter can be used for anything from a complex demonstration like the "flying through time" intro to a simple clock.

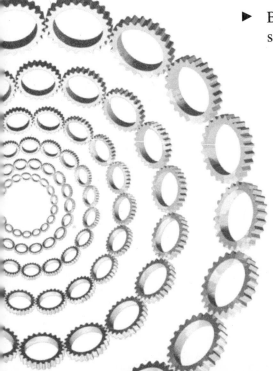

CHAPTER
15

Map Interface

As a vector-based program, Flash can be used to build user-interface designs with sharp graphics and smooth interaction. Most approaches to interface design use the traditional elements of scrolling text, windows that open and close, draggable boxes, and other interactive widgets.

In the presentation of text-based information, designers build conventional interfaces with the goal of allowing a user to view small parts of text in sequence, instead of cramming all of the text onto the screen at once. Usually a user can click a button to flip to the next page, or scroll down to read more text. However, the ActionScript language in Flash 5 provides designers with the opportunity to come up with new and innovative interface concepts that give the user a different kind of experience.

In some cases, interesting interface design requires a lot of programming—using mathematics, physics, and complex logic—to create advanced effects that involve motion and feedback. In other cases, a designer can implement an interesting and user-friendly interface with a good idea, some careful planning, and a sprinkling of programming. The map interface described in this chapter is an example of a simple Flash 5 project that incorporates an idea, some planning, and some unique techniques in advanced ActionScripting.

Components of the Map Interface

There are two components to the map interface: a main map, which contains large blocks of text for the user to read, and a mini-map, which contains a magnifying-glass pointer for the user to navigate through the map. The main map shows only the amount of text that will fit within its rectangular shape. To see the text that exists beyond the boundaries of the map's shape, the user can drag the pointer around the smaller rectangle (the mini-map), shifting the focus of the main map.

The key technique discussed in this chapter involves the use of ActionScript to move a movie clip beneath a mask. In the case of the map interface, the blocks of text exist inside a movie clip, which in turn exists beneath a mask layer.

The most important aspect of a masked movie clip is the shape of the mask. In Flash, masks can use only vector shapes, bitmaps cut with vector shapes, or graphic symbols. Movie clips do not work as masks. Many Flash designers make the common mistake of trying to use a movie clip to mask a layer. However, when you place a movie clip inside a mask layer, it will cease to behave as a movie clip, and the masking shape will not change if the movie clip's internal animation changes shape.

The chapter will also cover the important but tricky math concept of ratios, and how to combine ratios with the ActionScript getBounds() function to calculate the movement of the map.

mapInterface.fla

To see the final version of the interface, shown in Figure 15-1, open the mapInterface.fla file from the CD-ROM, save it to your local hard drive, and then run the Flash movie.

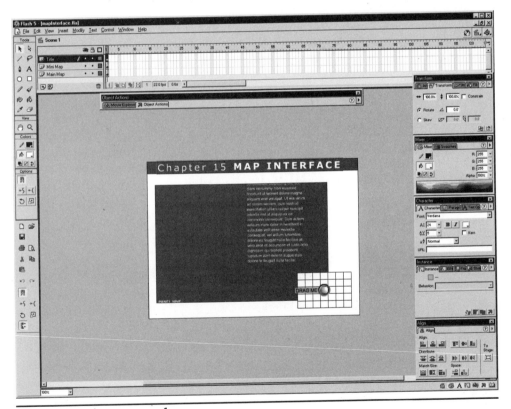

Figure 15-1   *The map interface*

Building the Graphics

mapInterface_01.fla

The graphics for the project include the interface title, the mini-map, and the main map. Create three layers from top to bottom with the following names: **Title**, **Mini Map**, and **Main Map**.

Adding the Title

Start by creating the interface title at the top of the screen. In the first keyframe of the Title layer, select the Rectangle tool with a black stroke and empty fill and draw a black border around the stage. Next, change the fill of the tool to dark gray, and draw a rectangle, 30 pixels high, across the top of the stage. Choose the Text tool and add **Chapter 15 Map Interface** as the title, in 24-point Verdana, as shown in Figure 15-2.

Building the Main Map

As explained at the beginning of the chapter, the map interface has a main map movie clip for text display and a mini-map movie clip for navigation. You need to build the main map first, so there will be something to navigate with the mini-map.

Start by creating a new Flash movie and setting the stage dimensions to 550 pixels by 400 pixels. The main map contains a large movie clip of text blocks and a mask shape.

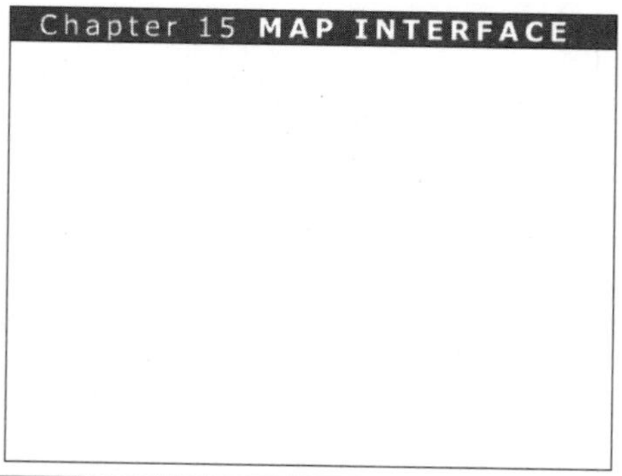

Figure 15-2   *Creating the map interface*

Begin building the main map by drawing a large, dark-gray rectangle, approximately 450 pixels by 300 pixels, on the layer named Main Map on the main timeline. Select the rectangle, and then convert it into a movie clip symbol by pressing F8 (or by selecting Insert | Convert to Symbol). Give this movie clip a symbol name of **MainMap**. In the main timeline, select the movie clip and give it an instance name of **MainMap** in the Instance panel.

Double-click the MainMap movie clip to edit its contents. At this point, only one layer exists for the gray rectangle. Rename this layer **Background**.

For the masked map movie clip, you need four layers:

▶ The bottom layer, which already exists, provides the background shape, so that the user can see the boundaries of the map area.

▶ The layer immediately above the background layer provides content for the map. It holds a very large movie clip containing blocks of text for the user to read as the navigation moves around the map.

▶ The layer above the text content layer acts as a masking layer, which defines the area in which the blocks of text will appear in the Flash movie.

▶ The topmost layer shows a black border around the mask area, so the user can see the boundaries of the map.

Creating the Content Layer

The bottom layer (Background) already exists, so the next step is to construct a large movie clip with blocks of text scattered throughout. The movie clip should contain blocks of text that exist outside the gray rectangle, because the purpose of the map interface is to allow the user to navigate among unseen areas of a large map to view different parts of the content.

Create the Content layer by inserting a new layer above the Background layer. Give the new layer the name **Content**, and then choose the Text tool. Before typing anything, make sure to choose the Arial font at 10 points in white. Next, draw several static text fields in the Content layer, making each text field approximately 160 by 240 pixels.

For this example, the text in the sample Flash file uses random Latin words to fill in the blocks of text. Make sure that the text blocks are scattered widely enough on the stage to give a sense of large spaces in the movie clip. You may want to zoom out on the stage in order to position text blocks farther away from the gray rectangle, as shown in Figure 15-3.

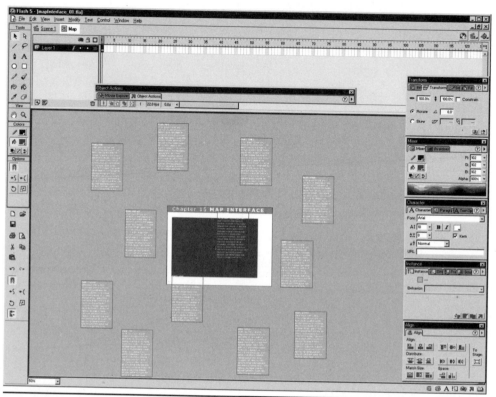

Figure 15-3   *Adding text blocks*

Convert all of the text fields into a single movie clip by selecting the Content layer, and then pressing F8. Define the new symbol as a new movie clip with the name **textmap**, and give the movie clip an instance name of **textmap** in the timeline as well.

Creating the Mask Layer

Now that the background shape and the text map have been defined, the next step is to create a mask layer to show only the portions of the text map that overlap the gray rectangle in the Background layer. Insert a new layer above the Content layer, and name the layer **Mask**.

Because the mask should hide portions of the text map that are outside the gray rectangle, the mask should have the same shape as the rectangle. Therefore, the mask is created by simply copying the rectangle in the Background layer, and then pasting the copy into the same position in the Mask layer.

NOTE

In Flash, there are two methods for cutting and pasting a graphic into the same position. To use the keyboard shortcuts, press CTRL-C (COMMAND-C for Macs) to copy the selected graphic, and then press CTRL-SHIFT-V (COMMAND-SHIFT-V for Macs) to paste the graphic into the same position. Alternatively, use the Edit menu commands: select Edit | Copy to make the copy, and then select Edit | Paste in Place to paste the copy into the same position.

So far, you've created three layers: Background, Content, and Mask. The Background layer and the Mask layer should contain the same gray rectangle. The rectangle in the Mask layer serves as a mask area that defines which portions of the textmap movie clip are visible in the Content layer.

Creating the Border Layer

Create the final layer by inserting a layer above the Mask layer and naming it **Border**. Copy the black border from the gray rectangle in the Background layer and paste it into the Border layer, as shown in Figure 15-4. It's necessary to create a new layer with a black border above all the other layers because the masked textmap movie clip will overlap the black border and gray rectangle in the Background layer below, causing that border to break in certain places.

Now, the large textmap movie clip is masked by a rectangular mask, with a corresponding gray rectangle beneath it. Even though the only visible parts of the text map are the areas that overlap the mask shape, the navigation system for this project will allow the user to move the text map around, so that the user can decide which parts of the text to show next.

Building the Mini-map

mapInterface_02.fla

The mini-map is the main component for the map interface's navigation. As the user drags the magnifying glass around the mini-map, the main map begins to move to the corresponding position, so that a user can navigate through the text map to read various text fields.

Creating the Minimap Clip

The first step in developing the navigation is creating the minimap movie clip, which consists of two parts: the shape of the mini-map and the magnifying glass. Return to the main timeline of the Flash movie and select the blank layer named Mini Map. This layer should be located between the top Title layer and the bottom Main Map layer.

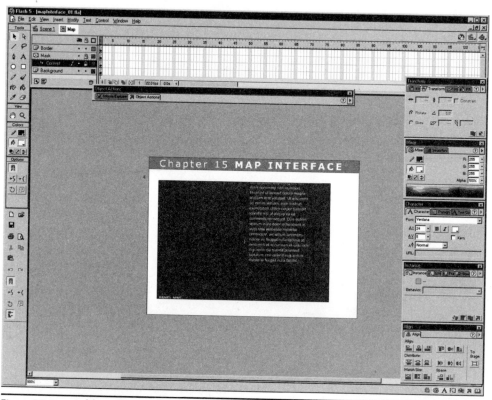

Figure 15-4 *Adding the Border layer*

Next, create the basic shape of the mini-map by drawing a small, white rectangle with black borders, approximately 140 pixels by 90 pixels. This white rectangle will provide the foundation for the mini-map. I also added some black lines to create a grid effect, but this is not necessary for the navigation to work.

Select the entire mini-map graphic, and then convert it into a movie clip symbol by pressing F8. Name the symbol **mapShape**, and give the movie clip an instance name of **mapShape** as well. The mapShape movie clip is only one part of the navigation, so select the mapShape movie clip and press F8 again to convert it into another movie clip, which now contains the mapShape movie clip. Name this new movie clip **minimap**, and give it an instance name of **minimap**.

You now have a movie clip named minimap, with an instance name of minimap. This movie clip has a single layer, which contains a rectangular movie clip called mapShape, as shown in Figure 15-5. The mapShape movie clip has an instance name of mapShape.

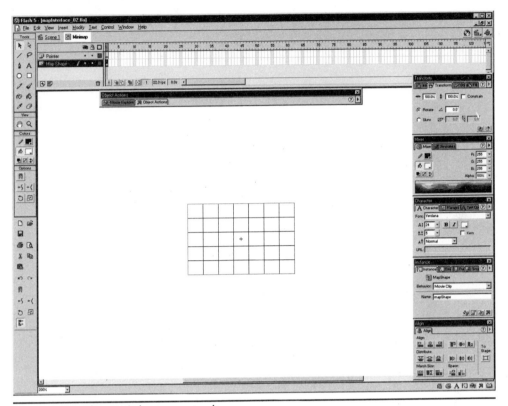

Figure 15-5 *The mapShape movie clip*

Building the Navigation Tool (the Pointer)

Now that the navigation area has been defined as the mapShape in the minimap movie clip, you can build the navigation tool that the user will drag around the small rectangle. This navigation tool resembles a magnifying glass, with a metallic ring and a semi-transparent dome covering the center of the ring. A small text box that reads "DRAG ME" appears to the left of the button, until the mouse cursor rolls over the button.

For the rest of the chapter, we'll refer to this navigation tool as the *pointer*, which is actually a button encapsulated inside a movie clip. The Pointer movie clip will exist in a layer above the mapShape movie clip. To begin, go inside the minimap movie clip and add a new layer named **Pointer** above the mapShape layer.

Next, select the Oval tool and change the fill to a linear gradient, from a light shade of gray to a dark shade of gray. Then create a circle at the center of the minimap movie clip, in the layer named Pointer. The result is a circle with a gradient fill. Select the circle and press F8 to convert it into a button symbol with the name **PointerButton**. Now you have a button with a basic circle shape and a gradient fill from light to dark.

In order to create a metallic effect for the button, open the Library (by selecting Window | Library) and double-click the PointerButton symbol to edit its contents. At this point, the PointerButton symbol contains one gradient circle. Creating a metallic bevel is a simple process that involves copying and pasting the same gradient circle.

Select the gradient circle and copy and paste into place. With the newly pasted circle still selected, choose Modify | Transform | Scale and Rotate. Set the value of the Scale transform to 80%, and the value of the Rotate transform to degrees. Click OK to perform the transformation. As a result, the graphic now appears as a beveled button with metallic gradients.

Now you need to create the inner bubble in translucent blue. Copy and paste in place the currently selected inner circle. Then repeat the same Transform operation on the circle to shrink it to 80% percent and rotate it 180 degrees. The translucent color of the middle bubble is achieved by changing the fill gradient of the middle bubble from a fully transparent white (white, Alpha = 0%) to a semi-transparent light blue (light blue, Alpha = 40%).

The button now has a complete set of graphics, but you must make some alterations in order to make it change appearance when the mouse rolls over it. You also need to add a text label to inform the user that the graphic can be dragged.

Name the current layer **Metallic Ring**, and then insert two new layers above the Metallic Ring layer. The top new layer should be named **Drag Label**, and the second layer should be named **Inner Bubble**. Then cut and paste the blue-tinged inner bubble onto the Inner Bubble layer. Add a blue rectangle and text field with the words "DRAG ME" to the top layer, positioned near the circle. Finally, change the appearance of the button in the over keyframe by inserting a blank keyframe on the top Drag Label layer and changing the tint of the bubble gradient in the Inner Bubble gradient. The effect when the mouse is over the pointer is shown in Figure 15-6.

The Pointer button has been created inside the minimap movie clip. However, in order for the user to be able to drag the pointer graphic, the button must be placed

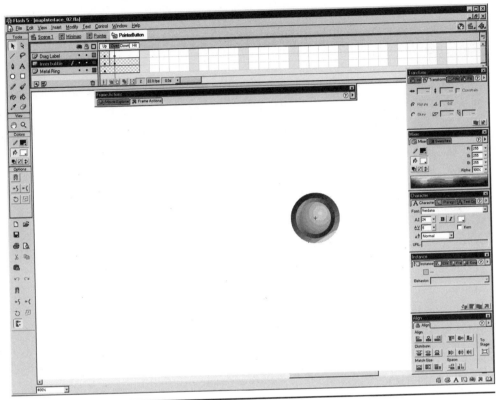

Figure 15-6   *The pointer when the mouse is over it*

inside its own movie clip. Double-click the minimap symbol in the Library to edit its contents, and then select the Pointer button. Press F8 to convert the Pointer button into a movie clip (now containing the Pointer button) and give the new symbol the name **Pointer**.

Adding ActionScript to the Interface

mapInterface_03.fla

Now it's time to add some ActionScript to make the map interactive by making use of the `getBounds()` and `startDrag()` functions. Before starting any programming, however, it's a good practice to review the sequence of actions for the interface, and then break down that sequence into small steps. Thinking through an interface from the topmost, general point of view all the way down to specific functions is an approach called *top-down design.*

To navigate through the many text fields located in the main map, the user first rolls the mouse over the Pointer movie clip. Then the user presses the mouse button down over the pointer and holds the mouse down while dragging it around the minimap movie clip. However, the user shouldn't be able to drag the pointer beyond the boundaries of the mini-map area. As the user drags the pointer around the mini-map, the content in the main map should move around according to the relative position of the Pointer movie clip in the minimap movie clip.

In the previous sections, you've taken care of the mouse rollover feature by changing the Pointer button graphics in the rollover keyframe. For the next step, you'll add some ActionScript that allows the user to drag the Pointer movie clip within the boundaries of the mini-map. Then you'll learn how to script the navigation with the Pointer movie clip.

Understanding Boundaries

If you run the mapInterface.fla file, you'll notice that the mouse can never drag the Pointer movie clip beyond the edges of the mini-map rectangle. It's obvious that the script is using the `startDrag()` function to allow the movie clip to be dragged with the mouse, but how do you find the coordinates of a movie clip's edges and use them to set the limits of the mouse-dragging action?

The key to constraining any mouse-dragging action to a movie clip's specific dimensions is a function called `getBounds()`. Even though a movie clip has four boundaries (top, bottom, left, and right), the `getBounds()` function actually returns a single object, called a Bounds object, that contains four properties corresponding to the top, bottom, left, and right edges of a movie clip. For example, in order to get the bounds of a movie clip with an instance name of myMovie, the ActionScript would look like this:

L 15-1
```
myBounds = myMovie.getBounds();
```

As a result, the `getBounds()` function would return an object to a variable named myBounds, which would become a new object containing information about the top, bottom, left, and right edges of the myMovie movie clip. This information is stored as properties of the `myBounds` object: `myBounds.xMax`, `myBounds.xMin`, `myBounds.yMax`, and `myBounds.yMin`. These properties can be accessed simply by referencing the property of the object; for example, the coordinates for the right edge of the movie clip would be `myBounds.xMax`.

Keep in mind, however, that Flash movie clips contain their own coordinate systems, where the origin (x = 0, y = 0) of each movie clip is located at the center of that movie clip's timeline. Therefore, Flash designers must be careful in determining which coordinate system they want to work within. If you're getting the bounds of a movie clip in another timeline, it's important to specify that you want the returned values of `xMin`, `xMax`, `yMin`, and `yMax` to correspond to the coordinates of your current movie clip.

For example, retrieving the bounds of a movie clip located in a parent timeline would require a path to the movie clip that looks like the following line of hypothetical code:

L 15-2
```
myBounds = _parent.otherMovieclip.getBounds();
```

Unfortunately, this ActionScript code would retrieve the `xMax`, `xMin`, `yMax`, and `yMin` edges of the movie clip, but the coordinates would actually refer to the maximum and minimum edges of the movie clip according to its parent timeline.

In order for a movie clip to get the bounds of another movie clip with useful coordinates, the `getBounds()` function must specify the scope of the calling movie clip by calling the function like so:

L 15-5
```
myBounds = _parent.otherMovieclip.getBounds(this);
```

Let's consider our hypothetical movie clip, myBounds, which is 360 pixels wide and 200 pixels tall. If its upper-left corner were located at the origin (x = 0, y = 0), then the right edge of the movie clip would be located at x = 360 and the bottom edge of the movie clip would be located at y = 200. Note that the upper edge of the movie clip would be located at y = 0, because the y coordinate increases downward along the vertical Y axis of the screen. The following diagram demonstrates how `yMin` corresponds to the top border of a movie clip, yMax corresponds to the bottom border, xMax corresponds to the right border, and xMin corresponds to the left border.

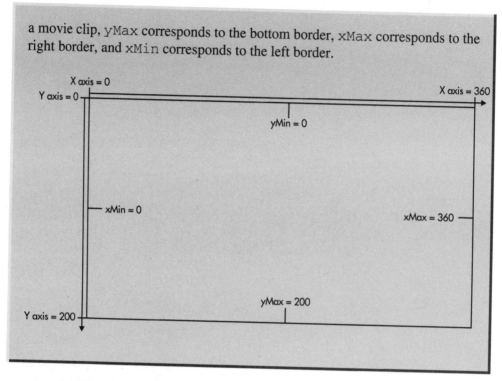

Applying the getBounds() function

By understanding how to retrieve the boundaries of a movie clip with the getBounds() function, you can use ActionScript to specify the limits for dragging a movie clip by providing the bounds of the movie clip as limits of the startDrag() function. For the map interface project, you want to apply the bounds of the mapShape movie clip, located inside the minimap movie clip, as the constraints for the startDrag() function of the Pointer button inside the Pointer movie clip.

To start off, add the startDrag() and stopDrag() functions to the Pointer button. Open the minimap movie clip by double-clicking the minimap movie clip in the Library. Once inside the minimap movie clip, double-click the Pointer movie clip to edit its button.

Open the Action panel for this button and add the following lines of code:

L 15-6
```
on (press) {
    bounds = _parent.mapShape.getBounds(_parent);
    startDrag (
```

```
    this, false, bounds.xMin, bounds.yMin, bounds.xMax, bounds.yMax
    );
}
on (release) {
    stopDrag ();
}
```

The `on (press)` event handler allows the lines of ActionScript within its curly braces to execute whenever the mouse button is pressed. The first line of code inside this event handler creates a new object variable called `bounds`, which contains the `xMax`, `xMin`, `yMax`, and `yMin` properties. These properties of the `bounds` object represent the coordinates of the movie clip's edges—the left, top, right, and bottom edges.

L 15-7
```
bounds = _parent.mapShape.getBounds(_parent);
```

These properties are then used in the second line of code to set the constraints of how far a user can drag the movie clip around the rectangle, by acting as parameters for the `startDrag()` function on the next line of code.

L 15-8
```
startDrag (
    this, false, bounds.xMin, bounds.yMin, bounds.xMax, bounds.yMax
);
```

The `startDrag()` function will reposition a movie clip to the location of the mouse cursor whenever the mouse is moved. There are six parameters required for the `startDrag()` function to define the limits of how a movie clip will be dragged around the screen:

▶ Which movie clip to drag

▶ Whether to lock the mouse to center

▶ The left border

▶ The top border

▶ The bottom border

▶ The right border

Because the `bounds` object already has properties for the coordinates of the boundaries, it's a simple matter to specify the Pointer movie clip as the target for dragging, and then replace the left, top, right, and bottom constraints of the startDrag() function with the xMin, yMin, xMax, and yMax properties of the bounds object.

The Pointer movie clip actually contains the Pointer button, so the Pointer movie clip exists within the same scope as the ActionScript for the Pointer button. As a result, the startDrag() function can simply refer to this as the target movie clip for dragging. Specifying false for the second parameter allows the startDrag() function to drag with the mouse cursor without locking its center to the mouse cursor.

The last two lines of code for the Pointer button simply stop the movie clip from dragging with the mouse. Once the ActionScript code calls the stopDrag() function, all movie clips previously locked to the mouse by the startDrag() function will cease to be draggable.

L 15-9
```
on (release) {
    stopDrag ();
}
```

At this point, the user can drag the Pointer movie clip within the boundaries of the mapShape movie clip because you've determined the coordinates of the movie clip boundaries and used those movie clips for the startDrag() function. Both the Pointer and mapShape movie clips actually exist inside the minimap movie clip.

Even though the user can drag the Pointer movie clip around, the map interface still lacks the ability to move the text beneath the mask of the MainMap movie clip in proportion to the location of the Pointer movie clip. The next section discusses how ActionScript can be used to link the location of the Pointer movie clip to the position of the textmap movie clip in the MainMap movie clip.

Scripting the Navigation

mapInterface_04.fla

So far, the user can drag the Pointer movie clip within the boundaries of the mini-map rectangle. Now you need to write some ActionScript to allow the user to navigate through the text blocks in the main map by dragging the pointer around the smaller map. As the user drags the pointer toward the left boundary of the minimap movie clip, the focus of the MainMap movie clip should also move toward the left of the textmap movie clip.

The navigation uses both the Pointer movie clip and the mapShape movie clip. Therefore, the ActionScript for the navigation control should exist inside the minimap movie clip, because it contains both the Pointer and mapShape movie clips, and provides a convenient way to reference both movie clips. The minimap movie clip can also act as a bridge between the MainMap movie clip, which exists on the main timeline, and the two movie clips inside its own timeline.

The minimap movie clip exists on the main timeline. To begin writing ActionScript for the navigation, go back to the main timeline and open the Action panel for the minimap movie clip. Then enter the following ActionScript code:

L 15-10
```
onClipEvent (load) {
        bounds = mapShape.getBounds(this);
}
onClipEvent (enterFrame) {
        mapWidth = bounds.xMax - bounds.xMin;
        mapHeight = bounds.yMax - bounds.yMin;
        xRatio = Pointer._x / mapWidth;
        yRatio = Pointer._y / mapHeight;
        _parent.mainmap.textmap._x = -1 * xRatio *
                _parent.mainmap.textmap._width;
        _parent.mainmap.textmap._y = -1 * yRatio *
                _parent.mainmap.textmap._height;
}
```

Again, the code makes use of the getBounds() function; and again, you want to get the bounds of the mapShape movie clip, because the rectangular shape of the mapShape movie clip provides the boundaries for the dragging behavior of the Pointer movie clip. The difference here is that you need to constantly track the position of the pointer relative to the boundaries of the mapShape and use the relative position of the Pointer movie clip to reposition the textmap movie clip inside the MainMap movie clip.

Calculating the Height and Width of the MapShape Movie Clip

The onClipEvent(enterFrame) handler executes code continuously, so this event handler will hold all of the code to perform the constant tracking and repositioning tasks. The first two lines inside the enterFrame code determine the height and width of the mapShape movie clip:

L 15-11
```
        mapWidth = bounds.xMax - bounds.xMin;
        mapHeight = bounds.yMax - bounds.yMin;
```

The calculation for the width of the movie clip is performed by subtracting the coordinate of the left edge from the coordinate of the right edge. Even though the _width property of a movie clip provides the same result, the actual position of a movie clip's edges might not be symmetrical, because the movie clip's inner graphics might lean off center. This code demonstrates the usefulness of the getBounds() method because it can retrieve the edges of a movie clip according to the coordinate space of the current movie clip. This way, you don't need to guess about whether the contents of the movie clip are centered or offset.

In the same way, the calculation for the width of the movie clip is performed by subtracting the coordinate of the bottom edge from the coordinate of the top edge. The difference between these two edges provides the actual distance, or height, of the movie clip's top and bottom edges. Note that it actually subtracts the *top* of the movie clip from the *bottom* of the movie clip, because the coordinate system increases from the top of the screen to the bottom of the screen.

Calculating Ratios

The next two lines of the enterFrame event handler calculate the horizontal and vertical ratios of the Pointer movie clip's position in relation to the edges of the mapShape movie clip.

L 15-12

```
xRatio = Pointer._x / mapWidth;
yRatio = Pointer._y / mapHeight;
```

It's easier to explain the reasoning behind these two lines of the code by referring to Figure 15-7. This diagram shows how the ratio is calculated by dividing the position of the Pointer's horizontal position by the total width of the mapShape movie clip. You need to calculate this ratio for the horizontal and vertical positions of the Pointer movie clip in order to move the textmap movie clip in the MainMap movie clip by a proportional distance.

For example, if you moved the pointer to the right until it reached a distance of 100 pixels from the center of the mapShape movie clip, then you would also expect the focus of the MainMap movie clip to shift a proportional amount of distance toward the right. However, because the MainMap movie clip is much bigger than the minimap movie clip, a user who drags the pointer around the mini-map will expect the text in the main map to move the same way, but at a much bigger proportion of the distance. In other words, moving the pointer by a little bit on the mini-map should move the text by a lot on the main map display. That's exactly what is done in the last two lines of ActionScript code:

L 15-13

```
_parent.mainmap.textmap._x = -1 * xRatio *
                    _parent.mainmap.textmap._width;
_parent.mainmap.textmap._y = -1 * yRatio *
                    _parent.mainmap.textmap._height;
```

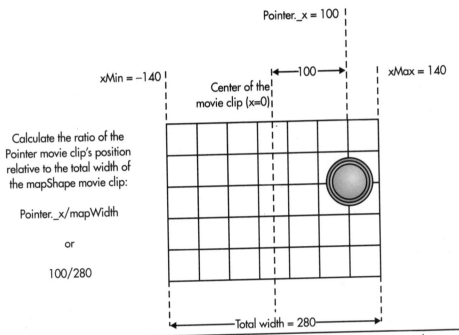

Figure 15-7 *Calculating the ratio of the distance moved on the mini-map. Here the pointer has been moved a distance of 100 pixels to the right of the origin.*

Several things happen on each line of code, so let's break it down into smaller portions for a more detailed examination. First, you want to change the x position of a movie clip called textmap, which is the movie clip containing all of the text blocks, located inside the MainMap movie clip's timeline. Change the y position with the same technique.

L 15-14
```
_parent.mainmap.textmap._x =
_parent.mainmap.textmap._y =
```

Next, you want to change the x position of the textmap movie clip in the opposite direction from which the Pointer movie clip has been dragged. This is accomplished by multiplying the rest of the ActionScript equation by –1. Follow the same techniques for the y position.

L 15-15
```
_parent.mainmap.textmap._x = -1 * xRatio
_parent.mainmap.textmap._y = -1 * yRatio
```

Because the textmap is a masked movie clip, the opposite direction of movement makes sense, because you would want to scroll toward the right side of the textmap if you drag the pointer toward the right side of the mapShape movie clip. If you dragged the pointer toward the left of the mapShape movie clip, you would want the textmap to move toward the right, so that the text hidden behind the left edge of the mask will start to appear on the screen.

NOTE

As an experiment, you can try removing the −1 from the ActionScript code and just setting the x position to xRatio, and the y position to yRatio. If you do so, you'll find that the textmap movie clip now moves in the same direction as the pointer, but the focus of the masked area moves in the opposite direction. This can be a disorienting way for users to navigate among the text boxes, which is why we multiply by −1 to reverse the direction of navigation.

Finally, multiplying the xRatio and yRatio by the width and height of the textmap movie clip will move the textmap movie clip at the same ratio of distance as the pointer inside the minimap movie clip.

L 15-16

```
_parent.mainmap.textmap._x = -1 * xRatio *
                    _parent.mainmap.textmap._width;
_parent.mainmap.textmap._y = -1 * yRatio *
                    _parent.mainmap.textmap._height;
```

This final key to the ActionScript code allows the Pointer clip to decide the current location of the text map underneath its mask layer in direct proportion to the sizes of the two movies.

Here's another way to look at the ActionScript code, based on Figure 15-7. Imagine that the pointer was located at the center of the minimap movie clip, where x = 0 and y = 0. If the user drags the pointer toward the right by a distance of 100 pixels, the pointer will move by a ratio of 100/280. However, the MainMap movie clip is much bigger than the minimap movie clip, so its textmap movie clip should move more than 100 pixels in order for the pointer to navigate correctly. Therefore, multiplying the ratio of 100/280 by the total width of the MainMap movie clip (let's say it's 450 pixels wide) yields a distance that's proportional to the size of the two movie clips: (100/280) * 450, or xRatio * _parent.mainmap.textmap._width.

What to Take Away from This Chapter

The map interface project demonstrates how a few lines of ActionScript and a nontraditional interface idea can combine to produce an interesting way to navigate through visual information. The unique capabilities of the Flash mask layer feature play a key role in the navigation's design.

There are few limits to what an interface designer can accomplish with Flash, given enough good ideas and enough ActionScript programming to provide the logic for the interface. For example, this map interface can be expanded to contain even more types of information by adding new graphics or buttons to the textmap movie clip. After reading this chapter, try adding some pictures or small movie clip animations inside the movie clip. Experiment with the source file, for example, by playing with the `getBounds()` function and `startDrag()` function to come up with new ways to navigate through the big textmap movie clip. There are many possibilities for exploration and experimentation when it comes to interface design in Flash 5.

The Links Generator Smart Clip

IN THIS CHAPTER:

► Discuss why reusability is important to your workflow and design process

► Introduce the concept of Smart Clips

► Use a simple Smart Clip

► Build a customized user-interface movie clip

► Integrate a customized user-interface movie clip into a Smart Clip

During the course of your life as a Flash designer, you'll find yourself rebuilding some of the same features from previous projects into new projects. More often than not, the task of rebuilding these features can get pretty boring by the sixth or seventh time!

Flash 5 introduces a new feature called Smart Clips, which allows designers to build reusable movie clips. "Reusable" doesn't mean much if it is just referring to copies. After all, you can put the same movie clip into different Flash movies simply by dragging the movie clip from the same Library onto the stage. The power of Smart Clips comes from their capability to be modified by a designer, so that you can adapt the movie clips to the requirements of your current project.

Modification of a Smart Clip can mean anything from changing a few variables in the movie clip to making major changes in how a movie looks and behaves. The range of possibilities depends on the complexity of the ActionScript programming behind the Smart Clip. At this point in the book, we have covered enough ActionScript and advanced Flash techniques to build a relatively useful Smart Clip tool. This chapter begins with an introduction to Smart Clips, and then describes a Smart Clip project that uses a customized interface.

How a Smart Clip Works

BasicSmartclip_01.fla

If you want to take advantage of the full power of Smart Clips, you need to understand how they work behind the scenes and how they rely on ActionScript.

At its most basic level, a Smart Clip has two parts. The first component of a Smart Clip is simply a movie clip whose ActionScript variables are defined by the second component of a Smart Clip, which is the Clip Parameters panel. The variables are never defined inside the movie clip itself.

NOTE

The help files and manuals from Macromedia don't take you directly to documentation about Smart Clips, but if you do a search for "Smart Clips" in the software help files, the resulting links will point to a few pages on Smart Clip construction. However, these pages in the documentation describe only the basic features of Smart Clips.

To get a closer look at the first component of a Smart Clip, open the Flash source file named BasicSmartclip_01.fla on the CD-ROM. The movie clip on stage contains two dynamic text fields above a gray rectangle, as shown in Figure 16-1. These text fields are named `textfield1` and `textfield2`. Now, test this movie clip in the Flash editor by choosing Control | Test Movie. You'll notice that the text fields remain empty in the Flash Player. This is because these text fields are empty by default, and their variable values haven't been defined by any ActionScript code.

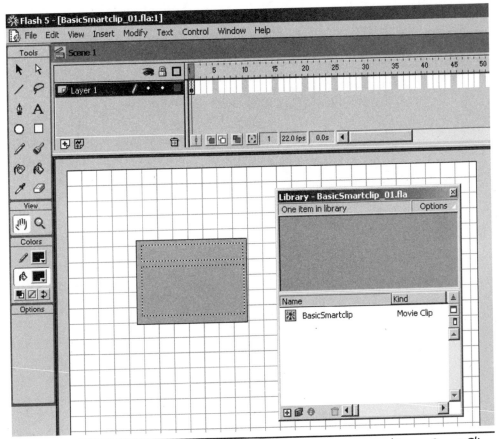

Figure 16-1   *The BasicSmartclip movie clip has not yet been converted into a Smart Clip. Note the regular movie clip icon in the Library Panel.*

Defining Clip Parameters

In the Library, find the movie clip symbol called BasicSmartclip and highlight that symbol with the mouse. You'll notice that the symbol has a standard movie clip icon in the Library. From the Library's drop-down Options menu (shown in Figure 16-2), select Define Clip Parameters. The Define Clip Parameters panel turns a regular movie clip into a Smart Clip by allowing you to specify which variables to modify for a movie clip.

Click the plus (+) button to add a new parameter to define. Then click the plus button again, so you can define two parameters for this Smart Clip. Click the Name, Value, and Type fields to define each parameter. The name of the first parameter should be Textfield1, with a default value of Hello and a type of Default. The

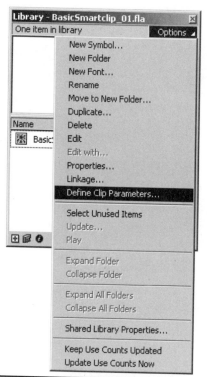

Figure 16-2   *Defining clip parameters for a movie clip*

name of the second parameter should be `Textfield2`, with a default value of `World` and a type of Default, as shown in Figure 16-3.

By specifying two parameters with names identical to the text fields in the movie clip, you've enabled this Smart Clip to modify the values of those two text fields. By giving default values to these two parameters, you've enabled the Smart Clip to automatically assign original values to the clip parameters if the user doesn't modify the clip parameters.

Click OK to save these parameters to the new Smart Clip. Now you'll notice that the symbol in the Library has a new icon that looks similar to the original movie clip icon, as shown in Figure 16-4. The new icon indicates that the movie clip has been changed into a Smart Clip and that it contains clip parameters.

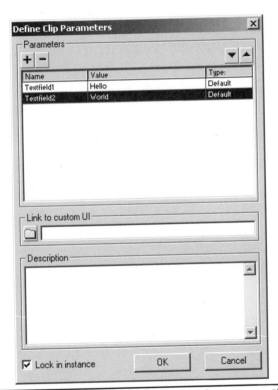

Figure 16-3 *Adding and defining new clip parameters for a Smart Clip*

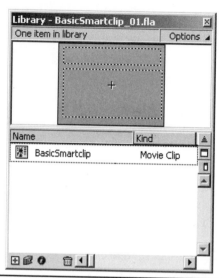

Figure 16-4   *The BasicSmartclip symbol has been converted to a Smart Clip.*

Now, delete all movie clips from the stage, and drag the new Smart Clip from the Library onto the stage. Try testing the movie by choosing Control | Test Movie. You'll notice that the Smart Clip version of this movie clip now displays the default values of `Hello` and `World`.

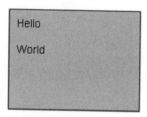

Modifying Smart Clip Parameters
BasicSmartclip_02.fla

You've learned how to define variables for a movie clip as Smart Clip parameters, and you've seen how the Smart Clip can define default values for those parameters. Next, you'll finish your exploration of how a Smart Clip works by modifying the value of each Smart Clip parameter. If you've skipped the previous steps up to this point, you can open the source file BasicSmartclip_02.fla to access a Flash file with a ready-made Smart Clip.

Once clip parameters have been defined for a Smart Clip in the Library, you can access the clip parameters for each Smart Clip instance on the stage through the Clip Parameters panel. If the test movie is still open, close it. Then select the Smart Clip on the stage and choose Window | Panels | Clip Parameters.

Even though the Smart Clip has the default values of `Hello` and `World`, you can assign new values to it through the Clip Parameters panel. In Figure 16-5, `Textfield1` and `Textfield2` have been assigned new values of `Ice` and `Cream`.

Try this with your own source file, and you'll see that the text fields now display the values of their corresponding clip parameters when you test the movie.

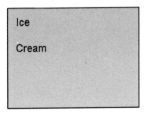

As you've seen, a Smart Clip consists of a movie clip whose variables can be defined by clip parameters. By modifying the values of a clip parameter, a Smart Clip can change the way it looks (such as from "Hello World" to "Ice Cream") or the way it behaves. Now you're ready to learn how to create a complex Smart Clip whose clip parameters change both the appearance and behavior of the Smart Clip.

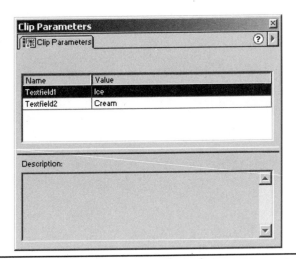

Figure 16-5   *Modifying the values for a Smart Clip's clip parameters*

How a Customized Smart Clip Interface Works

LinkMenu.fla, LinkGenerator_UI.fla, LinkGenerator_UI.swf

The project described in this chapter creates a customized user interface for the Clip Parameters panel. This allows a designer to use a graphical interface to modify the values of the clip parameters, instead of typing them in by hand.

First, save the LinkMenu.fla, LinkGenerator_UI.fla, and LinkGenerator_UI.swf files from the CD-ROM into the same directory on your hard drive. Then open the LinkMenu.fla file in the Flash editor, as shown in Figure 16-6.

Now you have a single movie clip called LinkMenu on the stage. A quick look at the Library will reveal that this movie clip is actually a Smart Clip, as indicated by its Smart Clip icon. Run the movie to see how it works by choosing Modify | Test Movie. The test movie shows a text-based list of Web sites inside a scrollable text panel. Clicking any of the underlined URL hyperlinks will open a Web browser to that Web site.

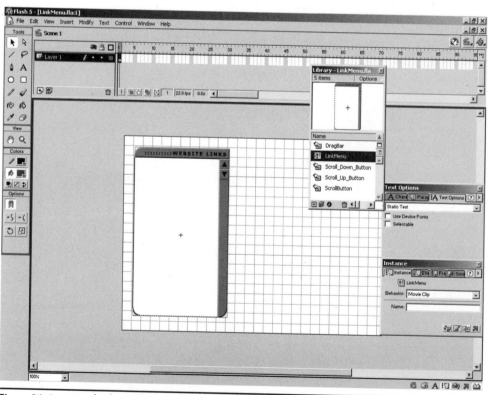

Figure 16-6 *Inside the LinkMenu.fla source file*

As a stand-alone feature, this scrollable list of links could be a useful part of any Web site. However, building a list of hyperlinks inside Flash usually requires a designer to create a text field and format all of the text to show a Web site title, URL, and description. It would take a lot of work to change the formatting of text inside a text field and assign URL hyperlinks for each additional Web site. Turning the LinkMenu movie clip into a Smart Clip allows any designer to drag and drop the Smart Clip from the Library onto the stage, and then add new Web sites to the links list through a user-friendly interface.

Exploring the Customized Smart Clip Interface

To see the customized interface, go back to the LinkMenu.fla source file, select the LinkMenu movie clip on the stage, and open its Clip Parameters panel. Rather than seeing a traditional Clip Parameters panel with text fields for the name, value, and type of each parameter, you now see a much richer interface, as shown in Figure 16-7. This kind of interactive Clip Parameters panel is called a *customized*

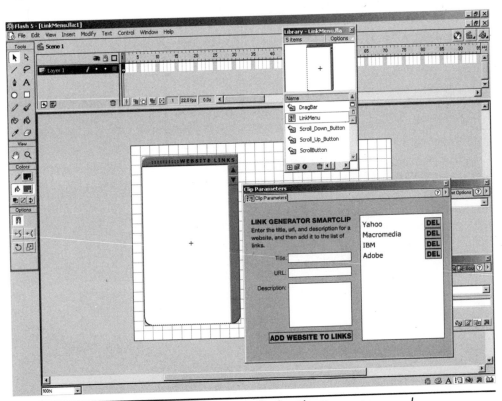

Figure 16-7   *A customized user interface inside the Clip Parameters panel*

Smart Clip interface, and it actually contains another Flash movie within the clip parameters to run the interface.

NOTE

If the customized Smart Clip interface seems small on your screen, enlarge the interface by dragging the corners of the panel.

You can play around with the customized Clip Parameters panel by adding or deleting new Web sites to the links list. Simply fill out the Title, URL, and Description text fields, and click the button to add the Web site to the links. Clicking a DEL button in the display list deletes a Web site from the list of links. Close the panel after you've finished making any changes to the Smart Clip.

If you made changes to the links list, you will see those changes appear when testing the movie in the Flash Player. When you open the Clip Parameters panel again, the list of links refreshes from the memory of that specific Smart Clip, so that each Smart Clip "remembers" the settings of its clip parameters.

Next, open the file named LinkGenerator_UI.fla, and you will see the Flash source file for the clip parameter interface. Select Control | Test Movie to test how the movie behaves on its own. The LinkGenerator_UI.fla file is just a regular Flash movie (shown in Figure 16-8), with its own timeline and library of symbols.

As you can see, the LinkGenerator movie behaves exactly like the customized clip parameter for the menu Smart Clip in the LinkMenu.fla file. Not surprisingly, the published LinkGenerator_UI.swf, which is published by the LinkGenerator_ UI.fla file, is the same Flash movie used to create a visual interface for the clip parameters of the menu Smart Clip.

Linking a Flash Movie to the Smart Clip's Clip Parameters Panel

Now that you know what clip parameters are and how they affect a Smart Clip, it's time to see how customized Flash movies can be embedded inside a Clip Parameters panel. Open the LinkMenu.fla file again and select the LinkMenu symbol in the Library. Choose the Define Clip Parameters command from the Library's drop-down Options menu.

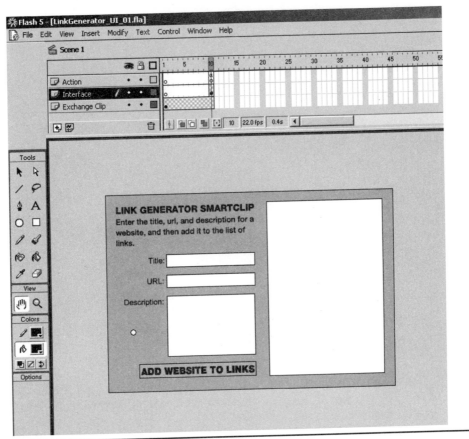

Figure 16-8   *Inside the LinkGenerator_UI.fla file*

In this Define Clip Parameters panel, the Link to Custom UI field contains LinkGenerator_UI.swf, as shown in Figure 16-9. This is the same Flash movie that is published from the LinkGenerator_UI.fla file. Specifying LinkGenerator_ UI.swf as the LinkMenu's custom user interface embeds the LinkGenerator_UI.swf movie clip inside the clip parameters, so that movie is used to modify the values of the clip parameters.

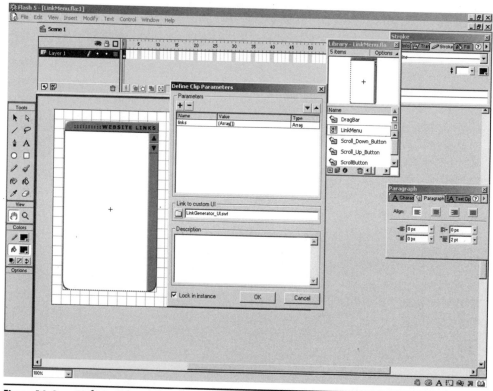

Figure 16-9 *Defining the Links clip parameter for the LinkMenu Smart Clip, with a default value set to an Array*

Examining the ActionScripting for the Smart Clip

To see what is actually going on in the LinkMenu Smart Clip, open the LinkMenu.fla file, and then double-click the LinkMenu Smart Clip in the Library to edit it. In the first frame of the layer named Action, double-click the keyframe to open the Action panel for that frame. The Action panel displays the following ActionScript code:

L 16-1
```
for(var i = 0; i < links.length; i++) {
        var information = links[i].split(",");
        var title       = information[0];
        var url         = information[1];
        var description = information[2];

        // Get the Web site's title
        textfield += "<p><b>" + title + "</b></p>";
```

```
// Get the Web site's URL and wrap it inside <a href> tag
textfield += "<p><u><a href='" + url + "'>" + url +
"</a></u></p>";

// Get the Web site's description and skip two lines.
textfield += "<i>" + description + "</i><p></p><p></p>";
}
```

There's relatively little code associated with this movie clip. Basically, it reads the title, URL, and description of each Web site from an array of data, and then it wraps those three pieces of information inside HTML tags. These tags change the appearance of each line of text and create a text hyperlink to the Web site's URL by using the <a href> tag. Let's break down this code to see how it works.

TIP

Dynamic text fields in Flash can be formatted with HTML tags from the HTML 1.0 specification.

The Links Array

First, the ActionScript code begins to loop through elements in an array called `links`.

L 16-2
```
for(var i = 0; i < links.length; i++) {
```

It's important to realize that the `links` array is not defined anywhere in the Smart Clip. Instead, the array will be defined by the Clip Parameters panel, and then assigned to the Smart Clip. This works in the same way that variables are passed from the clip parameters to the Smart Clip, as described in the previous section. (Later in the chapter, in the "Programming the LinkGenerator_UI Interface" section, we'll discuss how the information is actually passed between a customized clip parameter interface and a Smart Clip.)

In the case of this Smart Clip, the array being passed contains several elements, and each element contains information about the title, URL, and description of a Web site. These three pieces of information are stored in a single string, separated by commas. For example, the first and second elements in the `links` array might contain the following strings:

L 16-3
```
List[0] = "Yahoo, www.yahoo.com, Big web portal";
List[1] = "Macromedia, www.macromedia.com, Makers of Flash
software";
```

The clip parameters will pass the entire array into the movie clip, so that the movie clip can use the array to change its appearance and behavior.

The Information Array

The next line inside the `for` loop takes the string value of each element in the `links` array, splits each element into three elements, and puts the three elements into a new array called `information`.

L 16-4
```
var information = links[i].split(",");
```

Once the new array has been formed, each element is passed into a variable for easy access:

```
var title       = information[0];
var url         = information[1];
var description = information[2];
```

Variables to Text Fields

Once the title, URL, and description for the current element have been retrieved into matching variables, each variable is sent to the text field by appending itself to the end of the text field with the `+=` operator. The appended value is actually the value of the title, URL, or description, wrapped between HTML tags for formatting and hyperlink definition.

L 16-5
```
// Get the Web site's title
textfield += "<p><b>" + title + "</b></p>";

// Get the Web site's URL and wrap it inside <a href> tag
textfield += "<p><u><a href='" + url + "'>" + url + "</a></u></p>";

// Get the Web site's description and skip two lines.
textfield += "<i>" + description + "</i><p></p><p></p>";
```

For example, an array element with the values `Yahoo`, `www.yahoo.com`, `Big web portal` will result in a text field with the following value:

L 16-6
```
<p><b>Yahoo</b><p>
<p><u><a href='www.yahoo.com'>www.yahoo.com</a></u></p>
<i>Big web portal</i><p></p><p></p>
```

If a text field has been HTML enabled, clicking any of its text that has been tagged with the anchor tags (`<a href="url"></a>`) will send the browser to that Web site's address. The double `<p>` tags at the end of the HTML are an easy way to create double-spaced text in an HTML-enabled text field.

Creating a Customized Interface for a Smart Clip

You've seen how the Clip Parameters panel of a Smart Clip can use a customized user interface containing another Flash movie. You also already know how to link the LinkGenerator_UI.swf movie to the Clip Parameters panel of the LinkMenu Smart Clip in the LinkMenu.fla file. However, we haven't discussed how the LinkGenerator_UI.swf talks to the LinkMenu Smart Clip, or how the Link_GeneratorUI movie works in the first place. In order to understand how the Link_GeneratorUI movie works, you'll learn how to build it from scratch in this section.

Building the Link_GeneratorUI Interface

LinkGenerator_UI_01.fla

Open the LinkGenerator_UI_01.fla to begin building this interface. You'll see three layers named Action, Interface, and Exchange Clip, from the top down, as shown in Figure 16-10. Each layer serves its own special purpose:

▶ The Action layer contains a keyframe in the tenth frame to stop the movie from playing any further.

▶ The Interface layer contains all of the interface elements for this Smart Clip.

▶ The Exchange Clip layer contains a special movie clip called xch, which will be used to send information back and forth between this customized interface and the Clip Parameters panel of the LinkMenu Smart Clip.

Notice how the first nine frames of the top layers are blank, while the xch movie clip exists during the entire timeline of this movie. This is necessary because it provides enough time delay to make sure all of the necessary information has passed back and forth between the customized interface and the Smart Clip. According to the rules of customized interfaces for Smart Clips, the interface can communicate

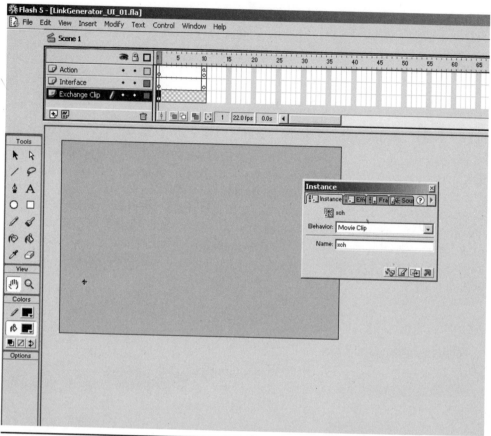

Figure 16-10   *The bare timeline of the customized interface movie*

with the Smart Clip only through a blank movie clip on the main timeline with the instance name of xch. It must have the specific instance name of xch; otherwise, the Smart Clip will not know where to retrieve information from inside the customized interface movie. Any variables, arrays, or objects existing inside the xch movie clip will be assigned to the Smart Clip movie clip, and vice versa.

Also, it's important to note that the complexity of objects or arrays passed through the xch movie clip must have only one layer. For example, arrays passed through xch can only be one-dimensional, and nested arrays or nested objects will not pass through xch. We will address this limitation later on in the chapter.

Defining the Interface Text Elements

Select the keyframe in the tenth frame of the Interface layer. This is where you will put the basic elements of the interface. The first elements to create are the required text fields. Choose the Text tool and open the Text Options panel. Choose the Input Text option from the drop-down menu in the Text Options panel and check the Border/Bg option. Add three text fields:

► Draw a single-line text field approximately 140 pixels wide on the screen. Give your new text field a variable name of **title** in the Text Options panel.

► Draw another text field below the `title` text field, with the same text options, and give it a variable name of **URL**.

► Draw a multi-line text field below the `URL` text field, and select Multi-Line from the drop-down menu in the Text Options panel. Give this final text field the variable name **description**.

Finally, add some static text labels beside each text field to show what information they should receive, and add some instructions to the upper-left corner of the movie. Use Figure 16-11 as a guide for how to align the text fields and labels.

Defining the Button and Display Panel

The next step is to create a button that allows the user to add the Web site to a list display, and then to create the display that lists all of the Web sites added so far.

Draw a static text field with the words "ADD WEBSITE TO LINKS" below the `description` text field, as shown in Figure 16-12. Then draw an orange rectangle over these words. Select both the rectangle and the text field, and then press F8 to convert the text and rectangle into a button symbol named **Button_Add**.

Draw a white rectangle with black borders, approximately 180 pixels wide and 265 pixels tall, on the right side of the screen. This rectangle will serve as

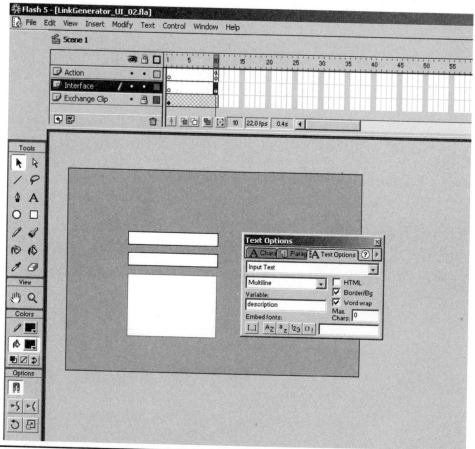

Figure 16-11 *Building input text fields and defining their variable names for the interface*

the background panel for the display panel, which will list all of the stored Web site links. Select both the rectangle and the black borders, and then press F8 to convert them into a movie clip symbol named **Display**. Then give this movie clip an instance name of **DisplayPanel**, as shown in Figure 16-13.

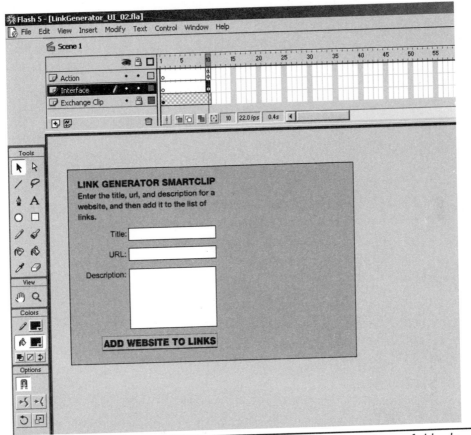

Figure 16-12   *Adding a button to the interface for the user to submit the text field values*

Defining the Title Movie Clip

Now you have all of the text fields required to enter information about a Web site and a button that you can program to add each Web site to the list in the DisplayPanel movie clip. However, the display panel is just a movie clip with a blank, white rectangle. In order to list all of the Web sites, the display panel will

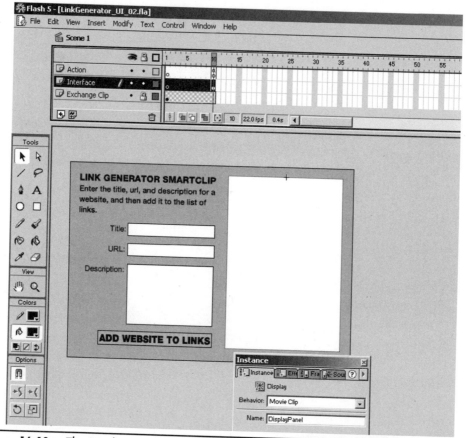

Figure 16-13   *The DisplayPanel movie clip*

need to attach a new movie clip, which should show a text field for the Web site title and a button that allows the user to delete the Web site from the list.

Choose Insert | New Symbol to create a new movie clip called **Title**. This movie clip will contain one text field and one button. Choose the Text tool, and then open the Text Options panel. Choose the Dynamic Text option from the drop-down menu of the Text Options panel, and then draw a text field approximately 140 pixels wide on the screen. Give this new text field a variable name of **textfield**.

Next, create a static text field with the letters "DEL" (for Delete). Draw an orange rectangle around the DEL text field. Select both the rectangle and the "DEL" text, and then press F8 to convert them into a button symbol named **Button_Delete**. Figure 16-14 shows the completed Title movie clip.

You'll need to attach new duplicates of the Title movie clip dynamically according to how many Web sites have been stored in the interface, so the movie clip must be linked externally from the Library. Open the Library, and then select the Title movie clip symbol. Choose the Linkage command from the Library's drop-down Options menu, and then select the Export This Symbol radio button. In the Identifier field, give the symbol an export identifier **TitleMovieclip**, as shown in Figure 16-15, and then click OK.

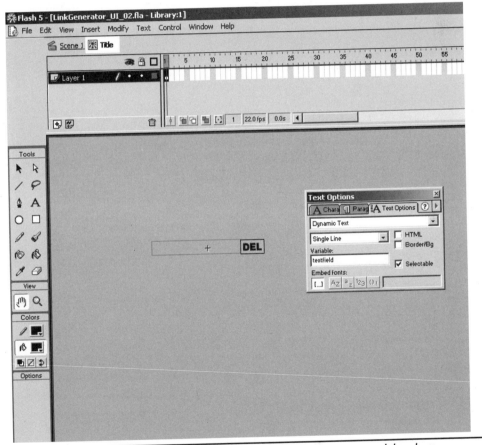

Figure 16-14   *The Title movie clip contains a text field and an orange delete button.*

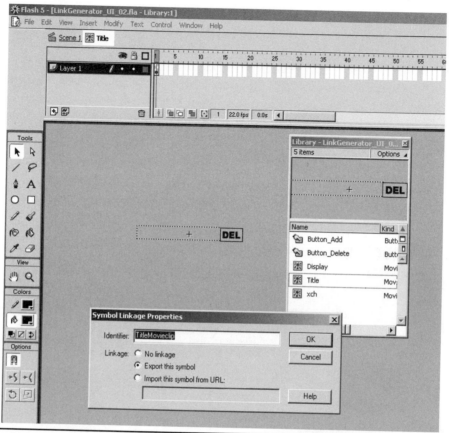

Figure 16-15 *Linking the Title movie clip in the library for export*

The Title movie clip doesn't appear in the LinkGenerator_UI movie clip right now. You haven't written the ActionScript code to receive information about a Web site for the link menu, or to list the Web sites in the display panel. The next section describes the ActionScripting for these tasks. Once a Web site has been added to the list, the display panel should attach another copy of the Title movie clip inside itself to show the title of the newly added Web site.

Programming the LinkGenerator_UI Interface

LinkGenerator_UI_02.fla

Now that the interface has been built, you can take the final step and add ActionScript code. In previous chapters, you've learned how you can simplify a project by containing several complex ActionScript commands inside a single function. The ActionScript for the LinkGenerator_UI interface takes this approach.

Here are the tasks that you'll need to perform with ActionScript:

▶ When the user clicks the Add Website To Links button, the interface should read the information from the text fields, send that information to the display panel, and then clear the text fields in preparation for the next Web site entry.

▶ The display panel receives the Web site information and adds it to an array of links.

▶ The display panel must refresh its display of sites to include the newly added link and attach a Title movie clip into the display panel for each link in the array.

▶ If the user clicks the DEL button in the Title movie clip, it should tell the display panel to remove that link from the array, and then refresh itself.

Reading and Sending Information

Because the user must click the button in order to add a Web site to the display panel, the first step of ActionScript programming should be placed on the button. Open the LinkGenerator_UI_02.fla file, which has the interface already built, and then open the Action panel for the button labeled Add Website To Links. Insert the following ActionScript code for the button:

L 16-7
```
on (release, keyPress "<Enter>") {
        DisplayPanel.addLink(title, url, description);
        title = "";
        url = "";
        description = "";
}
```

The code is triggered by two possible events: releasing the mouse over the button after it has been pressed or pressing the ENTER key after typing in all the information.

L 16-8
```
on (release, keyPress "<Enter>") {
```

Next, the button calls a function called addLink() in the movie clip named DisplayPanel. While calling the DisplayPanel.addLink function, the button also passes the values of the three text fields—title, url, and description—as parameters. Once the information has been passed, the form needs to be cleared again, so each text field is assigned a blank string value, " ".

Adding the Information to an Array of Links

Now the flow of information points toward the display panel, which is still just a white, rectangular movie clip. Select the display panel and open its Action panel. You need to define the addLink() function called by the button, so insert the following code:

L 16-9
```
onClipEvent (load) {
    function addLink(title, url, description) {
        if(links.length <= 11) {
            links.push(title + "," + url + "," + description);
            refresh();
        }
    }
}
```

Here, the addLink() function is defined inside the load event handler, which executes only once, when the movie clip loads into the Flash movie. Take a look at the first line of the function definition and you will see that the parameters of the addLink() function match the parameters passed by the button as it called this function: title, url, and description.

L 16-10
```
    function addLink(title, url, description) {
```

Passing information through function parameters is how the function can receive information from whatever object invokes that function.

Next, the function checks to see whether there are 11 or fewer links in the array called links. This allows the interface to stop adding any links if it has reached the maximum of 11.

L 16-11
```
        if(links.length <= 11) {
```

If there are 11 or fewer links in the array, the function adds another link to the links array in the following line of code, using the array's push() method. The push() method of an array merely pushes a new element to the top of the array, like adding a new pancake onto a stack of pancakes. In this case, a string of characters is formed by joining the values of the title, url, and description parameters into a single string, separated by commas.

L 16-12
```
        links.push(title + "," + url + "," + description);
```

Later you will write code to separate these commas into new arrays. As mentioned earlier in this chapter, the xch movie clip, through which a Smart Clip and its customized interface can communicate, cannot accept nested arrays or nested objects. Therefore, using commas to separate values in a single string is necessary because you will need to pass three separate values for each array element, to simulate the effect of having a nested (or two-dimensional) array.

The final line of code in the `addLinks()` function calls another function named `refresh()`, which will refresh the Title movie clips attached to the DisplayPanel movie clip.

L 16-13
```
refresh();
```

Refreshing the Display Panel and Attaching Title Movie Clips

When the `refresh()` function is called by the `addLinks()` function, it must perform three subtasks:

1. Delete all of the Title movie clips attached to the display panel.

2. Next, refresh the display panel with new Title movie clips.

3. Finally, send the links array to the xch movie clip in the main timeline, so that the xch movie clip can communicate with the Smart Clip.

The ActionScript for the `refresh()` function looks like this:

```
function refresh() {
    // Remove old attached movie clips
    for(var n in this) {
        if (typeof(this[n]) == "movieclip") {
            this[n].removeMovieClip();
        }
    }
    // Rebuild new bar movie clips
    for(var i = 0 ; i < links.length; i++) {
        attachMovie("TitleMovieclip", "bar" + i, i);
        var currentBar = this["bar" + i];
        var information = links[i].split(",");
        var title       = information[0];
        var url         = information[1];
        var description = information[2];
```

```
                    currentBar.textfield = title;
                    currentBar.identity = i;
                    currentBar._y = 20 + currentBar._height * (i);
            }
            _root.xch.links = new Array();
            _root.xch.links = this.links;
    }
```

Let's break this code down into understandable portions. First, it declares a function called `refresh()`, which does not receive any parameters.

```
    function refresh() {
```

Then it looks through all the possible objects inside the DisplayPanel movie clip to see whether they are movie clips. The command `typeof([object])` can receive an object and return a string value that describes that object's type. If the type matches the description of `"movieclip"`, the object is told to remove itself from the DisplayPanel movie clip.

```
        // Remove old attached movie clips
        for(var n in this) {
                if (typeof(this[n]) == "movieclip") {
                        this[n].removeMovieClip();
                }
        }
```

Now that all the attached movie clips have been removed, it's time to loop through the `links` array and attach a new Title movie clip from the Library for each link in the `links` array. The `for` loop will loop through all the elements in the `links` array, starting from zero and moving through the array to the last element.

```
        // Rebuild new bar movie clips
        for(var i = 0 ; i < links.length; i++) {
```

For every element in the array, the Title movie clip is attached to the DisplayPanel movie clip and given a new instance name of `"bar"` + i, where i increments from 0 to the last number of elements in the array. Remember that you gave the Title movie clip an external linkage identifier in the Library (as described in the "Defining the Title Movie Clip" section earlier in this chapter), and the Title movie clip had a linkage identifier of `TitleMovieclip`. Each new movie clip has a different instance name, so during each loop, a reference to that instance is assigned to a shortcut variable named `currentBar`.

```
attachMovie("TitleMovieclip", "bar" + i, i);
var currentBar = this["bar" + i];
```

When a Web site's information was added to the links array, the title, url, and description of the Web site were concatenated together into a single string, separated by commas. Each element in the links array is now split into three new array elements by separating them wherever the commas appear in the string. The three new array elements are assigned to a temporary array called information.

```
var information = links[i].split(",");
```

Once you've split the title, url, and description into the information array, each piece of the array is assigned to a temporary variable with a matching name: title, url, and description.

```
var title       = information[0];
var url         = information[1];
var description = information[2];
```

Okay, so far you've looped through the array and attached a new Title movie clip to the display panel. You've also extracted information from each element in the array. But how does the information go into the new Title movie clip? A few pages earlier, you inserted a dynamic text field into the Title movie clip, with a variable name of textfield. Assigning the value of the title variable to the textfield variable in each Title movie clip will make the title of that Web site link appear in the attached Title movie clip instance.

```
currentBar.textfield = title;
```

Next, add a new variable inside the Title movie clip, so that each attached Title movie clip knows which element it represents in the array. This will be helpful when you write a function to remove individual links from the links array by clicking a Title movie clip's DEL button.

```
currentBar.identity = i;
```

Attaching a new Title movie clip to the DisplayPanel movie clip is fine, but each movie clip is attached to the same position inside that movie clip. It's important to move each subsequent attachment downward, so that they appear in a vertical stack, instead of overlapping each other. Therefore, you will move each attached movie clip downward by a distance in proportion to how many movie clips have been attached so far. For example, if you've attached five Title movie clips, then the sixth attachment should appear beneath the fifth movie clip, or the equivalent of five times the height of a Title movie clip. Adding 20 pixels to the vertical position of each movie clip will reposition the entire stack 20 pixels lower, so that the movie clips are positioned well within the white rectangle of the display panel.

```
        currentBar._y = 20 + currentBar._height * (i);
    }
```

Finally, the `refresh()` function must send the array to the xch movie clip in the main timeline, in order for the Smart Clip to be able to receive this array.

```
        _root.xch.links = new Array();
        _root.xch.links = this.links;
    }
```

Deleting Movie Clips and Links

If the user clicks the DEL button, the Title movie clip should be removed, and the corresponding link must be deleted from the `links` array. The easiest way to perform this task is for the DEL button to call a function in the DisplayPanel movie clip named `removeLink()` and pass a reference to the movie clip as a parameter of the function.

L 16-14
```
function removeLink(targetMovieclip) {
    links.splice(targetMovieclip.identity, 1);
    targetMovieClip.removeMovieClip();
    refresh();
}
```

The parameter, `targetMovieclip`, provides a reference to that movie clip in the function definition. Remember that each attached movie clip was given a variable called `identity`, so that the movie clip would remember which element it represented inside the `links` array. Retrieving that `identity` variable from the `targetMoveclip` reference allows the ActionScript code to remove the corresponding element in the array. Removing an element from an array can be achieved by using the `splice()` array method.

The `splice()` method of an array allows you to specify the starting point from which you want to delete an element in the array and how many elements you would like to delete from that starting point. Because you need to delete only one element for each removed Title movie clip, use the `targetMovieclip.identity` variable as the starting point and specify 1 as the number of elements to remove from the array.

L 16-15

```
function removeLink(targetMovieclip) {
    links.splice(targetMovieclip.identity, 1);
```

After the element has been removed from the `links` array, the Title movie clip is removed from the display panel by calling the `removeMovieclip()` method. At this point, both the movie clip and array element have been removed, so it's time to call the `refresh()` function again to refresh the display panel.

L 16-16

```
    targetMovieClip.removeMovieClip();
    refresh();
```

After each addition or removal of a link from the `links` array, the `refresh()` function is called, and each call to the `refresh()` function causes the array to be sent into the xch movie clip on the main timeline.

Great! So now you have an interface that allows a user to add and delete Web site links from a visual link. The interface is easy to use and visually appealing, which makes it very useful as a customized Smart Clip interface. There is just one more interface element to consider.

Remembering Previous Smart Clip Settings

What if the Smart Clip already has a `links` array from previous changes to the clip parameters? If you add links to the Smart Clip, you would expect the interface to remember the information if you open the Clip Parameters panel again, right?

The solution is to write some code that runs as soon as the LinkGenerator_UI.swf movie clip loads into the Clip Parameters panel, so that it can retrieve information from the Smart Clip if that information already exists. The xch movie clip on the main timeline allows the Smart Clip to communicate with the Clip Parameters panel (and any customized Flash movies inside the panel), and vice versa. So, any clip parameters already defined in a Smart Clip can be retrieved from the xch movie clip.

The following code checks to see whether the `links` array has already been passed into the xch movie clip by the Smart Clip. If so, the code will assign the `links` array from the xch movie clip into the DisplayPanel movie clip's `links` array, and then refresh the display panel. Otherwise, nothing happens, and the `links` array is simply defined as an empty array.

L 16-17

```
// Initialize the list from the xch movie clip.
if(_root.xch.links.length > 0) {
    links = _root.xch.links;
    refresh();
} else {
```

```
        links = new Array();
}
```

What to Take Away from This Chapter

As you learned in this chapter, there are two different approaches to using Smart Clips. The easy approach, using the default clip parameters, allows a user to change values for a Smart Clip easily and quickly. However, some Smart Clips can require complex data, and complex data is best administered through a customized interface. Even though a custom Flash interface requires more work to build than using the default Clip Parameters panel, the ease of use that comes from an intuitive and well-designed interface can save you a lot of time in the long run.

Tackling the complexity of building Smart Clips is an investment that you, as the designer, should make based on your judgment of whether the Smart Clip is complex enough to require a customized interface, and whether you will be able to reuse this Smart Clip many times in the future. The LinkMenu Smart Clip described in this chapter can be dragged onto the stage from the Library, and then modified quickly and easily to create a new list of Web site links and Web site information.

XML Address Book

IN THIS CHAPTER:

▶ Discuss the origins and philosophy behind XML

▶ Understand why XML is an important addition to Flash 5

▶ Describe the structure of an XML document.

▶ Use XML in Flash 5 ActionScript

▶ Dynamically generate an XML interface

X ML (Extensible Markup Language) is a simple but powerful way to organize information for humans and computers. XML looks like HTML, but it is different in that it only tells a computer how the information is organized, not how to display that information.

XML is a subject that requires more than a single chapter to cover in any depth. In fact, the computer publishing world has produced many books on the subject of XML, and some of them weigh as much as a telephone book. The immense amount of information published on the subject of XML is ironic when you consider that XML was invented to simplify the transmission of information.

So why are we dedicating a chapter to XML at all? Because XML can be very useful, for both simple and complex Flash applications. For beginners who are new to XML, this chapter provides an introduction to XML. The basic techniques covered in this chapter are enough to help you get a jumpstart using XML for practical projects, and they'll give you some basic experience before moving on to more detailed topics in XML-oriented books. For advanced programmers who have already used XML with other Web technologies, this chapter explains how to bring your knowledge into Flash 5.

Why XML?

XML can be described as a small set of rules that enables you to organize information in a text-based document. As long as two pieces of software understand the same rules, they are able to send information to each other in the form of XML documents. The purpose of XML is to allow different people and organizations to agree on an XML structure, and then organize the information according to the structure, so that their machines can exchange information effectively. When its rules are followed, XML allows information exchange, no matter what kind of software or operating system is being used.

XML Versus HTML

XML was created with the intention of allowing information to be organized in a flexible, simple, and meaningful way. The creation of this standard was in response to a common complaint against the fact that HTML tags specified both the structure and the layout of the content. The world of computer science has long established the benefits of separating data from display, but HTML evolved too quickly to avoid that mistake.

For example, the HTML <ul> and <li> tags are used to specify a list of text, but they also specify how the list is displayed on a Web page.

L 17-1
```
<ul>GROCERY LIST
<li>APPLES
<li>MILK
<li>COOKIES
<li>EGGS
</ul>
```

If you try pasting the preceding code into an HTML page, you would see something like this in your browser:

L 17-2
```
GROCERY LIST
APPLES
MILK
COOKIES
EGGS
```

The preceding sample HTML code describes a structured list of grocery items. Unfortunately, you can't specify exactly how the browser should display the list, because the HTML tags already decide how the list will be shown in a browser.

Here's another example of how HTML and Cascading Style Sheets (CSS) can describe the structure of a document while simultaneously deciding how it will be displayed in the browser:

L 17-3
```
<div class="SpecialParagraph" <p>This is the beginning of a paragraph.
The paragraph tag in HTML does not allow you to decide where the
paragraph text will be positioned in the browser's screen. However,
the div tag specifies the paragraph as a separate data object, so
that the CSS class, "Special Paragraph", can be used to determine how
this paragraph's contents will be displayed.</p></div>
```

To the human eye, the source code behind a sophisticated HTML Web page is nearly unreadable because instructions for organizing the document are interwoven with instructions for displaying the document. In a typical high-quality Web page, you might see CSS, JavaScript, and HTML code occupying the same place in the source code.

The future of the Web will extend beyond computer browsers into portable devices, home appliances, and even wireless devices. Each new technology connected to the Web will have different limitations on how information can be displayed and used. If all future

Internet technologies relied on HTML, they would run into difficulties in implementing Cascading Style Sheets and JavaScript. Fortunately, XML provides a way to separate the data from the display, while also providing a meaningful description of its contents.

XML and Flash

Flash 5 includes the ability to read, manipulate, and send data encoded in the XML format. Flash is an excellent example of why XML's separation of the data and the display is so important. Even though Flash 5 movies can contain HTML-formatted text, Flash is limited to the original HTML 1.0 specification, which has only a handful

Design Goals of XML

XML is a standard recommended by the World Wide Web Consortium (W3C), the same committee that also established the standards for HTML, JavaScript, and CSS. The purpose of XML can be summed up by ten simple design goals listed in the following excerpt from the XML 1.0 Recommendation:

- ▶ XML shall be straightforwardly usable over the Internet.
- ▶ XML shall support a wide variety of applications.
- ▶ XML shall be compatible with SGML.
- ▶ It shall be easy to write programs which process XML documents.
- ▶ The number of optional features in XML is to be kept to the absolute minimum, ideally zero.
- ▶ XML documents should be human-legible and reasonably clear.
- ▶ The XML design should be prepared quickly.
- ▶ The design of XML shall be formal and concise.
- ▶ XML documents shall be easy to create.
- ▶ Terseness in XML markup is of minimal importance.

You can find the W3C's latest updated version of the XML 1.0 Recommendation at http://www.w3.org/TR/REC-xml.

of tags. For complex information, it makes a lot more sense to take advantage of Flash's vector-animation capabilities and use its multimedia features to display information in a more engaging way.

Because XML provides only the structure of data, Flash is able to receive complex information and convert that information into customized interfaces. As a result, XML allows Flash movies on desktops, laptops, and portable devices to display complex information in a way that takes advantage of each particular piece of hardware and software. Flash's XML features enable Flash movies to communicate with other data sources, such as server-side scripting languages and databases, in more complex ways.

Prior to Flash 5, ActionScript relied on the `loadVariables()` command to send and receive long strings of data in a flat format of simple name/value pairs. In other words, Flash 4 could only send and receive long lists of variable names and their values. This is the same approach used by HTML, specifically the POST and GET methods. It was fine for exchanging simple data such as a person's e-mail address or the price of an online purchase item. Here's an example of how information needed to be formatted before it could be sent to a SWF movie built in Flash 4:

L 17-4
```
Person1_FirstName=Santa
&Person1_LastName=Claus
&Person1_Description=He knows if you've been good or bad!
&Person2_FirstName=Snow
&Person2_LastName=White
&Person2_Description=A princess who is friends with seven dwarves.
```

These six lines are typical of what you might see in an ASP or PHP script that is preparing information to be sent to a Flash movie. Each line contains the name of a variable and the value of that variable (which is why they are called name/value pairs). Each name/value pair has its own line of text, and each pair is separated from the previous pair with an ampersand symbol (&).

The example describes information about two people, Santa Claus and Snow White. However, it's difficult to tell exactly what the information describes, because the relationship in the variables is identified only by differences in the variable names. For example, the variable `Person1_FirstName` exists in the same hierarchy as `Person2_FirstName`, and a single number is the only difference that tells you which person the variable is describing. This flatness poses a big problem if you are working on a project that requires more complex information than a simple name/value pair.

Very complex information, such as a hierarchical tree of data (like a family tree) or a list of entries in an address book, is more meaningful if it is organized into a structure that reflects the nature of the data:

L 17-5
```
<addressbook>
        <person firstname="Santa" lastname="Claus">
        He knows if you've been good or bad!
        </person>
        <person firstname="Snow" lastname="White">
        A princess who is friends with seven dwarves.
        </person>
</addressbook>
```

This is actually an XML document that can be recognized by Flash 5. Rather than separate a person's first name, last name, and description into a flat list of name/value pairs, all of the information associated with a person is organized into hierarchical groups of data. As you can see, this format presents information about people from an address book in a way that makes much more sense to human readers. It is also much more meaningful to software that can read XML documents, including Flash.

XML Elements

As you can see in the sample XML address book document in the previous section, the tags look a lot like the tags found in HTML. The main difference that you might notice at first glance are the tag names and attribute names within the tags. These names are not found in regular HTML tags, and if you used them within a regular HTML Web page, a browser would not recognize them as meaningful tags. This is because XML tags do not describe how the information should look on a Web page. Rather, they describe pieces of information as they relate to each other.

Nodes and Attributes

In XML, a *node* is an element that describes a piece of data. For example, in the case of the address book, the `<addressbook>` tag is a node, which describes a piece of data. All of the text between the opening tag, `<addressbook>`, and the closing tag, `</addressbook>`, belongs to the `addressbook` node. All nodes must have an opening and closing tag.

The `addressbook` node contains two *child nodes*, which have *node names* of `person`. Thus, the XML document describes two pieces of data, one for each person, and these two pieces of data belong to the parent addressbook node in the XML hierarchy.

Within each <person> tag are pieces of information called *attributes*, which provide some details about its current node. In the case of the address book, the firstname and lastname attributes provide more specific information about each person. Here are a few rules regarding attributes:

▶   Attributes must have an attribute name, such as firstname and lastname.

▶   The value of an attribute must be assigned by an equal sign (=) and be enclosed within quotation marks.

▶   The attribute name must be a continuous string name with no spaces or special characters.

For more specific naming rules, refer to the XML documentation listed in the upcoming section, "XML Resources."

Let's take a look at a simplified version of the XML example, with just the node elements and attributes:

L 17-6
```
<addressbook>
        <person firstname="Santa" lastname="Claus">
        </person>
</addressbook>
```

In this example, there are two nodes: addressbook and person. Each node is defined by an XML tag, so these types of nodes are called *element nodes*. The person is a child node of the addressbook. If you look at this relationship in another way, the addressbook is the parent node of the child node. The person node has two attributes, firstname and lastname. The value of the firstname attribute is "Santa" and the value of the lastname attribute is "Claus."

Text Nodes and Node Values

Bodies of text within the tags of an XML node are also considered nodes, just a different type of node called *text nodes*. This idea might be confusing at first, but when you consider that XML organizes documents into small pieces of structure, then it makes sense to think of text blocks as child nodes of the node tags. When you refer to the text between the tags of a node, the text, as a block of data, is still considered the child node of that tag. When you refer to the actual value of the text, or in other words, the characters and numbers that make up that text, it's considered the *node value* of the text node.

For example, consider the text between the `person` node tags in the address book code:

L 17-7
```
<addressbook>
      <person firstname="Santa" lastname="Claus">
      He knows if you've been good or bad!
      </person>
</addressbook>
```

The block of text makes up the text node, and the node value is the text itself: "He knows if you've been good or bad!"

This is a `person` node element containing a text node:

L 17-8
```
      <person firstname="Santa" lastname="Claus">
      He knows if you've been good or bad!
      </person>
```

The text node is a child node of the `person` node element. When you refer to the block of text, you can refer to it as the child node of the `person` node; but when you want to retrieve the actual value of the text, you would refer to the actual text as the "node value" of that child node.

When you consider how an XML document is designed, the XML rules produce a side effect that declares that all XML nodes may contain any number of child nodes, from zero on up. Another side effect is that an XML node may have only one parent node.

XML Resources

At this point in the chapter, you've learned why XML is significant for the Web, as well as why the universal portability of XML convinced Macromedia to include XML features in Flash 5. You've also seen what a simple XML document looks like and gotten a brief overview of some of the basic rules for building an XML document. Of course, XML documents can be many times more complex.

If you would like to learn more details about XML and its uses, you might want to check out some of the following resources:

- ▶ The W3C Recommendation for XML 1.0 (www.w3.org/TR/REC-xml)

- ▶ *XML: A Beginner's Guide* by Dave Mercer (Osborne/McGraw-Hill, 2001)

- ▶ W3C XML School (one of the free tutorials online at www.w3schools.com/xml/default.asp)

- ▶ Web Developers Virtual Library (wdvl.internet.com/Authoring/Languages/XML/Tutorials/Intro/)

Combining XML with Flash and ActionScript

AddressBook.fla

Now that you have the basic idea of how XML works, you're ready to learn some practical uses for XML with Flash 5. The rest of this chapter describes how to build a simple address book application in Flash, which allows a user to load various XML address books into the Flash movie and build a visual display of that information.

For a peek at the final version of the example, open the file named AddressBook.fla on the CD-ROM and test the movie. This Flash movie requires the accompanying XML files, too, so make sure to copy all of the files for this chapter into a new directory on your hard drive before you publish the movies for viewing.

Creating the XML Document

The addressbook.xml document looks similar to the example presented earlier in this chapter, but it contains more `person` nodes, and each `person` node contains more attributes. This is still a bare-bones XML document that doesn't use a lot of the frills found in more complex XML documents, but it does demonstrate some of the basic XML features in Flash 5.

L 17-9
```
<addressbook>
<person firstname="Santa" lastname="Claus" phonenumber="555-1001"
city="North Pole" state="Michigan">
   He knows if you've been bad or good!
</person>
<person firstname="Easter" lastname="Bunny" phonenumber="555-2022"
city="Chocolate City" state="Virginia">
   Too much candy is bad for your teeth!
```

```
</person>
<person firstname="Snow" lastname="White" phonenumber="555-3330"
city="Fairy Castle" state="California">
   Her best friends are the seven dwarves.
</person>
<person firstname="Bilbo" lastname="Baggins" phonenumber="555-4044"
city="Hobbitown" state="New Hampshire">
   Nobody has seen this elusive little hobbit fairy creature.
</person>
<person firstname="Jack" lastname="Frost" phonenumber="555-5555"
city="Minnesota" state="Minneapolis">
   Jack Frost roasting on an open fire, chestnuts nipping at your nose...
</person>
</addressbook>
```

The first node in this XML document is addressbook, and it has five child nodes. All five of these child nodes are person nodes, and each person node has the following attributes: firstname, lastname, phonenumber, city, and state. Each person node contains a child node, which is a text node.

Testing the Movie

AddressBook_01.fla

Before continuing, copy all of the files for this chapter from the CD-ROM to a new directory on your hard drive (if you haven't done so already). Testing the Flash movies will require access to the XML documents while running the movie, so it's important that they're all in the same directory.

Once you've copied the files to your computer, open the Flash source file named AddressBook_01.fla. The purpose of this file is to introduce the XML object in the ActionScript language by displaying the contents of the XML document in a text field in the Flash movie. Figure 17-1 shows the contents of AddressBook_01.fla, which contains a single large text field.

Try testing the movie by selecting Control | Test Movie. The movie displays two lines of text, as shown in Figure 17-2. The first line shows the name of the highest node in the XML hierarchy and the number of child nodes within that node. The highest node in an XML document is the document itself, and the name is null in this example, because the document doesn't have a node name. The second line shows the name of the first child of that node, as well as the number of child nodes within that node.

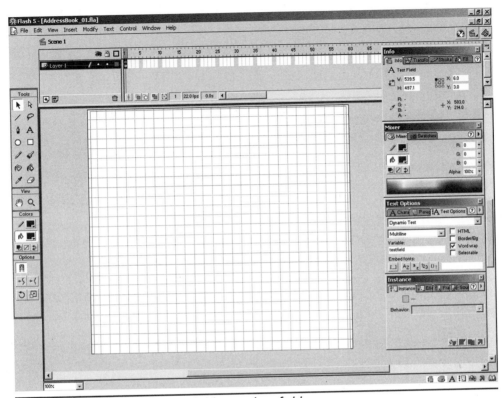

Figure 17-1   *Create a large text field named textfield*

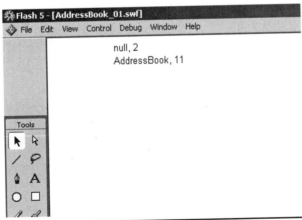

Figure 17-2   *Output from AddressBook_01.fla when testing the movie in the Flash editor*

Using the XML Object

In the address book file, you will find a single keyframe and a dynamic text field simply named `textfield`. The keyframe contains the following ActionScript:

L 17-10

```
objXML = new XML();
objXML.ignoreWhite = true;
objXML.onLoad = onLoadXML;

function onLoadXML() {
        nodeName1 = objXML.nodeName;
        nodeName2 = objXML.firstChild.nodeName;
        textfield += nodeName1 + ", " + objXML.childNodes.length + "\n";
        textfield += nodeName2 + ", "
                     + objXML.firstChild.childNodes.length + "\n";
}
objXML.load("addressbook.xml");
```

Declaring the XML Object

The first line of code in the keyframe declares a new XML object named `objXML`.

L 17-11

```
objXML = new XML();
```

The XML object is a native object from Flash 5 that allows ActionScript to read, manipulate, and send XML-encoded data. Each instance of the XML object contains methods and properties that allow you to interface with the data.

Ignoring White Space

The next line of code sets the `ignoreWhite` property of the `objXML` object to `true`. Some documents use a lot of empty space to format the tags with tabs and indentations, so that humans can read the document more easily. Unfortunately, these empty spaces in the XML document can sometimes create "ghost" nodes.

These ghost nodes occur because the Flash 5 editor is missing the XML feature that handles the empty spaces. Only the latest version of the Flash Player (5.0.41.0 or higher) can use XML documents properly without producing ghost nodes from the white space in an XML document.

If you test the movie within the Flash 5 editor, you will see an output of 11 child nodes for the `addressbook` node. However, the addressbook.xml document contains only five `person` child nodes. Now try this: press SHIFT-F12 to publish this movie with an accompanying HTML Web page named AddressBook_01.html. If you have updated your Flash Player to version 5.0.41.0 or higher, then viewing this Web page will cause the Flash movie to ignore the white space and remove the ghost nodes. Consequently, the Flash movie now correctly shows that the `addressbook` node contains only five child nodes, as shown in Figure 17-3.

NOTE

Lacking the `ignoreWhite` property in the Flash editor's player may cause errors when you try to test a movie that uses XML. Later on, in the "Looping Through Child Nodes" section of this chapter, you will see a quick fix to get rid of these ghost nodes during testing.

Overwriting the XML Object's On Load Method

The third line of code assigns a function to overwrite the `onLoad` method of the XML object.

L 17-12
```
objXML.onLoad = onLoadXML;
```

Ordinarily, loading external data into Flash raises the problem of knowing when the transfer has completed. Every XML object inherits a method called `onLoad`, which executes as soon as the XML document has completely loaded into the Flash Player. Assigning a new function called `onLoadXML()` to the `onLoad` method will overwrite that method and cause the `onLoadXML()` function to execute as soon as the XML document has completely loaded into the Flash Player.

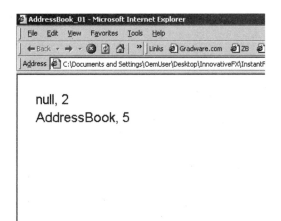

Figure 17-3   *The results of XML parsed to the textfield in a browser*

So, let's define the onLoadXML() function and see what will happen once the XML document has loaded:

L 17-13
```
function onLoadXML() {
        nodeName1 = objXML.nodeName;
        nodeName2 = objXML.firstChild.nodeName;
        textfield += nodeName1 + ", " + objXML.childNodes.length + "\n";
        textfield += nodeName2 + ", "
                    + objXML.firstChild.childNodes.length + "\n";
}
```

The onLoadXML() function performs a very simple task. It retrieves the name of the objXML object and the name of the first child in the XML object, which would be the addressbook node. These two names are assigned to the nodeName1 and nodeName2 variables, respectively.

After the names have been retrieved, the Flash movie displays the name of the node and the number of child nodes for that particular node. This is achieved by referencing an array called childNodes inside the objXML object. The childNodes array contains all of the child nodes. You can retrieve the number of child nodes in a node by using the length array method. For example, myNode.childNodes.length will return the length (or number of elements) in the childNodes array of the node called myNode.

Because objXML is just an object that represents the entire XML document and not a specific node, it does not have a node name. However, the first node, or firstChild, in the XML object is addressbook, which contains five person nodes. As a result, the following command will return a value of 5:

L 17-14
```
objXML.firstChild.childNodes.length
```

Looping Through Child Nodes

AddressBook_02.fla

So far, the ActionScript code for this project has only been able to refer directly to a node and its child node. The ability to loop through all of the child nodes in an XML node is a powerful and simple technique, because looping allows a single set of ActionScript commands to be applied to many child nodes, one after the other.

Open the file named AddressBook_02.fla and test the movie. You will see the same text field output, but this time, it displays the node name of each person node in the addressbook node, and the value of the firstname attribute for each person node (as shown in Figure 17-4).

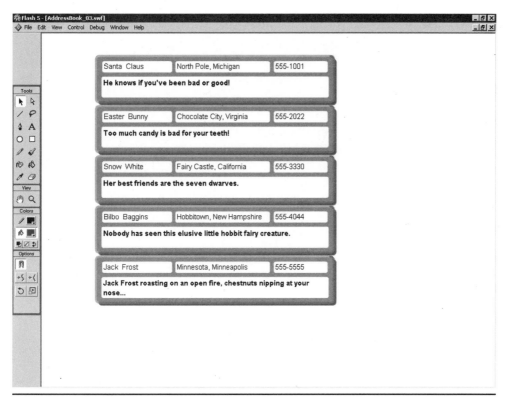

Figure 17-4   *Running the AddressBook_03.fla movie. The interface is dynamically generated by the XML.*

Open the Action panel for the first keyframe. Within that keyframe, you'll see the following ActionScript code:

17-15

```
objXML = new XML();
objXML.ignoreWhite = true;
objXML.onLoad = onLoadXML;

function onLoadXML() {
    addressBook = objXML.firstChild;
    currentNode = addressBook.childNodes[0];

    while(currentNode.nextSibling != null) {
        if(currentNode.nodeType == 1) {
            textfield += currentNode.nodeName + ", "
            textfield += currentNode.attributes.firstName
```

```
                                + "\n";
                }
                // Reassign the current node to its next sibling
                currentNode = currentNode.nextSibling;
        }
}
objXML.load("addressbook.xml");
```

The only significant difference between this code and the ActionScript from AddressBook_01.fla is the `onLoadXML()` function. Let's take a closer look at that function.

The first two lines of `onLoadXML()` create two variables: `addressBook` and `currentNode`.

L 17-16
```
        addressBook = objXML.firstChild;
        currentNode = addressBook.childNodes[0];
```

The first child node in the XML document is assigned to the `addressBook` variable because the first child in the XML document is the `addressbook` node. The first child node of the `addressbook` node is retrieved via the `childNodes` array in the `addressbook` node, and a reference to this first child is assigned to the `currentNode` variable. Because the `addressbook` node contains only `person` nodes, `currentNode` will point to the first `person` node inside the `addressbook` node.

Next, a series of ActionScript commands exists inside a `while` loop. The `while` loop executes all of the code within its curly brackets again and again while its condition is still true. In this case, the `while` loop will execute continuously as long as the `currentNode` variable is not null.

L 17-17
```
        while(currentNode.nextSibling != null) {
```

At the end of the `while` loop code, the `currentNode` variable is reassigned with a reference to its next sibling node. A *sibling node* is the next child node of its parent node. For example, this code will take the current `person` node referred to by the `currentNode` variable and reassign the `currentNode` variable to point to the next `person` node. If the `currentNode` reference points to the last child node `person` inside the `addressbook` node, then the `nextSibling` reference will return a null value, to let you know that it has reached the last `person` child node of the address book.

L 17-18
```
currentNode = currentNode.nextSibling;
```

Once the `currentNode` variable has shifted to the last sibling node, the next pointer to a node will be empty, and its null value allows the `while` loop to detect that it has looped through all of the child nodes.

Remember the problem with ghost nodes while testing XML Flash movies in the Flash editor? You can get rid of those ghost nodes because they're an error, which returns a null value as well. The main code in this function is nested inside an `if` statement, which tests to see whether the node type of the `currentNode` variable is 1. Node types have numeric values in ActionScript, and a node type value of 1 means that the node is a regular node element. If the `currentNode` variable shifted to the next sibling node and the next sibling were a ghost node, then the code would not execute within the `if` statement, because ghost nodes do not have a `nodeType` matching the node type 1.

L 17-19
```
if(currentNode.nodeType == 1) {
```

Finally, send the node name and the `firstname` attribute of each `person` node to the text field on the stage.

L 17-20
```
textfield += currentNode.nodeName + ", "
textfield += currentNode.attributes.firstName + "\n";
```

Customizing Flash's Display of XML

AddressBook_03.fla

Earlier in this chapter, you read about the difficulties of HTML and CSS in trying to define both document structure and document display at the same time. The case for separating data from display is even stronger when you consider that an XML document such as the addressbook.xml file can provide meaningful information to any number of technologies, including Flash, without dictating how the data should be represented.

The file named AddressBook_03.fla contains a way to customize the display of complex information through the Flash movie. Open this file in the Flash editor and test the movie to see what happens. First of all, you'll notice that all of the information from the XML document is displayed in the Flash movie (as shown in Figure 17-5), but the XML data has been fed into duplicated movie clips with customized graphics and layout.

The source file contains two layers. The first layer contains ActionScript, and the second layer contains a movie clip named Entry (as in Address Book Entry).

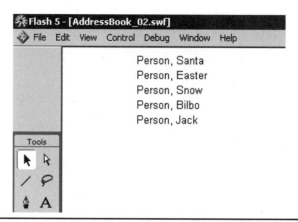

Figure 17-5 AddressBook_03.fla, showing the firstname attribute of each person node by sending them to a textfield

Double-click this movie to peek inside. There are a lot of rectangular blue-and-white decorations in the second layer, but what really matters is that the Entry movie clip contains four text fields in the Textfields layer. These four text fields allow the movie clip to receive and display attributes and text node values from each `person` node in the `addressbook` node.

Displaying Attributes

There are five attributes for each `person` node: `firstname`, `lastname`, `phonenumber`, `city`, and `state`. However, if you include the text description of each `person`, there are actually six pieces of data to display in the Entry movie clip, with only four text fields. So how do we cram six pieces of data into four text fields? The separation between data and display is most helpful here, because you can use ActionScript to join the `firstname` and `lastname` attributes and send them together into the `name` text field. You can also join the `city` and `state` attributes, and send them together into the `citystate` text field. The `phonenumber` attribute will be sent into the `phonenumber` text field, and the node value of the text node in each `person` node will be sent into the `description` text field.

By duplicating the Entry movie clip for each `person` child node, it's possible to display the attributes and text of each `person` child node in the `addressbook` node. In order for the movie clips to work properly, the following must occur:

1. Loop through all of the child nodes in the `addressbook` node.

2. Duplicate the Entry movie clip for each child node (`person` node).

3.   Send the information for each child node into the duplicated movie clip.

Duplicating the Entry Movie Clip

The ActionScript code actually hasn't changed much from the previous example, but the onLoadXML() function does contain additional commands to duplicate the Entry movie clip and send more information to the movie clip:

L 17-21
```
function onLoadXML() {
        addressBook = objXML.firstChild;
        duplicateCounter = 0;
        entry._visible = false;

        currentNode = addressBook.childNodes[0];
        while(currentNode != null) {
                // If the current node is a node element
                if(currentNode.nodeType == 1) {
                        duplicateMovieClip("entry", "entry" +
                                        duplicateCounter, duplicateCounter);
                        newHolder = eval("entry" + duplicateCounter);
                        newHolder._y = duplicateCounter * newHolder._height
                                        + entry._y;

                        // Create a shortcut variable for node attributes
                        var attributes = currentNode.attributes;

                        // Assign the node attributes to text fields
                        newHolder.name = attributes.firstname + "   "
                                        + attributes.lastname;
                        newHolder.phonenumber = attributes.phonenumber;
                        newHolder.citystate = attributes.city + ", "
                                        + attributes.state;
                        newHolder.description = currentNode.firstChild.nodeValue;
                        // Increment the duplicateCounter variable by 1
                        duplicateCounter ++;

                }
                // Get the text node's node value
                currentNode = currentNode.nextSibling;
        }
}
```

The two newest lines at the beginning of the function's code establish a variable called `duplicateCounter` to count how many Entry movie clips have been duplicated and to make the original Entry movie clip invisible:

L 17-22
```
duplicateCounter = 0;
entry._visible = false;
```

Inside the `while` loop, two lines of code perform the duplication of the Entry movie clip and use the `duplicateCounter` variable to make each name and depth of duplicate movie clips unique. Then a shortcut to the newest duplicated movie clip is assigned to the `newHolder` variable, which acts as a temporary shortcut variable that references the duplicated movie clip.

L 17-23
```
duplicateMovieClip("entry", "entry" +
                    duplicateCounter, duplicateCounter);
newHolder = eval("entry" + duplicateCounter);
newHolder._y = duplicateCounter * newHolder._height + entry._y;
```

The third line of code positions the duplicated movie clip farther down the screen, so that all the newest duplicated movie clips will be below the previously duplicated movie clip.

The purpose of the remaining code inside the `while` loop is to send all of the attributes and text nodes of each `person` node to specific text fields in the duplicated movie clip:

L 17-24
```
// Create a shortcut variable for node attributes
var attributes = currentNode.attributes;

// Assign the node attributes to text fields
newHolder.name = attributes.firstname + "  "
                    + attributes.lastname;
newHolder.phonenumber = attributes.phonenumber;
newHolder.citystate = attributes.city + ", " + attributes.state;
newHolder.description = currentNode.firstChild.nodeValue;
```

The `attributes` property acts as an array of an XML node, whose attribute values can be retrieved from the attribute array by the attribute name. For example, `currentNode.attributes.lastname` will retrieve the value of the `lastname` attribute from the node assigned to the `currentNode` variable.

The text from the text node of each `person` node is sent into the description text field of the movie clip in the last line:

L 17-25
```
newHolder.description = currentNode.firstChild.nodeValue;
```

Remember that blocks of text within a node element, such as
`<person>`*text*`</person>`, are also considered a child node in XML.
Therefore, the text description of each `person` node is considered the first
child node.

L 17-26
```
currentNode.firstChild
```

In order to retrieve the text value from this text node, you must make a reference
to the node value of the first child node.

L 17-27
```
currentNode.firstChild.nodeValue;
```

Finally, the `duplicateCounter` variable is incremented by a value of one,
so that the next cycle in the loop will be able to duplicate a movie clip with a new,
unique name:

L 17-28
```
// Increment the duplicateCounter variable by 1
duplicateCounter ++;
```

What to Take Away from This Chapter

XML is a very simple idea on how to organize information for electronic media.
However, this simple idea reaches into almost every aspect of Web technology,
including Flash. The practical applications of XML can range from simple address
books to very complex industry-wide standards in information exchange. As a result,
the concept of XML is simple, but the techniques for implementing XML-based
solutions can be extremely complex.

In this chapter, you learned the basic rules of XML as they apply to Flash
development, as well as some techniques to give you an introduction to using XML.
XML is presented from a practical standpoint, accompanied by some perspectives
on the more abstract reasons behind the invention of XML.

The address book projects described in this chapter demonstrate the hierarchical
relationship between XML nodes and child nodes, and how the XML structure can
contain descriptive information in the form of node structure, attribute values, and
text nodes. The final version demonstrates how Flash can receive XML data and
use the descriptive structure of an XML document to show the information with
a customized display.

Animating with ActionScript

IN THIS CHAPTER:

▶ Understand how to use ActionScript to program realistic, interactive motion

▶ Learn how to program math and physics functions in Flash

▶ Animate objects with a timer

U sing Flash's timeline to animate objects is an easy way to create animations; but if you want to develop realistic, interactive movement, you need to use ActionScript. The good news is that all those hours in your high school algebra and physics classes are about to pay off. The bad news is that if you were like I was in high school, you weren't exactly enthralled with Newton's Laws. Don't panic if you dozed off a little in physics class. We're going to begin this chapter with a quick and relatively painless review of the equations you'll need to get started animating with ActionScript.

Mathematics and Physics—The Keys to Interactive Movies

In the project described in this chapter, we're going to display the path a ball travels when the user throws it. Because we're going to be using ActionScript to control the movement of the ball instead of laying out our ball's position frame by frame in the timeline, we can make our Flash movie more interactive. In this movie, we'll let the user control the initial angle and velocity of the ball, and provide a target to aim for as well. Our final screen, once the user clicks the Throw Ball button, will look something like the one shown in Figure 18-1.

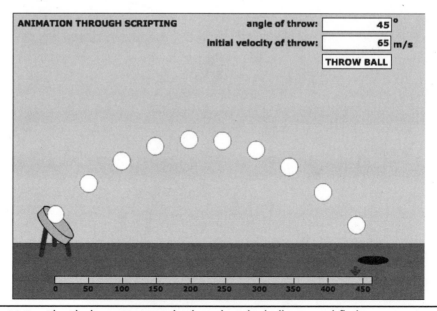

Figure 18-1   *The Flash movie stage display when the ball is in mid-flight*

Lets start with some basic principles from Physics 101. The ball the user is throwing here is a *projectile*, an object that has only one force acting upon it: *gravity*. (We're going to ignore air resistance for now, to keep this example from getting too complex.)

We know from Newton's Law of Inertia that ". . . an object in motion tends to stay in motion with the same speed and in the same direction unless acted upon by an unbalanced force." This means that if there were no gravity, the trajectory of a ball when thrown horizontally would look something like this:

You can see that a ball with no forces acting upon it remains in motion in the same direction at a constant velocity. *Velocity* is how we describe the change in position of an object over a specified amount of time (*velocity = change in position/time*).

The addition of gravity causes the ball to move in a parabolic trajectory, as shown in the following illustration.

Notice how the horizontal velocity of the ball (V_x) remains the same 30 (m/s) throughout the ball's travels, but the vertical velocity of the ball (V_y) changes by −10 m/s every second, due to the force of gravity. In physics terminology, this ball is moving with a *constant horizontal velocity* and a *downward vertical acceleration*.

These examples demonstrate that with projectiles, horizontal motion and vertical motion are independent of each other. This is why we will be using two different main equations in our ActionScript: one to represent the vertical movement of the ball and one to represent the horizontal movement of the ball.

The Physics Equations

For the project, we'll need to use several equations, including those to calculate the horizontal movement, vertical movement, initial horizontal velocity, and initial vertical velocity.

The Horizontal Movement Equation

The equation that describes the horizontal movement of the ball is as follows:

$$x = v_{ix} * t + 1/2 * a_x + t^2$$

Here, x represents the horizontal displacement of the ball over a period of time t, v_{ix} represents the initial horizontal velocity of the ball, and a_x represents the horizontal acceleration of the ball.

NOTE

Displacement is just a fancy way of describing an overall change of position. For example, if you moved forward 5 miles and then turned around and traveled back 2 miles, your displacement was (+ 5 miles) + (–2 miles), or 3 miles. This is not the same as distance, because the total distance you would have traveled is not 3 miles, but (5 miles + 2 miles), or 7 miles.

Because there is no horizontal force acting on our ball—there is only a vertical force (gravity)—a_x must equal zero. This cancels out a large portion of the previous equation and simplifies it into a much more straightforward formula:

$$x = v_{ix} * t$$

The Vertical Movement Equation

The equation that describes the vertical movement of the animated ball is very similar to the original horizontal movement equation:

$$y = v_{iy} * t + 1/2 * a_y + t^2$$

In this equation, y represents the vertical displacement of the ball over a period of time t, v_{iy} represents the initial vertical velocity of the ball, and a_y represents the vertical acceleration of the ball. In this case, because there is vertical acceleration on the ball (the acceleration of gravity, which we know to be –10 m/s/s), we cannot cancel out any parts of the equation. We will need the entire formula to help us determine the vertical movement of the ball.

The Initial Horizontal and Vertical Velocity Equations

Now all that's left to do is to understand how to determine the initial horizontal velocity and vertical velocity of the ball, so that we can plug those values into the horizontal and vertical movement equations. To find these two values, we're going to need to do a little trigonometry.

The initial horizontal velocity of the ball (v_{ix}) can be found using the following formula:

$$v_{ix} = v_i * \cos(\theta)$$

In this equation, v_i represents the initial velocity of the ball, and *theta* (θ) is the angle with which the ball is thrown with respect to the ground. A diagram showing the relationship between the angle theta and the velocity of the ball is shown here.

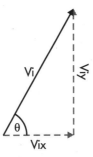

NOTE

Technically, theta represents the angle the velocity vector makes with respect to the horizontal vector. In our Flash movie, the ground is flat, so the simplified definition used here is sufficient for understanding how the equation works.

The initial vertical velocity of the ball can be determined using the following equation:

$$v_{iy} = v_i * \sin(\theta)$$

That's all you need to know about physics calculations for the animation project. Now you'll learn how to apply them in Flash.

The Math Equations

Including complex mathematical equations in Flash 4's Actions window was incredibly difficult because the scripting syntax in that version of Flash was very limited. Fortunately, Macromedia has greatly expanded the scripting language in Flash 5.

For this project, the ball's movement is affected by its angle and velocity. Suppose that the user throws the ball at a 45-degree angle with an initial velocity of 30 m/s, and we want to calculate where the ball is located after 1 second. No problem! First we need to calculate the initial horizontal velocity (v_{ix}) and initial vertical velocity (v_{iy}) of the ball. As explained in the previous section, we can calculate these values as follows:

$$v_{ix} = v_i * \cos(\theta)$$
$$v_{iy} = v_i * \sin(\theta)$$

The example says that the angle the ball is thrown (θ) is 45 degrees, and the initial velocity (v_i) of the ball is 30 m/s, so we have all of the information we need. The good news is that Flash 5 has a built-in Math object that contains methods for determining sine and cosine values. Use this simple ActionScript expression:

L 18-1   `myCosineValue = Math.cos(θ)`

This will set a variable named `myCosineValue` to the cosine value of an angle theta.

The not-so-good news is that Flash expects the theta value to be in radians, not degrees. The angle in the example is in degrees, so the first thing we need to do is convert that value to radians.

A *radian* is simply another way to measure angles. Fortunately, it's easy to convert the measurement of an angle from degrees to radians. There are 2π radians in a 360-degree circle. Because 2π radians = 360 degrees, then 1 radian = $180/\pi$ degrees, and therefore, 1 degree = $\pi/180$ degrees. To determine how many radians are equivalent to 45 degrees, multiply both sides of the equation by 45, as follows:

$$(45) * 1 \text{ degree} = (45) * \pi/180 = \pi/4 \text{ radians}$$

According to these calculations, there are $\pi/4$ radians in 45 degrees.

NOTE

π is the symbol for pi. A lot of people find pi to be confusing, but pi is really just a number. Technically, pi is an infinite decimal, which means it goes on forever, but you're more likely to see pi's value rounded to about five decimal places, to 3.14159. Why does this particular value have a name? This number represents the ratio of the circumference of a circle to its diameter. Because this ratio is always the same, mathematicians decided to assign a name to it to make their equations easier to write. Thus, pi was born.

Now that you know the mathematical equations for both calculating the ball's path and converting angles (what the user enters) to radians (what the Flash Math object uses), you're ready to get started on the animation project.

Outlining the Structure of the Application

Let's quickly review what we want our Flash application to do. We want a user to be able to enter values for an angle and an initial velocity, and when the user clicks the Throw Ball button, a ball placed on a platform should travel according to the equations reviewed in the previous sections. To keep track of how far the ball has traveled, we'll place a ruler on the bottom of the screen, with an arrow "thumb" that moves toward the right side of the Flash movie at the same pace as the ball moves.

Defining the Functions

For this project, we'll need to write the following functions to position and move the ball:

▶   `initVariables()`   This function, called at the very beginning of the Flash movie, will initialize the variables we need throughout the application. This includes creating variables to hold the starting x and y position of the ball and the ruler thumb.

▶   `throwBall()`   This function is called when the user clicks the Throw Ball button. It will make sure that the angle value the user enters is converted to radians, tilt the platform the ball is resting on to the proper angle, solve for the initial horizontal and vertical velocity of the ball (so we can plug those values into our main equations), and call the function to move the ball.

▶   `moveBall()`   This function is initially called from the `throwBall()` function. Then it is called from the `onClipEvent(enterFrame)` script of the ball at regular intervals, to continually update the ball's position. It calculates the elapsed time since the ball was first thrown, passes that value to the functions listed below to calculate the ball's horizontal and vertical displacement at that time, duplicates the ball movie clip, and places the duplicate at the appropriate x and y coordinates.

▶   `convertDegreesToRadians()`   This function simply takes the angle in degrees the user entered as an argument, converts it into radians (as described earlier, in "The Math Equations," and returns the angle in radians (the format the Flash Math object requires).

▶ `getInitialHorizontalVelocity()` and `getInitialVerticalVelocity()` These two functions calculate the horizontal and vertical velocity of the ball when it is first thrown. As you learned earlier, we need these values to help us determine the location of the ball at any given point in time.

▶ `getHorizontalDisplacement()` and `getVerticalDisplacement()` These two functions use the initial horizontal and vertical velocities calculated in the previous functions, and the elapsed time since the ball was first thrown, to determine where the ball should be placed on the screen.

Now let's set up our Flash movie and look at each of these functions in more detail.

Setting Up Assets in the Movie
ch18_01.fla

As you can see in Figure 18-2, or if you open up the ch18_01.fla file on the CD-ROM, each symbol for this project is in its own layer. These layers are named actions, ball, platform, platform legs, hole, throw button, text fields, ruler thumb, ruler, title, sky, grass, and border. Notice that the platform and its legs are kept as separate symbols. This is because only the top of the platform will be rotated in response to the user's throw.

All of the movie clips are named with an mc_ prefix: mc_hole, mc_platform, mc_ruler, and so on. The objects we will be controlling programmatically are the ball, the platform, and the ruler thumb. Figure 18-3 shows each movie clip symbol (mc_ball, mc_platform, and mc_ruler_thumb) from the Flash Library.

These three objects need instance names when placed on the stage, so that we can reference them using ActionScript. In this project, all of the instance names begin with the inst_ prefix. The ball movie clip instance is named inst_ball in the Instance panel, as shown in Figure 18-4. The platform instance is named inst_platform, and the ruler thumb instance is named inst_ruler_thumb.

Figure 18-2   *The layers of the Flash movie*

We will also need to be able to access the values the user enters for both the initial angle of the throw and the initial velocity. This is handled by two single-line input text fields, placed in the upper-right corner of the Flash stage. The first text field has

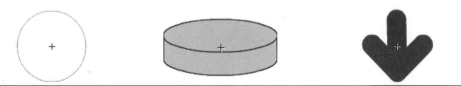

Figure 18-3   *The ball (mc_ball), platform (mc_platform), and ruler thumb (mc_ruler_thumb) movie clip symbols, from left to right*

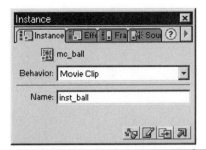

Figure 18-4   *The ball movie clip Instance window*

the variable name angle_degrees, as shown in Figure 18-5. The second text field is set up the same way, with the variable name initial_velocity.

Writing the ActionScript Code

Once all the symbols we need are on the Flash movie stage, we can open the Action panel for the first frame of our movie and start coding some of our functions.

The initVariables() Function

As its name suggests, the initVariables() function is used to initialize all of the global variables we will need for our interactive animation. The code for this function is as follows:

L 18-2
```
function initVariables () {
        ball_is_thrown = "false";
        counter = 2;
        myTimerFlag = 0;
        endOfRuler = 520;

        _root.orig_ball_x = _root.inst_ball._x;
        _root.orig_ball_y = _root.inst_ball._y;
        _root.orig_ruler_thumb_x = _root.inst_ruler_thumb._x;
}
```

The first line of this function initializes a ball_is_thrown flag to "false". This will be updated to "true" when the user clicks the Throw Ball button, and set back to "false" again if the ball moves out of the boundaries of the movie stage. In the throwBall() function (described in the next section), the ball checks to see

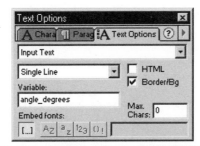

Figure 18-5   *The Text Options panel settings for the angle_degrees user input text field*

whether it is currently supposed to be moving or not, based on whether the value of this `ball_is_thrown` variable is set to `"true"` or `"false"`.

Next, a variable named `counter` is created. We will use this variable to display the trail of the ball's path when the ball is in motion. This will be explained in more detail in the section detailing the `moveBall()` function.

The `myTimerFlag` variable is another flag. This variable is set so that we know whether or not to reset the ball timer.

The `endOfRuler` variable is set to `520`, which is the x coordinate of the rightmost edge of the ruler. This establishes the limit that the arrow ruler thumb can travel. (We wouldn't want the arrow to shoot off the side of the ruler!)

Finally, we need to store the original x and y coordinate values of the ball in variables that are easy to access, so that we can plug those values into the physics equations (covered in "The Physics Equations," earlier in this chapter). We also will record the original x position of our ruler thumb in a variable, so that we can move it toward the right side of the Flash stage at the same pace as the ball. These variables are created and given initial values by the following three lines in the `initVariables()` function:

L 18-3
```
_root.orig_ball_x = _root.inst_ball._x;
_root.orig_ball_y = _root.inst_ball._y;
_root.orig_ruler_thumb_x = _root.inst_ruler_thumb._x;
```

The throwBall() Function

When the movie is playing and the user clicks the Throw Ball button, the `throwBall()` function is called. You can see this by right-clicking (CONTROL-clicking on Macs) on the Throw Ball button on the stage and choosing Actions. A script window appears, as shown in Figure 18-6, displaying code that uses an

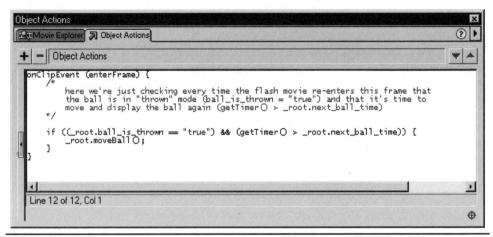

Figure 18-6   *The actions attached to the Throw Ball button*

onClipEvent() event handler to direct the Flash movie, on release of the button, to call the throwBall() function.

The throwBall() function itself performs a few tasks. First, it performs error checking, using the following code snippet:

L 18-4

```
if ((angle_degrees < 0) || (angle_degrees == "???") ||
(angle_degrees == "") || (angle_degrees > 90)) {
        angle_degrees = "???";
        ball_is_thrown = "false";
}
```

As explained earlier in the chapter, angle_degrees is the name assigned to the input text field where the user types the angle for the ball to be thrown. If the user has entered a negative value for the angle or left the field blank, or if the text field contains ???, we set the value of the field to be "???". We hope that the user will see the question marks and reenter a value for the angle of the ball throw.

The ball_is_thrown flag is also set to "false", so that the ball understands it cannot go anywhere just yet, because it doesn't have all the information it needs to properly calculate its path.

Assuming the user did enter the value of the initial angle of trajectory correctly, the throwBall() function continues to its else clause, which is shown here.

L 18-5

```
else {
        ball_is_thrown = "true";
```

```
ay = -10;
theta = convertDegreesToRadians (angle_degrees);
inst_platform._rotation = angle_degrees;

vix = getInitialHorizontalVelocity (theta,
initial_velocity);
viy = getInitialVerticalVelocity (theta,
initial_velocity);

}
```

First, this clause sets the `ball_is_thrown` variable to `"true"`, so that the ball knows it is currently in flight. As explained earlier, `ay` represents the vertical acceleration of the ball. In this case, we use the value of gravity, which is –10 m/s/s, so we assign the `ay` variable the value `-10`.

Next, we need to convert the angle that the user entered in degrees to radians so Flash's Math object can use it. This is done with the following line within the `else` clause:

L 18-6   `theta = convertDegreesToRadians (angle_degrees);`

In the preceding line of code, we are calling our `convertDegreesToRadians()` function and passing it the degrees value the user entered in the text field. The value returned is assigned to a new variable, `theta`.

The instance of the mc_platform movie clip on the Flash stage (`inst_platform`) is then rotated to reflect the angle at which the ball is about to be thrown. This is not necessary, but it adds an interesting effect.

Finally, because we now know the initial angle of the ball in radians, as well as its initial velocity, the last two lines of the `throwBall()` function call the functions `getInitialHorizontalVelocity()` and `getInitialVerticalVelocity()` to solve for the initial horizontal and vertical velocity of the ball.

L 18-7   `vix = getInitialHorizontalVelocity (theta, initial_velocity);`
          `viy = getInitialVerticalVelocity (theta, initial_velocity);`

We can plug those values into our main equations and begin calculating the ball's path.

The Math and Physics Functions

In the first few sections of this chapter, we covered all of the physics and mathematical equations necessary to determine the trajectory of a ball thrown by the user. The following five functions just incorporate those equations into individual methods, so that we separate the confusing stuff from the rest of the movie and return the values needed to determine the ball's path.

L 18-8

```
function convertDegreesToRadians (angle_degrees) {
    angle_radians = angle_degrees * (Math.PI/180);
    return angle_radians;
}

function getInitialHorizontalVelocity (angle_radians,
initial_velocity) {
    initialHorizontalVelocity = initial_velocity *
    Math.cos(angle_radians);
    return initialHorizontalVelocity;
}

function getInitialVerticalVelocity (angle_radians,
initial_velocity) {
    initialVerticalVelocity = initial_velocity *
    Math.sin(angle_radians);
    return initialVerticalVelocity;
}

function getHorizontalDisplacement (vix, elapsed_time) {
    horizontalDisplacement = vix * elapsed_time;
    return horizontalDisplacement;
}

function getVerticalDisplacement (viy, elapsed_time, ay) {
    verticalDisplacement = viy * elapsed_time + 0.5 * ay *
    elapsed_time * elapsed_time;
    return verticalDisplacement;
}
```

The moveBall() Function

The moveBall() function is the most interesting utility of all, because it is responsible for making the ball travel along the user-defined path. It is called from the onClipEvent (enterFrame) script of the ball and is a bit complex, so we will review it step by step. (The ball's script will be covered in more depth in the next section.)

The first task the moveBall() function performs is to record the time at which the ball is initially thrown by the user in a variable called start_time.

L 18-9
```
if (myTimerFlag == 0) {
    my_date = new Date();
    start_time = my_date.getTime();
    myTimerFlag = 1;
}
```

This is done so that we have a starting point to use later in calculating how much time the ball has been traveling at any moment. To accomplish this, we create the new Date() object, and use its built-in getTime() method to determine the time the ball was first thrown.

Next, we need to find out what time it is now.

L 18-10
```
new_date = new Date();
now = new_date.getTime();
```

A Date object is also used here to detect the current time and to store that value in a variable named now. Keep in mind that the moveBall() function is called many times by the ball. The start_time variable will always have the same value during any one throw, but the now variable value will change, depending on how long it has been since the ball was first thrown.

Now we can subtract the time the ball was thrown from the current time and divide that value by 1000 to convert the elapsed time to seconds. (Flash's getTime() method returns a number in milliseconds.)

L 18-11
```
elapsed_time = now - start_time;
elapsed_time /= 1000;
```

Once we have determined how many seconds it has been since the ball was first thrown, we can pass these values to the getHorizontalDisplacement() and getVerticalDisplacement() functions in order to calculate the ball's horizontal and vertical displacement after elapsed_time seconds.

L 18-12
```
x_disp = getHorizontalDisplacement (vix, elapsed_time);
y_disp = getVerticalDisplacement (viy, elapsed_time, ay);
```

The new values assigned to x_disp and y_disp tell us how far the ball should have traveled at this point.

Next, it's time to duplicate the ball movie clip, and place the new ball and ruler thumb at the correct x and y coordinates.

L 18-13
```
duplicateMovieClip ("inst_ball", "inst_ball" + counter, counter);

if (orig_ruler_thumb_x + x_disp <= endOfRuler) {
    inst_ruler_thumb._x = orig_ruler_thumb_x + x_disp;
} else {
    inst_ruler_thumb._x = endOfRuler;
}

["inst_ball" + counter]._x = inst_ball._x;
["inst_ball" + counter]._y = inst_ball._y;
["inst_ball" + counter]._alpha = 20;

inst_ball._x = orig_ball_x + x_disp;
inst_ball._y = _root.orig_ball_y - y_disp;
```

TIP

If you don't wish to show the ball's trail, you can just comment out the `duplicateMovieClip()` *line in the preceding code block.*

There's something important to notice here that you'll probably come across quite often in your Flash programming. In the Cartesian coordinate system (which is the system we typically use to plot objects) x values increase as you move further right, and y values increase as you move further up. However, in the Flash coordinate system, while x values still increase as you move toward the right, y values increase as you move further *down* the stage, as shown in Figure 18-7.

We added the x_disp value that we calculated to the inst_ball x value so that the ball would move in the correct direction (to the right of the stage). We *subtracted* the y_disp value from the current y coordinate of the inst_ball clip so that the ball moves vertically in the right direction at any point in time.

The next line of the moveBall() function increments the counter variable by one, so that we can create a new, unique ball movie clip in the next moveBall() cycle.

L 18-14
```
counter++;
```

At this point, we specify how often we want the ball to move. Here, we've programmed it to change its position every 1000 milliseconds (or every second).

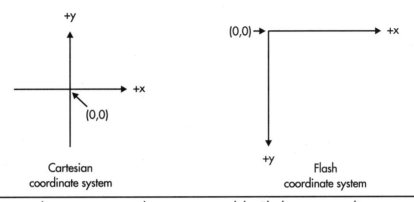

Figure 18-7 *The Cartesian coordinate system and the Flash stage coordinate system*

Specifying an action based on a timer rather than relying on the movie's frame rate is much more exact, because the frame rate can vary based on a lot of uncontrollable factors.

L 18-15
```
next_ball_time = getTimer() + 1000;
```

Finally, we check to make sure the ball is still within the boundaries of the Flash movie. If it is, we run through the whole moveBall() function again. If not, we set the ball_is_thrown flag to "false", and this throw cycle is complete.

L 18-16
```
if ((inst_ball._x >= 563) || (inst_ball._x <= 10) || (inst_ball._y <=
10) || (inst_ball._y >= 390)) {
    ball_is_thrown = "false";
} else {
    gotoAndPlay (1);
}
```

The Ball's Script

The ball needs to know only two things at any point in time. First, it checks to make sure it is currently in "thrown" mode (ball_is_thrown = "true"). Second, the ball checks to see whether enough time has passed since its last advance (getTimer() > _root.next_ball_time). If so, the ball can move again.

L 18-17
```
onClipEvent (enterFrame) {
    if ((_root.ball_is_thrown == "true") && (getTimer() > _root.next_ball_time))
    {
```

```
                    _root.moveBall();
              }
        }
```

This code is contained in the ball's `onClipEvent(enterFrame)` method, and so it is run every time Flash's playback head enters the frame.

What to Take Away from This Chapter

That's all there is to it! In this chapter, you've learned how to program mathematical functions in Flash and how to use the built-in Date object to animate objects with a timer, and even discovered some useful physics equations. Programming realistic, interactive movement in ActionScript is not so difficult, and the techniques covered here can be applied to a wide range of projects.

Have fun!

19

Programming a Game in Flash

IN THIS CHAPTER:

▶ Program a fully functional maze game in Flash

▶ Understand how to use arrays and multidimensional arrays

▶ Learn how and when to create reusable functions

One of the great advantages to Flash is the way it allows you to build games much easier and faster than hand-coding them in Java or C++. In this chapter, we'll cover the theory and code needed to program a game similar to Pac-Man in Flash.

The Game Play

The game we will build in this chapter includes a maze, good bugs, and bad bugs. Figure 19-1 shows the finished game. The groovy bugs and maze were designed by my friend Nelson Wong, who is currently Director of the New Media Lab at Sony Music.

In the game, the user will press the left, right, up, and down arrow keys to maneuver the good bug (the red bug in the grid) around the maze. Along the way, this good bug can eat dots, as well as kill the bad, blue bugs by smacking into them.

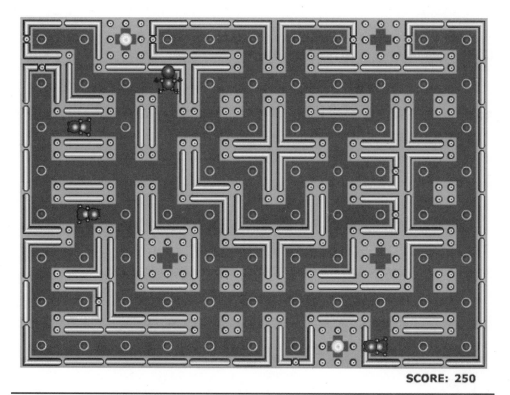

SCORE: 250

Figure 19-1   *The finished game*

good bug   bad bug   bad bug   dot
                         dying

The user's score increases by 10 points for every dot eaten, and by 50 points every time the good bug catches a bad bug. To promote positive self-esteem, I have programmed the game so that the good bug never dies, but you could easily modify this game to make it more challenging.

Building the Maze

The first step in creating the game is to think about how you should lay out the maze. One possibility is to create a movie clip that contains a graphic of the background of the maze, removing the portions that correspond to wherever the creatures are allowed to travel. Then you could use the movie clip object's `hitTest()` method to determine whether or not each creature has hit a wall before letting it progress further through the maze. (For more details on the `hitTest()` function, see "Coding the Good Bug's Actions," later in this chapter.)

Using a single background for the entire grid would work, but for maze games like this, I usually prefer to use a grid of tiles to create the maze instead. There are a few reasons why I like this technique better, even though it's a bit more complex to set up at the outset:

▶ It provides more flexibility in the design. If you want to add new levels, you don't need to create new background graphics. You can simply write an algorithm that sets up a new level by randomly rearranging the tiles in the grid a different way whenever the user completes a stage of the game. To make the maze smaller or bigger, you can reduce or increase the number of tiles in the grid.

▶ You can add functionality to allow users to create their own mazes without extensive alterations to the Flash file. You'll see later in the chapter how this technique makes it easy to customize the layout of the maze.

▶ It saves coding time. Once you enter information about each of the tile's structures into an array, you never need to worry about it again. As long as you keep track of which tile is in each slot in the grid, the bugs always know where they can and cannot go, and the dots understand which tiles they can and cannot be placed in.

Creating the Tiles

Creating the tiles for the maze is a lot of fun, but it takes a bit of patience. For this example, I've made each of the tiles for the game 50 pixels high by 50 pixels wide. It's important to keep your tiles uniform so that the paths and edges in the maze line up properly. To check that your tiles are correctly drawn, place a few of them side by side and see if the walls and open areas look perfectly aligned.

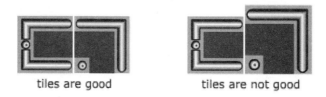

tiles are good   tiles are not good

For four-sided tiles (which is what I typically use when creating maze games), there are 16 possible distinct tile patterns. Looking at the tiles in Figure 19-2, you

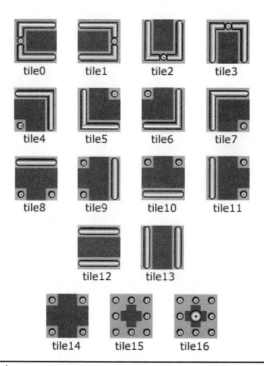

Figure 19-2 *All 17 tile patterns*

can see that the first four tiles (tile0 through tile3) each has three sides blocked by walls and one side open. Tile4 through tile7 have two sides closed off and two sides open for the bugs to crawl through, as do tile12 and tile13. Tile8 through tile11 have three sides open and one side blocked. Tile14 is the only tile with all four sides open. Finally, tile15 and tile16 are both completely closed off to our creatures.

NOTE

You probably noticed that there are 17 different tiles, not 16. You don't need two different tile designs to represent a tile with all four sides closed off, but Nelson (the designer) put an extra one in there to make the design of the maze a little more interesting. Technically, to adequately represent every possible combination of open and closed walls for a four-sided tile, you need only 16 different tiles. But if you're feeling creative, go ahead and make as many tile designs as you like!

Using Arrays to Hold Tile Data

You may be wondering why I named the first tile tile0 instead of tile1. This is because arrays in ActionScript (as in most programming languages) are zero based. As a result, in Flash 5, the first element in any array you create (unless you specify otherwise) automatically has an index value of 0.

NOTE

An array is a container. It contains a bunch of elements, and each element (which is referred to by an index) has a value.

Once you've created all 16 (well, in this case, 17) tile types, you can set up an array to hold the 17 tile objects. Each tile object describes which sides of an individual tile are open and which are blocked off by walls. The data in the array is whether or not the left, top, right, and bottom sides of each individual tile are open for the bugs to pass through. If the side is open, give it a value of 1. If the side of the tile is blocked, assign it a value of 0.

The code to create each of the tile objects is placed in a frame script in the first frame of the Flash movie and reads as follows:

L 19-1
```
function tile(left, top, right, bottom) {
    this.left = left;
    this.top = top;
    this.right = right;
    this.bottom = bottom;
}
```

The createTileInfoArray() function (placed in the same frame script as the tile() function just listed) generates an array called tileInfoArray and populates it with information about the 17 types of tiles.

L 19-2
```
function createTileInfoArray() {
    tileInfoArray = new Array();
    tileInfoArray[0]  = new tile(0, 0, 1, 0);
    tileInfoArray[1]  = new tile(1, 0, 0, 0);
    tileInfoArray[2]  = new tile(0, 1, 0, 0);
    tileInfoArray[3]  = new tile(0, 0, 0, 1);
    tileInfoArray[4]  = new tile(1, 0, 0, 1);
    tileInfoArray[5]  = new tile(0, 1, 1, 0);
    tileInfoArray[6]  = new tile(1, 1, 0, 0);
    tileInfoArray[7]  = new tile(0, 0, 1, 1);
    tileInfoArray[8]  = new tile(1, 0, 1, 1);
    tileInfoArray[9]  = new tile(1, 1, 0, 1);
    tileInfoArray[10] = new tile(1, 1, 1, 0);
    tileInfoArray[11] = new tile(0, 1, 1, 1);
    tileInfoArray[12] = new tile(1, 0, 1, 0);
    tileInfoArray[13] = new tile(0, 1, 0, 1);
    tileInfoArray[14] = new tile(1, 1, 1, 1);
    tileInfoArray[15] = new tile(0, 0, 0, 0);
    /* this is just an extra "blinking" tile with no openings for
    design purposes */
    tileInfoArray[16] = new tile(0, 0, 0, 0);
}
```

The createTileInfoArray() function begins by building a new array object called tileInfoArray, using the following line:

L 19-3
```
tileInfoArray = new Array();
```

Next, assign each array element (starting with 0) the properties of one of the 17 tile objects. For example, in Figure 19-2, you can see that tile0 has its top, left, and bottom edges closed off, but its right face is open. Therefore, create a tile object as follows:

L 19-4
```
tileInfoArray[0] = new tile(0, 0, 1, 0);
```

The first 0 passed to the tile() function in the preceding line of code records in the array that tile0 has its left side blocked by a wall. The second argument sent to the tile() function represents the condition (blocked or open) of the top of the tile. In this case, the second argument passed is 0; therefore, a wall blocks the top edge of tile0, too. The third argument for the `tile()` function, which represents the right side of tile0, is `1`, which denotes an open side. Therefore, a bug can enter and exit from the right side of this tile. The final `0` indicates that the bottom of tile0 is also walled off. This single line of code records everything you need to know about tile0.

The same recording of data is done for tile1 through tile16. However, while `tileInfoArray` now contains all of the information about each of the tile's structures, you still need more information before the bugs will be able to determine when they are smashing into walls. You need to understand how the tiles are laid out in the grid.

Assembling the Grid

Arranging the tiles in a grid can make even the most design-challenged programmer feel creative. You can come up with almost any design you like for the maze, but you need to make sure that the connections between the tiles are "legal," meaning that the open and closed spaces of adjacent tiles line up appropriately.

"illegal"   "legal"

In the illegal illustration, the tile on the left has its right side open, but the tile immediately to the right of it has its left side blocked off. In that configuration, even though a bug should be able to enter the first tile from the right side, it is now prevented from doing so. The two tiles in the legal illustration line up correctly. The tile with the opening on the right side is adjacent to a tile that is open on its left side, leaving a clear path for bugs to travel.

In this example, the grid is 550 pixels wide by 400 pixels high. Because the tiles are 50 pixels by 50 pixels, this means that the maze contains exactly 11 tiles across by 8 tiles down. To calculate these values, I used the following equations:

11 tiles each at 50 pixels width = 11 × 50 = 550 pixels wide maze
8 tiles each at 50 pixels height = 8 × 50 = 400 pixels high maze

Figure 19-3 illustrates the layout of the tiles in the grid.

Once you've laid out your tiles, you need to create another array that holds data on which tile design is placed in each square of the grid. This is handled by the `createMazeGrid()` function. This function is called from the `initVariables()`

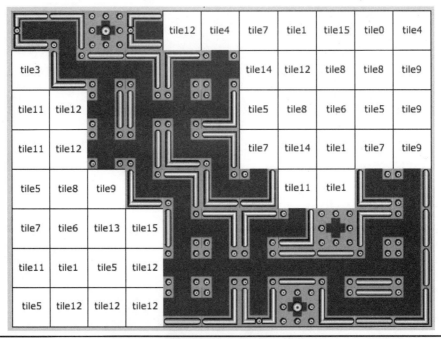

Figure 19-3 *Laying out the tiles in the grid*

function (covered in "Coding the InitVariables() Function and Movie Parameters," later in this chapter) when the movie is first launched, because one of the first things you want the Flash movie to do is draw your maze.

L 19-5
```
function createMazeGrid() {
        mazeGridArray = new Array();
        mazeGridArray[0] = new Array(0, 4, 16, 0, 12, 4, 7, 1, 15, 0, 4);
        mazeGridArray[1] = new Array(3, 5, 8, 4, 7, 14, 14, 12, 8, 8, 9);
        mazeGridArray[2] = new Array(11, 12, 9, 11, 14, 6, 5, 8, 6, 5, 9);
        mazeGridArray[3] = new Array(11, 12, 14, 9, 5, 4, 7, 14, 1, 7, 9);
        mazeGridArray[4] = new Array(5, 8, 9, 5, 4, 5, 6, 11, 1, 5, 9);
        mazeGridArray[5] = new Array(7, 6, 13, 15, 11, 4, 7, 6, 15, 7, 9);
        mazeGridArray[6] = new Array(11, 1, 5, 12, 14, 14, 14, 12, 8, 10, 9);
```

```
        mazeGridArray[7] = new Array(5, 12, 12, 12, 10, 6, 2, 16, 5, 12, 6);
}
```

In the `mazeGridArray`, each index represents a row of the grid. For example, the following line populates the first row in the grid:

19-6

```
mazeGridArray[0] = new Array(0, 4, 16, 0, 12, 4, 7, 1, 15, 0, 4);
```

The 0 inside the brackets specifies the grid's first row, and the numbers inside the parentheses mean that, from left to right, the tiles in the first row are tile0, tile4, tile16, tile0, tile12, tile4, tile7, tile1, tile15, tile0, and tile4.

This function populates all eight rows of the grid (row 0 through row 7) with the proper tiles. Now that you have the data you need on where the openings are within each tile and where all the tiles are positioned in the grid, you can arrange your bugs and dots.

I mentioned at the beginning of this chapter that one advantage of using a grid of tiles rather than a single image as the maze background is that it provides you with an easy way to change the maze layout as often as you like. This is true—you could code the `createMazeGrid()` function so that it contains an algorithm that randomly places the tiles in the grid (checking to make sure they are placed in a legal pattern, of course). However, to keep things straightforward in this example, I simply specified exactly where I wanted to situate each tile.

Creating the Bad Bugs

ch19_01.fla

If you open the ch19_01.fla game file, you will see that the good, red bug has already been placed in the grid. However, the bad bugs and red dots will be positioned using ActionScript. This is to guarantee that the bad bugs always start out in random tiles and the dots are only placed where it is appropriate. You wouldn't want a dot placed in a tile that had all four walls blocked off—how would a bug get to the dot to eat it? (There is no reason to torture the good bug that way.)

First, place a movie clip of a bad bug on the stage and give it an instance name of **badbug1**. Now you need to write a function that positions all the bad bugs you want to include in the maze on the screen. There are a few things you should keep in mind when writing this script.

First, you want to be able to easily change the number of bad bugs that appear on the screen whenever you create a new maze, so you should be able to pass the function an integer that corresponds to the number of blue bugs you wish to include.

Second, you need to make sure that the bugs are positioned above the dots so that they don't appear to be crawling underneath them. That's easy enough when you're duplicating movie clips. You just need to make sure that the level you assign to each movie clip that you've cloned is higher than the levels assigned to the dots. However, the original bad bug movie clip you are duplicating to create the other bugs will, by default, have a level of 0, so you will need to use the swapDepths() method to swap the level of the first bad bug movie clip with a movie clip that is at a higher level, in this case, a movie clip with the instance name **dummyClip2**.

The code for creating the bad bugs is as follows:

L 19-7
```
function layoutBadBugs(numBugs) {
    _root.numBadBugs = numBugs;
    for (i = 2; i <= numBadBugs; i++){
        badbug1.duplicateMovieClip("badbug" + i, 5000 + i);
    }
    /*
        This just makes sure that our initial bad bug is
        on top of the dots like all the other bugs.
    */
    duplicateMovieClip("dummyClip", "dummyClip2", 5000);
    badbug1.swapDepths(dummyClip2);
}
```

This code uses a for statement to duplicate the badbug1 movie clip so that you end up with the number of bugs you specify in the argument you pass to the layoutBadBugs() function.

In this case, because you want to have four bad bugs in the game annoying the good bug, call the layoutBadBugs() function from the initVariables() function, as follows:

L 19-8
```
layoutBadBugs(4);
```

The layoutBadBugs() function understands from the preceding line of code to duplicate the first bad bug three times, so that there are a total of four bad bugs running around the grid.

This is the first step in creating the bad bugs. However, there is still something missing. You haven't yet specified where the bad bugs should be placed in the grid. At this point, they are just sitting in the same x and y location as badbug1.

Checking for Walls and Openings in Tiles

To figure out where it is legal to place bugs in the grid, create a new function called checkMove(). You may be wondering why this functionality isn't included inside the layoutBadBug() function. The reason is that you can use this same checkMove() function for many different tasks, including the following:

▶ Making sure that the red dots are placed only in tiles with at least one opening for bugs to enter and exit

▶ Making sure that the bad bugs are initially placed only in tiles with at least one opening for bugs to enter and exit, so they don't just sit in a completely walled-off tile the entire game

▶ Checking to see whether the user has led the good bug into a wall or an open direction

▶ Making sure that each of the bad bug's random movements has it turn around when it hits a wall

Because this functionality is useful for several different situations, it is better to keep the ActionScript that checks for openings and walls within tiles in a separate frame script. This way, all of your movie clips can easily call it.

The checkMove() function is a bit complex, so I've added line numbers to simplify code review.

19-9
```
1 function checkMove(direction, bugxloc, bugyloc) {
2     /*
3         These are the x and y coordinates of where the bug is now
4     */
5     xloc = bugxloc;
6     yloc = bugyloc;
7     dir = direction;
8     /*
9         Using these coordinates, we determine what part of the
10        maze the bug is currently in.
11    */
12        colnum = Math.floor((xloc - _root.halfTileWidth) /
_root.tileWidth);
13        rownum = Math.floor((yloc -_ root.halfTileWidth) /
_root.tileWidth);
14    /*
15        Once we find that the bug is in column number "colnum"
```

```
16          and row number "rownum", then we figure out which of the
17          17 possible types of tiles it is in.
18     */
19     tileType = mazeGridArray[rownum][colnum];
20     /*
21          Finally, we check to see if the direction the bug wishes
22          to move is legal for that type of tile. If it is, we'll
23          pass back a "yes" to the bug. If it's not legal (i.e., it
24          would be running into a wall), then we pass back a "no" to
25          the bug, and the bug stays where it is.
26     */
27
28     /*
29          More useful debugging code if you want to uncomment out
30          the trace statements below...
31
32              trace("the bug is currently in tile " + colnum + ","
33              + rownum + " of the grid");
34              trace("the tile design the bug is in is " + tileType);
35              trace("the bug wants to move " + dir);
36              trace("nochecking if this is legal...");
37              trace(tileInfoArray[tileType][dir]);
38
39     */
40
41     moveIsLegal = tileInfoArray[tileType][dir];
42     if (moveIsLegal == 1) {
43         return "yes";
44     } else {
45         return "no";
46     }
47
48 }
```

Line 1 sets up the checkMove() function so that it takes three arguments:

▶ direction is the direction ("left", "top", "right", or "bottom") you wish to determine to be open or closed in the tile the object is currently in.

▶ bugxloc is the current x location of the bug (or whatever movie clip you're checking; it could be a dot, too).

▶ bugyloc is the current y location of the bug or dot.

Lines 5, 6, and 7 assign the arguments that were passed to the `checkMove()` function to the newly created variables `xloc`, `yloc`, and `dir`.

Now that you know the coordinates of the bug or dot you are examining, you can calculate where that object is in the grid. This is what lines 12 and 13 do. Line 12 calculates the number of the column in the grid where the movie clip is currently placed.

L 19-10
```
colnum = Math.floor((xloc - _root.halfTileWidth) / _root.tileWidth);
```

It uses the `floor()` method of the built-in Math object to round the number you get in your calculation down to the nearest integer value. For example, if the bug has an `xloc` of 25, then the equation is `colnum = Math.floor((25 - 25) / 50)`, or 0. This means that the bug is located in column 0 (the first column) of the grid.

A similar calculation is done in line 13 for the row number of where the bug or dot is.

L 19-11
```
rownum = Math.floor((yloc - _root.halfTileWidth) / _root.tileWidth);
```

The only difference here is the use of `yloc` (the y location of the movie clip) to determine the row number.

Once you have calculated that your object is in column number `colnum` and row number `rownum`, you can easily determine which of the 17 possible types of tiles the bug or dot is in. This is because the tile number located in each section of the grid is already stored in the `mazeGridArray` (described in "Assembling the Grid," earlier in the chapter).

Line 19 of the `checkMove()` function sets a variable called `tileType` equal to the number of the tile design found in row `rownum` and column `colnum` in the maze.

L 19-12
```
tileType = mazeGridArray[rownum][colnum];
```

For example, if you determined from the previous equations that the object is in row 3 and column 4, you could look up what tile type number is found in `mazeGridArray[3][4]` and see that the bug or dot is located in a `tile9` type.

Because you've established the type of tile that the object is located in, all you need to do now is check to see whether the direction the bug wishes to move (or the initial position where you wish to place the dot or bad bug) is legal for that type of tile. If it is, you will pass back a `"yes"` to the bug or dot. If it's not legal (because the bug would be running into a wall or a dot, or the bug would be initially placed in a completely walled-off tile), then the `checkMove()` function passes back a `"no"` to the bug or dot object, and the bug or dot cannot move in that direction. This is accomplished with the code in lines 41 through 46, shown here.

L 19-13
```
moveIsLegal = tileInfoArray[tileType][dir];
if (moveIsLegal == 1) {
    return "yes";               '
} else {
    return "no";
}
```

This code uses the `tileInfoArray` (described in the "Assembling the Grid" section earlier in this chapter) to find out whether the direction the bug wishes to move is legal or illegal. This works for both the good bug being controlled by the user or the bad bug randomly running around.

Positioning the Bad Bugs

As mentioned in the previous section, not only can the `checkMove()` function be used to determine whether or not a bug can move in a particular direction, but it also can be used to confirm that the initial location where you place the bad bugs and dots is acceptable. All you need to do is pass the `tileInfoArray` all four possible directions (`"left"`, `"top"`, `"right"`, `"bottom"`) until you find a side of the tile that is open. If the tile is completely blocked off, try to place the bug or dot in another tile. Why? Because if at least any one side of a tile is open, then it is a legal place for a dot or bug to be plopped down in at the start of the game.

If you right-click (CONTROL-click for Macs) on the blue bug in the Flash movie and click Actions, you will see two `onClipEvent()` handlers. One handles the actions for the bad bug clip when it is first loaded, and one controls what happens to the bad bug every time the Flash movie enters the frame.

Let's look at the handler that is run when each of the bad bugs is initially loaded.

L 19-14
```
onClipEvent (load) {
    this._x = _root.halfTileWidth + (random(11) * _root.tileWidth);
    this._y = _root.halfTileWidth + (random(8) * _root.tileWidth);
    isLegalMove = _root.checkMove("left", this._x, this._y);
    while (isLegalMove != "yes") {
        this._x = _root.halfTileWidth + (random(11) *
        _root.tileWidth);
        this._y = _root.halfTileWidth + (random(8) *
        _root.tileWidth);
        isLegalMove = _root.checkMove("left", this._x, this._y);
```

```
        }
        this.bugspeed = 50;
        this.alive = 1;
    }
```

First, the function chooses a random x and y coordinate for the initial bug position. This is done with the following two lines:

L 19-15
```
this._x = _root.halfTileWidth + (random(11) * _root.tileWidth);
this._y = _root.halfTileWidth + (random(8) * _root.tileWidth);
```

`_root.halfTileWidth` and `_root.tileWidth` correspond to the centerpoint and width of the tiles, and they are initialized in the `initVariables()` function (see the "Coding the InitVariables() Function and Movie Parameters" section later in the chapter for details on this function.)

Next, call the same `checkMove()` function to make sure that at least one direction of the tile you placed the bad bug in is open.

L 19-16
```
isLegalMove = _root.checkMove("left", this._x, this._y);
```

NOTE

To simplify the code here, only the left side of the tile is checked for an opening. However, you could check all directions. As long as at least one side of the tile is open, it's okay for the bug to start there.

Then use a `while` loop to continue resetting the location of this bad bug until it's in a place that is acceptable (in this case, a tile that has its left side open).

L 19-17
```
while (isLegalMove != "yes") {
        this._x = _root.halfTileWidth + (random(11) *
        _root.tileWidth);
        this._y = _root.halfTileWidth + (random(8) *
        _root.tileWidth);
        isLegalMove = _root.checkMove("left", this._x, this._y);
    }
```

This ensures that each of our bad bugs starts off in a legal tile within the maze.

The `onClipEvent(load)` handler is also typically used to initialize any variables specific to that particular movie clip. In this case, there are two variables you want to set: the speed of the bad bug (set to 50 pixels per frame) and whether or not it is alive.

L 19-18
```
this.bugspeed = 50;
this.alive = 1;
```

Each bad bug starts out with its `alive` property set to `1`. If it is killed, this value is set to `0`.

Creating the Dots

Now that you've placed the bad bugs in the maze, you need to create the dots for the good bug to eat. Dots are pretty simple, because they never really move and have only two states: visible (not eaten) and invisible (eaten). At the start of the game, all dots are visible. The two dot states are contained in a movie clip (named mc_dot) with two frames, as shown in Figure 19-4.

Within the dot movie clip, label the first frame of the dot movie clip **visible** and place a dot graphic on the stage. Label the second frame **invisible** and remove the dot from view. Both frames have a `stop()` action attached to them, so that the dot doesn't flip between states without being directed to. All of the dots will initially be at their visible frame when the game is loaded, and the appropriate ones will be told to go to their invisible frame as they are eaten. The code to control the state of the dots will be covered later in the chapter, in the "Coding the Good Bug's Actions" section.

Positioning the Dots

It's time to write the code to position the dots. First, set some variables for this code in the `initVariables()` function. You've already determined that the maze has 11 columns and 8 rows. Because this is useful information that you may need to use or change during the game, set up two variables in the `initVariables()` function to hold these values:

L 19-19
```
rows = 8;
cols = 11;
```

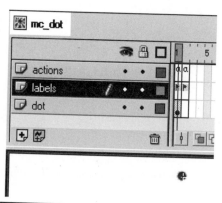

Figure 19-4   *The dot movie clip*

The layoutDots() function is similar to the layoutBadBugs() function used to position the blue bugs, but it is a bit more complex because it requires more math. You want to place a dot in every square of the grid that the good bug can get to. Therefore, you need some way to determine which squares of the grid are completely closed off, and then place one dot in every square that doesn't meet that criteria. The following code accomplishes this task.

L 19-20
```
function layoutDots() {
counter=1;
for (i = 0; i < cols; i++) {
    for (j = 0; j < rows; j++) {
        if ((checkMove("left", (halfTileWidth + (tileWidth * i)),
        (halfTileWidth + (tileWidth * j))) == "yes") ||
        (checkMove("right", (halfTileWidth + (tileWidth * i)),
        (halfTileWidth + (tileWidth * j))) == "yes") ||
        (checkMove("top", (halfTileWidth + (tileWidth * i)),
        (halfTileWidth + (tileWidth * j))) == "yes") ||
        (checkMove("bottom", (halfTileWidth + (tileWidth * i)),
        (halfTileWidth + (tileWidth * j))) == "yes")){
                        dot.duplicateMovieClip("dot" + counter, counter);
        setProperty ("dot" + counter, _x, halfTileWidth + (tileWidth * i));
        setProperty ("dot" + counter, _y, halfTileWidth + (tileWidth * j));
            }
        counter += 1;
    }
}
}
```

This code uses a nested for loop (a for loop that contains another for loop inside it) to loop through the tiles in each of the rows and columns, calling the checkMove() function to check to see whether any direction within any of the tiles is open, and therefore can contain a dot. If a tile has at least one open side, the dot movie clip is duplicated and added to the maze in the center of that tile. If not, the tile is skipped over, and no dot is placed there.

Coding the Good Bug's Actions

At this point, you have initialized all the variables you need, laid out the maze, put the grid and tile information into arrays, and placed the dots and bad bugs where appropriate. It's time to add the functionality that allows users to play the game.

If you open the Actions window for the good, red bug—the one controlled by the user—you again see two `onClipEvent()` handlers, as shown in Figure 19-5. As in the bad bug's scripts, one event handler is for when the bug is first loaded, and the other is run every time the Flash playback head enters the frame.

The `onClipEvent(load)` function is straightforward. All it does is set the speed of the good bug to 50 pixels per frame, which is the same rate as the speed used for the bad bugs.

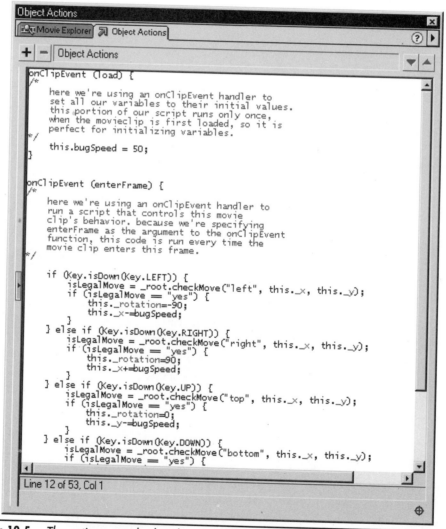

Figure 19-5   *The actions attached to the good bug movie clip*

The onClipEvent(enterFrame) handler for the good bug, shown next, is a bit more complex because it handles multiple tasks. First, it captures keys pressed by the user and moves the good bug accordingly. Next, it checks to see whether the movement of the good bug caused it to collide with a bad bug. Finally, it checks to see whether the movement of the good bug caused it to run over a dot.

L 19-21
```
onClipEvent (enterFrame) {
    if (Key.isDown(Key.LEFT)) {
        isLegalMove = _root.checkMove("left", this._x, this._y);
        if (isLegalMove == "yes") {
            this._rotation = -90;
            this._x -= bugSpeed;
        }
    } else if (Key.isDown(Key.RIGHT)) {
        isLegalMove = _root.checkMove("right", this._x, this._y);
        if (isLegalMove == "yes") {
            this._rotation = 90;
            this._x += bugSpeed;
        }
    } else if (Key.isDown(Key.UP)) {
        isLegalMove = _root.checkMove("top", this._x, this._y);
        if (isLegalMove == "yes") {
            this._rotation = 0;
            this._y -= bugSpeed;
        }
    } else if (Key.isDown(Key.DOWN)) {
        isLegalMove = _root.checkMove("bottom", this._x, this._y);
        if (isLegalMove == "yes") {
            this._rotation = 180;
            this._y += bugSpeed;
        }
    }

    _root.checkBadBugCollision();
    _root.checkDotCollision();
}
```

The Key object in Flash has an isDown() method that returns "true" if the key specified in the argument you pass it is pressed down. In this case, the code checks the four arrow keys: Key.DOWN (the down arrow key), Key.UP (the up arrow key), Key.LEFT (the left arrow key), and Key.RIGHT (the right arrow key).

Here, the code first checks to see whether any of these keys are down. If so, use the incredibly useful `checkMove()` function to see whether the direction the user wants to move the good bug in is a legal move. If the answer is yes, the bug clip is rotated to face the right direction (it would be silly if the bug were moving up toward the top of the maze but facing down!) and moved forward the number of pixels specified in its `bugSpeed` property (in this case, 50).

Next, call the `checkBadBugCollision()` method that is included in the main frame script of the Flash movie. This function checks to see whether the good bug has collided with a bad bug. In the game, this a good thing—the bad bug dies, and the user's score is increased by 50.

L 19-22
```
function checkBadBugCollision() {
    for (i = 1; i <= _root.numBadBugs; i++){
        if (goodbug.hitTest(_root["badbug" + i]) &&
        (_root["badbug" + i].alive == 1)) {
            _root.score += 50;
            _root["badbug" + i].alive = 0;
            _root["badbug" + i].gotoAndPlay("die");
        }
    }
}
```

NOTE

You can change the game to make it so that when the good bug hits a bad bug, it loses a life instead. However, in this example, the user always wins.

The first line in the `checkBadBugCollision()` function begins with a `for` loop:

L 19-23
```
for (i = 1; i <= _root.numBadBugs; i++){
```

This tells the movie to loop through all the bad bugs in the maze.

The next line uses the `hitTest()` method, a built-in method for movie clip objects:

L 19-24
```
if (goodbug.hitTest(_root["badbug"+i]) && (_root["badbug"+i].alive
== 1)) {
```

This tests to see whether the good bug has collided with one of the bad bugs. If it has, and the bad bug is alive, the score is increased by 50 points, and the bad bug's `alive` property is set to 0. As the instance of the bad bug is sent to its `"die"` frame, you see a sad animation of the bad, blue bug fading away.

The form of hitTest() used here is *movieClipName*.hitTest(*target*), which is the method commonly used for games, because typically you wish to determine whether one movie clip has hit another movie clip. Another form of hitTest() is *movieClipName*.hitTest(*x, y, shapeFlag*). This method allows you to determine whether the instance *movieClipName* has intersected with a particular point (*x, y*) on the stage. If *shapeFlag* is set to true, the exact shape of the *movieClipName* instance is checked against the (*x, y*) coordinate. If shapeFlag is set to false, only the bounding box of the *movieClipName* instance is checked against those coordinates.

The checkDotCollision() function, used to see whether the good bug rams into a dot, is very similar to the checkBadBugCollision() function.

19-25
```
function checkDotCollision() {
for (i = 1; i <= (rows * cols); i++) {
        if (goodbug.hitTest(_root["dot" + i])) {
            _root.score += 10;
            _root["dot" + i].gotoAndPlay("invisible");
        }
    }
}
```

Here, the for statement loops through all of the dots that remain visible on the board. If the good bug collides with a dot, the score is increased by 10 points, and that instance of the dot is told to go to its "invisible" frame.

NOTE

If a movie clip is invisible, the hitTest() *function won't recognize it, so you don't need to worry about setting an* alive *property for your dots. Setting them to invisible prevents users from accumulating extra points when they roll over the same dot multiple times.*

Coding the Bad Bug's Actions

While the user controls the good bug, the bad bugs are basically on their own. Place the logic to move the bad bugs in the onClipEvent(enterFrame) handler for each instance of the blue bug, as shown in Figure 9-6.

You could extend this script to make the bad bugs smarter, perhaps to have them stalk the good bug or approach it if they come within a certain distance. For now

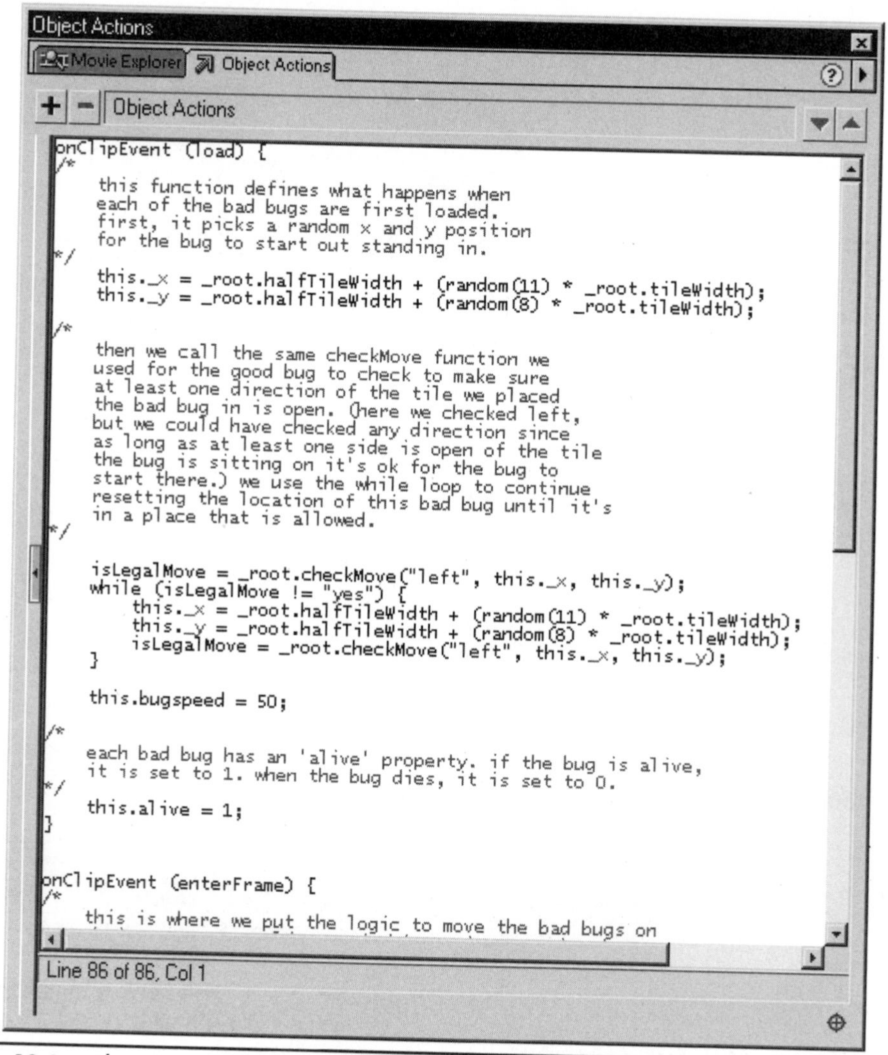

```
Object Actions                                                    x
[Movie Explorer] [Object Actions]                               (?) ▶
[+] [-] | Object Actions                                        ▼ ▲
onClipEvent (load) {
/*
    this function defines what happens when
    each of the bad bugs are first loaded.
    first, it picks a random x and y position
    for the bug to start out standing in.
*/
    this._x = _root.halfTileWidth + (random(11) * _root.tileWidth);
    this._y = _root.halfTileWidth + (random(8) * _root.tileWidth);

/*
    then we call the same checkMove function we
    used for the good bug to check to make sure
    at least one direction of the tile we placed
    the bad bug in is open. (here we checked left,
    but we could have checked any direction since
    as long as at least one side is open of the tile
    the bug is sitting on it's ok for the bug to
    start there.) we use the while loop to continue
    resetting the location of this bad bug until it's
    in a place that is allowed.
*/
    isLegalMove = _root.checkMove("left", this._x, this._y);
    while (isLegalMove != "yes") {
        this._x = _root.halfTileWidth + (random(11) * _root.tileWidth);
        this._y = _root.halfTileWidth + (random(8) * _root.tileWidth);
        isLegalMove = _root.checkMove("left", this._x, this._y);
    }

    this.bugspeed = 50;

/*
    each bad bug has an 'alive' property. if the bug is alive,
    it is set to 1. when the bug dies, it is set to 0.
*/
    this.alive = 1;
}

onClipEvent (enterFrame) {
/*
    this is where we put the logic to move the bad bugs on
```
Line 86 of 86, Col 1
```
```

Figure 19-6   *The actions attached to the bad bug movie clip*

though, the bad bugs are pretty dumb. They just wander around in random directions, bumping into walls and each other, using the code listed here.

L 19-26
```
onClipEvent (enterFrame) {
    if (this.alive) {
```

```
tempDir = random(4);
if (tempDir == 0) {
    isLegalMove = _root.checkMove("left", this._x,
    this._y);
    if (isLegalMove == "yes") {
        this._rotation = -90;
        this._x -= bugSpeed;
    }
} else if (tempDir == 1) {
    isLegalMove = _root.checkMove("right", this._x,
    this._y);
    if (isLegalMove == "yes") {
        this._rotation = 90;
        this._x+ = bugSpeed;
    }
} else if (tempDir == 2) {
    isLegalMove = _root.checkMove("top", this._x, this._y);
    if (isLegalMove == "yes") {
        this._rotation = 0;
        this._y -= bugSpeed;
    }
} else if (tempDir == 3) {
    isLegalMove = _root.checkMove("bottom", this._x,
    this._y);
    if (isLegalMove == "yes") {
        this._rotation = 180;
        this._y += bugSpeed;
    }
    }
}
}
```

First, the bug is checked to see whether it's alive. If it is, a random number between 0 and 3 is assigned to a variable named tempDir. The random numbers represent directions: 0 for right, 1 for left, 2 for top, and 3 for bottom. If tempDir contains a legal direction for the bug to move, the bug is rotated so it faces the direction it is to progress, and then it runs one tile in the direction specified. If tempDir does not contain a legal direction for the bug to move, then the process starts all over again.

Keeping Score

It's not really a game unless the user can measure how wonderful (or horrendous) he or she is doing. That's why scoring is important.

To keep score, I put two text fields on the stage. The first one is a simple static text box (a text box that doesn't change throughout the duration of the movie) that holds the label SCORE:. A second text box is set to Dynamic Text in its Text Options panel (shown in Figure 19-7), given an instance name of score, and initialized to 0.

Both the checkBadBugCollision() and checkDotCollision() functions include code to increase the users' score if they collided with a bad bug or a dot. Here is that code in the checkDotCollision() function:

L 19-27
```
if (goodbug.hitTest(_root["dot" + i])) {
    _root.score += 10;
    _root["dot" + i].gotoAndPlay("invisible");
}
```

And here is the code for increasing the user's score in the checkBadBugCollision() function:

L 19-28
```
if (goodbug.hitTest(_root["badbug" + i]) && (_root["badbug" +
i].alive
== 1)) {
    _root.score += 50;
_root["badbug"+i].alive = 0;
    _root["badbug" + i].gotoAndPlay("die");
}
```

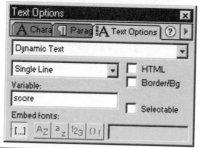

Figure 19-7 *Setting up the text field for the score*

As you can see, these functions (which are called by the good bug every time the Flash movie reenters the frame) check to see whether the good bug hit either a dot or a bad bug, If so, they increase the value of the `_root.score` variable (the variable that is assigned to the `score` text field on the stage) by either 10 points for colliding with a dot or 50 points for squishing a bad bug.

Coding the InitVariables() Function and Movie Parameters

Although I set up the `initVariables()` function to be the first function called when the movie is played, I've saved its discussion for last. This is because I typically finish up programming a game in Flash by cleaning up my `initVariables()` function.

The `initVariables()` function serves two main roles:

▶ It is the first function run by the Flash movie, so it is a perfect place to initialize all the variables used globally throughout the application.

▶ It is the function that calls all the other functions needed to set up the game.

The final code listing for this function (with comments removed) is as follows:

L 19-29
```
function initVariables() {
rows = 8;
    cols = 11;
    tileWidth = 50;
    halftileWidth = tileWidth / 2;
    _root.score = 0;
    createTileInfoArray();
    createMazeGrid();
    duplicateMovieClip("dummyClip", "dummyClip1", 10001);
    goodBug.swapDepths(dummyClip1);
    layoutBadBugs(4);
    layoutDots();
}
```

Setting Global Variables

When I want to figure out what properties I should assign to global variables, I usually start by sitting down and thinking about what values I am going to be using multiple times in the Flash file, and which ones may need to be accessed by different objects.

The first two variables that are initialized in the `initVariables()` function are the number of rows in the grid (`rows`) and the number of columns (`cols`). Because I use those values quite a few times in the code, and I may want to change them at a later time, they make excellent candidates for global variables.

The `tileWidth` and `halfTileWidth` variables are also used quite often throughout the code. They are used in the `layoutDots()` function to help determine where it is legal to place the dots and in a similar way in the `layoutBadBugs()` function.

As you learned in the previous section, `_root.score` is the variable assigned to the text field that contains the user's score. This is initialized to `0` in the `initVariables()` function (so the users need to earn their points!).

Calling the Functions

Using the code shown next, I call the various functions needed to set up the array of tiles, lay out the tiles in a grid, swap the goodBug movie clip instance with a dummyClip1, so that it is at a higher level than any other object in the movie, and distribute the bad bugs and dots within the maze.

L 19-30
```
createTileInfoArray();
createMazeGrid();
duplicateMovieClip("dummyClip", "dummyClip1", 10001);
goodBug.swapDepths(dummyClip1);
layoutBadBugs(4);
layoutDots();
```

Setting the Movie's Parameters

Finally, the movie is set to full-screen mode, scaling is turned off, and the `initVariables()` function is itself called from the main frame script of the movie, as follows:

L 19-31
```
fscommand ("allowscale", "false");
fscommand ("fullscreen", "true");
initVariables();
```

What to Take Away from This Chapter

Congratulations, you've just programmed a fully functional maze game in Flash! Not that it's very exciting as it is, but there are many ways to make it even better. Here are some ideas:

▶ Add more levels.

▶ Add a high score list.

▶ Add sound effects.

▶ Add the ability for bugs to "wrap around" to the other side of the maze.

▶ Make the maze scrollable.

▶ Add different behaviors for evil bug squishers.

▶ Change maze designs between levels.

  Using the Flash techniques you've learned in this book, you can enhance the game in these and many other ways.

APPENDIX

Flash Web Sites

The following is a list of Web sites that offer more Flash information, and may provide creative inspiration as well.

Innovative FX (www.innovativefx.com) Open-source Flash experiments by Jim Caldwell, author of this book.

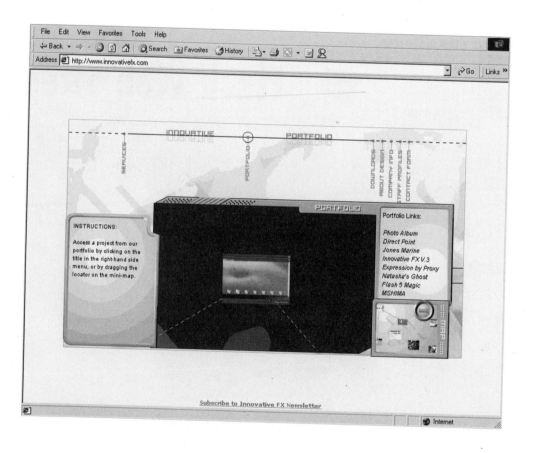

Deconcept (www.deconcept.com) Open-source Flash experiments by Geoff Stearns.

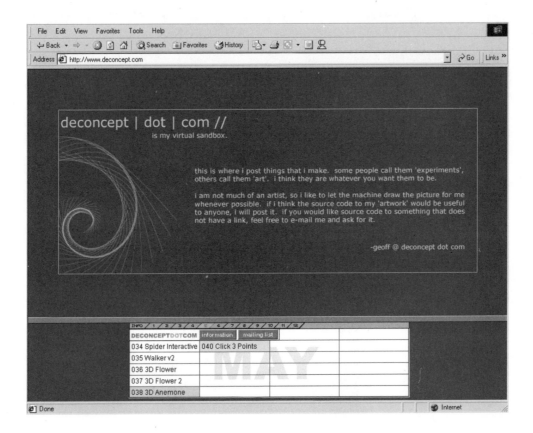

Were-Here (www.were-here.com) Online forums dedicated to Flash design.

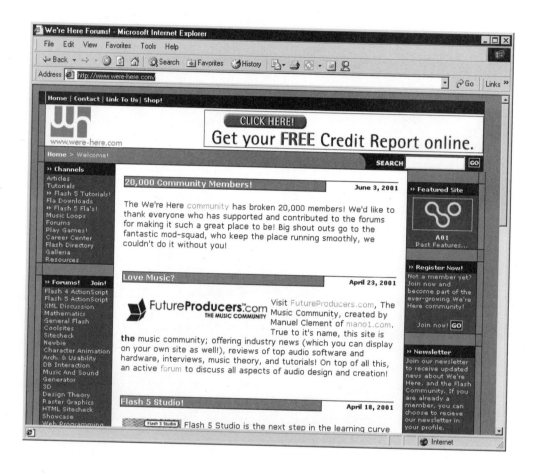

UltraShock (www.ultrashock.com)   Flash forums, tutorials, and open-source
FLA files contributed by some of the most astounding designers.

Flashmove (www.flashmove.com) Flash forums dedicated to new concepts and gaming in Flash.

Shockfusion (www.shockfusion.com)   Flash forums made in Flash.
The entire site runs in Flash, with much backend integration.

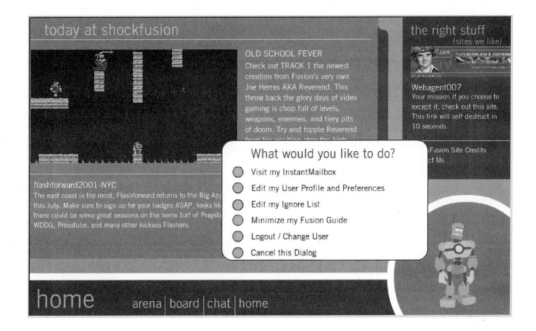

Virtual-FX (www.virtual-fx.net) Flash tutorials and articles on the latest events.

Flashmagazine (**www.flashmagazine.com**)   Online Flash magazine covering all the latest news and events. Several people dedicate their time to write articles and reviews.

Ming php Module (www.opaque.net/ming)   Open-source php module for Flash that allows you to build dynamic Flash content using php coding.

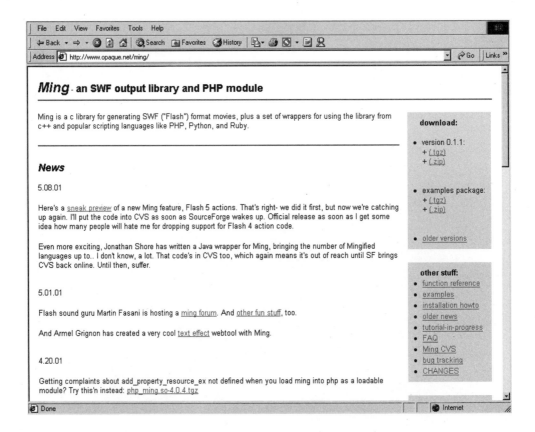

Index

INTERNATIONAL CONTACT INFORMATION

AUSTRALIA
McGraw-Hill Book Company Australia Pty. Ltd.
TEL +61-2-9417-9899
FAX +61-2-9417-5687
http://www.mcgraw-hill.com.au
books-it_sydney@mcgraw-hill.com

CANADA
McGraw-Hill Ryerson Ltd.
TEL +905-430-5000
FAX +905-430-5020
http://www.mcgrawhill.ca

GREECE, MIDDLE EAST, NORTHERN AFRICA
McGraw-Hill Hellas
TEL +30-1-656-0990-3-4
FAX +30-1-654-5525

MEXICO (Also serving Latin America)
McGraw-Hill Interamericana Editores S.A. de C.V.
TEL +525-117-1583
FAX +525-117-1589
http://www.mcgraw-hill.com.mx
fernando_castellanos@mcgraw-hill.com

SINGAPORE (Serving Asia)
McGraw-Hill Book Company
TEL +65-863-1580
FAX +65-862-3354
http://www.mcgraw-hill.com.sg
mghasia@mcgraw-hill.com

SOUTH AFRICA
McGraw-Hill South Africa
TEL +27-11-622-7512
FAX +27-11-622-9045
robyn_swanepoel@mcgraw-hill.com

UNITED KINGDOM & EUROPE (Excluding Southern Europe)
McGraw-Hill Education Europe
TEL +44-1-628-502500
FAX +44-1-628-770224
http://www.mcgraw-hill.co.uk
computing_neurope@mcgraw-hill.com

ALL OTHER INQUIRIES Contact:
Osborne/McGraw-Hill
TEL +1-510-549-6600
FAX +1-510-883-7600
http://www.osborne.com
omg_international@mcgraw-hill.com

About the CD-ROM

The CD-ROM contains the source files used for each chapter of this book. The files are organized by chapter number. Throughout the book, CD-ROM icons point out the names of the associated files for each project so you can locate them on the CD-ROM. Having the files open while reading the chapters can help you visualize the projects.

All FLA files located on the CD-ROM were created with Macromedia Flash 5. Some chapters include the use of HTML files, which are also stored within the same directories. All files have been tested on multiple platforms, including Windows and Macintosh, with the Macromedia Flash 5 plug-in installed.

WARNING: BEFORE OPENING THE DISC PACKAGE, CAREFULLY READ THE TERMS AND CONDITIONS OF THE FOLLOWING COPYRIGHT STATEMENT AND LIMITED CD-ROM WARRANTY.

Copyright Statement

This software is protected by both United States copyright law and international copyright treaty provision. Except as noted in the contents of the CD-ROM, you must treat this software just like a book. However, you may copy it into a computer to be used and you may make archival copies of the software for the sole purpose of backing up the software and protecting your investment from loss. By saying, "just like a book," The McGraw-Hill Companies, Inc. ("Osborne/McGraw-Hill") means, for example, that this software may be used by any number of people and may be freely moved from one computer location to another, so long as there is no possibility of its being used at one location or on one computer while it is being used at another. Just as a book cannot be read by two different people in two different places at the same time, neither can the software be used by two different people in two different places at the same time.

Limited Warranty

Osborne/McGraw-Hill warrants the physical compact disc enclosed herein to be free of defects in materials and workmanship for a period of sixty days from the purchase date. If you live in the U.S. and the CD included in your book has defects in materials or workmanship, please call McGraw-Hill at 1-800-217-0059, 9 A.M. to 5 P.M., Monday through Friday, Eastern Standard Time, and McGraw-Hill will replace the defective disc. If you live outside the U.S., please contact your local McGraw-Hill office. You can find contact information for most offices on the International Contact Information page immediately following the index of this book, or send an e-mail to omg_international@mcgraw-hill.com.

The entire and exclusive liability and remedy for breach of this Limited Warranty shall be limited to replacement of the defective disc, and shall not include or extend to any claim for or right to cover any other damages, including but not limited to, loss of profit, data, or use of the software, or special incidental, or consequential damages or other similar claims, even if Osborne/McGraw-Hill has been specifically advised of the possibility of such damages. In no event will Osborne/McGraw-Hill's liability for any damages to you or any other person ever exceed the lower of the suggested list price or actual price paid for the license to use the software, regardless of any form of the claim.

OSBORNE/McGRAW-HILL SPECIFICALLY DISCLAIMS ALL OTHER WARRANTIES, EXPRESS OR IMPLIED, INCLUDING BUT NOT LIMITED TO, ANY IMPLIED WARRANTY OF MERCHANTABILITY OR FITNESS FOR A PARTICULAR PURPOSE. Specifically, Osborne/McGraw-Hill makes no representation or warranty that the software is fit for any particular purpose, and any implied warranty of merchantability is limited to the sixty-day duration of the Limited Warranty covering the physical disc only (and not the software), and is otherwise expressly and specifically disclaimed.

This limited warranty gives you specific legal rights; you may have others which may vary from state to state. Some states do not allow the exclusion of incidental or consequential damages, or the limitation on how long an implied warranty lasts, so some of the above may not apply to you.

This agreement constitutes the entire agreement between the parties relating to use of the Product. The terms of any purchase order shall have no effect on the terms of this Agreement. Failure of Osborne/McGraw-Hill to insist at any time on strict compliance with this Agreement shall not constitute a waiver of any rights under this Agreement. This Agreement shall be construed and governed in accordance with the laws of New York. If any provision of this Agreement is held to be contrary to law, that provision will be enforced to the maximum extent permissible, and the remaining   will remain in force and effect.

NO TECHNICAL SUPPORT IS PROVIDED WITH THIS CD-ROM.